PROFILE OF
THE NATION
AN AMERICAN PORTRAIT

ISSN 1538-6627

PROFILE OF THE NATION

AN AMERICAN PORTRAIT

Paul Connors

INFORMATION PLUS® REFERENCE SERIES
Formerly published by Information Plus, Wylie, Texas

THOMSON

GALE

Detroit • New York • San Francisco • San Diego • New Haven, Conn. • Waterville, Maine • London • Munich

Profile of the Nation: An American Portrait
Paul Connors

Project Editor
Ellice Engdahl

Editorial
Beverly Baer, Paula Cutcher-Jackson, Pamela A. Dear, Kathleen Edgar, Debra Kirby, Prindle LaBarge, Elizabeth Manar, Kathleen Meek, Charles B. Montney, Heather Price

Permissions
Margaret Abendroth, William Sampson, Sheila Spencer

Composition and Electronic Prepress
Evi Seoud

Manufacturing
Keith Helmling

LIBRARY OF CONGRESS CATALOGING-IN-PUBLICATION DATA

ISBN 0-7876-5103-6 (set)
ISBN 0-7876-7522-9
ISSN 1538-6627

Printed in the United States of America
10 9 8 7 6 5 4 3 2 1

TABLE OF CONTENTS

PREFACE vii
ACKNOWLEDGMENTS ix

CHAPTER 1
Population Characteristics 1
From the first national census conducted in 1790 to the present day, the United States has experienced phenomenal population growth. This chapter details the characteristics of that population growth, including the fastest growing states, counties, and cities. The rural population, race and Hispanic origin, geographic mobility, birth and death rates, and life expectancy are also covered.

CHAPTER 2
Families and Households 25
This chapter describes the types of households and family structures most commonly found in the United States today. Topics covered include family size, median age of householders, households headed by women, marital status, and the living arrangements of children and young adults.

CHAPTER 3
Labor Force 33
The number of workers in the labor force nearly doubled between 1965 and 2002. This chapter discusses the changing economy (from manufacturing- to service-oriented), the fastest growing occupations, unemployment, and characteristics of workers and workplaces.

CHAPTER 4
Income and Poverty 53
This chapter covers income and poverty, average pay, median income, distribution of income, personal worth, debt, and demographics of those living in poverty.

CHAPTER 5
Health 67
Health care costs are rising at an incredible rate every year. This chapter covers heath-care spending by individuals and the government (including Medicare and Medicaid), insurance coverage, hospitalization, the rate of doctor and dentist visits by Americans, and major causes of death.

CHAPTER 6
Education. 83
The United States is one of the most highly educated nations in the world. This chapter discusses school enrollment, attendance of public elementary and secondary schools, private school enrollment, college and university attendance and degrees conferred, the influence of education on earnings, and spending on education.

CHAPTER 7
Voter Participation 113
This chapter covers suffrage for blacks and women, felony disenfranchisement laws, low voter turnout, and voter turnout at presidential and congressional elections. The chapter also includes sections on the 2000 presidential election and the 2002 congressional elections.

CHAPTER 8
Crime. 123
Crime is a problem that plagues the nation. This chapter discusses the number and rate of crimes, types of crime, victims of crime, and terrorism. A section detailing the September 11, 2001, terrorist attacks on America is also included.

CHAPTER 9
Spending Our Money 143
The amount of income earned determines in large part how much Americans spend. This chapter details the spending and saving habits of Americans.

IMPORTANT NAMES AND ADDRESSES 149
RESOURCES 151
INDEX 153

PREFACE

Profile of the Nation: An American Portrait is one of the latest volumes in the Information Plus Reference Series. The purpose of each volume of the series is to present the latest facts on a topic of pressing concern in modern American life. These topics include today's most controversial and most studied social issues: abortion, capital punishment, care for the elderly, crime, health care, the environment, immigration, minorities, social welfare, women, youth, and many more. Although written especially for the high school and undergraduate student, this series is an excellent resource for anyone in need of factual information on current affairs.

By presenting the facts, it is Thomson Gale's intention to provide its readers with everything they need to reach an informed opinion on current issues. To that end, there is a particular emphasis in this series on the presentation of scientific studies, surveys, and statistics. These data are generally presented in the form of tables, charts, and other graphics placed within the text of each book. Every graphic is directly referred to and carefully explained in the text. The source of each graphic is presented within the graphic itself. The data used in these graphics are drawn from the most reputable and reliable sources, in particular from the various branches of the U.S. government and from major independent polling organizations. Every effort has been made to secure the most recent information available. The reader should bear in mind that many major studies take years to conduct, and that additional years often pass before the data from these studies are made available to the public. Therefore, in many cases the most recent information available in 2004 dated from 2001 or 2002. Older statistics are sometimes presented as well if they are of particular interest and no more recent information exists.

Although statistics are a major focus of the Information Plus Reference Series, they are by no means its only content. Each book also presents the widely held positions and important ideas that shape how the book's subject is discussed in the United States. These positions are explained in detail and, where possible, in the words of their proponents. Some of the other material to be found in these books includes: historical background; descriptions of major events related to the subject; relevant laws and court cases; and examples of how these issues play out in American life. Some books also feature primary documents or have pro and con debate sections giving the words and opinions of prominent Americans on both sides of a controversial topic. All material is presented in an even-handed and unbiased manner; the reader will never be encouraged to accept one view of an issue over another.

HOW TO USE THIS BOOK

America is known as a melting pot, a place where many diverse groups come together to form one people and one nation. This book attempts to chart the ways citizens maintain their own individual identities and yet still make up a very unique and cohesive group—Americans. The book also presents a snapshot of today's America—where Americans live, work, play, and learn, along with statistics on the earnings of Americans, the crime problem, and health issues.

Profile of the Nation: An American Portrait consists of nine chapters and three appendices. Each of the chapters is devoted to a particular aspect of the American people. For a summary of the information covered in each chapter, please see the synopses provided in the Table of Contents at the front of the book. Chapters generally begin with an overview of the basic facts and background information on the chapter's topic, then proceed to examine subtopics of particular interest. For example, Chapter 3, Labor Force, begins with a discussion of the number of Americans in the workforce. It then examines the trend toward a service economy, the different occupations of Americans, statistics on unemployment, and how many hours Americans work.

Also covered are various kinds of nontraditional work arrangements, contingent work, accidents on the job, unions, and employee benefit plans. Readers can find their way through a chapter by looking for the section and subsection headings, which are clearly set off from the text. They can also refer to the book's extensive index if they already know what they are looking for.

Statistical Information

The tables and figures featured throughout *Profile of the Nation: An American Portrait* will be of particular use to the reader in learning about this issue. These tables and figures represent an extensive collection of the most recent and important statistics on the diversity of America and related issues—for example, graphics in the book cover U.S. cities with a population of 100,000 or more, life expectancy at birth, the employment status of U.S. citizens, Medicaid coverage, educational levels, voter registration, and the number and types of crimes committed in the United States over the past decade. Thomson Gale believes that making this information available to the reader is the most important way in which we fulfill the goal of this book: to help readers understand the issues and controversies surrounding the modern-day United States and to reach their own conclusions.

Each table or figure has a unique identifier appearing above it for ease of identification and reference. Titles for the tables and figures explain their purpose. At the end of each table or figure, the original source of the data is provided.

In order to help readers understand these often complicated statistics, all tables and figures are explained in the text. References in the text direct the reader to the relevant statistics. Furthermore, the contents of all tables and figures are fully indexed. Please see the opening section of the index at the back of this volume for a description of how to find tables and figures within it.

Appendices

In addition to the main body text and images, *Profile of the Nation: An American Portrait* has three appendices. The first is the Important Names and Addresses directory. Here the reader will find contact information for a number of government and private organizations that can provide further information on American demographics. The second appendix is the Resources section, which can also assist the reader in conducting his or her own research. In this section, the author and editors of *Profile of the Nation: An American Portrait* describe some of the sources that were most useful during the compilation of this book. The final appendix is the detailed Index, which facilitates reader access to specific topics in this book.

ADVISORY BOARD CONTRIBUTIONS

The staff of Information Plus would like to extend their heartfelt appreciation to the Information Plus Advisory Board. This dedicated group of media professionals provides feedback on the series on an ongoing basis. Their comments allow the editorial staff who work on the project to make the series better and more user-friendly. Our top priority is to produce the highest-quality and most useful books possible, and the Advisory Board's contributions to this process are invaluable.

The members of the Information Plus Advisory Board are:

- Kathleen R. Bonn, Librarian, Newbury Park High School, Newbury Park, California

- Madelyn Garner, Librarian, San Jacinto College—North Campus, Houston, Texas

- Anne Oxenrider, Media Specialist, Dundee High School, Dundee, Michigan

- Charles R. Rodgers, Director of Libraries, Pasco-Hernando Community College, Dade City, Florida

- James N. Zitzelsberger, Library Media Department Chairman, Oshkosh West High School, Oshkosh, Wisconsin

COMMENTS AND SUGGESTIONS

The editors of the Information Plus Reference Series welcome your feedback on *Profile of the Nation: An American Portrait*. Please direct all correspondence to:

Editors
Information Plus Reference Series
27500 Drake Rd.
Farmington Hills, MI 48331-3535

ACKNOWLEDGMENTS

The editors wish to thank the copyright holders of material included in this volume and the permissions managers of many book and magazine publishing companies for assisting us in securing reproduction rights. We are also grateful to the staffs of the Detroit Public Library, the Library of Congress, the University of Detroit Mercy Library, Wayne State University Purdy/Kresge Library Complex, and the University of Michigan Libraries for making their resources available to us.

Following is a list of the copyright holders who have granted us permission to reproduce material in Profile of the Nation: An American Portrait. *Every effort has been made to trace copyright, but if omissions have been made, please let us know.*

For more detailed source citations, please see the sources listed under each individual table and figure.

Centers for Disease Control and Prevention, National Center for Health Statistics: Table 1.15, Table 1.16, Table 5.1, Table 5.2, Table 5.3, Table 5.4, Table 5.5, Table 5.7, Table 5.8, Table 5.9

Federal Bureau of Investigation: Table 8.1, Table 8.2, Table 8.3, Table 8.4

Federal Bureau of Investigation, Counterterrorism Threat Assessment and Warning Unit, Counterterrorism Division: Figure 8.1, Figure 8.2

Federal Election Commission: Figure 7.2, Figure 7.3, Table 7.4

Federal Interagency Forum on Child and Family Statistics: Table 2.4, Figure 4.3

Federal Reserve Board: Table 4.1

The Sentencing Project: Table 7.1

U.S. Census Bureau: Figure 1.1, Figure 1.2, Figure 1.3, Figure 1.4, Table 1.2, Table 1.5, Table 1.6, Table 1.7, Table 1.10, Table 1.13, Table 1.14, Table 2.1, Table 2.2, Table 2.3, Table 2.5, Figure 4.1, Figure 4.2, Table 4.2, Table 4.3, Table 4.4, Table 5.6, Figure 7.1, Table 7.2, Table 7.3

U.S. Census Bureau, Population Division: Table 1.1, Table 1.3, Table 1.4, Table 1.8, Table 1.9, Table 1.14

U.S. Department of Agriculture, National Agricultural Statistics Service: Table 1.11, Table 1.12

U.S. Department of Education, Institute of Education Sciences: Figure 6.2, Figure 6.3, Figure 6.5, Table 6.6, Table 6.10

U.S. Department of Education, National Center for Education Statistics: Figure 6.1, Figure 6.4, Table 6.1, Table 6.2, Table 6.3, Table 6.4, Table 6.5, Table 6.7, Table 6.8, Table 6.9, Table 6.11, Table 6.12, Table 6.13, Table 6.14, Table 6.15, Table 6.16, Table 6.17, Table 6.18

U.S. Department of Justice, Bureau of Justice Statistics: Table 8.5, Table 8.6, Table 8.7, Table 8.8

U.S. Department of Labor: Figure 3.1

U.S. Department of Labor, Bureau of Labor Statistics: Table 3.1, Table 3.2, Table 3.3, Table 3.4, Table 3.5, Table 3.6, Table 3.7, Table 3.8, Table 3.9, Table 3.10, Table 3.11, Table 9.1, Table 9.2, Table 9.3, Table 9.4

U.S. Department of State: Figure 8.3, Figure 8.4

CHAPTER 1
POPULATION CHARACTERISTICS

The United States has expanded from a small nation of fewer than 4 million persons scattered along the eastern seaboard into a country of more than 280 million extending halfway across the Pacific Ocean to Hawaii and north of the Arctic Circle in Alaska. America's movement westward is reflected in the gradual shift of the center of the U.S. population.

In 1790, the year of the first national census, the mean population center for the United States lay just east of Baltimore, Maryland. By the Civil War (1861–65), the population center had moved well into Ohio, and by the end of World War II (1945), the center had reached westward to Illinois. (See Figure 1.1.)

Reflecting the movement of population out of the Northeast toward the Southwest, the 1980 census located the population center in Jefferson County, Missouri, near the city of DeSoto, approximately 40 miles south-southwest of the Gateway Arch in St. Louis, Missouri. The 1990 census moved the population center 39.5 miles farther southwest of DeSoto to a heavily wooded area in Crawford County, Missouri. Steelville (population 1,429), the closest town to the 1990 population center, lies 9.7 miles to the northwest. By 2000 the mean center of population had moved some 30 miles farther southwest, to Phelps County, Missouri, 2.8 miles east of the rural community of Edgar Springs, population 190. (See Figure 1.1.)

CURRENT POPULATION FIGURES

The official 2000 census, performed by the U.S. Census Bureau, counted the population of the United States (including armed forces overseas) at 281.4 million people. In September 2003 the Census Bureau estimated that the U.S. population had risen to 291.1 million. There is 1 birth every 8 seconds and 1 death every 13 seconds in the United States; one international migrant (net; those entering minus those leaving) enters every 42 seconds and one federal U.S. citizen (net)

returns every 3,508 seconds for a net gain of 1 person every 13 seconds.

As to the count itself, beginning with the first census in 1790, everyone in the country was counted—including slaves, even though they were not considered U.S. citizens. As a result, today's national census counts all persons, whether or not they are legal citizens of the United States.

Census counts are particularly important because the apportionment of local, state, and federal representatives to Congress is based on Census Bureau counts, as are the formation of political districts and the funding of government grants. Unfortunately, the decennial census is not an exact science. The Census Bureau estimates that the Census 2000 net undercount rate was 1.18 percent, totaling nearly 3.3 million missing persons. While 1.18 percent may not seem like much, most of those not counted live in the larger cities where the miscount may be as high as 4 to 5 percent. An increase of 4 or 5 percent in federal grant monies is significant, particularly since Congress allocates approximately $185 billion in federal funds each year based on each state's respective share of the U.S. population, as determined every 10 years by the census. For example, the professional services firm PricewaterhouseCoopers estimates that the Census 2000 undercount will result in the loss of nearly $3.5 billion in Medicaid spending to 31 adversely affected states for the fiscal years 2002 to 2012. Medicaid is important because it provides medical assistance to low-income children and pregnant women, low-income persons with disabilities, and low-income elderly persons.

U.S. AND WORLD POPULATION

Following China, with 1.3 billion people, and India, with 1.06 billion, the United States ranked third in the world in population in 2002. Indonesia was fourth with 220 million, Brazil fifth with 178 million, Pakistan sixth with 178 million, Bangladesh seventh with 147 million,

FIGURE 1.1

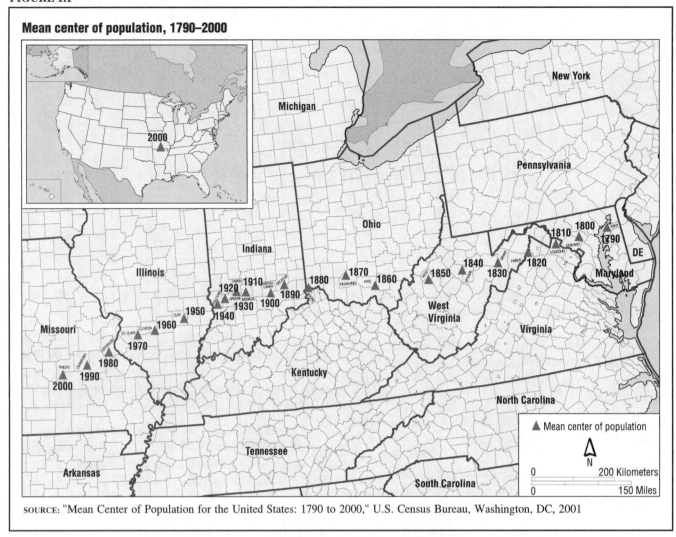

Mean center of population, 1790–2000

2000

Michigan

New York

Pennsylvania

Ohio

Indiana

1800
1810
1790
DE

Illinois

1870
1860
1840
1850
1830
1820
Maryland

1880
1910
1920
1890
1930
1900
1940
1950
1960

West
Virginia

Virginia

Missouri

1970
1980
1990
2000

Kentucky

North Carolina

▲ Mean center of population

Tennessee

N

0   200 Kilometers
0   150 Miles

Arkansas

South Carolina

SOURCE: "Mean Center of Population for the United States: 1790 to 2000," U.S. Census Bureau, Washington, DC, 2001

Russia eighth with 143 million, Japan ninth with 128 million, and Nigeria tenth with 124 million people. Of the 6.3 billion people worldwide in 2002, more than half live in Asia. In fact, China and India account for approximately 38 percent of the world's population compared to the United States, which comprises about 5 percent of the world's population.

POPULATION GROWTH

The 281.4 million people counted in Census 2000 represented an increase of 13.2 percent from the 1990 census count of 248.7 million. That represents a growth in population of some 32.7 million people between 1990 and 2000, the largest census-to-census increase in U.S. history. During that decade, the population growth rate in the West was highest, at 19.7 percent, followed by the South at 17.3 percent and the Midwest at 7.9 percent. The population in the Northeast region of the United States grew at the lowest rate, 5.5 percent.

The next highest recent growth rate over a 10-year census period was 18.4 percent between 1950 and 1960.

This period included the peak years of the post–World War II "baby boom" (1946–1964), during which the average rate of childbirth was more than three births per woman, leading to a large population increase. Population growth steadily declined for the next three decades, from 13.4 percent between 1960 and 1970, to 11.4 percent between 1970 and 1980, to 9.8 percent between 1980 and 1990—the second lowest growth rate in U.S. history. (See Figure 1.2.) This drop in population growth was caused mainly by a lower rate of childbearing. During the two decades from 1980 to 2000 this rate averaged about two births per woman. Only the 7.3 percent population growth rate during the 1930s, the decade of the Great Depression, was lower than that of the decade between 1980 and 1990. During the Great Depression, many people were reluctant to have children because they were not sure they could afford to take care of them.

Population growth rates increased much more slowly in the 20th century than in the 19th century, largely because of a long-term drop in the number of births. At the beginning of the 19th century, the average childbear-

FIGURE 1.2

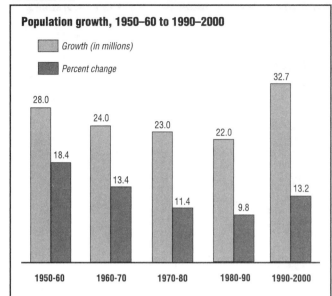

Population growth, 1950–60 to 1990–2000

Growth (in millions)

Percent change

SOURCE: Marc J. Perry and Paul J. Mackun, et al., "Figure 1. U.S. Population Growth: 1950–60 to 1990–2000," in *Population Change and Distribution: 1990 to 2000,* U.S. Census Bureau, Washington, DC, April 2001

ing rate was seven births per woman, more than three times as many as today; however, many children died during infancy. Nonetheless, despite the average number of births dropping, the population growth rate increased in the late 19th and early 20th centuries. During this period, the number of people who died from disease and other causes was declining, while the rate of immigration was increasing from the 1840s to the 1920s.

STATE AND COUNTY POPULATIONS

According to Census 2002 state population estimates, the 10 most populous states contained over half (54 percent) of the U.S. population. California was the most populous with 35.1 million people—12 percent of the nation's population. Texas was the second most populous state, with 21.7 million people, followed by New York, with 19.1 million. Rounding out the top 10 most populous states, in order, were Florida, Illinois, Pennsylvania, Ohio, Michigan, New Jersey, and Georgia, which collectively accounted for about 28 percent of the nation's population. (See Table 1.1.)

Of the 10 least populous states, 3 were in the Northeast (New Hampshire, Rhode Island, and Vermont), 2 in the Midwest (North Dakota and South Dakota), 1 in the Middle Atlantic (Delaware), and 4 in the West (Hawaii, Montana, Alaska, and Wyoming). All together, these states accounted for about 3 percent of the national population.

The Fastest Growing States

In sheer numbers, California grew the fastest from 2000 to 2002, adding 1,244,385 million people to its pop-

ulation. Rounding out the top five fastest growing states, Texas grew by 928,081 people, Florida by 730,749 people, Georgia by 373,824 people, and Arizona by 325,821 people.

By percentage, Nevada showed the highest growth rate of all states between April 2000 and July 2002, at 8.8 percent, followed by Arizona (6.4 percent), Colorado (4.8 percent), Florida (4.6 percent), and Georgia (4.6 percent). North Dakota and West Virginia had the lowest growth rates, at -1.3 percent and -0.4 percent, respectively. They were followed by Louisiana (0.3 percent), Iowa (0.4 percent), and Pennsylvania (0.4 percent).

Of nonstates counted, Puerto Rico grew by an estimated 50,196 people, or 1.3 percent, to 3,858,806 people from April 2000 to July 2002. Over the same period of time, the District of Columbia declined by an estimated 0.2 percent to 570,898 people.

Top Counties

Between 1990 and 2000 Douglas County, Colorado, located south of Denver, had the highest rate of population growth, at an astounding 191 percent. Following Douglas were Forsyth County, Georgia (north of Atlanta), up 123 percent; Elbert County, Colorado (southeast of Denver), up 106 percent; Henry County, Georgia (east of Atlanta), up 103 percent; and Park County, Colorado (southwest of Denver), where the population rose by 102 percent. (See Table 1.2.)

Between July 2001 and July 2002 Rockwall County, Texas, located 25 miles northeast of Dallas, was the fastest growing county in the nation with a population growth of 7.9 percent. Following Rockwall were Loudoun County, Virginia, located 25 miles south of Washington, D.C., up 7.3 percent; Henry County, Georgia, up 7.1 percent; Forsyth County, Georgia, up 7.1 percent; and Flagler County, Florida, located on the eastern side of central Florida, up 6.9 percent. (See Table 1.3.)

According to the Census Bureau, Los Angeles County, California, is the largest county in the United States with an estimated population of 9.8 million in July 2002. After Los Angeles County is Cook County, Illinois, which includes Chicago, with 5.4 million residents; Harris County, Texas, which includes Houston, with 3.5 million inhabitants; Maricopa, Arizona, which includes Phoenix, with 3.3 million people; and Orange County, California, which includes Anaheim, with 2.9 million residents. (See Table 1.4.)

According to Census 2000, among the nation's 3,141 counties there was rapid population growth in the interior West and across the South in counties located in Florida, northern Georgia, North Carolina, Tennessee, southwestern Missouri, and eastern, central, and southern Texas. Despite overall population declines in much

TABLE 1.1

State population estimates, April 1, 2000 to July 1, 2002

State	July 1, 2002 population	July 1, 2001 population	July 1, 2000 population	April 1, 2000 population estimates base	Census 2000 population
United States	288,368,698	285,317,559	282,224,348	281,422,509	281,421,906
Alabama	4,486,508	4,468,912	4,451,975	4,447,100	4,447,100
Alaska	643,786	633,630	627,697	626,931	626,932
Arizona	5,456,453	5,306,966	5,167,142	5,130,632	5,130,632
Arkansas	2,710,079	2,694,698	2,678,668	2,673,398	2,673,400
California	35,116,033	34,600,463	34,010,375	33,871,648	33,871,648
Colorado	4,506,542	4,430,989	4,326,758	4,301,331	4,301,261
Connecticut	3,460,503	3,434,602	3,411,956	3,405,565	3,405,565
Delaware	807,385	796,599	786,512	783,600	783,600
District of Columbia	570,898	573,822	571,641	572,059	572,059
Florida	16,713,149	16,373,330	16,051,395	15,982,400	15,982,378
Georgia	8,560,310	8,405,677	8,234,373	8,186,486	8,186,453
Hawaii	1,244,898	1,227,024	1,212,670	1,211,537	1,211,537
Idaho	1,341,131	1,320,585	1,299,721	1,293,953	1,293,953
Illinois	12,600,620	12,520,227	12,440,846	12,419,296	12,419,293
Indiana	6,159,068	6,126,743	6,091,950	6,080,485	6,080,485
Iowa	2,936,760	2,931,967	2,928,742	2,926,327	2,926,324
Kansas	2,715,884	2,702,125	2,692,557	2,688,418	2,688,418
Kentucky	4,092,891	4,068,816	4,048,832	4,042,209	4,041,769
Louisiana	4,482,646	4,470,368	4,469,768	4,468,979	4,468,976
Maine	1,294,464	1,284,470	1,277,284	1,274,923	1,274,923
Maryland	5,458,137	5,386,079	5,312,461	5,296,483	5,296,486
Massachusetts	6,427,801	6,401,164	6,361,720	6,349,097	6,349,097
Michigan	10,050,446	10,006,266	9,956,115	9,938,444	9,938,444
Minnesota	5,019,720	4,984,535	4,934,248	4,919,479	4,919,479
Mississippi	2,871,782	2,859,733	2,848,829	2,844,658	2,844,658
Missouri	5,672,579	5,637,309	5,605,067	5,595,211	5,595,211
Montana	909,453	905,382	903,416	902,195	902,195
Nebraska	1,729,180	1,720,039	1,713,375	1,711,263	1,711,263
Nevada	2,173,491	2,097,722	2,018,828	1,998,257	1,998,257
New Hampshire	1,275,056	1,259,359	1,240,472	1,235,786	1,235,786
New Jersey	8,590,300	8,511,116	8,433,276	8,414,350	8,414,350
New Mexico	1,855,059	1,830,935	1,821,767	1,819,046	1,819,046
New York	19,157,532	19,084,350	18,999,760	18,976,457	18,976,457
North Carolina	8,320,146	8,206,105	8,082,261	8,049,474	8,049,313
North Dakota	634,110	636,550	641,131	642,200	642,200
Ohio	11,421,267	11,389,785	11,363,568	11,353,008	11,353,140
Oklahoma	3,493,714	3,469,577	3,454,408	3,450,656	3,450,654
Oregon	3,521,515	3,473,441	3,431,137	3,421,405	3,421,399
Pennsylvania	12,335,091	12,303,104	12,286,107	12,281,054	12,281,054
Rhode Island	1,069,725	1,059,659	1,050,698	1,048,319	1,048,319
South Carolina	4,107,183	4,062,125	4,023,725	4,012,010	4,012,012
South Dakota	761,063	758,324	755,783	754,844	754,844
Tennessee	5,797,289	5,749,398	5,703,246	5,689,277	5,689,283
Texas	21,779,893	21,370,983	20,955,248	20,851,812	20,851,820
Utah	2,316,256	2,278,712	2,243,406	2,233,169	2,233,169
Vermont	616,592	612,978	609,952	608,827	608,827
Virginia	7,293,542	7,196,750	7,105,900	7,078,499	7,078,515
Washington	6,068,996	5,993,390	5,911,803	5,894,119	5,894,121
West Virginia	1,801,873	1,800,975	1,807,326	1,808,350	1,808,344
Wisconsin	5,441,196	5,405,947	5,374,367	5,363,701	5,363,675
Wyoming	498,703	493,754	494,086	493,782	493,782
Puerto Rico	3,858,806	3,838,361	3,815,893	3,808,610	3,808,610

SOURCE: "State Population Estimates: April 1, 2000 to July 1, 2002," in *State Population Estimates,* U.S. Census Bureau, Population Division, Washington, DC, December 20, 2002

of the Midwest, counties in Sioux Falls, South Dakota, and Minneapolis–St. Paul, Minnesota, showed strong growth. The Minneapolis–St. Paul metropolitan area showed a growth pattern of slow expansion in the central counties and more rapid growth in outlying counties. This pattern was also apparent in the Atlanta, Georgia, metropolitan area.

Between 1990 and 2000 the population in U.S. counties along the Mexican border increased by 21 percent, while the population in U.S. counties neighboring Canada remained more or less stable, increasing by less than 1 percent. Nationwide, coastal counties had an 11 percent overall growth rate in population, while the population of noncoastal counties rose by 15 percent.

MOST AMERICANS LIVE IN METROPOLITAN STATISTICAL AREAS

A metropolitan statistical area (MSA) includes a large population center with at least 50,000 residents, together with surrounding communities that are economically and

TABLE 1.2

Counties ranked by percent change in population, 1990–2000

Rank (of 3,141 counties)	State and county FIPS codes	County name	State	Census population		Change, 1990 to 2000	
				April 1, 1990	April 1, 2000	Number	Percent
1	08035	Douglas County	CO	60,391	175,766	115,375	191.0
2	13117	Forsyth County	GA	44,083	98,407	54,324	123.2
3	08039	Elbert County	CO	9,646	19,872	10,226	106.0
4	13151	Henry County	GA	58,741	119,341	60,600	103.2
5	08093	Park County	CO	7,174	14,523	7,349	102.4
6	51107	Loudoun County	VA	86,129	169,599	83,470	96.9
7	13223	Paulding County	GA	41,611	81,678	40,067	96.3
8	49043	Summit County	UT	15,518	29,736	14,218	91.6
9	16015	Boise County	ID	3,509	6,670	3,161	90.1
10	08037	Eagle County	CO	21,928	41,659	19,731	90.0
11	48085	Collin County	TX	264,036	491,675	227,639	86.2
12	49053	Washington County	UT	48,560	90,354	41,794	86.1
13	32003	Clark County	NV	741,459	1,375,765	634,306	85.5
14	08007	Archuleta County	CO	5,345	9,898	4,553	85.2
15	08117	Summit County	CO	12,881	23,548	10,667	82.8
16	32023	Nye County	NV	17,781	32,485	14,704	82.7
17	08027	Custer County	CO	1,926	3,503	1,577	81.9
18	08113	San Miguel County	CO	3,653	6,594	2,941	80.5
19	48491	Williamson County	TX	139,551	249,967	110,416	79.1
20	13123	Gilmer County	GA	13,368	23,456	10,088	75.5
21	16081	Teton County	ID	3,439	5,999	2,560	74.4
22	12035	Flagler County	FL	28,701	49,832	21,131	73.6
23	21215	Spencer County	KY	6,801	11,766	4,965	73.0
24	32019	Lyon County	NV	20,001	34,501	14,500	72.5
25	13085	Dawson County	GA	9,429	15,999	6,570	69.7
26	08053	Hinsdale County	CO	467	790	323	69.2
27	12119	Sumter County	FL	31,577	53,345	21,768	68.9
28	48397	Rockwall County	TX	25,604	43,080	17,476	68.3
29	18057	Hamilton County	IN	108,936	182,740	73,804	67.7
30	48019	Bandera County	TX	10,562	17,645	7,083	67.1
31	13135	Gwinnett County	GA	352,910	588,448	235,538	66.7
32	29043	Christian County	MO	32,644	54,285	21,641	66.3
33	13183	Long County	GA	6,202	10,304	4,102	66.1
34	04015	Mohave County	AZ	93,497	155,032	61,535	65.8
35	13077	Coweta County	GA	53,853	89,215	35,362	65.7
36	42103	Pike County	PA	27,966	46,302	18,336	65.6
37	12021	Collier County	FL	152,099	251,377	99,278	65.3
38	08119	Teller County	CO	12,468	20,555	8,087	64.9
39	35057	Torrance County	NM	10,285	16,911	6,626	64.4
40	39041	Delaware County	OH	66,929	109,989	43,060	64.3
41	56039	Teton County	WY	11,172	18,251	7,079	63.4
42	08091	Ouray County	CO	2,295	3,742	1,447	63.1
43	48259	Kendall County	TX	14,589	23,743	9,154	62.7
44	49021	Iron County	UT	20,789	33,779	12,990	62.5
45	51065	Fluvanna County	VA	12,429	20,047	7,618	61.3

Note: 1990 populations shown in this table do not include subsequent revisions due to boundary or other changes.

SOURCE: Adapted from "Table 4. Counties Ranked by Percent Change in Population: 1990 to 2000," in *Ranking Tables for Counties: Population in 2000 and Population Change from 1990 to 2000*, PHC-T-4, U.S. Census Bureau, Washington, DC, April 2001 [Online] http://www.census.gov/population/www/cen2000/phc-t4.html [accessed November 10, 2003]

socially tied together. Generally, a metropolitan area is made up of a sizable city with its suburbs and a total population of at least 100,000 people. Most metropolitan areas cross over county lines and may also include some rural areas.

In 2000 some 226 million Americans—just over 80 percent—lived in metropolitan areas, up from 198.4 million (79.8 percent) in 1990. From 1990 to 2000 metropolitan areas showed a population growth rate of nearly 14 percent, versus nonmetropolitan areas at slightly over 10 percent.

Metropolitan areas of at least 5 million people were home to almost one-third of all Americans, while those with populations of between 2 and 5 million held 14 percent of the population. According to Census 2000, 13 percent of the population resided in metropolitan areas of 1 to 2 million people, 16 percent in MSAs of 1 million, and 7 percent in MSAs with fewer than 250,000.

The fastest growing metropolitan areas in 2000 were those with populations of between 2 and 5 million, up 20 percent. An 11 percent growth rate was seen in both the largest and the smallest metropolitan areas nationwide.

TABLE 1.3

Ten fastest growing counties with 10,000 or more population in 2002, April 1, 2000 to July 1, 2002

County	State	July 1, 2002 population	July 1, 2001 population	Numerical population change	Percent population change
Rockwall	Texas	50,858	47,130	3,728	7.9
Loudoun	Virginia	204,054	190,180	13,874	7.3
Henry	Georgia	139,699	130,419	9,280	7.1
Forsyth	Georgia	116,924	109,183	7,741	7.1
Flagler	Florida	57,377	53,658	3,719	6.9
Douglas	Colorado	211,091	197,611	13,480	6.8
Newton	Georgia	71,594	67,143	4,451	6.6
Scott	Minnesota	103,681	97,465	6,216	6.4
Stafford	Virginia	104,823	98,703	6,120	6.2
Delaware	Ohio	125,399	118,225	7,174	6.1

SOURCE: Adapted from "100 Fastest Growing U.S. Counties with 10,000 or more Population in 2002: April 1, 2001 to July 1, 2002," in *State Population Estimates,* U.S. Census Bureau, Population Division, Washington, DC, April 17, 2003

New York was the most populous MSA, with a population of 21.2 million, followed by Los Angeles (16.4 million), Chicago (9.2 million), Washington, D.C. (7.6 million), and San Francisco (7 million). Philadelphia had 6.2 million people, and the Boston, Detroit, and Dallas MSAs each had populations of between 5 and 6 million. (See Table 1.5.)

The fastest growing metropolitan areas between 1990 and 2000 were Las Vegas, Nevada-Arizona, up by 83 percent, and Naples, Florida, up by 65 percent. Growth rates of between 44 and 50 percent were seen in Yuma and Phoenix, Arizona; McAllen, Austin, and Laredo, Texas; Fayetteville, Arkansas; and Boise City, Idaho. Provo, Utah, the 10th fastest growing metropolitan area, grew at a rate of 40 percent. (See Table 1.6.)

CITIES

Between 1990 and 2000, 8 of the 10 largest cities in the United States gained population. Of those, New York City had the highest numeric gain, with an increase of 685,714, followed by Phoenix (337,642), Houston (323,078), Los Angeles (209,422), and San Antonio (208,713). Phoenix showed the highest rate of gain, at 34.3 percent, followed by San Antonio (22.3 percent), Houston (19.8 percent), Dallas (18 percent), and San Diego (10.2 percent). (See Table 1.7.)

Between 2001 and 2002 Gilbert, Arizona (135,005), was the fastest growing city with a population of over 100,000 residents with a rate of gain of 10.3 percent. After Gilbert, the fastest growing cities with a population over 100,000 people were North Las Vegas (135,902), with a rate of gain of 6.7 percent; Rancho Cucamonga, California (143,711), with a rate of gain of 6.3 percent; Henderson, Nevada (206,153), with a rate of gain of 6.3 percent; and Joliet, Illinois (118,423), with a gain rate of 5.7 percent. (See Table 1.8.)

In 2002 the largest U.S. city was New York, with an estimated population of 8,084,316 million. Following the Big Apple, the largest cities are Los Angeles, with 3,798,981 million; Chicago, with 2,886,251 million; Houston, with 2,009,834 million; Philadelphia, with 1,492,231 million; Phoenix, with 1,371,960 million; San Diego, with 1,259,532 million; Dallas, with 1,211,467 million; San Antonio, with 1,194,222 million; and Detroit, with 925,051 million. (See Table 1.9.)

From 1990 to 2000, 2 cities among the nation's 10 largest had declines in their populations, the largest of which was Detroit, where the population fell by 76,704 (7.5 percent), followed by Philadelphia, down by 68,027 (4.3 percent). (See Table 1.10.) Between 2001 and 2002 Detroit's population fell an estimated 10,813, a rate change of -1.2 percent. Over the same period, Philadelphia lost an estimated 9,546, a rate change of -0.6 percent. Of the cities in the United States with a population of 100,000 or more, San Francisco experienced the largest percentage rate decline at -1.5 percent or 11,929.

TABLE 1.4

Population estimates for the 10 largest counties, April 1, 2000 to July 1, 2002

County	State	July 1, 2002 population	July 1, 2001 population	July 1, 2000 population	April 1, 2000 population estimates base	Census 2000 population
Los Angeles	California	9,806,577	9,677,220	9,549,068	9,519,330	9,519,338
Cook	Illinois	5,377,507	5,383,211	5,378,702	5,376,741	5,376,741
Harris	Texas	3,557,055	3,483,847	3,416,816	3,400,578	3,400,578
Maricopa	Arizona	3,303,876	3,201,841	3,097,299	3,072,149	3,072,149
Orange	California	2,938,507	2,900,200	2,857,286	2,846,289	2,846,289
San Diego	California	2,906,660	2,869,900	2,825,493	2,813,833	2,813,833
Kings	New York	2,488,194	2,479,923	2,467,778	2,465,326	2,465,326
Miami-Dade	Florida	2,332,599	2,296,625	2,261,716	2,253,362	2,253,362
Dallas	Texas	2,283,953	2,266,112	2,226,824	2,218,899	2,218,899
Queens	New York	2,237,815	2,238,024	2,231,842	2,229,379	2,229,379

SOURCE: "Population Estimates for the 100 Largest U.S. Counties: April 1, 2000 to July 1, 2002," in *State Population Estimates,* U.S. Census Bureau, Population Division, April 17, 2003

TABLE 1.5

Metropolitan areas ranked by population, 2000

MSA/ CMSA Code	Rank	Area Name	Census Population		Change, 1990 to 2000	
			April 1, 2000	April 1, 1990	Number	Percent
5602	1	New York—Northern New Jersey—Long Island, NY—NJ—CT—PA CMSA	21,199,865	19,549,649	1,650,216	8.4%
4472	2	Los Angeles—Riverside—Orange County, CA CMSA	16,373,645	14,531,529	1,842,116	12.7%
1602	3	Chicago—Gary—Kenosha, IL—IN—WI CMSA	9,157,540	8,239,820	917,720	11.1%
8872	4	Washington—Baltimore, DC—MD—VA—WV CMSA	7,608,070	6,727,050	881,020	13.1%
7362	5	San Francisco—Oakland—San Jose, CA CMSA	7,039,362	6,253,311	786,051	12.6%
6162	6	Philadelphia—Wilmington—Atlantic City, PA—NJ—DE—MD CMSA	6,188,463	5,892,937	295,526	5.0%
1122	7	Boston—Worcester—Lawrence, MA—NH—ME—CT CMSA	5,819,100	5,455,403	363,697	6.7%
2162	8	Detroit—Ann Arbor—Flint, MI CMSA	5,456,428	5,187,171	269,257	5.2%
1922	9	Dallas—Fort Worth, TX CMSA	5,221,801	4,037,282	1,184,519	29.3%
3362	10	Houston—Galveston—Brazoria, TX CMSA	4,669,571	3,731,131	938,440	25.2%
0520	11	Atlanta, GA MSA	4,112,198	2,959,950	1,152,248	38.9%
4992	12	Miami—Fort Lauderdale, FL CMSA	3,876,380	3,192,582	683,798	21.4%
7602	13	Seattle—Tacoma—Bremerton, WA CMSA	3,554,760	2,970,328	584,432	19.7%
6200	14	Phoenix—Mesa, AZ MSA	3,251,876	2,238,480	1,013,396	45.3%
5120	15	Minneapolis—St. Paul, MN—WI MSA	2,968,806	2,538,834	429,972	16.9%
1692	16	Cleveland—Akron, OH CMSA	2,945,831	2,859,644	86,187	3.0%
7320	17	San Diego, CA MSA	2,813,833	2,498,016	315,817	12.6%
7040	18	St. Louis, MO—IL MSA	2,603,607	2,492,525	111,082	4.5%
2082	19	Denver—Boulder—Greeley, CO CMSA	2,581,506	1,980,140	601,366	30.4%
7442	20	San Juan—Caguas—Arecibo, PR CMSA	2,450,292	2,270,808	179,484	7.9%

Note: 1990 Census population counts are as published in 1990 census reports and do not include changes published subsequently due to boundary or other changes. Metropolitan Areas are as defined on June 30, 1999 by the Office of Management and Budget. Eight new metropolitan areas were announced between 1993 and 1999: Auburn-Opelika, AL MSA; Corvallis, OR MSA; Flagstaff, AZ-UT MSA; Grand Junction, CO MSA; Hattiesburg, MS MSA; Jonesboro, AR MSA; Missoula, MT MSA: Pocatello, ID MSA.

SOURCE: Adapted from "Table 3. Metropolitan Areas Ranked by Population: 2000" in *Ranking Tables for Metropolitan Areas: Population in 2000 and Population Change from 1990 to 2000*, PHC-T-3, U.S. Census Bureau, Washington, DC, April 2001 [Online] http://www.census.gov/population/www/cen2000/phc-t3.html [accessed November 10, 2003]

TABLE 1.6

Metropolitan areas ranked by percent population change, 1990–2000

MSA/ CMSA code	Rank	Metropolitan area name	Census population		Change, 1990 to 2000	
			April 1, 2000	April 1, 1990	Number	Percent
4120	1	Las Vegas, NV—AZ MSA	1,563,282	852,737	710,545	83.3%
5345	2	Naples, FL MSA	251,377	152,099	99,278	65.3%
9360	3	Yuma, AZ MSA	160,026	106,895	53,131	49.7%
4880	4	McAllen—Edinburg—Mission, TX MSA	569,463	383,545	185,918	48.5%
0640	5	Austin—San Marcos, TX MSA	1,249,763	846,227	403,536	47.7%
2580	6	Fayetteville—Springdale—Rogers, AR MSA	311,121	210,908	100,213	47.5%
1080	7	Boise City, ID MSA	432,345	295,851	136,494	46.1%
6200	8	Phoenix—Mesa, AZ MSA	3,251,876	2,238,480	1,013,396	45.3%
4080	9	Laredo, TX MSA	193,117	133,239	59,878	44.9%
6520	10	Provo—Orem, UT MSA	368,536	263,590	104,946	39.8%
0520	11	Atlanta, GA MSA	4,112,198	2,959,950	1,152,248	38.9%
6640	12	Raleigh—Durham—Chapel Hill, NC MSA	1,187,941	855,545	332,396	38.9%
5330	13	Myrtle Beach, SC MSA	196,629	144,053	52,576	36.5%
9200	14	Wilmington, NC MSA	233,450	171,269	62,181	36.3%
2670	15	Fort Collins—Loveland, CO MSA	251,494	186,136	65,358	35.1%
5960	16	Orlando, FL MSA	1,644,561	1,224,852	419,709	34.3%
6720	17	Reno, NV MSA	339,486	254,667	84,819	33.3%
5790	18	Ocala, FL MSA	258,916	194,833	64,083	32.9%
0580	19	Auburn—Opelika, AL MSA	115,092	87,146	27,946	32.1%
2700	20	Fort Myers—Cape Coral, FL MSA	440,888	335,113	105,775	31.6%

Note: 1990 Census population counts are as published in 1990 census reports and do not include changes published subsequently due to boundary or other changes. Metropolitan Areas are as defined on June 30, 1999 by the Office of Management and Budget. Eight new metropolitan areas were announced between 1993 and 1999: Auburn-Opelika, AL MSA; Corvallis, OR MSA; Flagstaff, AZ-UT MSA; Grand Junction, CO MSA; Hattiesburg, MS MSA; Jonesboro, AR MSA; Missoula, MT MSA: Pocatello, ID MSA.

SOURCE: Adapted from "Table 5: Metropolitan Areas Ranked by Percent Population Change: 1990 to 2000," in *Ranking Tables for Metropolitan Areas: Population in 2000 and Population Change from 1990 to 2000*, PHC-T-3, U.S. Census Bureau, Washington, DC, April 2001 [Online] http://www.census.gov/population/www/cen2000/phc-t3.html [accessed November 10, 2003]

TABLE 1.7

Cities with a population over 100,000 by numeric population change, 1990–2000

Rank (of 243 places)	Place name	Area	Population		Change, 1990 to 2000	
			April 1, 2000	April 1, 1990	Number	Percent
1	New York city[1]	NY	8,008,278	7,322,564	685,714	9.4
2	Phoenix city	AZ	1,321,045	983,403	337,642	34.3
3	Houston city	TX	1,953,631	1,630,553	323,078	19.8
4	Las Vegas city	NV	478,434	258,295	220,139	85.2
5	Los Angeles city	CA	3,694,820	3,485,398	209,422	6.0
6	San Antonio city	TX	1,144,646	935,933	208,713	22.3
7	Austin city	TX	656,562	465,622	190,940	41.0
8	Dallas city	TX	1,188,580	1,006,877	181,703	18.0
9	Augusta-Richmond County[2]	GA	199,775	44,639	155,136	347.5
10	Charlotte city	NC	540,828	395,934	144,894	36.6
11	San Diego city	CA	1,223,400	1,110,549	112,851	10.2
12	San Jose city	CA	894,943	782,248	112,695	14.4
13	Chicago city	IL	2,896,016	2,783,726	112,290	4.0
14	Henderson city	NV	175,381	64,942	110,439	170.1
15	Mesa city	AZ	396,375	288,091	108,284	37.6
16	Jacksonville city	FL	735,617	635,230	100,387	15.8
17	Vancouver city	WA	143,560	46,380	97,180	209.5
18	Plano city	TX	222,030	128,713	93,317	72.5
19	Portland city	OR	529,121	437,319	91,802	21.0
20	Fort Worth city	TX	534,694	447,619	87,075	19.5
21	Denver city[3]	CO	554,636	467,610	87,026	18.6
22	Chandler city	AZ	176,581	90,533	86,048	95.0
23	Tucson city	AZ	486,699	405,390	81,309	20.1
24	Gilbert town	AZ	109,697	29,188	80,509	275.8
25	Colorado Springs city	CO	360,890	281,140	79,750	28.4
26	Columbus city	OH	711,470	632,910	78,560	12.4
27	Fresno city	CA	427,652	354,202	73,450	20.7
28	Scottsdale city	AZ	202,705	130,069	72,636	55.8
29	Bakersfield city	CA	247,057	174,820	72,237	41.3
30	Pembroke Pines city	FL	137,427	65,452	71,975	110.0
31	Arlington city	TX	332,969	261,721	71,248	27.2
32	Glendale city	AZ	218,812	148,134	70,678	47.7
33	Raleigh city	NC	276,093	207,951	68,142	32.8
34	North Las Vegas city	NV	115,488	47,707	67,781	142.1
35	Albuquerque city	NM	448,607	384,736	63,871	16.6
36	Anaheim city	CA	328,014	266,406	61,608	23.1
37	Oklahoma City city	OK	506,132	444,719	61,413	13.8
38	Boise City city	ID	185,787	125,738	60,049	47.8
39	Nashville-Davidson[4]	TN	569,891	510,784	59,107	11.6
40	Peoria city	AZ	108,364	50,618	57,746	114.1
41	Athens-Clarke County[5]	GA	101,489	45,734	55,755	121.9
42	Aurora city	CO	276,393	222,103	54,290	24.4
43	Omaha city	NE	390,007	335,795	54,212	16.1
44	Laredo city	TX	176,576	122,899	53,677	43.7
45	San Francisco city[6]	CA	776,733	723,959	52,774	7.3
46	Durham city	NC	187,035	136,611	50,424	36.9
47	Indianapolis city	IN	791,926	741,952	49,974	6.7
48	Corona city	CA	124,966	76,095	48,871	64.2
49	El Paso city	TX	563,662	515,342	48,320	9.4
50	Palmdale city	CA	116,670	68,842	47,828	69.5

Note: 1990 Census population counts are as published in 1990 census reports and do not include changes published subsequently due to boundary or other changes. In Puerto Rico, a zona urbana represents the governmental center of a municipio (which is the equivalent of a county). Zonas urbanas are treated as Census Designated Places, as there are no incorporated places in Puerto Rico. See additional documentation at bottom of table.

[1] The five boroughs of New York city are coextensive with the five counties that constitute New York city: Bronx borough (Bronx County), Brooklyn borough (Kings County), Manhattan borough (New York County), Queens borough (Queens County), and Staten Island borough (Richmond County).

[2] In 2000, Richmond County and the incorporated place of Augusta-Richmond County are coextensive. The 1990 population is for the incorporated place of Augusta city before consolidation of the city and county governments.

[3] Denver city is coextensive with Denver County.

[4] Nashville-Davidson city is consolidated with Davidson County.

[5] In 2000, Clarke County and the incorporated place of Athens-Clarke County are coextensive. The 1990 population is for the incorporated place of Athens city before consolidation of the city and county governments.

[6] San Francisco city is coextensive with San Francisco County.

SOURCE: Adapted from "Table 3. Incorporated Places of 100,000 or More, Ranked by Numeric Population Change: 1990 to 2000," in *Ranking Tables for Incorporated Places of 100,000 or More: Population in 2000 and Population Change from 1990 to 2000*, PHC-T-5, U.S. Census Bureau, Washington, DC, April 2001 [Online] http://www.census.gov/population/www/cen2000/phc-t5.html [accessed November 10, 2003]

TABLE 1.8

Population estimates for incorporated places over 100,000, ranked by percent change, July 1, 2001 to July 1, 2002

Rank	Place	State	July 1, 2002 population	July 1, 2001 population	Numerical population change	Percent population change
1	Gilbert town	Arizona	135,005	122,372	12,633	10.3
2	North Las Vegas city	Nevada	135,902	127,409	8,493	6.7
3	Rancho Cucamonga city	California	143,711	135,198	8,513	6.3
4	Henderson city	Nevada	206,153	194,005	12,148	6.3
5	Joliet city	Illinois	118,423	112,066	6,357	5.7
6	Chandler city	Arizona	202,016	191,426	10,590	5.5
7	Chula Vista city	California	193,919	183,778	10,141	5.5
8	Olathe city	Kansas	101,413	96,312	5,101	5.3
9	Cape Coral city	Florida	112,899	107,743	5,156	4.8
10	Peoria city	Arizona	123,239	117,880	5,359	4.5
11	Aurora city	Illinois	156,974	150,563	6,411	4.3
12	Fontana city	California	143,607	137,745	5,862	4.3
13	Corona city	California	138,326	132,810	5,516	4.2
14	McAllen city	Texas	113,877	109,388	4,489	4.1
15	Irvine city	California	162,122	156,229	5,893	3.8
16	Bakersfield city	California	260,969	251,690	9,279	3.7
17	Raleigh city	North Carolina	306,944	296,538	10,406	3.5
18	Modesto city	California	203,555	196,827	6,728	3.4
19	Brownsville city	Texas	150,425	145,486	4,939	3.4
20	Laredo city	Texas	191,538	185,506	6,032	3.3
21	Stockton city	California	262,835	254,774	8,061	3.2
22	Pembroke Pines city	Florida	146,637	142,180	4,457	3.1
23	Sacramento city	California	435,245	422,075	13,170	3.1
24	Palmdale city	California	124,346	120,726	3,620	3.0
25	Moreno Valley city	California	150,773	146,436	4,337	3.0
26	Coral Springs city	Florida	125,674	122,072	3,602	3.0
27	Riverside city	California	274,226	266,642	7,584	2.8
28	Overland Park city	Kansas	158,430	154,074	4,356	2.8
29	Fairfield city	California	101,935	99,144	2,791	2.8
30	Thousand Oaks city	California	122,700	119,533	3,167	2.6
31	Fort Worth city	Texas	567,516	553,341	14,175	2.6
32	Lancaster city	California	124,592	121,500	3,092	2.5
33	Santa Clarita city	California	160,554	156,828	3,726	2.4
34	Mesa city	Arizona	426,841	416,953	9,888	2.4
35	Scottsdale city	Arizona	215,779	210,973	4,806	2.3
36	Arlington city	Texas	349,944	342,180	7,764	2.3
37	Naperville city	Illinois	135,389	132,430	2,959	2.2
38	Tampa city	Florida	315,140	308,394	6,746	2.2
39	Albuquerque city	New Mexico	463,874	454,109	9,765	2.2
40	Grand Prairie city	Texas	135,303	132,544	2,759	2.1
41	Fresno city	California	445,227	436,389	8,838	2.0
42	Durham city	North Carolina	195,914	192,036	3,878	2.0
43	San Antonio city	Texas	1,194,222	1,170,820	23,402	2.0
44	Pasadena city	California	139,712	136,987	2,725	2.0
45	Ontario city	California	165,064	161,857	3,207	2.0
46	Fort Collins city	Colorado	124,665	122,268	2,397	2.0
47	Las Vegas city	Nevada	508,604	498,935	9,669	1.9
48	Reno city	Nevada	190,248	186,633	3,615	1.9
49	Anchorage municipality	Alaska	268,983	264,015	4,968	1.9
50	Phoenix city	Arizona	1,371,960	1,347,458	24,502	1.8
51	Simi Valley city	California	116,562	114,482	2,080	1.8
52	Sioux Falls city	South Dakota	130,491	128,178	2,313	1.8
53	Madison city	Wisconsin	215,211	211,448	3,763	1.8
54	San Buenaventura (Ventura) city	California	103,619	101,813	1,806	1.8
55	Jacksonville city	Florida	762,461	749,201	13,260	1.8
56	Plano city	Texas	238,091	233,954	4,137	1.8
57	El Monte city	California	119,918	117,853	2,065	1.8
58	Salem city	Oregon	140,977	138,647	2,330	1.7
59	Miami city	Florida	374,791	368,614	6,177	1.7
60	Santa Rosa city	California	153,489	151,019	2,470	1.6
61	Charlotte city	North Carolina	580,597	571,288	9,309	1.6
62	Vancouver city	Washington	149,811	147,417	2,394	1.6
63	Chesapeake city	Virginia	206,665	203,377	3,288	1.6
64	Huntsville city	Alabama	162,536	159,954	2,582	1.6
65	Tucson city	Arizona	503,151	495,506	7,645	1.5
66	Carrollton city	Texas	115,107	113,359	1,748	1.5
67	Lincoln city	Nebraska	232,362	228,850	3,512	1.5
68	Norfolk city	Virginia	239,036	235,446	3,590	1.5

TABLE 1.8

Population estimates for incorporated places over 100,000, ranked by percent change, July 1, 2001 to July 1, 2002 [CONTINUED]

Rank	Place	State	July 1, 2002 population	July 1, 2001 population	Numerical population change	Percent population change
69	San Bernardino city	California	191,631	188,769	2,862	1.5
70	Oxnard city	California	177,984	175,514	2,470	1.4
71	Pomona city	California	153,555	151,426	2,129	1.4
72	Burbank city	California	102,913	101,515	1,398	1.4
73	Houston city	Texas	2,009,834	1,983,065	26,769	1.3
74	Clarksville city	Tennessee	105,898	104,524	1,374	1.3
75	Hollywood city	Florida	143,213	141,389	1,824	1.3
76	Amarillo city	Texas	177,010	174,763	2,247	1.3
77	Oklahoma City city	Oklahoma	519,034	512,497	6,537	1.3
78	Oceanside city	California	165,880	163,807	2,073	1.3
79	Long Beach city	California	472,412	466,530	5,882	1.3
80	Los Angeles city	California	3,798,981	3,751,815	47,166	1.3
81	Pasadena city	Texas	145,034	143,256	1,778	1.2
82	Salinas city	California	148,744	146,925	1,819	1.2
83	Fullerton city	California	128,842	127,348	1,494	1.2
84	Westminster city	Colorado	103,599	102,415	1,184	1.2
85	Mesquite city	Texas	128,776	127,328	1,448	1.1
86	El Paso city	Texas	577,415	570,997	6,418	1.1
87	Honolulu CDP	Hawaii	378,155	374,000	4,155	1.1
88	Torrance city	California	141,615	140,062	1,553	1.1
89	Tallahassee city	Florida	155,171	153,471	1,700	1.1
90	Virginia Beach city	Virginia	433,934	429,223	4,711	1.1
91	Huntington Beach city	California	193,799	191,697	2,102	1.1
92	Tacoma city	Washington	197,553	195,412	2,141	1.1
93	West Covina city	California	107,694	106,530	1,164	1.1
94	Omaha city	Nebraska	399,357	395,092	4,265	1.1
95	San Diego city	California	1,259,532	1,246,252	13,280	1.1
96	Inglewood city	California	114,959	113,780	1,179	1.0
97	Downey city	California	109,840	108,717	1,123	1.0
98	Glendale city	California	199,430	197,399	2,031	1.0
99	Fort Lauderdale city	Florida	158,194	156,629	1,565	1.0
100	Waco city	Texas	115,749	114,620	1,129	1.0
101	Sterling Heights city	Michigan	126,146	124,923	1,223	1.0
102	Irving city	Texas	196,119	194,350	1,769	0.9
103	Lubbock city	Texas	203,715	201,879	1,836	0.9
104	Norwalk city	California	106,084	105,140	944	0.9
105	Eugene city	Oregon	140,395	139,146	1,249	0.9
106	Athens-Clarke County (balance)	Georgia	102,663	101,755	908	0.9
107	Boise City city	Idaho	189,847	188,190	1,657	0.9
108	Elizabeth city	New Jersey	123,279	122,223	1,056	0.9
109	Stamford city	Connecticut	119,850	118,846	1,004	0.8
110	Orlando city	Florida	193,722	192,102	1,620	0.8
111	Glendale city	Arizona	230,564	228,671	1,893	0.8
112	West Valley City city	Utah	111,254	110,351	903	0.8
113	Newark city	New Jersey	277,000	274,788	2,212	0.8
114	Portland city	Oregon	539,438	535,186	4,252	0.8
115	Concord city	California	125,225	124,243	982	0.8
116	Wichita city	Kansas	355,126	352,466	2,660	0.8
117	Greensboro city	North Carolina	228,217	226,550	1,667	0.7
118	Orange city	California	131,606	130,651	955	0.7
119	Winston-Salem city	North Carolina	188,934	187,586	1,348	0.7
120	Pueblo city	Colorado	103,411	102,675	736	0.7
121	Costa Mesa city	California	110,126	109,350	776	0.7
122	Corpus Christi city	Texas	278,520	276,691	1,829	0.7
123	Providence city	Rhode Island	175,901	174,785	1,116	0.6
124	Garland city	Texas	219,646	218,259	1,387	0.6
125	Aurora city	Colorado	286,028	284,253	1,775	0.6
126	Santa Ana city	California	343,413	341,360	2,053	0.6
127	Anaheim city	California	332,642	330,660	1,982	0.6
128	Rockford city	Illinois	151,068	150,170	898	0.6
129	Garden Grove city	California	167,429	166,443	986	0.6
130	Columbus city	Ohio	725,228	721,139	4,089	0.6
131	Worcester city	Massachusetts	174,962	174,017	945	0.5
132	Atlanta city	Georgia	424,868	422,673	2,195	0.5
133	Spokane city	Washington	196,305	195,308	997	0.5
134	Dallas city	Texas	1,211,467	1,205,897	5,570	0.5
135	Escondido city	California	135,908 1	35,299	609	0.5
136	Lexington-Fayette	Kentucky	263,618	262,478	1,140	0.4

TABLE 1.8

Population estimates for incorporated places over 100,000, ranked by percent change, July 1, 2001 to July 1, 2002 [CONTINUED]

Rank	Place	State	July 1, 2002 population	July 1, 2001 population	Numerical population change	Percent population change
137	Paterson city	New Jersey	150,750	150,106	644	0.4
138	Tempe city	Arizona	159,508	158,856	652	0.4
139	Vallejo city	California	119,798	119,342	456	0.4
140	Newport News city	Virginia	180,272	179,596	676	0.4
141	Hialeah city	Florida	228,149	227,331	818	0.4
142	St. Petersburg city	Florida	248,546	247,693	853	0.3
143	Richmond city	California	102,553	102,216	337	0.3
144	New Haven city	Connecticut	124,176	123,788	388	0.3
145	Lafayette city	Louisiana	111,272	110,929	343	0.3
146	Ann Arbor city	Michigan	115,213	114,861	352	0.3
147	Springfield city	Massachusetts	151,915	151,466	449	0.3
148	Waterbury city	Connecticut	107,883	107,574	309	0.3
149	New York city	New York	8,084,316	8,062,027	22,289	0.3
150	Little Rock city	Arkansas	184,055	183,566	489	0.3
151	Columbia city	South Carolina	117,394	117,110	284	0.2
152	Cedar Rapids city	Iowa	122,514	122,235	279	0.2
153	Montgomery city	Alabama	201,425	201,024	401	0.2
154	Manchester city	New Hampshire	108,398	108,186	212	0.2
155	Kansas City city	Missouri	443,471	442,608	863	0.2
156	Abilene city	Texas	115,225	115,012	213	0.2
157	Bridgeport city	Connecticut	140,104	139,869	235	0.2
158	Seattle city	Washington	570,426	569,494	932	0.2
159	Peoria city	Illinois	112,670	112,493	177	0.2
160	Springfield city	Illinois	111,834	111,665	169	0.2
161	Bellevue city	Washington	112,894	112,748	146	0.1
162	Hartford city	Connecticut	124,558	124,404	154	0.1
163	Memphis city	Tennessee	648,882	648,202	680	0.1
164	Chattanooga city	Tennessee	155,404	155,266	138	0.1
165	Hampton city	Virginia	145,921	145,872	49	-
166	Yonkers city	New York	197,234	197,181	53	-
167	Alexandria city	Virginia	130,804	130,828	−24	-
168	Fort Wayne city	Indiana	210,070	210,122	−52	-
169	Arlington CDP	Virginia	189,927	190,092	−165	−0.1
170	Indianapolis city (balance)	Indiana	783,612	784,343	−731	−0.1
171	Colorado Springs city	Colorado	371,182	371,563	−381	−0.1
172	Nashville-Davidson (balance)	Tennessee	545,915	546,496	−581	−0.1
173	Warren city	Michigan	137,672	137,823	−151	−0.1
174	Arvada city	Colorado	102,190	102,310	−120	−0.1
175	Tulsa city	Oklahoma	391,908	392,407	−499	−0.1
176	Salt Lake City city	Utah	181,266	181,509	−243	−0.1
177	Independence city	Missouri	113,027	113,194	−167	−0.1
178	Fayetteville city	North Carolina	124,286	124,471	−185	−0.1
179	Richmond city	Virginia	197,456	197,762	−306	−0.2
180	Hayward city	California	142,718	142,940	−222	−0.2
181	Beaumont city	Texas	112,871	113,047	−176	−0.2
182	Austin city	Texas	671,873	672,974	−1,101	−0.2
183	Lakewood city	Colorado	143,754	143,990	−236	−0.2
184	Columbus city	Georgia	185,948	186,263	−315	−0.2
185	Knoxville city	Tennessee	173,661	174,047	−386	−0.2
186	Livonia city	Michigan	100,341	100,570	−229	−0.2
187	Lansing city	Michigan	118,588	118,891	−303	−0.3
188	South Bend city	Indiana	106,558	106,851	−293	−0.3
189	Shreveport city	Louisiana	199,033	199,593	−560	−0.3
190	Chicago city	Illinois	2,886,251	2,894,581	−8,330	−0.3
191	Green Bay city	Wisconsin	101,515	101,809	−294	−0.3
192	Springfield city	Missouri	151,010	151,457	−447	−0.3
193	Provo city	Utah	105,170	105,495	−325	−0.3
194	Allentown city	Pennsylvania	106,105	106,450	−345	−0.3
195	Syracuse city	New York	145,164	145,658	−494	−0.3
196	Kansas City city	Kansas	146,978	147,491	−513	−0.3
197	Clearwater city	Florida	108,313	108,698	−385	−0.4
198	Lowell city	Massachusetts	104,901	105,280	−379	−0.4
199	Milwaukee city	Wisconsin	590,895	593,093	−2,198	−0.4
200	Jersey City city	New Jersey	240,100	240,999	−899	−0.4
201	Grand Rapids city	Michigan	196,595	197,345	−750	−0.4
202	Topeka city	Kansas	122,103	122,576	−473	−0.4
203	Rochester city	New York	217,158	218,022	−864	−0.4
204	Evansville city	Indiana	119,081	119,569	−488	−0.4

TABLE 1.8

Population estimates for incorporated places over 100,000, ranked by percent change, July 1, 2001 to July 1, 2002 [CONTINUED]

Rank	Place	State	July 1, 2002 population	July 1, 2001 population	Numerical population change	Percent population change
205	Boston city	Massachusetts	589,281	591,707	−2,426	−0.4
206	Wichita Falls city	Texas	102,926	103,373	−447	−0.4
207	Fremont city	California	206,856	207,784	−928	−0.4
208	Santa Clara city	California	101,867	102,324	−457	−0.4
209	Oakland city	California	402,777	404,633	1,856	−0.5
210	Cambridge city	Massachusetts	101,807	102,281	−474	−0.5
211	Des Moines city	Iowa	198,076	199,031	−955	−0.5
212	Berkeley city	California	103,640	104,155	−515	−0.5
213	Augusta-Richmond County (balance)	Georgia	193,101	194,073	−972	−0.5
214	Denver city	Colorado	560,415	563,238	−2,823	−0.5
215	Washington city	District of Columbia	570,898	573,822	−2,924	−0.5
216	Akron city	Ohio	214,349	215,458	−1,109	−0.5
217	Baton Rouge city	Louisiana	225,702	226,941	−1,239	−0.5
218	Jackson city	Mississippi	180,881	181,990	−1,109	−0.6
219	Birmingham city	Alabama	239,416	240,905	−1,489	−0.6
220	San Jose city	California	900,443	906,183	−5,740	−0.6
221	Philadelphia city	Pennsylvania	1,492,231	1,501,777	−9,546	−0.6
222	Buffalo city	New York	287,698	289,663	−1,965	−0.7
223	Erie city	Pennsylvania	102,122	102,843	−721	−0.7
224	Toledo city	Ohio	309,106	311,391	−2,285	−0.7
225	Dayton city	Ohio	162,669	163,885	−1,216	−0.7
226	Louisville city	Kentucky	251,399	253,367	−1,968	−0.8
227	Gary city	Indiana	100,945	101,738	−793	−0.8
228	Pittsburgh city	Pennsylvania	327,898	330,541	−2,643	−0.8
229	St. Paul city	Minnesota	284,037	286,372	−2,335	−0.8
230	Cleveland city	Ohio	467,851	472,031	−4,180	−0.9
231	Savannah city	Georgia	127,691	128,876	−1,185	−0.9
232	New Orleans city	Louisiana	473,681	478,427	−4,746	−1.0
233	Minneapolis city	Minnesota	375,635	379,513	−3,878	−1.0
234	Baltimore city	Maryland	638,614	645,305	−6,691	−1.0
235	Mobile city	Alabama	194,862	196,939	−2,077	−1.1
236	Daly City city	California	101,901	102,990	−1,089	−1.1
237	Detroit city	Michigan	925,051	935,864	−10,813	−1.2
238	Cincinnati city	Ohio	323,885	327,739	−3,854	−1.2
239	St. Louis city	Missouri	338,353	342,773	−4,420	−1.3
240	Flint city	Michigan	121,763	123,450	−1,687	−1.4
241	Sunnyvale city	California	129,687	131,517	−1,830	−1.4
242	San Francisco city	California	764,049	775,978	−11,929	−1.5

Dash (-) represents zero or rounds to zero.

SOURCE: "Table 2. Population Estimates for Incorporated Places over 100,000, Ranked by Percent Change: July 1, 2001 to July 1, 2002," State Population Estimates, U.S. Census Bureau, Population Division, July 10, 2003

FARMS

In 2002 the nation's 2.1 million farms covered 941.4 million acres. The average farm was 436 acres. (See Table 1.11.) According to the *1997 Census of Agriculture* (U.S. Department of Agriculture, National Agricultural Statistics Service, 1999), the number of large farms (those with sales of $100,000 or more) increased sixfold from 1969 to 1997. While total farm count dwindled from 2.7 million in 1969 to 1.9 million in 1997, the number of large farms jumped from 51,995 in 1969 to 345,988 in 1997. In 2002 there were 348,160 large farms in the United States, more than half of which (183,600) were situated in the north central region consisting of Illinois, Indiana, Iowa, Kansas, Michigan, Minnesota, Missouri, Nebraska, North Dakota, Ohio, South Dakota, and Wisconsin. (See Table 1.12.)

In 2002, 54.4 percent of all farms sold less than $10,000 worth of farm products. These farms accounted for only 13.3 percent of total land. On the other hand, larger farms with sales of $100,000 or more made up only 16 percent of all farms but accounted for 57.6 percent of all land. Larger farms averaged 2,049 acres, compared to 118 acres for smaller farms.

Corporations are more likely to own large farms, while families or individuals are more likely to own small farms. Individual or family ownership is the most common type of organization for both groups. Of all corporate farms in 1997, 58 percent were large farms.

Rural Population

Until the early part of the 20th century, the nation's population was mainly rural (open countryside and places with fewer than 2,500 inhabitants that were not suburbs). In 1790, when the first census was taken, 19 out of every 20 persons had a rural residence. The 1920 census was the first one that showed a majority of people living in urban

TABLE 1.9

Population estimates for incorporated places over 100,000, ranked by July 1, 2002 population, April 1, 2000 to July 1, 2002

Rank	Place	State	July 1, 2002 Population	July 1, 2001 Population	July 1, 2000 Population	April 1, 2000 Population Estimates Base	Census 2000 Population
1	New York city	New York	8,084,316	8,062,027	8,018,546	8,008,278	8,008,278
2	Los Angeles city	California	3,798,981	3,751,815	3,705,510	3,694,742	3,694,820
3	Chicago city	Illinois	2,886,251	2,894,581	2,896,095	2,896,047	2,896,016
4	Houston city	Texas	2,009,834	1,983,065	1,959,379	1,953,633	1,953,631
5	Philadelphia city	Pennsylvania	1,492,231	1,501,777	1,514,029	1,517,550	1,517,550
6	Phoenix city	Arizona	1,371,960	1,347,458	1,326,124	1,321,190	1,321,045
7	San Diego city	California	1,259,532	1,246,252	1,227,970	1,223,416	1,223,400
8	Dallas city	Texas	1,211,467	1,205,897	1,191,272	1,188,589	1,188,580
9	San Antonio city	Texas	1,194,222	1,170,820	1,155,313	1,151,268	1,144,646
10	Detroit city	Michigan	925,051	935,864	948,048	951,270	951,270
11	San Jose city	California	900,443	906,183	898,149	895,005	894,943
12	Indianapolis city (balance)	Indiana	783,612	784,343	781,850	781,870	781,870
13	San Francisco city	California	764,049	775,978	776,855	776,733	776,733
14	Jacksonville city	Florida	762,461	749,201	736,534	735,617	735,617
15	Columbus city	Ohio	725,228	721,139	713,778	711,548	711,470
16	Austin city	Texas	671,873	672,974	660,657	656,562	656,562
17	Memphis city	Tennessee	648,882	648,202	649,958	650,100	650,100
18	Baltimore city	Maryland	638,614	645,305	648,75	651,154	651,154
19	Milwaukee city	Wisconsin	590,895	593,093	596,125	596,974	596,974
20	Boston city	Massachusetts	589,281	591,707	589,403	589,141	589,141
21	Charlotte city	North Carolina	580,597	571,288	561,081	558,549	540,828
22	El Paso city	Texas	577,415	570,997	565,374	563,657	563,662
23	Washington city	District of Columbia	570,898	573,822	571,641	572,059	572,059
24	Seattle city	Washington	570,426	569,494	564,030	563,372	563,374
25	Fort Worth city	Texas	567,516	553,341	541,925	539,167	534,694
26	Denver city	Colorado	560,415	563,238	556,577	554,636	554,636
27	Nashville-Davidson (balance)	Tennessee	545,915	546,496	545,641	545,534	545,524
28	Portland city	Oregon	539,438	535,186	529,743	529,148	529,121
29	Oklahoma City city	Oklahoma	519,034	512,497	507,461	506,129	506,132
30	Las Vegas city	Nevada	508,604	498,935	483,937	479,644	478,434
31	Tucson city	Arizona	503,151	495,506	489,572	487,285	486,699
32	New Orleans city	Louisiana	473,681	478,427	483,667	484,674	484,674
33	Long Beach city	California	472,412	466,530	462,432	461,522	461,522
34	Cleveland city	Ohio	467,851	472,031	476,398	477,459	478,403
35	Albuquerque city	New Mexico	463,874	454,109	449,480	448,607	448,607
36	Fresno city	California	445,227	436,389	430,085	428,806	427,652
37	Kansas City city	Missouri	443,471	442,608	441,828	441,545	441,545
38	Sacramento city	California	435,245	422,075	409,375	407,018	407,018
39	Virginia Beach city	Virginia	433,934	429,223	426,674	425,257	425,257
40	Mesa city	Arizona	426,841	416,953	401,479	397,763	396,375
41	Atlanta city	Georgia	424,868	422,673	417,550	416,267	416,474
42	Oakland city	California	402,777	404,633	400,787	399,484	399,484
43	Omaha city	Nebraska	399,357	395,092	391,171	390,159	390,007
44	Tulsa city	Oklahoma	391,908	392,407	392,824	393,120	393,049
45	Honolulu CDP	Hawaii	378,155	374,000	371,313	371,657	371,657
46	Minneapolis city	Minnesota	375,635	379,513	382,104	382,618	382,618
47	Miami city	Florida	374,791	368,614	363,678	362,470	362,470
48	Colorado Springs city	Colorado	371,182	371,563	361,346	360,979	360,890
49	Wichita city	Kansas	355,126	352,466	351,211	351,028	344,284
50	Arlington city	Texas	349,944	342,180	334,719	332,969	332,969
51	Santa Ana city	California	343,413	341,360	338,684	337,977	337,977
52	St. Louis city	Missouri	338,353	342,773	346,948	348,189	348,189
53	Anaheim city	California	332,642	330,660	328,620	328,07	328,014
54	Pittsburgh city	Pennsylvania	327,898	330,541	333,806	334,563	334,563
55	Cincinnati city	Ohio	323,885	327,739	330,510	331,285	331,285
56	Tampa city	Florida	315,140	308,394	304,123	303,463	303,447
57	Toledo city	Ohio	309,106	311,391	313,279	313,782	313,619
58	Raleigh city	North Carolina	306,944	296,538	284,724	281,915	276,093
59	Buffalo city	New York	287,698	289,663	292,034	292,648	292,648
60	Aurora city	Colorado	286,028	284,253	277,576	275,922	276,393
61	St. Paul city	Minnesota	284,037	286,372	287,030	287,151	287,151
62	Corpus Christi city	Texas	278,520	276,691	277,288	277,492	277,454
63	Newark city	New Jersey	277,000	274,788	272,878	272,537	273,546
64	Riverside city	California	274,226	266,642	257,258	255,175	255,166
65	Anchorage municipality	Alaska	268,983	264,015	260,571	260,283	260,283
66	Lexington-Fayette	Kentucky	263,618	262,478	260,975	260,512	260,512
67	Stockton city	California	262,835	254,774	245,421	243,771	243,771
68	Bakersfield city	California	260,969	251,690	244,516	243,072	247,057
69	Louisville city	Kentucky	251,399	253,367	255,598	256,231	256,231

TABLE 1.9

Population estimates for incorporated places over 100,000, ranked by July 1, 2002 population, April 1, 2000 to July 1, 2002 [CONTINUED]

Rank	Place	State	July 1, 2002 Population	July 1, 2001 Population	July 1, 2000 Population	April 1, 2000 Population Estimates Base	Census 2000 Population
70	St. Petersburg city	Florida	248,546	247,693	248,301	248,408	248,232
71	Jersey City city	New Jersey	240,100	240,999	240,085	240,055	240,055
72	Birmingham city	Alabama	239,416	240,905	242,516	242,820	242,820
73	Norfolk city	Virginia	239,036	235,446	234,456	234,403	234,403
74	Plano city	Texas	238,091	233,954	224,108	222,008	222,030
75	Lincoln city	Nebraska	232,362	228,850	226,503	225,640	225,581
76	Glendale city	Arizona	230,564	228,671	220,730	218,815	218,812
77	Greensboro city	North Carolina	228,217	226,550	224,553	224,035	223,891
78	Hialeah city	Florida	228,149	227,331	226,576	226,419	226,419
79	Baton Rouge city	Louisiana	225,702	226,941	228,318	228,518	227,818
80	Garland city	Texas	219,646	218,259	216,153	215,794	215,768
81	Rochester city	New York	217,158	218,022	219,500	219,773	219,773
82	Scottsdale city	Arizona	215,779	210,973	204,336	202,736	202,705
83	Madison city	Wisconsin	215,211	211,448	208,856	208,126	208,054
84	Akron city	Ohio	214,349	215,458	216,854	217,074	217,074
85	Fort Wayne city	Indiana	210,070	210,122	210,493	210,415	205,727
86	Fremont city	California	206,856	207,784	204,424	203,413	203,413
87	Chesapeake city	Virginia	206,665	203,377	200,472	199,184	199,184
88	Henderson city	Nevada	206,153	194,005	179,558	175,750	175,381
89	Lubbock city	Texas	203,715	201,879	199,732	199,572	199,564
90	Modesto city	California	203,555	196,827	190,066	188,856	188,856
91	Chandler city	Arizona	202,016	191,426	179,563	176,652	176,581
92	Montgomery city	Alabama	201,425	201,024	201,447	201,587	201,568
93	Glendale city	California	199,430	197,399	195,424	194,973	194,973
94	Shreveport city	Louisiana	199,033	199,593	200,004	200,114	200,145
95	Des Moines city	Iowa	198,076	199,031	198,775	198,709	198,682
96	Tacoma city	Washington	197,553	195,412	193,840	193,556	193,556
97	Richmond city	Virginia	197,456	197,762	197,477	197,790	197,790
98	Yonkers city	New York	197,234	197,181	196,414	196,086	196,086
99	Grand Rapids city	Michigan	196,595	197,345	197,826	197,800	197,800
100	Spokane city	Washington	196,305	195,308	195,493	195,629	195,629
101	Irving city	Texas	196,119	194,350	192,027	191,615	191,615
102	Durham city	North Carolina	195,914	192,036	188,339	187,364	187,035
103	Mobile city	Alabama	194,862	196,939	198,582	198,915	198,915
104	Chula Vista city	California	193,919	183,778	175,559	173,566	173,556
105	Huntington Beach city	California	193,799	191,697	190,032	189,594	189,594
106	Orlando city	Florida	193,722	192,102	190,235	189,752	185,951
107	Augusta-Richmond County (balance)	Georgia	193,101	194,073	194,950	195,182	195,182
108	San Bernardino city	California	191,631	188,769	185,866	185,260	185,401
109	Laredo city	Texas	191,538	185,506	178,939	177,322	176,576
110	Reno city	Nevada	190,248	186,633	181,419	180,480	180,480
111	Arlington CDP	Virginia	189,927	190,092	189,445	189,453	189,453
112	Boise City city	Idaho	189,847	188,190	186,331	185,898	185,787
113	Winston-Salem city	North Carolina	188,934	187,586	186,053	185,779	185,776
114	Columbus city	Georgia	185,948	186,263	186,488	186,291	185,781
115	Little Rock city	Arkansas	184,055	183,566	183,205	183,135	183,133
116	Salt Lake City city	Utah	181,266	181,509	181,758	181,767	181,743
117	Jackson city	Mississippi	180,881	181,990	183,766	184,256	184,256
118	Newport News city	Virginia	180,272	179,596	180,106	180,150	180,150
119	Oxnard city	California	177,984	175,514	171,429	170,359	170,358
120	Amarillo city	Texas	177,010	174,763	173,995	173,627	173,627
121	Providence city	Rhode Island	175,901	174,785	173,800	173,618	173,618
122	Worcester city	Massachusetts	174,962	174,017	173,003	172,648	172,648
123	Knoxville city	Tennessee	173,661	174,047	174,448	174,501	173,890
124	Garden Grove city	California	167,429	166,443	165,461	165,196	165,196
125	Oceanside city	California	165,880	163,807	161,564	161,029	161,029
126	Ontario city	California	165,064	161,857	158,704	158,011	158,007
127	Dayton city	Ohio	162,669	163,885	165,740	166,197	166,179
128	Huntsville city	Alabama	162,536	159,954	158,751	158,430	158,216
129	Irvine city	California	162,122	156,229	145,706	143,072	143,072
130	Santa Clarita city	California	160,554	156,828	153,088	152,192	151,088
131	Tempe city	Arizona	159,508	158,856	158,634	158,625	158,625
132	Overland Park city	Kansas	158,430	154,074	150,247	149,080	149,080
133	Fort Lauderdale city	Florida	158,194	156,629	154,690	154,198	152,397
134	Aurora city	Illinois	156,974	150,563	144,450	143,078	142,990
135	Chattanooga city	Tennessee	155,404	155,266	155,620	155,704	155,554
136	Tallahassee city	Florida	155,171	153,471	151,794	151,401	150,624
137	Pomona city	California	153,555	151,426	149,781	149,473	149,473

TABLE 1.9

Population estimates for incorporated places over 100,000, ranked by July 1, 2002 population, April 1, 2000 to July 1, 2002 [CONTINUED]

Rank	Place	State	July 1, 2002 Population	July 1, 2001 Population	July 1, 2000 Population	April 1, 2000 Population Estimates Base	Census 2000 Population
138	Santa Rosa city	California	153,489	151,019	148,622	147,854	147,595
139	Springfield city	Massachusetts	151,915	151,466	152,062	152,082	152,082
140	Rockford city	Illinois	151,068	150,170	150,376	150,323	150,115
141	Springfield city	Missouri	151,010	151,457	151,650	151,720	151,580
142	Moreno Valley city	California	150,773	146,436	143,129	142,379	142,381
143	Paterson city	New Jersey	150,750	150,106	149,331	149,222	149,222
144	Brownsville city	Texas	150,425	145,486	140,795	139,715	139,722
145	Vancouver city	Washington	149,811	147,417	144,170	143,593	143,560
146	Salinas city	California	148,744	146,925	144,373	143,776	151,060
147	Kansas City city	Kansas	146,978	147,491	146,823	146,866	146,866
148	Pembroke Pines city	Florida	146,637	142,180	138,344	137,415	137,427
149	Hampton city	Virginia	145,921	145,872	146,494	146,437	146,437
150	Syracuse city	New York	145,164	145,658	146,262	146,435	147,306
151	Pasadena city	Texas	145,034	143,256	141,968	141,674	141,674
152	Lakewood city	Colorado	143,754	143,990	144,143	144,137	144,126
153	Rancho Cucamonga city	California	143,711	135,198	129,160	127,743	127,743
154	Fontana city	California	143,607	137,745	130,619	128,938	128,929
155	Hollywood city	Florida	143,213	141,389	139,901	139,530	139,357
156	Hayward city	California	142,718	142,940	140,704	140,031	140,030
157	Torrance city	California	141,615	140,062	138,345	137,946	137,946
158	Salem city	Oregon	140,977	138,647	137,349	136,971	136,924
159	Eugene city	Oregon	140,395	139,146	138,552	138,319	137,893
160	Bridgeport city	Connecticut	140,104	139,869	139,679	139,529	139,529
161	Pasadena city	California	139,712	136,987	134,521	133,936	133,936
162	Corona city	California	138,326	132,810	126,696	125,251	124,966
163	Warren city	Michigan	137,672	137,823	138,317	138,247	138,247
164	Escondido city	California	135,908	135,299	133,958	133,643	133,559
165	North Las Vegas city	Nevada	135,902	127,409	117,975	115,488	115,488
166	Naperville city	Illinois	135,389	132,430	129,246	128,420	128,358
167	Grand Prairie city	Texas	135,303	132,544	128,365	127,427	127,427
168	Gilbert town	Arizona	135,005	122,372	112,384	109,920	109,697
169	Orange city	California	131,606	130,651	129,198	128,821	128,821
170	Alexandria city	Virginia	130,804	130,828	129,229	128,283	128,283
171	Sioux Falls city	South Dakota	130,491	128,178	125,243	124,293	123,975
172	Sunnyvale city	California	129,687	131,517	131,853	131,760	131,760
173	Fullerton city	California	128,842	127,348	126,281	126,003	126,003
174	Mesquite city	Texas	128,776	127,328	125,003	124,523	124,523
175	Savannah city	Georgia	127,691	128,876	130,933	131,555	131,510
176	Sterling Heights city	Michigan	126,146	124,923	124,606	124,471	124,471
177	Coral Springs city	Florida	125,674	122,072	118,449	117,549	117,549
178	Concord city	California	125,225	124,243	122,152	121,780	121,780
179	Fort Collins city	Colorado	124,665	122,268	119,314	118,716	118,652
180	Lancaster city	California	124,592	121,500	119,227	118,718	118,718
181	Hartford city	Connecticut	124,558	124,404	124,177	124,121	121,578
182	Palmdale city	California	124,346	120,726	117,584	116,829	116,670
183	Fayetteville city	North Carolina	124,286	124,471	124,967	125,024	121,015
184	New Haven city	Connecticut	124,176	123,788	123,600	123,626	123,626
185	Elizabeth city	New Jersey	123,279	122,223	120,847	120,568	120,568
186	Peoria city	Arizona	123,239	117,880	110,495	108,685	108,364
187	Thousand Oaks city	California	122,700	119,533	117,538	117,005	117,005
188	Cedar Rapids city	Iowa	122,514	122,235	121,547	121,296	120,758
189	Topeka city	Kansas	122,103	122,576	122,698	122,685	122,377
190	Flint city	Michigan	121,763	123,450	124,728	124,943	124,943
191	El Monte city	California	119,918	117,853	116,322	115,965	115,965
192	Stamford city	Connecticut	119,850	118,846	117,514	117,083	117,083
193	Vallejo city	California	119,798	119,342	117,445	116,760	116,760
194	Evansville city	Indiana	119,081	119,569	121,174	121,582	121,582
195	Lansing city	Michigan	118,588	118,891	119,111	119,213	119,128
196	Joliet city	Illinois	118,423	112,066	107,462	106,334	106,221
197	Columbia city	South Carolina	117,394	117,110	116,349	116,278	116,278
198	Simi Valley city	California	116,562	114,482	112,014	111,365	111,351
199	Waco city	Texas	115,749	114,620	114,056	113,880	113,726
200	Abilene city	Texas	115,225	115,012	115,841	115,930	115,930
201	Ann Arbor city	Michigan	115,213	114,861	114,336	114,111	114,024
202	Carrollton city	Texas	115,107	113,359	110,259	109,578	109,576
203	Inglewood city	California	114,959	113,780	112,801	112,580	112,580
204	McAllen city	Texas	113,877	109,388	107,041	106,419	106,414
205	Independence city	Missouri	113,027	113,194	113,298	113,288	113,288

TABLE 1.9

Population estimates for incorporated places over 100,000, ranked by July 1, 2002 population, April 1, 2000 to July 1, 2002 [CONTINUED]

Rank	Place	State	July 1, 2002 Population	July 1, 2001 Population	July 1, 2000 Population	April 1, 2000 Population Estimates Base	Census 2000 Population
206	Cape Coral city	Florida	112,899	107,743	103,221	102,286	102,286
207	Bellevue city	Washington	112,894	112,748	112,595	112,638	109,569
208	Beaumont city	Texas	112,871	113,047	113,694	113,866	113,866
209	Peoria city	Illinois	112,670	112,493	112,901	112,970	112,936
210	Springfield city	Illinois	111,834	111,665	111,482	111,486	111,454
211	Lafayette city	Louisiana	111,272	110,929	110,863	111,385	110,257
212	West Valley City city	Utah	111,254	110,351	109,199	108,896	108,896
213	Costa Mesa city	California	110,126	109,350	108,888	108,756	108,724
214	Downey city	California	109,840	108,717	107,583	107,323	107,323
215	Manchester city	New Hampshire	108,398	108,186	107,203	107,006	107,006
216	Clearwater city	Florida	108,313	108,698	108,773	108,789	108,787
217	Waterbury city	Connecticut	107,883	107,574	107,306	107,271	107,271
218	West Covina city	California	107,694	106,530	105,352	105,080	105,080
219	South Bend city	Indiana	106,558	106,851	107,764	107,919	107,789
220	Allentown city	Pennsylvania	106,105	106,450	106,532	106,632	106,632
221	Norwalk city	California	106,084	105,140	103,643	103,298	103,298
222	Clarksville city	Tennessee	105,898	104,524	103,952	103,478	103,455
223	Provo city	Utah	105,170	105,495	105,117	105,168	105,166
224	Lowell city	Massachusetts	104,901	105,280	105,250	105,167	105,167
225	Berkeley city	California	103,640	104,155	103,085	102,743	102,743
226	San Buenaventura (Ventura) city	California	103,619	101,813	101,123	100,920	100,916
227	Westminster city	Colorado	103,599	102,415	101,325	100,928	100,940
228	Pueblo city	Colorado	103,411	102,675	102,119	102,129	102,121
229	Wichita Falls city	Texas	102,926	103,373	103,917	104,197	104,197
230	Burbank city	California	102,913	101,515	100,538	100,316	100,316
231	Athens-Clarke County (balance)	Georgia	102,663	101,755	100,566	100,266	100,266
232	Richmond city	California	102,553	102,216	99,712	99,216	99,216
233	Arvada city	Colorado	102,190	102,310	102,309	102,271	102,153
234	Erie city	Pennsylvania	102,122	102,843	103,492	103,717	103,717
235	Fairfield city	California	101,935	99,144	96,894	96,178	96,178
236	Daly City city	California	101,901	102,990	103,654	103,621	103,621
237	Santa Clara city	California	101,867	102,324	102,461	102,361	102,361
238	Cambridge city	Massachusetts	101,807	102,281	101,579	101,355	101,355
239	Green Bay city	Wisconsin	101,515	101,809	102,263	102,313	102,313
240	Olathe city	Kansas	101,413	96,312	93,765	92,998	92,962
241	Gary city	Indiana	100,945	101,738	102,522	102,746	102,746
242	Livonia city	Michigan	100,341	100,570	100,564	100,545	100,545

SOURCE: "Table 1. Population Estimates for Incorporated Places over 100,000, Ranked by July 1, 2002 Population: April 1, 2000 to July 1, 2002," in *State Population Estimates,* U.S. Census Bureau, Population Division, July 10, 2003

areas (51.2 percent). In 1997 only 20 percent of families lived in nonmetropolitan areas.

In 1920 farm residents made up 30.2 percent of the total population. This proportion fell to 15.3 percent in 1950, 4.8 percent in 1970, and 2.7 percent in 1980. By 1991, the last year statistics were kept on residents of farms and rural areas, 1 of every 51 persons (about 1.9 percent) lived on a farm.

RACE AND HISPANIC ORIGIN

The Census Bureau bases its population estimates on three components of population change: births, deaths, and immigration. The number of births minus the number of deaths is the "natural increase" in the population. The bureau researchers then add the number of immigrants (persons coming into a country from another country or region) minus the number of emigrants (persons who have left one country or region to settle in another) to the "natural increase" and arrive at a total increase in population.

The Census Bureau estimated the U.S. population, as of July 1, 2002, at 288 million people; 232.6 million were white; 36.7 million, black; 2.7 million, Native American, Eskimo, and Aleut; and 11.5 million, Asian and Pacific Islander. The Hispanic population, which includes people of any race but of Latin American descent (mainly Cuban, Mexican, and Puerto Rican), living in the United States as of July 1, 2002, numbered 38.7 million.

The general population rose by about 16 million people from April 1990 to November 2000. During the same period, the white population rose from 208.7 million to 226.9 million, an increase of 8 percent, but representing a decrease from 84 percent of the total population in 1990 to 82 percent in 2000. The white non-Hispanic population decreased from about 75.7 of the total population in 1990 to about 69.1 percent in 2000.

From April 2000 to July 2002 the U.S. population increased by 6.9 million people. During this period, the

TABLE 1.10

Top 50 incorporated places of 100,000 or more ranked by population, 1990 and 2000

Rank	Place name	Area	Population April 1, 2000	Population April 1, 1990	Change, 1990 to 2000 Number	Change, 1990 to 2000 Percent
1	New York city[1]	NY	8,008,278	7,322,564	685,714	9.4
2	Los Angeles city	CA	3,694,820	3,485,398	209,422	6.0
3	Chicago city	IL	2,896,016	2,783,726	112,290	4.0
4	Houston city	TX	1,953,631	1,630,553	323,078	19.8
5	Philadelphia city[2]	PA	1,517,550	1,585,577	−68,027	−4.3
6	Phoenix city	AZ	1,321,045	983,403	337,642	34.3
7	San Diego city	CA	1,223,400	1,110,549	112,851	10.2
8	Dallas city	TX	1,188,580	1,006,877	181,703	18.0
9	San Antonio city	TX	1,144,646	935,933	208,713	22.3
10	Detroit city	MI	951,270	1,027,974	−76,704	−7.5
11	San Jose city	CA	894,943	782,248	112,695	14.4
12	Indianapolis city	IN	791,926	741,952	49,974	6.7
13	San Francisco city[3]	CA	776,733	723,959	52,774	7.3
14	Jacksonville city	FL	735,617	635,230	100,387	15.8
15	Columbus city	OH	711,470	632,910	78,560	12.4
16	Austin city	TX	656,562	465,622	190,940	41.0
17	Baltimore city	MD	651,154	736,014	−84,860	−11.5
18	Memphis city	TN	650,100	610,337	39,763	6.5
19	Milwaukee city	WI	596,974	628,088	−31,114	−5.0
20	Boston city	MA	589,141	574,283	14,858	2.6
21	Washington city[4]	DC	572,059	606,900	−34,841	−5.7
22	Nashville-Davidson[5]	TN	569,891	510,784	59,107	11.6
23	El Paso city	TX	563,662	515,342	48,320	9.4
24	Seattle city	WA	563,374	516,259	47,115	9.1
25	Denver city[6]	CO	554,636	467,610	87,026	18.6
26	Charlotte city	NC	540,828	395,934	144,894	36.6
27	Fort Worth city	TX	534,694	447,619	87,075	19.5
28	Portland city	OR	529,121	437,319	91,802	21.0
29	Oklahoma City city	OK	506,132	444,719	61,413	13.8
30	Tucson city	AZ	486,699	405,390	81,309	20.1
31	New Orleans city	LA	484,674	496,938	−12,264	−2.5
32	Las Vegas city	NV	478,434	258,295	220,139	85.2
33	Cleveland city	OH	478,403	505,616	−27,213	−5.4
34	Long Beach city	CA	461,522	429,433	32,089	7.5
35	Albuquerque city	NM	448,607	384,736	63,871	16.6
36	Kansas City city	MO	441,545	435,146	6,399	1.5
37	Fresno city	CA	427,652	354,202	73,450	20.7
38	Virginia Beach city	VA	425,257	393,069	32,188	8.2
39	San Juan zona urbana	Puerto Rico	421,958	426,832	−4,874	−1.1
40	Atlanta city	GA	416,474	394,017	22,457	5.7
41	Sacramento city	CA	407,018	369,365	37,653	10.2
42	Oakland city	CA	399,484	372,242	27,242	7.3
43	Mesa city	AZ	396,375	288,091	108,284	37.6
44	Tulsa city	OK	393,049	367,302	25,747	7.0
45	Omaha city	NE	390,007	335,795	54,212	16.1
46	Minneapolis city	MN	382,618	368,383	14,235	3.9
47	Honolulu CDP[7]	HI	371,657	365,272	6,385	1.7
48	Miami city	FL	362,470	358,548	3,922	1.1
49	Colorado Springs city	CO	360,890	281,140	79,750	28.4
50	St. Louis city	MO	348,189	396,685	−48,496	−12.2

[1]The five boroughs of New York city are coextensive with the five counties that constitute New York city: Bronx borough (Bronx County), Brooklyn borough (Kings County), Manhattan borough (New York County), Queens borough (Queens County), and Staten Island borough (Richmond County).
[2]Philadelphia city is coextensive with Philadelphia County.
[3]San Francisco city is coextensive with San Francisco County.
[4]Washington city is coextensive with the District of Columbia.
[5]Nashville-Davidson city is consolidated with Davidson County.
[6]Denver city is coextensive with Denver County.
[7]Honolulu Census Designated Place; by agreement with the State of Hawaii, the Census Bureau does not show data separately for the city of Honolulu, which is coextensive with Honolulu County.
Note: 1990 Census population counts are as published in 1990 census reports and do not include changes published subsequently due to boundary or other changes. In Puerto Rico, a zona urbana represents the governmental center of a municipio (which is the equivalent of a county). Zonas urbanas are treated as Census Designated Places, as there are no incorporated places in Puerto Rico.

SOURCE: Adapted from "Table 2. Incorporated Places of 100,000 or more, ranked by population: 2000," in *Census 2000 PHC-T-5. Ranking Tables for Incorporated Places of 100,000 or More: 1990 and 2000*, U.S. Census Bureau, Washington, DC, April 2, 2001 [Online] http://www.census.gov/population/cen2000/phc-t5/tab02.pdf [accessed March 5, 2004]

white population rose from 228.1 million to 232.6 million, an increase of 2 percent, but representing a decrease from 82 percent of the total population in 2000 to 81 percent in July 2002. The white non-Hispanic population decreased from about 75.7 of the total population in 1990 to 68 percent in July 2002.

TABLE 1.11

Number of farms, land in farms, and average size of farm, 1993–2002

Year	Farms[1] (number)	Land in farms (1,000 acres)	Average size farm (acres)
1993	2,201,590	968,845	440
1994	2,197,690	965,935	440
1995	2,196,400	962,515	438
1996	2,190,500	958,675	438
1997	2,190,510	956,010	436
1998	2,191,360	953,500	435
1999	2,192,070	947,440	432
2000	2,172,280	943,090	434
2001	2,155,680	941,310	437
2002[2]	2,158,090	941,480	436

[1]A farm is any establishment from which $1,000 or more of agricultural products were sold or would normally be sold during the year.
[2]Preliminary.
Note: The farm definition was changed in 1993 to include maple syrup, short rotation woody crops, and places with 5 or more horses.

SOURCE: "Table 9-2. Farms: Land, land in farms, and average size of farm, U.S., 1993–2002," in *Agricultural Statistics 2003,* U. S. Department of Agriculture, National Agricultural Statistics Service, Washington, DC, 2003

Hispanic-Origin Population

The Hispanic-origin population, from April 1, 1990, to November 2000, rose by 46 percent, from 22.4 million to 32.8 million. From April 1, 2000, to July 1, 2002, the Hispanic-origin population rose by almost 11 percent, from 35.3 million to 38.7 million. The Hispanic-origin population accounted for almost 13 percent of the total population of the United States in July 2002. Hispanics are expected to number 98.2 million in 2050. By then the Census Bureau projects that nearly one in four Americans will be of Hispanic origin. A higher birth rate for Hispanics than for non-Hispanics and high levels of immigration are two of the major reasons for the expected rapid increase in the Hispanic population.

In 2000 almost two-thirds of all Hispanics were of Mexican origin.

Asian and Pacific Islander Population

From April 1, 1990, to November 2000 the number of non-Hispanic Asians and Pacific Islanders in the United States rose from 7.5 million to 11 million, an increase of almost 50 percent. By July 1, 2002, the number of non-Hispanic Asians and Pacific Islanders in the United States rose to 11.6 million. Immigration to the United States accounted for much of this growth. In 2000 the total Asian and Pacific Islander population accounted for 4 percent of America's population. By 2050 the proportion of Asians and Pacific Islanders is projected to be 9.3 percent of the total U.S. populace.

Native American, Eskimo, and Aleut Population

The non-Hispanic Native American, Eskimo, and Aleut populations rose from 2 million to 2.5 million

FIGURE 1.3

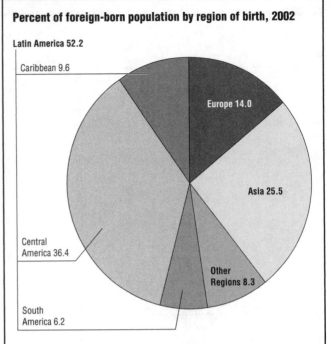

Percent of foreign-born population by region of birth, 2002

Latin America 52.2

Caribbean 9.6

Europe 14.0

Asia 25.5

Central America 36.4

Other Regions 8.3

South America 6.2

SOURCE: Dianne Schmidley, "Figure 1. Foreign Born by Region of Birth: 2002," in "The Foreign-Born Population in the United States: March 2002," *Current Population Reports,* vol. P20-539, February 2003

between April 1990 and November 2000, an increase of 25 percent. In 2002 these groups accounted for about 1 percent of the total U.S. population, a proportion that is projected to remain relatively constant through 2050.

Black Population

From April 1990 to November 2000 the non-Hispanic black population increased from 30.5 million to 35.5 million, a gain of 16 percent. The total black population increased from 30.5 million to 37.1 million. The black population accounted for approximately 13 percent of the total population in July 2002, up somewhat from 12.3 percent in 1990 and 11.7 percent in 1980. According to the Census Bureau's projection, the black population will likely be 14.7 percent of the total population by 2050. Most of the growth in the black population since 1980 (84 percent) has been due to natural increase (births minus deaths). Immigration accounted for the remaining 16 percent.

Children

In 2000, 64 percent of U.S. children were non-Hispanic white, down from 74 percent in 1980. About 15 percent were non-Hispanic black; 16 percent, Hispanic; 4 percent, Asian and Pacific Islander; and 1 percent, Native American or Alaska Native. The percentages of the child population of blacks and Native American or Alaska Natives were fairly stable from 1980 to 2000.

Meanwhile, the percentage of Hispanics increased more rapidly than that of other racial and ethnic groups, growing

TABLE 1.12

Economic sales class of farms by region, 2000–02

Region and year	Economic sales class						Total
	$1,000–$9,999 (number)	$10,000–$99,999 (number)	$100,000 & over (number)	$100,000 $249,999 (number)	$250,000 $499,999	$500,000 & over	
Northeast:[1]							
2000	73,900	38,000	22,000	—	—	—	133,900
2001	72,800	38,100	22,200	—	—	—	133,100
2002[5]	74,000	34,780	23,820	14,140	5,870	3,810	132,600
North central:[2]							
2000	333,800	297,200	183,800	—	—	—	814,800
2001	330,200	289,200	185,900	—	—	—	805,300
2002	332,400	286,000	183,600	109,600	47,600	26,400	802,000
South:[3]							
2000	601,500	227,220	89,280	—	—	—	918,000
2001	598,240	228,580	89,580	—	—	—	916,400
2002	605,410	230,330	86,360	41,900	22,524	21,936	922,100
West:[4]							
2000	164,350	87,130	54,100	—	—	—	305,580
2001	159,750	86,830	54,300	—	—	—	300,880
2002	160,960	86,050	54,380	24,230	13,250	16,900	301,390
US:							
2000	1,173,550	649,550	349,180	—	—	—	2,172,280
2001	1,160,990	642,710	351,980	—	—	—	2,155,680
2002	1,172,770	637,160	348,160	189,870	89,244	69,046	2,158,090

[1] CT, ME, MA, NH, NJ, NY, PA, RI, and VT.
[2] IL, IN, IA, KS, MI, MN, MO, NE, ND, OH, SD, WI.
[3] AL, AR, DE, FL, GA, KY, LA, MD, MS, NC, OK, SC, TN, TX, VA, WV.
[4] AK, AZ, CA, CO, HI, ID, MT, NV, NM, OR, UT, WA, WY.
[5] Number of farms estimated for 3 sales classes above $100,000 beginning in 2002.

SOURCE: "Table 9-4. Number of farms: Economic sales class by region and United States, 2000–2002," in *Agricultural Statistics 2003*, U.S. Department of Agriculture, National Agricultural Statistics Service, Washington, DC, 2003

from 9 percent of the child population in 1980 to 16 percent in 2000. By 2020 it is projected that more than one in five children will be Hispanic. The percentage of Asian and Pacific Islander children doubled from 2 to 4 percent between 1980 and 2000. This percentage is expected to continue to grow in the coming decades to 6 percent by 2020.

FOREIGN-BORN POPULATION

In March 2002, 32.5 million people in the United States were foreign born, representing 11.5 percent of the population, according to the Census Bureau. That figure is more than double the 4.7 percent of the total population that the foreign born comprised in 1970. Between 1990 and 2002 the foreign-born population increased much more quickly than the native population. "Natives" are persons born in the United States, Puerto Rico, or an outlying area of the United States, such as Guam or the U.S. Virgin Islands, and persons who were born in a foreign country but who had at least one parent who was a U.S. citizen. All other persons born outside the United States, including naturalized citizens, resident legal aliens, and resident illegal aliens, are foreign born. Fifty-two percent of foreign-born persons living in the United States in 2002 were born in Latin America. Slightly more than one-fourth (25.5 percent) of the foreign born were born in Asia. Fourteen percent were born in Europe, down signifi-

cantly from 1970 when almost 62 percent of the foreign born were from Europe. (See Figure 1.3.)

The foreign-born population is not distributed evenly throughout the country. In 2002, 38.1 percent of foreign-born residents lived in the West, followed by 28.2 percent in the South, 23.1 percent in the Northeast, and 10.6 percent in the Midwest. (See Figure 1.4.) The highest concentration of the foreign born from Latin America (40.6 percent) and Asia (44.6 percent) was in the West, more than in any other region of the United States. Central America's foreign born, who represent more than two-thirds of foreign born from Latin America, were concentrated in the West and the South (54.7 percent and 30.1 percent, respectively). In contrast, the Latin American foreign born from South America and the Caribbean were concentrated in the Northeast (45.5 percent and 50.5 percent, respectively) and the South (36 percent and 44.4 percent, respectively).

According to the Census Bureau, about 39.5 percent of the foreign-born people living in the United States in 2000 entered in the 1990s. Twenty-eight percent arrived in the 1980s and 16 percent in the 1970s. Of those who arrived before 1970, 80.4 percent had obtained U.S. citizenship by 2000. Some 61.9 percent of those entering between 1970 and 1979 were U.S. citizens by 2000, compared to 38.9 percent of those who entered from

FIGURE 1.4

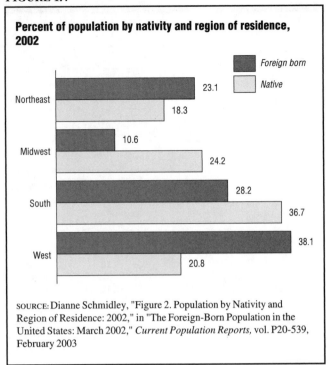

Percent of population by nativity and region of residence, 2002

- Foreign born
- Native

Northeast
 23.1
 18.3

Midwest
 10.6
 24.2

South
 28.2
 36.7

West
 38.1
 20.8

SOURCE: Dianne Schmidley, "Figure 2. Population by Nativity and Region of Residence: 2002," in "The Foreign-Born Population in the United States: March 2002," *Current Population Reports,* vol. P20-539, February 2003

1980 to 1989 and 8.9 percent of those who entered during the 1990s.

IMMIGRATION

According to the Census Bureau's *Statistical Abstract of the United States: 2002,* in 2000, 849,800 people immigrated to the United States. Mexico was the leading country of origin, with 173,900 persons coming to the United States from that nation. Other leading countries were China (45,700), the Philippines (42,500), India (42,000), Vietnam (26,700), Nicaragua (24,000) and El Salvador (22,600). (See Table 1.13.)

In 2000 about 40 percent of the immigrants settled in just two states: California (217,753) and New York (106,061). Florida (98,391), Texas (63,840), New Jersey (40,013), and Illinois (36,180) were also popular destinations for immigrants. (See Table 1.14.) Since 1971 these six states have been the principal states of intended residence for new immigrants, with California the leading state since 1976. These figures do not include refugees and asylum seekers.

GEOGRAPHIC MOBILITY

Fifteen percent of the population one year old and over moved in the one-year period between 1999 and 2000. Of those who moved, almost 60 percent moved from one residence to another within the same county; 20 percent moved to a different county within the same state; and 20 percent relocated to a different state. During that same one-year period, about 1 percent of the population moved into the United States from abroad.

In 2000 young adults in their 20s had the highest mobility rates. Moving rates declined as age increased; only 5 percent of those 65 years and older moved. In the West 18 percent of the population moved between 1998 and 1999, followed by 17 percent in the South, 15 percent in the Midwest, and 11 percent in the Northeast. During the same period, renters moved at a rate of 32 percent, compared to only 8 percent of home owners.

AN AGING POPULATION

In the 20th century, the rate of growth of the elderly population (persons 65 years old and over) greatly exceeded the growth rate of the population of the country as a whole. The elderly increased by a factor of 11, from 3 million in 1900 to 35 million in 2000. In comparison, the total population increased 3.5 times. However, Census 2000 was the first time since census data on the 65 and over population was first tracked in 1790 that this group did not grow faster than the total population. Between 1990 and 2000 the total population increased by 13.2 percent, from 248.7 million to 281.4 million people. In comparison, the population 65 years and over increased by only 12 percent.

According to Census Bureau projections, the number of people 65 years old and over will more than double, to 79 million, by the middle of the 21st century. About one in eight Americans was elderly in 1990; by 2050 about one in five will be elderly.

Persons 85 years old and over are a small but rapidly growing group, accounting for 1.5 percent of the U.S. population. This population was 4.2 million in 2000, an increase of 38 percent from the 3.1 million in 1990, which is about 34 times larger than in 1900. On November 1, 2000, the nation had an estimated 68,000 people aged 100 years or more. Fifty-six thousand were women and 12,000 were men.

In 2000 children made up almost 26 percent of the population, down from a peak of 36 percent in 1960. Since 1960 the proportion of children in the U.S. population has been decreasing. They are projected to make up 24 percent of the population in 2020. On the other hand, the elderly have increased as a percentage of the total population. They are expected to comprise 16 percent of the population by 2020.

Median Age

Since the proportion of elderly Americans is projected to increase dramatically, it should not be surprising that the median age (half are older; half are younger) in the United States is increasing. In 2000 the median age was 35.9, up from 32.8 a decade earlier. The average (the number achieved by adding a set of figures and dividing the sum by the number of figures) age of the U.S. population in

TABLE 1.13

Immigrants by country of birth, 1981–2000

[In thousands (7,338.1 represents 7,338,100). For fiscal years ending Sept. 30.]

Country of birth	1981-90, total	1991-98, total	1999	2000	Country of birth	1981-90, total	1991-98, total	1999	2000
All countries	**7,338.1**	**7,599.0**	**646.6**	**849.8**	Thailand	64.4	42.3	2.4	3.8
Europe[1]	**705.6**	**1,086.2**	**92.7**	**132.5**	Turkey	20.9	21.5	2.2	2.6
Bosnia and					Vietnam	401.4	374.0	20.4	26.7
Herzegovina	(X)	[2]21.9	5.4	11.8	**Africa[1]**	**192.3**	**301.6**	**36.7**	**44.7**
France	23.1	21.8	2.2	3.5	Egypt	31.4	37.8	4.4	4.5
Germany	70.1	54.9	5.2	7.6	Ethiopia	27.2	41.0	4.3	4.1
Greece	29.1	11.9	0.7	1.0	Ghana	14.9	27.6	3.7	4.3
Ireland	32.8	56.8	0.8	1.3	Nigeria	35.3	52.7	6.8	7.9
Italy	32.9	18.5	1.5	2.5	South Africa	15.7	18.2	1.6	2.8
Poland	97.4	150.7	8.8	10.1	**Oceania[1]**	**(NA)**	**39.2**	**3.7**	**5.1**
Portugal	40.0	20.3	1.1	1.4	Australia	13.9	14.8	1.1	2.1
Romania	38.9	45.0	5.7	6.9	**North America[1]**	**3,125.0**	**3,301.2**	**271.4**	**344.8**
Russia	(X)	[2]98.6	12.3	17.1	Canada	119.2	112.5	8.9	16.2
Soviet Union[3]	84.0	95.5	5.1	3.3	Mexico	1,653.3	1,929.9	147.6	173.9
Ukraine	(X)	[2]115.4	10.1	15.8	Caribbean[1]	892.7	836.2	71.7	88.2
United Kingdom	142.1	114.8	7.7	13.4	Cuba	159.2	145.9	14.1	20.8
Yugoslavia[3]	19.2	21.2	1.5	2.8	Dominican				
Asia[1]	**2,817.4**	**2,427.4**	**199.4**	**265.4**	Republic	251.8	305.5	17.9	17.5
Afghanistan	26.6	15.5	0.9	1.0	Haiti	140.2	142.9	16.5	22.4
Bangladesh	15.2	52.7	6.0	7.2	Jamaica	213.8	142.8	14.7	16.0
Cambodia	116.6	15.0	1.4	2.1	Trinidad and				
China	[4]388.8	346.7	32.2	45.7	Tobago	39.5	52.3	4.3	6.7
Hong Kong	63.0	63.7	4.9	5.4	Central America[1]	458.7	422.2	43.2	66.4
India	261.9	311.0	30.2	42.0	El Salvador	214.6	180.2	14.6	22.6
Indonesia	14.3	12.3	1.2	1.8	Guatemala	87.9	85.8	7.3	10.0
Iran	154.8	96.9	7.2	8.5	Honduras	49.5	56.0	4.8	5.9
Iraq	19.6	32.2	3.4	5.1	Nicaragua	44.1	60.3	13.4	24.0
Israel	36.3	27.3	1.9	2.8	Panama	29.0	20.5	1.6	1.8
Japan	43.2	50.2	4.2	7.1	**South America[1]**	**455.9**	**442.2**	**41.6**	**56.1**
Jordan	32.6	32.5	3.3	3.9	Argentina	25.7	20.6	1.4	2.3
Korea	338.8	142.7	12.8	15.8	Brazil	23.7	41.4	3.9	7.0
Laos	145.6	41.4	0.9	1.4	Chile	23.4	14.1	1.1	1.7
Lebanon	41.6	36.8	3.0	3.7	Colombia	124.4	106.5	10.0	14.5
Pakistan	61.3	96.5	13.5	14.5	Ecuador	56.0	59.8	8.9	7.7
Philippines	495.3	432.1	31.0	42.5	Guyana	95.4	64.8	3.3	5.7
Syria	20.6	21.7	2.1	2.4	Peru	64.4	87.7	8.4	9.6
Taiwan	([4])	90.6	6.7	9.0	Venezuela	17.9	22.7	2.5	4.7

Note: NA Not available. X Not applicable.
[1]Includes countries not shown separately.
[2]Covers years 1992-1998.
[3]Prior to 1992, data include independent republics; beginning in 1992, data are for unknown republic only.
[4]Data for Taiwan included with China.

SOURCE: "No. 7. Immigrants by County of Birth: 1981 to 1998," in *Statistical Abstract of the United States 2002: The National Data Book,* U.S. Census Bureau, Washington, DC, 2002

2000 was 36.6. According to projections by the Census Bureau, the median age of the population will peak at 38.7 in 2035 and then decrease slightly to 38.1 in 2050.

Baby Boom

The increasing median age is driven by the aging of the population born during the baby boom. About 29 percent of the population in 1999 was born during the baby boom. As this population ages, the median age will rise. People born during the baby boom were between the ages of 36 and 54 in 2000. In 2011 the first members of the baby boom will reach 65, and the baby boom population will have decreased to 25 percent of the total population. The last of the baby boom population will reach 65 in 2029. By that time, the baby boom population is projected to be only 16 percent of the total population.

GENDER

In 2000 the United States had 141 million women and 134.9 million men. At the youngest ages (under 15 years), boys slightly outnumbered girls. The higher number of males continued until about age 25, when the situation reversed. The female edge then kept getting larger with increasing age. Among those 85 years and over, there were more than two women for every man. In November 2000 men had a median age of 34.6 years and women 37.0 years.

BIRTHS AND BIRTH RATES

According to the Census Bureau, as of June 2003 there is one birth about every eight seconds in the United States. That works out to 11,011 births per day, or about 4,019,280 births per year.

TABLE 1.14

Immigrants admitted by state and leading country of birth, 2000

[For year ending September 30.]

State and other area	Total	Mexico	China	Philip-pines	India	Vietnam	Nicara-gua	El Salvador	Haiti
Total	849,807	173,919	45,652	42,474	42,046	26,747	24,029	22,578	22,364
Alabama	1,904	259	172	66	230	78	16	6	5
Alaska	1,374	136	47	327	12	21	4	27	1
Arizona	11,980	6,301	304	335	374	464	62	81	10
Arkansas	1,596	606	93	75	124	77	12	89	4
California	217,753	85,551	13,232	16,773	9,313	10,251	5,176	9,987	81
Colorado	8,216	2,915	503	151	286	351	31	101	6
Connecticut	11,346	278	544	441	594	208	114	51	497
Delaware	1,570	182	117	49	153	33	5	10	80
District of Columbia	2,542	39	122	75	53	65	79	544	35
Florida	98,391	4,597	1,119	1,922	1,438	994	14,400	651	11,044
Georgia	14,778	2,099	659	310	1,323	752	106	166	127
Hawaii	6,056	62	551	3,053	23	196	—	1	1
Idaho	1,922	1,083	100	41	18	35	8	6	4
Illinois	36,180	8,600	1,475	2,738	3,239	433	112	135	98
Indiana	4,128	759	333	185	328	99	34	35	7
Iowa	3,052	699	90	64	145	298	13	27	3
Kansas	4,582	1,794	226	129	190	350	52	57	5
Kentucky	2,989	164	176	88	149	144	9	3	8
Louisiana	3,016	194	229	97	211	335	154	40	13
Maine	1,133	29	81	40	32	49	1	4	1
Maryland	17,705	487	1,102	748	1,228	379	475	1,480	194
Massachusetts	23,483	193	2,023	267	1,227	902	79	290	1,943
Michigan	16,773	935	832	783	1,490	320	36	33	21
Minnesota	8,671	591	505	208	441	536	48	43	9
Mississippi	1,083	127	109	163	122	48	16	5	12
Missouri	6,053	636	394	227	359	331	18	43	15
Montana.	493	44	25	39	11	2	4	1	2
Nebraska	2,230	834	86	64	70	281	9	47	1
Nevada	7,827	3,120	283	859	141	173	278	322	11
New Hampshire	2,001	40	116	123	101	43	4	6	26
New Jersey	40,013	700	1,862	1,845	4,364	428	431	712	2,101
New Mexico	3,973	2,717	139	82	77	138	9	14	2
New York	106,061	1,883	8,930	1,927	3,581	665	741	2,548	5,507
North Carolina	9,251	1,390	514	386	785	352	137	152	24
North Dakota	420	15	9	10	21	12	—	1	5
Ohio	9,263	345	712	281	804	280	44	19	5
Oklahoma	4,586	1,565	210	174	288	365	12	24	3
Oregon	8,543	2,699	597	286	345	511	24	46	5
Pennsylvania	18,148	1,081	1,494	464	1,714	879	93	42	269
Rhode Island	2,526	49	85	55	44	25	11	30	68
South Carolina	2,267	191	167	165	201	72	15	9	7
South Dakota	465	26	26	27	7	16	3	1	2
Tennessee	4,882	504	326	364	352	148	20	31	6
Texas	63,840	31,211	2,293	2,025	3,528	2,275	644	2,677	21
Utah	3,710	1,036	146	79	57	152	30	52	3
Vermont	810	11	54	17	32	56	1	1	1
Virginia	20,087	777	868	1,046	1,465	827	329	1,794	29
Washington	18,486	3,256	1,058	1,216	578	1,216	39	89	8
West Virginia	573	24	47	35	35	10	—	4	3
Wisconsin	5,057	952	290	148	308	57	68	22	6
Wyoming	248	60	20	18	3	3	1	2	—
Guam	1,556	—	54	1,267	11	11	1	—	—
Northern Mariana Islands	122	—	12	83	—	—	—	—	—
Puerto Rico	2,649	71	85	6	6	1	21	17	1
Virgin Islands	1,328	1	4	5	13	—	—	—	24
Armed Services posts	116	1	2	23	2	—	—	—	—

Note: — Represents zero.
*Includes other countries, not shown separately.

SOURCE: "No. 9. Immigrants Admitted by State and Leading County of Birth: 2000," in *Statistical Abstract of the United States 2002: The National Data Book,* U.S. Census Bureau, Washington, DC, 2002

The birth rates, which increased dramatically in the 1940s and 1950s, declined in the 1960s and early 1970s. In 2002 the birth rate for all races in the United States was 13.9 births per 1,000 women, down 17 percent since 1990. From 2001 to 2002 the birth rate fell 1 percent to 14.1. This is the lowest birth rate reported for the United

TABLE 1.15

Deaths, age-adjusted death rates, and life expectancy at birth, by race and sex; and infant deaths and mortality rates by race, 2000 and preliminary 2001

[Death rates are based on populations enumerated in the 2000 census as of April 1 for 2000 and estimated as of July 1 for 2001.]

Measure and sex	All races[1]		White		Black	
	2001	2000	2001	2000	2001	2000
All deaths	2,417,762	2,403,351	2,081,842	2,071,287	287,110	285,826
Age-adjusted death rate[2]	855.0	869.0	837.3	849.8	1,098.8	1,121.4
Male	1,029.5	1,053.8	1,006.9	1,029.4	1,372.4	1,403.5
Female	722.4	731.4	707.5	715.3	910.4	927.6
Life expectancy at birth[3]	77.2	77.0	77.7	77.6	72.2	71.9
Male	74.4	74.3	75.0	74.9	68.6	68.3
Female	79.8	79.7	80.2	80.1	75.5	75.2
All infant deaths	27,801	28,035	18,094	18,144	8,563	8,771
Infant mortality rate[4]	6.9	6.9	5.7	5.7	14.2	14.1

[1]Includes races other than white and black.
[2]Age-adjusted death rates are per 100,000 U.S. standard population, based on the year 2000 standard.
[3]Life expectancy at birth stated in years.
[4]Infant mortality rates are deaths under 1 year per 1,000 live births in specified group.

SOURCE: Elizabeth Arias and Betty L. Smith, "Table A. Deaths, age-adjusted death rates, and life expectancy at birth, by race and sex; and infant deaths and mortality rates, by race: United States, final 2000 and preliminary 2001," in "Deaths: Preliminary Data for 2001," *National Vital Statistics Reports,* vol. 51, no. 5, March 14, 2003

States since national data have been available. In 2002 the birth rate was down 1 percent from the previous year to 64.8 live births per 1,000 women aged 15 to 44. This rate is 9 percent lower than 1990.

The infant mortality rate reached a record low in 2001 to 6.8 infant deaths per 1,000 live births, down 10.5 percent (7.6) since 1995. Among blacks the infant mortality rate in 2001 was 13.3, a decrease from 13.5 in 2000—and significantly higher than the infant death rate for whites in 2001 of 5.7, down from 6.0 in 1998.

DEATH RATES

The death rate dropped from 945 per 100,000 population in 1970 to 860 in 1977 and remained in the range of 850 to 880 per 100,000 through most of the 1980s and 1990s—the lowest levels ever achieved in the United States. The 2001 age-adjusted death rate was 855.0 deaths per 100,000. Males had a death rate of 1,029.5 per 100,000 in 2001, down from 1,053.8 in 2000. The death rate for women in 2001 was lower than that of males at 722.4. (See Table 1.15.)

LIFE EXPECTANCY

In 2000 life expectancy at birth reached a record high of 76.9 years. A century before, life expectancy at birth was 47.3 years. Life expectancy for males in 2000 increased slightly to 74.1, up from 73.9 in 1999. Among women, life expectancy reached 79.5 in 2000, up slightly from 79.4 from the year before. (See Table 1.16.)

TABLE 1.16

Life expectancy at birth, at 65 years of age, and at 75 years of age, according to race and sex, selected years 1900–2000

[Data are based on death certificates]

Specified age and year	All races			White			Black or African American[1]		
	Both sexes	Male	Female	Both sexes	Male	Female	Both sexes	Male	Female
At birth				Remaining life expectancy in years					
1900[2,3]	47.3	46.3	48.3	47.6	46.6	48.7	33.0	32.5	33.5
1950[3]	68.2	65.6	71.1	69.1	66.5	72.2	60.8	59.1	62.9
1960[3]	69.7	66.6	73.1	70.6	67.4	74.1	63.6	61.1	66.3
1970	70.8	67.1	74.7	71.7	68.0	75.6	64.1	60.0	68.3
1980	73.7	70.0	77.4	74.4	70.7	78.1	68.1	63.8	72.5
1985	74.7	71.1	78.2	75.3	71.8	78.7	69.3	65.0	73.4
1990	75.4	71.8	78.8	76.1	72.7	79.4	69.1	64.5	73.6
1991	75.5	72.0	78.9	76.3	72.9	79.6	69.3	64.6	73.8
1992	75.8	72.3	79.1	76.5	73.2	79.8	69.6	65.0	73.9
1993	75.5	72.2	78.8	76.3	73.1	79.5	69.2	64.6	73.7
1994	75.7	72.4	79.0	76.5	73.3	79.6	69.5	64.9	73.9
1995	75.8	72.5	78.9	76.5	73.4	79.6	69.6	65.2	73.9
1996	76.1	73.1	79.1	76.8	73.9	79.7	70.2	66.1	74.2
1997	76.5	73.6	79.4	77.1	74.3	79.9	71.1	67.2	74.7
1998	76.7	73.8	79.5	77.3	74.5	80.0	71.3	67.6	74.8
1999	76.7	73.9	79.4	77.3	74.6	79.9	71.4	67.8	74.7
2000	76.9	74.1	79.5	77.4	74.8	80.0	71.7	68.2	74.9
At 65 years									
1950[2]	13.9	12.8	15.0	—	12.8	15.1	13.9	12.9	14.9
1960[2]	14.3	12.8	15.8	14.4	12.9	15.9	13.9	12.7	15.1
1970	15.2	13.1	17.0	15.2	13.1	17.1	14.2	12.5	15.7
1980	16.4	14.1	18.3	16.5	14.2	18.4	15.1	13.0	16.8
1985	16.7	14.5	18.5	16.8	14.5	18.7	15.2	13.0	16.9
1990	17.2	15.1	18.9	17.3	15.2	19.1	15.4	13.2	17.2
1991	17.4	15.3	19.1	17.5	15.4	19.2	15.5	13.4	17.2
1992	17.5	15.4	19.2	17.6	15.5	19.3	15.7	13.5	17.4
1993	17.3	15.3	18.9	17.4	15.4	19.0	15.5	13.4	17.1
1994	17.4	15.5	19.0	17.5	15.6	19.1	15.7	13.6	17.2
1995	17.4	15.6	18.9	17.6	15.7	19.1	15.6	13.6	17.1
1996	17.5	15.7	19.0	17.6	15.8	19.1	15.8	13.9	17.2
1997	17.7	15.9	19.2	17.8	16.0	19.3	16.1	14.2	17.6
1998	17.8	16.0	19.2	17.8	16.1	19.3	16.1	14.3	17.4
1999	17.7	16.1	19.1	17.8	16.1	19.2	16.0	14.3	17.3
2000	17.9	16.3	19.2	17.9	16.3	19.2	16.2	14.5	17.4
At 75 years									
1980	10.4	8.8	11.5	10.4	8.8	11.5	9.7	8.3	10.7
1985	10.6	9.0	11.7	10.6	9.0	11.7	10.1	8.7	11.1
1990	10.9	9.4	12.0	11.0	9.4	12.0	10.2	8.6	11.2
1991	11.1	9.5	12.1	11.1	9.5	12.1	10.2	8.7	11.2
1992	11.2	9.6	12.2	11.2	9.6	12.2	10.4	8.9	11.4
1993	10.9	9.5	11.9	11.0	9.5	12.0	10.2	8.7	11.1
1994	11.0	9.6	12.0	11.1	9.6	12.0	10.3	8.9	11.2
1995	11.0	9.7	11.9	11.1	9.7	12.0	10.2	8.8	11.1
1996	11.1	9.8	12.0	11.1	9.8	12.0	10.3	9.0	11.2
1997	11.2	9.9	12.1	11.2	9.9	12.1	10.7	9.3	11.5
1998	11.3	10.0	12.2	11.3	10.0	12.2	10.5	9.2	11.3
1999	11.2	10.0	12.1	11.2	10.0	12.1	10.4	9.2	11.1
2000	11.3	10.1	12.1	11.3	10.1	12.1	10.5	9.4	11.2

[1]Data shown for 1900–60 are for the nonwhite population.
[2]Death registration area only. The death registration area increased from 10 States and the District of Columbia in 1900 to the coterminous United States in 1933.
[3]Includes deaths of persons who were not residents of the 50 States and the District of Columbia.

SOURCE: V.M. Freid, K. Prager, A.P. MacKay, and H. Xia, "Table 27. Life expectancy at birth, at 65 years of age, and at 75 years of age, according to race and sex: United States, selected years 1900–2000," in *Health, United States, 2003, with Chartbook on Trends in the Health of Americans,* Centers for Disease Control and Prevention, National Center for Health Statistics, Hyattsville, MD, September 2003

CHAPTER 2
FAMILIES AND HOUSEHOLDS

TYPES OF HOUSEHOLDS

The U.S. Census Bureau has two major categories of households: family and nonfamily. A family household consists of the householder (the person who represents the entire household) and at least one additional person related to the householder through marriage, birth, or adoption. A nonfamily household is made up of a householder who either lives alone or exclusively with persons unrelated to the householder.

In 2000 the Census Bureau counted 104.7 million households, an increase of about 12 percent from the 93.3 million households counted in 1990. During the 1970s the number of households rose by a total of 17.4 million, an average of 1.7 million per year. From 1980 to 1990 the number of households increased by 12.5 million, or by 16 percent. (See Table 2.1.)

FAMILY HOUSEHOLDS

There were 72 million family households in 2000. Their share of households (68.7 percent) fell steadily over the previous 40 years, from about 85 percent in 1960, to 81 percent in 1970, 74 percent in 1980, and 71 percent in 1990. Married-couple families made up just over half (53 percent) of all households in 2000. This number also dropped, down from 61 percent in 1980, 71 percent in 1970, and 74.5 percent in 1960. In 2000 family households included 55.3 million married-couple families (three-quarters of all family households), 4 million families with a male householder (no wife present), and 12.6 million families with a female householder (no husband present). (See Table 2.1.)

Married couples living with their own children represented 24.1 percent of all households in 2000, dropping by almost half since 1970, when they represented 40.3 percent of all households. There were 30 million married-couple households without their own children, about 28.7

percent of all households in 2000. (See Table 2.1.) These couples had not yet had children, were "empty nesters" whose children had grown up and left home, chose to remain childless, or were unable to have children.

About 37.4 million family households did not have any of their own children under age 18 present in the home in 2000. However, families without their own children under 18 at home might not be childless. They might have grandchildren, unrelated foster children, or adult children living in the household. In 2000, 34.7 million family households did not have any related children under age 18 present in the home.

Racial and Ethnic Differences

In 2000 approximately 75.3 percent of all households were maintained by white non-Hispanic householders, 12.3 percent by black householders, 9 percent by Hispanic householders, and the remaining by householders of other races.

Significant racial and ethnic differences emerged among the proportion of married-couple family households. While about 83 percent of the white non-Hispanic family households were married-couple families, 68 percent of Hispanic family households and fewer than half (48 percent) of black family households were married-couple families.

NONFAMILY HOUSEHOLDS

There were approximately 32.7 million nonfamily households in 2000, about three times as many as the 11.9 million in 1970. Meanwhile, the proportion of all households that were nonfamily households climbed from 19 percent in 1970 to 31 percent in 2000. In later years, however, the rate of increase of this type of household slowed significantly. During the 1970s nonfamily households increased at an average annual rate of 5.7 percent per year. This rate of increase fell to 2.5 percent per year during the

TABLE 2.1

Households, families, subfamilies, and married couples, 1980–2000

[In thousands, except as indicated (80,776 represents 80,776,000). Includes members of Armed Forces living off post or with their families on post, but excludes all other members of Armed Forces. Minus sign (-) indicates decrease]

Type of unit	1980	1985	1990	1995	1997	1998	1999	2000	Percent change 1980-90	Percent change 1990-2000
Households	**80,776**	**86,789**	**93,347**	**98,990**	**101,018**	**102,528**	**103,874**	**104,705**	16	12
Average size	2.76	2.69	2.63	2.65	2.64	2.62	2.61	2.62	(X)	(X)
Family households	59,550	62,706	66,090	69,305	70,241	70,880	71,535	72,025	11	9
Married couple	49,112	50,350	52,317	53,858	53,604	54,317	54,770	55,311	7	6
Male householder[1]	1,733	2,228	2,884	3,226	3,847	3,911	3,976	4,028	66	40
Female householder[1]	8,705	10,129	10,890	12,220	12,790	12,652	12,789	12,687	25	17
Nonfamily households	21,226	24,082	27,257	29,686	30,777	31,648	32,339	32,680	28	20
Male householder	8,807	10,114	11,606	13,190	13,707	14,133	14,368	14,641	32	26
Female householder	12,419	13,968	15,651	16,496	17,070	17,516	17,971	18,039	26	15
One person	18,296	20,602	22,999	24,732	25,402	26,327	26,606	26,724	26	16
Families	**59,550**	**62,706**	**66,090**	**69,305**	**70,241**	**70,880**	**71,535**	**72,025**	11	9
Average size	3.29	3.23	3.17	3.19	3.19	3.18	3.18	3.17	(X)	(X)
With own children[2]	31,022	31,112	32,289	34,296	34,665	34,760	34,613	34,605	4	7
Without own children[2]	28,528	31,594	33,801	35,009	35,575	36,120	36,922	37,420	18	11
Married couple	49,112	50,350	52,317	53,858	53,604	54,317	4,770	55,311	7	6
With own children[2]	24,961	24,210	24,537	25,241	25,083	25,269	25,066	25,248	-2	3
Without own children[2]	24,151	26,140	27,780	28,617	28,521	29,048	29,703	30,062	15	6
Male householder[1]	1,733	2,228	2,884	3,226	3,847	3,911	3,976	4,028	66	40
With own children[2]	616	896	1,153	1,440	1,709	1,798	1,706	1,786	87	55
Without own children[2]	1,117	1,332	1,731	1,786	2,138	2,113	2,270	2,242	55	30
Female householder[1]	8,705	10,129	10,890	2,220	12,790	2,652	2,789	12,687	25	17
With own children[2]	5,445	6,006	6,599	7,615	7,874	7,693	7,841	7,571	21	15
Without own children[2]	3,261	4,123	4,290	4,606	4,916	4,960	4,948	5,116	32	19
Unrelated subfamilies.	360	526	534	674	615	575	522	571	48	7
Married couple	20	46	68	64	50	41	50	37	(B)	(B)
Male reference persons[1]	36	85	45	59	77	72	64	57	(B)	(B)
Female reference persons[1]	304	395	421	550	487	463	408	477	9	13
Related subfamilies	1,150	2,228	2,403	2,878	2,907	2,870	2,901	2,984	109	24
Married couple	582	719	871	1,015	1,012	947	1,029	1,149	50	32
Father-child[1]	54	116	153	195	244	250	281	201	(B)	31
Mother-child[1]	512	1,392	1,378	1,668	1,651	1,673	1,591	1,634	169	19
Married couples	**49,714**	**51,114**	**53,256**	**54,937**	**54,666**	**55,305**	**55,849**	**56,497**	7	6
With own household	49,112	50,350	52,317	53,858	53,604	54,317	54,770	55,311	7	6
Without own household	602	764	939	1,079	1,062	988	1,079	1,186	56	26
Percent without	1.2	1.5	1.8	2.0	1.9	1.8	1.9	2.1	(X)	(X)

Note: B Not shown; base less than 75,000.   X Not applicable.
[1] No spouse present.
[2] Under 18 years old.

SOURCE: "No. 51. Households, Families, Subfamilies, and Married Couples: 1980 to 2000," in *Statistical Abstract of the United States 2002: The National Data Book*, U.S. Census Bureau, Washington, DC, 2002

1980s and declined further to 1.8 percent per year during the 1990s.

In 2000 women maintained more than half of nonfamily households. About 18 million female and 14.6 million male householders lived in nonfamily households in 2000. The proportion of male nonfamily households to all households doubled from 6 percent in 1970 to 14 percent in 1998, while the proportion of female nonfamily households increased from 12 percent to 17 percent.

HOUSEHOLD AND FAMILY SIZE

Household size is closely related to the type of household. Over the past generation, changes in household composition and childbearing patterns have resulted in households that, on average, include fewer persons than in the past. The trends toward fewer children per family, more one-parent families, and increased numbers of people living alone are among the major factors contributing to smaller households.

In 1790, the year of the first national census, there were 5.79 persons per household. In 1890 there were 4.76 persons per household. The average had declined by about one member per household over a period of 100 years. It took only another 50 years for household size to drop an additional person (3.76 persons per household in 1940).

Household size fell to 3.14 persons in 1970 and 2.76 persons in 1980. The average number of persons per household in the United States reached a new low of 2.62 persons per household in 1989, where it has remained. Of family households in 2000, the average family size was 3.24 overall, and 3.26 for married couples. Nonfamily households tended to be smaller, with an overall average size of 1.25.

The proportion of the largest households (those with five persons or more) fell from 21 percent in 1970 to about 10 percent in 2000. Medium-sized households, with three or four persons, accounted for about one-third of households, a proportion that has remained constant over the past two decades. Finally, the smallest households, those comprising only one or two persons, increased their share of the total from 46 percent in 1970 to 59 percent in 2000.

AGE OF HOUSEHOLDER

The median age of householders dropped from 48.1 years in 1970 to 46.1 years in 1980, reaching 45.1 years in 1989 and then increasing to 46.3 years in 1998. This leveling off is primarily attributable to the decline in the number of householders in the youngest age categories since 1980. After 1980 the number of households maintained by persons under 25 years of age declined from 8 percent of all households to approximately 5 percent in 2000.

The recent decline in the number of young adult householders is mainly the result of the aging of the 1946–1964 baby boom generation. The leading edge of the baby boom generation first began forming households during the 1960s. By 1990 baby boomers ranged from 26 to 44 years of age. This group accounted for a large number of households formed during the two decades between 1970 and 1990. As they increased their share of the total, the median age of householders dropped from 48.1 years to 45.3 years during the same period.

The youngest baby boomers turned 39 in 2003. As this large segment of the population continues to grow older and is replaced by the comparatively smaller generation that follows, the median age of householders can be expected to reverse its decline. This turnaround has probably begun, as the median age of householders has increased slightly since 1990 to 46.3 years in 1998. The number of households maintained by persons 45 to 54 years of age increased from nearly 20.2 million in 1999 to 20.9 million in 2000. Meanwhile, the number of households maintained by those aged 30 to 34 decreased during that period.

Another factor contributing to the decline in the number of younger householders is that today's young adults are not forming their own households at as high a rate as previous generations. Instead, many are returning to or remaining in their parents' homes.

FAMILIES MAINTAINED BY WOMEN

One of the most dramatic changes in the composition of family households during the last three decades of the 20th century was the tremendous increase in the number of families maintained by women. In fact, the number of female-headed families doubled between 1970 and 1987. By 2000 about 18 percent of all families were maintained by women, up from 15 percent in 1980 and 11 percent in 1970. (See Table 2.1.)

Blacks and whites show a significant difference in the proportion of families maintained by women. In 2000 about 44 percent of black family households were maintained by women, compared to 13 percent for whites. Among Hispanics, women maintained about 1 in 4 families (24 percent) in 2000.

MARRIED POPULATION

Marriage

The number of marriages in the United States soared from 1.6 million in 1945 to 2.3 million in 1946 as the World War II veterans returned to civilian life. In the 1950s the number of marriages averaged about 1.5 million annually, rising to 2.3 million in 1972. Since 1980 the number of marriages has averaged around 2.4 million annually. In 2002 the National Center for Health Statistics (NCHS) reported approximately 2.3 million marriages.

From January to March 2003 the NCHS reported 421,000 marriages in the United States, a rate of 7.8 per 1,000 population. This rate is slightly lower than the 8.1 rate in 2002 (the lowest rate since 1963), the 8.2 rate in 2001, and the 8.5 rate in 2000. This decline in the marriage rate is not a recent phenomena, but is part of an overall trend since the 1980s. Over the last quarter of the 20th century, marriage rates went through two periods of decline. Marriage rates rose from the early 1960s through 1972, when the rate reached 10.9 per 1,000. Beginning in 1973 the rate dropped, reaching 9.9 per 1,000 in 1977. The rate increased again, reaching 10.6 per 1,000 between 1980 and 1982. Beginning in the early 1980s, the marriage rate once again began to decline. One reason for this decline was that the majority of the very large baby boom generation had aged past their 20s and early 30s, the peak marriage years.

In 2000, according to the Census Bureau, about 53 percent of the population 15 years and over were married and living with their spouses. Married people in the age group of 55 to 64 years old were the most likely to be living with their spouses, at a rate of about 70 percent. The percentages among those 65 years and older decreased as the number of widows increased.

Postponing Marriage

In 1890 the estimated median age at first marriage was 26.1 years for men and 22 years for women. Since that time, the median age at first marriage declined until 1956, when the median age at first marriage reached a low of

TABLE 2.2

Marital status of the population by sex, race, and Hispanic origin, 1980–2000

[In millions, except percent (159.5 represents 159,500,000).Persons 18 years old and over. Excludes members of Armed Forces except those living off post or with their families on post.]

Marital status, race, and Hispanic origin	Total				Male				Female			
	1980	1990	1995	2000	1980	1990	1995	2000	1980	1990	1995	2000
Total[1]	159.5	181.8	191.6	201.8	75.7	86.9	92.0	96.9	83.8	95.0	99.6	104.9
Never married	32.3	40.4	43.9	48.2	18.0	22.4	24.6	26.1	14.3	17.9	19.3	22.1
Married	104.6	112.6	116.7	120.1	51.8	55.8	57.7	59.6	52.8	56.7	58.9	60.4
Widowed	12.7	13.8	13.4	13.7	2.0	2.3	2.3	2.6	10.8	11.5	11.1	11.1
Divorced	9.9	15.1	17.6	19.8	3.9	6.3	7.4	8.5	6.0	8.8	10.3	11.3
Percent of total	100.0	100.0	100.0	100.0	100.0	100.0	100.0	100.0	100.0	100.0	100.0	100.0
Never married	20.3	22.2	22.9	23.9	23.8	25.8	26.8	27.0	17.1	18.9	19.4	21.1
Married	65.5	61.9	60.9	59.5	68.4	64.3	62.7	61.5	63.0	59.7	59.2	57.6
Widowed	8.0	7.6	7.0	6.8	2.6	2.7	2.5	2.7	12.8	12.1	11.1	10.5
Divorced	6.2	8.3	9.2	9.8	5.2	7.2	8.0	8.8	7.1	9.3	10.3	10.8
White, total	139.5	155.5	161.3	168.1	66.7	74.8	78.1	81.6	72.8	80.6	83.2	86.6
Never married	26.4	31.6	3.2	6.0	15.0	18.0	19.2	20.3	11.4	13.6	14.0	15.7
Married	93.8	99.5	102.0	104.1	46.7	49.5	50.6	51.8	47.1	49.9	51.3	52.2
Widowed	10.9	11.7	11.3	11.5	1.6	1.9	1.9	2.2	9.3	9.8	9.4	9.3
Divorced	8.3	12.6	14.8	16.5	3.4	5.4	6.3	7.2	5.0	7.3	8.4	9.3
Percent of total	100.0	100.0	100.0	100.0	100.0	100.0	100.0	100.0	100.0	100.0	100.0	100.0
Never married	18.9	20.3	20.6	21.4	22.5	24.1	24.6	24.9	15.7	16.9	16.9	18.1
Married	67.2	64.0	63.2	62.0	70.0	66.2	64.9	63.5	64.7	61.9	61.7	60.2
Widowed	7.8	7.5	7.0	6.8	2.5	2.6	2.5	2.7	12.8	12.2	11.3	10.7
Divorced	6.0	8.1	9.1	.8	5.0	7.2	8.1	8.8	6.8	9.0	10.1	10.7
Black, total	16.6	20.3	22.1	24.0	7.4	9.1	9.9	10.7	9.2	11.2	12.2	13.3
Never married	5.1	7.1	8.5	9.5	2.5	3.5	4.1	4.3	2.5	3.6	4.4	5.1
Married	8.5	9.3	9.6	10.1	4.1	4.5	4.6	5.0	4.5	4.8	4.9	5.1
Widowed	1.6	1.7	1.7	1.7	0.3	0.3	0.3	0.3	1.3	1.4	1.4	1.4
Divorced	1.4	2.1	2.4	2.8	0.5	0.8	0.8	1.1	0.9	1.3	1.5	1.7
Percent of total	100.0	100.0	100.0	100.0	100.0	100.0	100.0	100.0	100.0	100.0	100.0	100.0
Never married	30.5	35.1	38.4	39.6	34.3	38.4	41.7	40.2	27.4	32.5	35.8	38.3
Married	51.4	45.8	43.2	42.1	54.6	49.2	46.7	46.7	48.7	43.0	40.4	38.3
Widowed	9.8	8.5	7.6	7.1	4.2	3.7	3.1	2.8	14.3	12.4	11.3	10.5
Divorced	8.4	10.6	10.7	11.7	7.0	8.8	8.5	10.3	9.5	12.0	12.5	12.8
Hispanic,[2] total	7.9	13.6	17.6	21.1	3.8	6.7	8.8	10.4	4.1	6.8	8.8	10.7
Never married	1.9	3.7	5.0	5.9	1.0	2.2	3.0	3.4	0.9	1.5	2.1	2.5
Married	5.2	8.4	10.4	12.7	2.5	4.1	5.1	6.2	2.6	4.3	5.3	6.5
Widowed	0.4	0.5	0.7	0.9	0.1	0.1	0.2	0.2	0.3	0.4	0.6	0.7
Divorced	0.5	1.0	1.4	1.6	0.2	0.4	0.6	0.7	0.3	0.6	0.8	1.0
Percent of total	100.0	100.0	100.0	100.0	100.0	100.0	100.0	100.0	100.0	100.0	100.0	100.0
Never married	24.1	27.2	28.6	28.0	27.3	32.1	33.8	32.7	21.1	22.5	23.5	23.4
Married	65.6	61.7	59.3	60.2	67.1	60.9	57.9	59.6	64.3	62.4	60.7	60.7
Widowed	4.4	4.0	4.2	4.2	1.6	1.5	1.8	1.9	7.1	6.5	6.6	6.5
Divorced	5.8	7.0	7.9	7.6	4.0	5.5	6.6	6.7	7.6	8.5	9.2	9.3

[1] Includes persons of other races, not shown separately.
[2] Hispanic persons may be of any race.

SOURCE: "No. 46. Marital Status of the Population by Sex, Race, and Hispanic Origin: 1980 to 2000," in *Statistical Abstract of the United States 2002: The National Data Book,* U.S. Census Bureau, Washington, DC, 2002

22.5 years for men and 20.1 years for women. By 1990 the median age had returned to the 1890 level of 26.1 years for men and an even higher 23.9 years for women. The median age continued to rise. In 1996 the age increased to 27.1 for men and 24.8 for women. In 1998 the median age for men at first marriage dropped slightly to 26.7, while the median age for women was at a high of 25 years.

Delayed marriage may lessen the chance of divorce. Studies show that marriages at younger ages have a higher probability of divorce than marriages at older ages. However, delayed marriage is an important reason for steep increases in the number of out-of-wedlock births from 1940 to 1990. Although the number of unmarried women continues to rise, the number of out-of-wedlock births has leveled off or slowed its rate of increase during the 1990s.

Never Married

In 2000 the never-married, over 15 years of age segment accounted for 28.1 percent of the population. Out of all males, 31.3 percent were never married. Never-married females represented 25.1 percent of all females. These rates slowly increased after 1970, when 24.9 percent of the population was never married. In 1970, 28.1 percent of males were unmarried, compared to 22.1 percent of females. Conversely, the percentage of married males and females steadily declined during that same period.

TABLE 2.3

Married couples of same or mixed races and origins, 1980–2000

[In thousands (49,714 represents 49,714,000). Persons 15 years old and over. Persons of Hispanic origin may be of any race.]

Race and origin of spouses	1980	1990	1995	1999	2000
Married couples, total	**49,714**	**53,256**	**54,937**	**55,849**	**56,497**
Race					
White/White	44,910	47,202	48,030	48,455	48,917
Black/Black	3,354	3,687	3,703	3,868	3,989
Black/White	167	211	328	364	363
Black husband/White wife	122	150	206	240	268
White husband/Black wife	45	61	122	124	95
White/other race*	450	720	988	1,086	1,051
Black/other race*	34	33	76	31	50
All other couples*	799	1,401	1,811	2,045	2,127
Hispanic Origin					
Hispanic/Hispanic	1,906	3,085	3,857	4,480	4,739
Hispanic/other origin (not Hispanic)	891	1,193	1,434	1,647	1,743
All other couples (not of Hispanic origin)	46,917	48,979	49,646	49,722	50,015

*Excluding White and Black.

SOURCE: "No. 47. Married Couples of Same or Mixed Races and Origins: 1980 to 2000," in *Statistical Abstract of the United States 2002: The National Data Book*, U.S. Census Bureau, Washington, DC, 2002

As of 2000 a much higher proportion of black women (38 percent) and black men (40 percent) age 18 and older were never married than white women (18 percent) and white men (25 percent). (See Table 2.2.) The increase in the percentage of adults who have never been married may reflect the increase in adults in nonmarital, joint living arrangements rather than an increase in traditional "singles."

Interracial Marriages

In 2000, in the vast majority of married couples in the United States, both partners were of the same race. Interracial married couples accounted for fewer than 5 percent of all married couples. Of 56.5 million married couples in 2000, there were 363,000 black-white marriages, 1,051,000 white-other races marriages, and 50,000 black-other races marriages. Between 1980 and 2000 the number of black-white marriages increased by 196,000, white-other race marriages increased by over 600,000, and black-other race marriages increased by 16,000. (See Table 2.3.)

DIVORCE

In 2000 the divorce rate per 1,000 population was 4.1, down slightly from a rate of 4.2 in 1998 and the same as in 1999, maintaining the lowest divorce rate in over two decades. During the 1950s and early 1960s the divorce rate was lower, ranging between 2.1 and 2.6 per 1,000 people. Beginning in 1967 the divorce rate increased almost yearly until it peaked at 5.3 per 1,000 in 1979. The rate was 5.3 per 1,000 again in 1981, but then began to decline, reaching 4.8 per 1,000 by 1987. After 1987 the rate varied only slightly each year.

The NCHS reports that, based on the current figures, statistically half of all marriages will end in divorce. It should be noted, however, that a certain percentage of people get married and divorced two or more times, adding to the number of divorces. For those not among this group, less than half of marriages will end in divorce.

UNMARRIED-COUPLE HOUSEHOLDS

In 1999 there were more than 4.4 million unmarried-couple households, a number that steadily increased from 523,000 in 1970, to 1,589,000 in 1980, and to 2,856,000 in 1990. An unmarried-couple household is composed of two unrelated adults of the opposite sex (one of whom is the householder) living together in a housing unit with or without children under 15 years old. The count of unmarried-couple households is intended mainly to estimate the number of cohabiting couples, but it may also include households with a roommate, boarder, or paid employee of the opposite sex.

In 1999 there were 8 unmarried couples for every 100 married couples, compared to only 1 for every 100 in 1970 and 6 for every 100 in 1993. About one-third (36 percent) had children under 15 years old present in the home. These children might have resulted from the union of the two people in the relationship, or they might have come from earlier marriages or relationships, or both.

LIVING ALONE

In 2000, 26.7 million persons—about 13 percent of all adults—lived alone. Of those, 15.5 million were women and 11.1 million were men. Between 1980 and 2000 the number of women living alone increased by 4.2 million. During the same period the number of men living alone also increased by 4.2 million. Older women are more likely than older men to live alone because they are more likely to outlive their spouses.

TABLE 2.4

Percent of children under age 18 by presence of married parents in household, race, and Hispanic origin, selected years 1980–2002

Race, Hispanic origin, and family type	1980	1985	1990	1995	1996	1997	1998	1999	2000	2001	2002
Total											
Two married parents[1]	77	74	73	69	68	68	68	68	69	69	69
Mother only[2]	18	21	22	23	24	24	23	23	22	22	23
Father only[2]	2	2	3	4	4	4	4	4	4	4	5
No parent	4	3	3	4	4	4	4	4	4	4	4
White, non-Hispanic											
Two married parents[1]	—	—	81	78	77	77	76	77	77	78	77
Mother only[2]	—	—	15	16	16	17	16	16	16	16	16
Father only[2]	—	—	3	3	4	4	5	4	4	4	4
No parent	—	—	2	3	3	3	3	3	3	2	3
Black											
Two married parents[1]	42	39	38	33	33	35	36	35	38	38	38
Mother only[2]	44	51	51	52	53	52	51	52	49	48	48
Father only[2]	2	3	4	4	4	5	4	4	4	5	5
No parent	12	7	8	11	9	8	9	10	9	10	8
Hispanic[3]											
Two married parents[1]	75	68	67	63	62	64	64	63	65	65	65
Mother only[2]	20	27	27	28	29	27	27	27	25	25	25
Father only[2]	2	2	3	4	4	4	4	5	4	5	5
No Parent	3	3	3	4	5	5	5	5	5	6	5

[1] Excludes families where parents are not living as a married couple.
[2] Because of data limitations, includes some families where both parents are present in the household but living as unmarried partners.
[3] Persons of Hispanic origin may be of any race.
Note: – not available. Family structure refers to the presence of biological, adoptive, and stepparents in the child's household. Thus, a child with a biological mother and stepfather living in the household is said to have two married parents.

SOURCE: "Table POP6. Family structure and children's living arrangements: percentage of children under age 18 by presence of parents in household, race, and Hispanic origin, selected years 1980–2002," in *America's Children: Key National Indicators of Well-Being 2003*, Federal Interagency Forum on Child and Family Statistics, Washington, DC, July 2003

LIVING ARRANGEMENTS OF YOUNG ADULTS

Significant changes in the living arrangements of young adults have occurred in the past few decades. More young adults are living at home with their parents, more are living alone or sharing their home with a roommate or other nonrelative, more are living in the homes of others, and fewer are maintaining families of their own. Between 1970 and 2000 the proportion of persons under 24 years old maintaining a family (married couples or other persons maintaining families, family householder, or spouse of householder) dropped from 38 to about 5 percent. The proportion of nonfamily householders (persons living alone or sharing the home they owned/rented with a roommate or other nonrelative) increased from 5 percent to 7 percent.

After 1970 the proportion of adults aged 25 to 34 who maintained their own families also declined by some 20 percent. In 2000 the older group was about three times more likely to maintain a family than the younger group. In 1970, in contrast, the older group was about twice as likely to maintain a family than its younger cohorts.

The proportion of 25- to 34-year-olds living alone or sharing their homes with nonrelatives increased from 5 percent in 1970 to 14 percent in 1998. The total proportion living in the home of someone other than relatives increased from 4 to 22 percent. Between 1970 and 1980 the proportion of 18- to 24-year-olds living in their parents' homes remained virtually unchanged (47 percent in 1970 and 48 percent in 1980). During the 1980s the proportion rose 5 percentage points to 53 percent in 1990. In 1998 the proportion living in their parents' homes remained at 53 percent (59 percent of young men and 48 percent of young women).

The pattern among adults aged 25 to 34 is similar. Some 8 percent of these adults lived with their parents in 1970, 9 percent in 1980, and 12 percent in 1990 and 1998. Increases in the proportion living at home occurred for both men and women, but in all years, men were more likely to live at home than women.

LIVING ARRANGEMENTS OF CHILDREN

Nearly 7 of 10 Children Live with Two Parents

Children are considerably more likely to be living with only one parent today than they were two decades ago. In 2002, 69 percent of U.S. children under 18 lived with two married parents, down from 77 percent in 1980 and 85 percent in 1970. In 2002, 23 percent of children under 18 lived with only their mothers, while 5 percent lived with only their fathers; 4 percent lived with neither parent. The rise in divorce and the increase in unwed

TABLE 2.5

Characteristics of children who coreside with grandparents by presence of parents, March 2002[1]

(In thousands)

Characteristic	Total	With grandparents present														
			Grandparent is householder									Grandparent is not householder				
				Parent present				No parents present				Parent is householder				
		Total with grand parents	Total in grand parent's household	Total	Grandmother and grandfather	Grandmother only	Grandfather only	Total	Grandmother and grandfather	Grandmother only	Grandfather only	Total	Grandmother and grandfather	Grandmother only	Grandfather only	Parent is not householder
Total	72,321	5,601	3,683	2,409	1,204	1,021	184	1,274	614	591	69	1,801	258	1,231	312	118
Age of child																
Under 6 years old	23,363	2,339	1,644	1,309	721	506	82	335	171	138	26	635	109	393	133	61
6 to 11 years old	24,623	1,770	1,118	656	307	293	56	462	240	201	21	619	90	428	101	33
12 to 17 years old	24,335	1,493	920	444	175	223	46	476	202	252	22	547	59	410	78	25
Race and ethnicity of child[2]																
White	56,276	3,674	2,418	1,701	947	601	153	717	429	245	43	1,177	180	784	213	81
Non-Hispanic	44,235	2,408	1,671	1,130	624	405	101	541	332	169	40	707	88	481	138	30
Black	11,646	1,445	1,077	576	178	381	17	501	153	327	21	339	27	253	59	29
Asian and Pacific Islander	3,223	361	89	67	44	16	7	22	19	3	-	262	48	176	38	9
Hispanic (of any race)	12,817	1,341	787	591	328	210	53	196	101	87	8	504	93	324	87	51
Presence of parents																
Two parents	49,666	1,706	477	477	255	155	67	(X)	(X)	(X)	(X)	1,217	164	840	213	12
Mother only	16,473	2,249	1,658	1,658	807	753	98	(X)	(X)	(X)	(X)	503	74	337	92	89
Father only	3,297	373	275	275	142	114	19	(X)	(X)	(X)	(X)	81	21	53	7	17
Neither parent	2,885	1,273	1,274	(X)	(X)	(X)	(X)	1,274	614	591	69	(X)	(X)	(X)	(X)	-
Family income																
Under $15,000	9,516	611	508	178	33	132	13	330	59	256	15	88	-	78	10	14
$15,000 to $29,999	12,094	995	704	389	111	254	24	315	138	154	23	270	28	190	52	21
$30,000 to $49,999	15,140	1,278	911	626	249	307	70	285	161	113	11	330	66	217	47	37
$50,000 to $74,999	14,414	1,190	718	556	298	218	40	162	119	38	54	56	61	305	90	16
$75,000 and over	21,157	1,527	840	659	513	110	36	181	137	30	14	657	103	441	113	30
Poverty status																
Below 100 percent of poverty	12,239	988	743	362	106	217	39	381	98	270	13	217	24	158	35	28
100 to 199 percent of poverty	15,686	1,512	1,088	696	287	357	52	392	174	192	26	382	59	256	67	42
200 percent of poverty and above	44,396	3,101	1,851	1,350	810	447	93	501	342	129	30	1,203	176	817	210	48
Health insurance coverage																
Covered by health insurance	63,907	4,293	2,673	1,856	914	802	140	817	378	394	45	1,539	213	1,053	273	81
Not covered by health insurance	8,414	1,309	1,008	551	289	219	43	457	236	197	24	262	46	177	39	38
Household receives public assistance																
Receives assistance	3,372	506	417	202	94	98	10	215	59	146	10	60	2	46	12	28
Does not receive assistance	68,949	5,096	3,265	2,206	1,110	923	173	1,059	555	445	59	1,741	256	1,185	300	92
Household receives food stamps																
Receives food stamps	7,873	908	702	467	174	252	41	235	48	178	9	159	9	128	22	45
Does not receive food stamps	64,448	4,694	2,980	1,942	1,029	770	143	1,038	565	413	60	1,642	249	1,103	290	73

mothers are two major factors contributing to the growing proportion of children living in one-parent families. Another factor contributing to rising proportions of children in single-parent families is the greater likelihood of married couples remaining childless or having fewer children than in the past.

In 2002, 77 percent of white, non-Hispanic children lived with two parents, compared to 38 percent of black children and 65 percent of children of Hispanic origin. The percentage of black children living with two parents in 2002 showed a decline from the 42 percent recorded in 1980 but was up from a low of 33 percent in 1995 and 1996. (See Table 2.4.)

Marital Status of Parents

In 2000 there were 9.7 million single mothers and 2 million single fathers. Of those, 4.8 million single mothers were white non-Hispanic, 3.1 million were black, and 1.6 million were Hispanic. White non-Hispanic single fathers accounted for 1.3 million single parents, followed by 335,000 black single fathers and 313,000 Hispanic single fathers.

TABLE 2.5

Characteristic	Total	Total with grand-parents	Grandparent is householder										Grandparent is not householder				
			Total in grand-par-ent's house-hold	Parent present				No parents present				Parent is householder					Parent is not house-holder
				Total	Grand-mother and grand-father	Grand-mother only	Grand-father only	Total	Grand-mother and grand-father	Grand-mother only	Grand-father only	Total	Grand-mother and grand-father	Grand-mother only	Grand-father only	
Household tenure																
Owns/buying	48,542	4,091	2,723	1,818	1,019	647	152	905	528	329	48	1,304	202	870	232	64
Rents	22,512	1,448	925	564	165	368	31	361	84	257	20	474	51	349	74	49
No cash rent	1,266	62	34	27	20	6	1	7	2	5	-	22	5	11	6	5
Type of residence[3]																
Central city, in MSA	20,971	2,042	1,376	893	346	487	60	483	189	279	15	602	104	409	89	63
Outside central city, in MSA	38,194	2,641	1,577	1,098	647	367	84	479	260	186	33	1,022	137	708	177	42
Outside MSA	13,155	919	727	417	211	167	39	310	165	125	20	178	17	114	47	15

Note:-Represents zero or rounds to zero. X Not applicable
[1]All people under age 18, excluding group quarters, householders, subfamily reference people, and their spouses.
[2]Data are not shown separately for the American Indian and Alaska Native population because of the small sample size.
[3]"MSA" refers to Metropolitan Statistical Area

SOURCE: Jason Fields, "Table 3. Characteristics of Children Who Coreside With Grandparents by Presence of Parents: March 2002," in "Children's Living Arrangements and Characteristics: March 2002," *Current Population Reports,* vol. P20-547, June 2003

Among the children who lived with one parent, the proportion who lived with a never-married parent grew from 25 percent in 1985 to 41 percent in 2002, while the proportion who lived with a divorced parent declined from 41 to 35 percent. In 1985 a child in a one-parent family was more likely to be living with a divorced parent than with a never-married parent. In 2002 the child was more likely to be living with a never-married parent than with a divorced parent. The proportion of children living with a separated parent decreased from 23 to 15 percent between 1985 and 2002, and the proportion living with a widowed parent dropped from 8 to 4 percent.

Grandparents

Grandparents play an important role in raising a small but significant proportion of children. In 2002, 5.6 million grandchildren under 18 lived in households with a grandparent present (parent's household), and 3.6 million lived in the grandparent's home. (See Table 2.5.)

After 1970 the proportion of children living with their grandparents rose from about 3 percent to nearly 8 percent in 2002. Most of the increase in the number of grandchildren living with grandparents was among children with only a mother present in the household. The proportion of grandchildren living with their grandparents with neither parent present declined from 43 percent in 1970 to 23 percent in 2002, while the proportion with only the mother present increased from 37 percent to 40 percent. Continued high levels of divorce and the rise in out-of-wedlock childbearing were the main reasons for these changes.

CHAPTER 3

LABOR FORCE

The number of workers in the U.S. civilian noninstitutionalized labor force (not in the army, school, jail, or mental health facilities) grew rapidly over the past generation, almost doubling from 74.4 million in 1965 to 144.8 million in 2002. During this period, the proportion of the population of working age rose from 58.9 to 66.6 percent. (See Table 3.1.) This growth was mainly attributable to the entrance into the workforce of the post–World War II baby boom children and the growth in the number and percentage of women entering the workforce.

While the proportion of men in the labor force remained steady throughout the 1990s and the early 2000s at around 75 percent, participation by women rose slightly from 56.0 percent in 1987 to 59.6 percent in 2002. (See Table 3.2.) In 1969 only two out of five women were in the workforce, compared to nearly three out of five women in 2002.

Ninety-one percent of men 25 to 54 years of age and 75.9 percent of women of the same age group were in the workforce during 2002, compared to 69.2 percent of men and 55.2 percent of women between 55 and 64 years of age. The proportion of men in the latter age group in the labor force generally declined in recent years, while the percentage of women increased. A growing percentage of jobs held by this age group are part time instead of full time. The low unemployment rate of 3.9 percent in 2002 among this older group reflected the fact that many of these older workers had given up looking for a job—and were therefore not counted—or they had retired and were no longer in the labor force. (See Table 3.3.)

Older workers leave the workforce for many reasons, ranging from disability to a genuine desire to retire. For many older people, however, leaving the workforce is not a voluntary act. Companies trying to cut expenses sometimes find it in their financial interest to force older, more highly paid workers into retirement and replace them with younger, lower paid workers. Older workers are also more

expensive to insure. The increasing desire of many companies to cut down the size of their staffs, frequently by eliminating many middle-management positions, has been particularly detrimental to this age group. Older workers are frequently offered early retirement with some fringe benefits, but they may be laid off with no benefits if they refuse the early retirement.

SERVICE ECONOMY

The U.S. economy has moved away from a goods-producing, or manufacturing, economy toward a service economy. Over the past generation, the service sector has accounted for an increasing proportion of workers. Since 1969 the number of workers in goods-producing industries has remained virtually unchanged, while the number working in the service-producing sector has doubled. In 1960, for every goods-producing worker, there were about 1.7 service-producing workers. By 1970 the ratio was 1 to 2, by 1980 it was 1 to 3, and by 2000 it was nearly 1 to 4.

Over the 2000–2010 period, the Bureau of Labor Statistics (BLS) expects the service-producing industries will account for virtually all job growth. Ten industries are projected to grow the fastest during this period. Half belong to four industry groups: health services, business services, social services, and engineering, management, and related services. These four industries are expected to account for nearly half of all nonfarm wage and salary jobs added to the economy over the next decade.

From 1947 to 2000 the proportion of manufacturing jobs fell from 35 percent of all jobs to 13 percent, a trend expected to continue through 2010. During the 1990s, in the goods-producing area, only the construction industry employed a growing number of workers, while the numbers working in mining fell significantly and manufacturing managed to stay somewhat level. Construction is the only goods-producing industry predicted to add jobs in the near future.

TABLE 3.1

Employment status of the civilian noninstitutional population, 1940–2002

(Numbers in thousands)

Year	Civilian noninstitutional population	Civilian labor force Total	Percent of population	Employed Total	Agriculture	Nonagricultural industries	Unemployed Number	Percent of force	Not in labor force
				Persons 14 years of age and over					
1940	*	55,640	*	47,520	9,540	37,980	8,120	14.6	*
1941	*	55,910	*	50,350	9,100	41,250	5,560	9.9	*
1942	98,640	56,410	57.2	53,750	9,250	44,500	2,660	4.7	42,230
1943	94,640	55,540	58.7	54,470	9,080	45,390	1,070	1.9	39,100
1944	93,220	54,630	58.6	53,960	8,950	45,010	670	1.2	38,590
1945	94,090	3,860	57.2	52,820	8,580	44,240	1,040	1.9	40,230
1946	103,070	57,520	55.8	55,250	8,320	46,930	2,270	3.9	45,550
1947	106,018	60,168	56.8	57,812	8,256	49,557	2,356	3.9	45,850
				Persons 16 years of age and over					
1947	101,827	59,350	58.3	57,038	7,890	49,148	2,311	3.9	42,477
1948	103,068	60,621	58.8	58,343	7,629	50,714	2,276	3.8	42,447
1949	103,994	61,286	58.9	57,651	7,658	49,993	3,637	5.9	42,708
1950	104,995	62,208	59.2	58,918	7,160	51,758	3,288	5.3	42,787
1951	104,621	62,017	59.2	59,961	6,726	53,235	2,055	3.3	42,604
1952	105,231	62,138	59.0	60,250	6,500	53,749	1,883	3.0	43,093
1953	107,056	63,015	58.9	61,179	6,260	54,919	1,834	2.9	44,041
1954	108,321	63,643	58.8	60,109	6,205	53,904	3,532	5.5	44,678
1955	109,683	65,023	59.3	62,170	6,450	55,722	2,852	4.4	44,660
1956	110,954	66,552	60.0	63,799	6,283	57,514	2,750	4.1	44,402
1957	112,265	66,929	59.6	64,071	5,947	58,123	2,859	4.3	45,336
1958	113,727	67,639	59.5	63,036	5,586	57,450	4,602	6.8	46,088
1959	115,329	68,369	59.3	64,630	5,565	59,065	3,740	5.5	46,960
1960	117,245	69,628	59.4	65,778	5,458	60,318	3,852	5.5	47,617
1961	118,771	70,459	59.3	65,746	5,200	60,546	4,714	6.7	48,312
1962	120,153	70,614	58.8	66,702	4,944	61,759	3,911	5.5	49,539
1963	122,416	71,833	58.7	67,762	4,687	63,076	4,070	5.7	50,583
1964	124,485	73,091	58.7	69,305	4,523	64,782	3,786	5.2	51,394
1965	126,513	74,455	58.9	71,088	4,361	66,726	3,366	4.5	52,058
1966	128,058	75,770	59.2	72,895	3,979	68,915	2,875	3.8	52,288
1967	129,874	77,347	59.6	74,372	3,844	70,527	2,975	3.8	52,527
1968	132,028	78,737	59.6	75,920	3,817	72,103	2,817	3.6	53,291
1969	134,335	80,734	60.1	77,902	3,606	74,296	2,832	3.5	53,602
1970	137,085	82,771	60.4	78,678	3,463	75,215	4,093	4.9	54,315
1971	140,216	84,382	60.2	79,367	3,394	75,972	5,016	5.9	55,834
1972	144,126	87,034	60.4	82,153	3,484	78,669	4,882	5.6	57,091
1973	147,096	89,429	60.8	85,064	3,470	81,594	4,365	4.9	57,667
1974	150,120	91,949	61.3	86,794	3,515	83,279	5,156	5.6	58,171
1975	153,153	93,775	61.2	85,846	3,408	82,438	7,929	8.5	59,377
1976	156,150	96,158	61.6	88,752	3,331	85,421	7,406	7.7	59,991
1977	159,033	99,008	62.3	92,017	3,283	88,734	6,991	7.1	60,025
1978	161,910	102,250	63.2	96,048	3,387	92,661	6,202	6.1	59,659
1979	164,863	104,962	63.7	98,824	3,347	95,477	6,137	5.8	59,900
1980	167,745	106,940	63.8	99,302	3,364	95,938	7,637	7.1	60,806
1981	170,130	108,670	63.9	100,397	3,368	97,030	8,273	7.6	61,460
1982	172,271	110,204	64.0	99,526	3,401	96,125	10,678	9.7	62,067
1983	174,215	111,550	64.0	100,834	3,383	97,450	10,717	9.6	62,665
1984	176,383	113,544	64.4	105,005	3,321	101,685	8,539	7.5	62,839
1985	178,206	115,461	64.8	107,150	3,179	103,971	8,312	7.2	62,744
1986	180,587	117,834	65.3	109,597	3,163	106,434	8,237	7.0	62,752
1987	182,753	119,865	65.6	112,440	3,208	109,232	7,425	6.2	62,888
1988	184,613	121,669	65.9	114,968	3,169	111,800	6,701	5.5	62,944
1989	186,393	123,869	66.5	117,342	3,199	114,142	6,528	5.3	62,523
1990	189,164	125,840	66.5	118,793	3,223	115,570	7,047	5.6	63,324
1991	190,925	126,346	66.2	117,718	3,269	114,449	8,628	6.8	64,578
1992	192,805	128,105	66.4	118,492	3,247	115,245	9,613	7.5	64,700
1993	194,838	129,200	66.3	120,259	3,115	117,144	8,940	6.9	65,638
1994	196,814	131,056	66.6	123,060	3,409	119,651	7,996	6.1	65,758
1995	198,584	132,304	66.6	124,900	3,440	121,460	7,404	5.6	66,280
1996	200,591	133,943	66.8	126,708	3,443	123,264	7,236	5.4	66,647
1997	203,133	136,297	67.1	129,558	3,399	126,159	6,739	4.9	66,836

TABLE 3.1

Employment status of the civilian noninstitutional population, 1940–2002 [CONTINUED]

(Numbers in thousands)

Year	Civilian noninstitutional population	Civilian labor force								Not in labor force
					Employed			Unemployed		
		Total	Percent of population	Total	Agri culture	Nonagricultural industries	Number	Percent of force	
1998	205,220	137,673	67.1	131,463	3,378	128,085	6,210	4.5	67,547
1999	207,753	139,368	67.1	133,488	3,281	130,207	5,880	4.2	68,385
2000	212,577	142,583	67.1	136,891	3,382	133,509	5,692	4.0	69,994
2001	215,092	143,734	66.8	136,933	3,231	133,702	6,801	4.7	71,359
2002	217,570	144,863	66.6	136,485	3,340	133,145	8,378	5.8	72,707

*Not available.

SOURCE: "1. Employment status of the civilian noninstitutional population, 1940 to date," in *Employment and Earnings,* U.S. Department of Labor, Bureau of Labor Statistics, Washington, DC, June 2003

OCCUPATIONS

In 2000 an almost equal proportion of workers were employed in managerial or professional areas as were in sales or administrative support fields (29.1 percent and 27.1 percent, respectively). Service occupations accounted for 17.9 percent of all employment, an increase of 4.2 percent in two years. Other leading occupational categories were production (9.0 percent), construction and extraction (5.1 percent), and installation, maintenance, and repair (4.0 percent).

It is important to understand the difference between a service industry and a service occupation. A service industry provides service to the economy but employs more than service workers. For example, a restaurant is a service industry. It may employ workers involved in service, but it also employs secretaries, managers, and accountants, whose occupations are not considered service occupations.

Of the 10 occupations projected to grow the fastest over the next decade, the top 6 are computer-related (often referred to as information technology occupations). The 10 occupations expected to add the most jobs between 2000 and 2010 will account for nearly one-fourth of total employment growth.

Women are far more likely than men to work in administrative support, including clerical, and in service occupations. Men dominate such categories as precision production, craft, and repair; operators, fabricators, and laborers; and farming, forestry, and fishing.

Blacks are less likely than whites to work in managerial and professional specialties, sales, and precision production positions. Blacks are more likely than whites to work as operators, fabricators, and laborers and in service occupations. Black women are more likely to be in managerial and professional specialties and sales and administrative support than black men.

THE UNEMPLOYED

The U.S. unemployment rate reached a post–World War II high of 9.7 percent in 1982. In 1983 it remained high at 9.6 percent as the result of the most severe economic recession since the Great Depression of the 1930s. The unemployment rate then dropped, approaching 5 percent in 1989, but again began increasing, staying just under 7 percent for most of 1991 and rising to 8 percent in 1992. As the economy improved, the rate fell to 7 percent in 1993. From 1997 until the fourth quarter of 2001, the U.S. unemployment rate was under 5 percent, indicating a robust economy. After the September 11, 2001, terrorist attacks on New York, Washington, D.C., and Pennsylvania, the unemployment rate jumped to 5.4 percent in October 2001, the sharpest increase in unemployment in 23 years. From the fourth quarter of 2001 to the second quarter of 2003 the unemployment rate averaged 5.9 percent. In fact, in the second quarter of 2003, the unemployment rate climbed to its highest point (6.2 percent) since 1993 (6.9 percent).

Prior to September 11, 2001, the United States had one of the lowest unemployment rates of the industrialized countries. Netherlands (2.4 percent) had the lowest rate followed by Austria and Norway (3.6 percent). Among the larger European economies, Spain was the highest (10.7 percent), followed by Italy (9.6), France (8.5 percent), and Germany (8.0 percent). (See Figure 3.1.) Despite the economic slowdown that plagued much of 2002, the U.S. unemployment rate remains lower than that of France and Germany (9.2 percent each), as well as Italy (8.8 percent).

Unemployment rates in the United States vary from state to state. In August 2003 Alaska and Oregon (8.0 percent each) and Washington (7.5 percent) had the highest unemployment rates. South Dakota (3.4 percent), Virginia (3.7 percent), and Nebraska and North Dakota (3.8 percent each) had the lowest rates.

TABLE 3.2

Employment status of the civilian noninstitutional population 16 years and over by sex, 1971–2002

(Numbers in thousands)

Year	Civilian noninsti- tutional population	Civilian labor force Total	Percent of population	Employed Total	Agri- culture	Nonagri- cultural industries	Unemployed Number	Percent of labor force	Not in labor force
				Men					
1971	65,942	52,180	79.1	49,390	2,795	46,595	2,789	5.3	13,762
1972	67,835	53,555	78.9	50,896	2,849	48,047	2,659	5.0	14,280
1973	69,292	54,624	78.8	52,349	2,847	49,502	2,275	4.2	14,667
1974	70,808	55,739	78.7	53,024	2,919	50,105	2,714	4.9	15,069
1975	72,291	56,299	77.9	51,857	2,824	49,032	4,442	7.9	15,993
1976	73,759	57,174	77.5	53,138	2,744	50,394	4,036	7.1	16,585
1977	75,193	58,396	77.7	54,728	2,671	52,057	3,667	6.3	16,797
1978	76,576	59,620	77.9	56,479	2,718	53,761	3,142	5.3	16,956
1979	78,020	60,726	77.8	57,607	2,686	54,921	3,120	5.1	17,293
1980	79,398	61,453	77.4	57,186	2,709	54,477	4,267	6.9	17,945
1981	80,511	61,974	77.0	57,397	2,700	54,697	4,577	7.4	18,537
1982	81,523	62,450	76.6	56,271	2,736	53,534	6,179	9.9	19,073
1983	82,531	63,047	76.4	56,787	2,704	54,083	6,260	9.9	19,484
1984	83,605	63,835	76.4	59,091	2,668	56,423	4,744	7.4	19,771
1985	84,469	64,411	76.3	59,891	2,535	57,356	4,521	7.0	20,058
1986	85,798	65,422	76.3	60,892	2,511	58,381	4,530	6.9	20,376
1987	86,899	66,207	76.2	62,107	2,543	59,564	4,101	6.2	20,692
1988	87,857	66,927	76.2	63,273	2,493	60,780	3,655	5.5	20,930
1989	88,762	67,840	76.4	64,315	2,513	61,802	3,525	5.2	20,923
1990	90,377	69,011	76.4	65,104	2,546	62,559	3,906	5.7	21,367
1991	91,278	69,168	75.8	64,223	2,589	61,634	4,946	7.2	22,110
1992	92,270	69,964	75.8	64,440	2,575	61,866	5,523	7.9	22,306
1993	93,332	70,404	75.4	65,349	2,478	62,871	5,055	7.2	22,927
1994	94,354	70,817	75.1	66,450	2,554	63,896	4,367	6.2	23,538
1995	95,178	71,360	75.0	67,377	2,559	64,818	3,983	5.6	23,818
1996	96,206	72,086	74.9	68,207	2,573	65,634	3,880	5.4	24,119
1997	97,715	73,261	75.0	69,685	2,552	67,133	3,577	4.9	24,454
1998	98,758	73,959	74.9	70,693	2,553	68,140	3,266	4.4	24,799
1999	99,722	74,512	74.7	71,446	2,432	69,014	3,066	4.1	25,210
2000	101,964	76,280	74.8	73,305	2,502	70,803	2,975	3.9	25,684
2001	103,282	76,886	74.4	73,196	2,353	70,843	3,690	4.8	26,396
2002	104,585	77,500	74.1	72,903	2,473	70,430	4,597	5.9	27,085
				Women					
1971	74,274	32,202	43.4	29,976	599	29,377	2,227	6.9	42,072
1972	76,290	33,479	43.9	31,257	635	30,622	2,222	6.6	42,811
1973	77,804	34,804	44.7	32,715	622	32,093	2,089	6.0	43,000
1974	79,312	36,211	45.7	33,769	596	33,173	2,441	6.7	43,101
1975	80,860	37,475	46.3	33,989	584	33,404	3,486	9.3	43,386
1976	82,390	38,983	47.3	35,615	588	35,027	3,369	8.6	43,406
1977	83,840	40,613	48.4	37,289	612	36,677	3,324	8.2	43,227
1978	85,334	42,631	50.0	39,569	669	38,900	3,061	7.2	42,703
1979	86,843	44,235	50.9	41,217	661	40,556	3,018	6.8	42,608
1980	88,348	45,487	51.5	42,117	656	41,461	3,370	7.4	42,861
1981	89,618	46,696	52.1	43,000	667	42,333	3,696	7.9	42,922
1982	90,748	47,755	52.6	43,256	665	42,591	4,499	9.4	42,993
1983	91,684	48,503	52.9	44,047	680	43,367	4,457	9.2	43,181
1984	92,778	49,709	53.6	45,915	653	45,262	3,794	7.6	43,068
1985	93,736	51,050	54.5	47,259	644	46,615	3,791	7.4	42,686
1986	94,789	52,413	55.3	48,706	652	48,054	3,707	7.1	42,376
1987	95,853	53,658	56.0	50,334	666	49,668	3,324	6.2	42,195
1988	96,756	54,742	56.6	51,696	676	51,020	3,046	5.6	42,014
1989	97,630	56,030	57.4	53,027	687	52,341	3,003	5.4	41,601
1990	98,787	56,829	57.5	53,689	678	53,011	3,140	5.5	41,957
1991	99,646	57,178	57.4	53,496	680	52,815	3,683	6.4	42,468
1992	100,535	58,141	57.8	54,052	672	53,380	4,090	7.0	42,394
1993	101,506	58,795	57.9	54,910	637	54,273	3,885	6.6	42,711
1994	102,460	60,239	58.8	56,610	855	55,755	3,629	6.0	42,221
1995	103,406	60,944	58.9	57,523	881	56,642	3,421	5.6	42,462
1996	104,385	61,857	59.3	58,501	871	57,630	3,356	5.4	42,528
1997	105,418	63,036	59.8	59,873	847	59,026	3,162	5.0	42,382

TABLE 3.2

Employment status of the civilian noninstitutional population 16 years and over by sex, 1971–2002 [CONTINUED]

(Numbers in thousands)

| Year | Civilian noninsti-tutional population | Civilian labor force | | | | | | | | Not in labor force |
| | | Total | Percent of population | Employed | | | Unemployed | | | |
				Total	Agri-culture	Nonagri-cultural industries	Number	Percent of labor force		
1998	106,462	63,714	59.8	60,771	825	59,945	2,944	4.6		42,748
1999	108,031	64,855	60.0	62,042	849	61,193	2,814	4.3		43,175
2000	110,613	66,303	59.9	63,586	880	62,706	2,717	4.1		44,310
2001	111,811	66,848	59.8	63,737	878	62,859	3,111	4.7		44,962
2002	112,985	67,363	59.6	63,582	867	62,715	3,781	5.6		45,621

SOURCE: "2. Employment status of the civilian noninstitutional population, 16 years and over by sex, 1971 to date," in *Employment and Earnings,* U.S. Department of Labor, Bureau of Labor Statistics, Washington, DC, June 2003

FIGURE 3.1

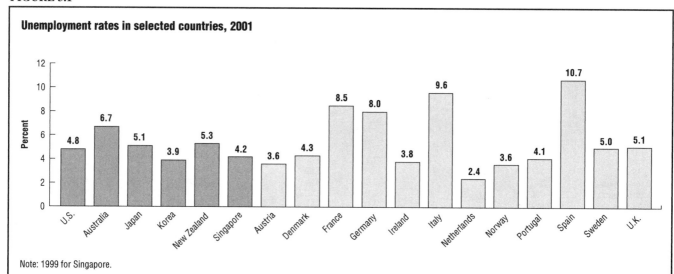

Unemployment rates in selected countries, 2001

Note: 1999 for Singapore.

SOURCE: Elaine L. Chao, "Chart 9. Unemployment Rates, 2001," in *A Chartbook of International Labor Comparisons: United States, Europe, and Asia,* U.S. Department of Labor, Washington, DC, April 2003

Age

Unemployment does not occur evenly in all occupations or sectors of society. Workers under 25 years of age are far more likely to be unemployed than older workers. Their jobs are frequently more marginal, and younger workers leave their jobs more often than older ones do. They also have less seniority to protect themselves against layoffs.

Race

Race plays a role in unemployment rates. Many blacks traditionally worked in occupations that have suffered from the change from an industrial to a service economy. According to the BLS, in 2001 the unemployment rates for blacks (8.6 percent) and Hispanics (6.6 percent) were higher than that for whites (4.2 percent). The economy slowed over the following year, and in 2002 the unemployment rate for whites was 6.1 percent, while it had risen to 10.2 percent for

blacks and 7.5 percent for Hispanics. By September 2003 the unemployment rate for whites was 5.3 percent, 11.2 percent for blacks, and 7.5 percent for Hispanics.

Gender

Historically, females usually have higher unemployment rates than males. However, in September 2002 the unemployment rate for males over 20 years of age was higher (5.3 percent) than the rate for females over 20 years of age (5.0 percent). In September 2003 the unemployment rate for females over 20 years of age continued below the rate of their male counterparts (5.3 percent and 5.7 percent, respectively). Unemployment differences between males and females are affected by family status. For example, in September 2003 those married men and women with spouses present had unemployment rates of 3.7 percent and 4.0 percent, respectively. Furthermore,

TABLE 3.3

Employment status of the civilian noninstitutional population by age, sex, and race, 2002

(Numbers in thousands)

		2002								
		Civilian labor force								
				Employed				**Unemployed**		
Age, sex, and race	**Civilian noninstitutional population**	**Total**	**Percent of population**	**Total**	**Percent of population**	**Agriculture**	**Nonagricultural industries**	**Number**	**Percent of labor force**	**Not in labor force**
Total										
16 years and over	217,570	144,863	66.6	136,485	62.7	3,340	133,145	8,378	5.8	72,707
16 to 19 years	15,994	7,585	47.4	6,332	39.6	212	6,120	1,253	16.5	8,409
16 to 17 years	8,099	2,870	35.4	2,330	28.8	91	2,239	540	18.8	5,229
18 to 19 years	7,895	4,715	59.7	4,002	50.7	121	3,880	714	15.1	3,180
20 to 24 years	19,348	14,781	76.4	13,351	69.0	369	12,982	1,430	9.7	4,567
25 to 54 years	122,077	101,719	83.3	96,823	79.3	2,029	94,794	4,896	4.8	20,358
25 to 34 years	38,472	32,196	83.7	30,306	78.8	635	29,672	1,890	5.9	6,276
25 to 29 years	18,188	15,182	83.5	14,204	78.1	298	13,906	978	6.4	3,006
30 to 34 years	20,284	17,014	83.9	16,103	79.4	337	15,766	911	5.4	3,270
35 to 44 years	43,894	36,926	84.1	35,235	80.3	764	34,471	1,691	4.6	6,968
35 to 39 years	21,338	17,887	83.8	17,022	79.8	398	16,625	864	4.8	3,451
40 to 44 years	22,556	19,040	84.4	18,213	80.7	366	17,846	827	4.3	3,516
45 to 54 years	39,711	32,597	82.1	31,281	78.8	630	30,651	1,315	4.0	7,114
45 to 49 years	21,073	17,666	83.8	16,944	80.4	348	16,596	722	4.1	3,407
50 to 54 years	18,638	14,931	80.1	14,337	76.9	282	14,055	594	4.0	3,707
55 to 64 years	26,343	16,309	61.9	15,674	59.5	426	15,248	635	3.9	10,034
55 to 59 years	14,901	10,531	70.7	10,125	68.0	238	9,887	405	3.8	4,370
60 to 64 years	11,442	5,779	50.5	5,549	48.5	187	5,361	230	4.0	5,664
65 years and over	33,808	4,469	13.2	4,306	12.7	305	4,001	163	3.6	29,339
65 to 69 years	9,492	2,474	26.1	2,379	25.1	140	2,239	95	3.8	7,019
70 to 74 years	8,507	1,191	14.0	1,144	13.4	89	1,055	47	4.0	7,316
75 years and over	15,809	804	5.1	783	5.0	75	708	21	2.6	15,005
Men										
16 years and over	104,585	77,500	74.1	72,903	69.7	2,473	70,430	4,597	5.9	27,085
16 to 19 years	8,146	3,870	47.5	3,169	38.9	160	3,009	700	18.1	4,276
16 to 17 years	4,140	1,431	34.6	1,130	27.3	71	1,058	301	21.1	2,709
18 to 19 years	4,006	2,439	60.9	2,040	50.9	89	951	399	16.4	1,567
20 to 24 years	9,627	7,769	80.7	6,978	72.5	287	6,691	792	10.2	1,857
25 to 54 years	59,939	54,568	91.0	51,923	86.6	1,489	50,434	2,645	4.8	5,372
25 to 34 years	19,037	17,596	92.4	16,573	87.1	482	16,091	1,023	5.8	1,441
25 to 29 years	9,031	8,253	91.4	7,722	85.5	229	7,493	531	6.4	778
30 to 34 years	10,005	9,343	93.4	8,851	88.5	253	8,598	492	5.3	662
35 to 44 years	21,523	19,828	92.1	18,932	88.0	565	18,367	897	4.5	1,695
35 to 39 years	10,471	9,705	92.7	9,259	88.4	299	8,960	445	4.6	766
40 to 44 years	11,053	10,124	91.6	9,672	87.5	265	9,407	451	4.5	929
45 to 54 years	19,379	17,143	88.5	16,419	84.7	442	15,976	725	4.2	2,236
45 to 49 years	10,289	9,277	90.2	8,881	86.3	245	8,635	397	4.3	1,012
50 to 54 years	9,090	7,866	86.5	7,538	82.9	197	7,341	328	4.2	1,224
55 to 64 years	12,641	8,751	69.2	8,378	66.3	310	8,068	373	4.3	3,890
55 to 59 years	7,201	5,617	78.0	5,382	74.7	171	5,212	235	4.2	1,583
60 to 64 years	5,440	3,133	57.6	2,996	55.1	140	2,856	137	4.4	2,307
65 years and over	14,233	2,542	17.9	2,455	17.2	227	2,228	87	3.4	11,690
65 to 69 years	4,388	1,415	32.2	1,365	31.1	105	1,261	49	3.5	2,974
70 to 74 years	3,772	664	17.6	637	16.9	68	570	27	4.0	3,108
75 years and over	6,073	464	7.6	452	7.4	55	397	12	2.5	5,609
Women										
16 years and over	112,985	67,363	59.6	63,582	56.3	867	62,715	3,781	5.6	45,621
16 to 19 years	7,848	3,715	47.3	3,162	40.3	52	3,111	553	14.9	4,133
16 to 17 years	3,959	1,439	36.3	1,200	30.3	19	1,181	238	16.6	2,520
18 to 19 years	3,889	2,277	58.5	1,962	50.4	32	1,930	315	13.8	1,613
20 to 24 years	9,721	7,012	72.1	6,374	65.6	82	6,291	638	9.1	2,710
25 to 54 years	62,137	47,151	75.9	44,900	72.3	540	44,360	2,252	4.8	14,986
25 to 34 years	19,435	14,600	75.1	13,733	70.7	153	13,581	866	5.9	4,835
25 to 29 years	9,156	6,929	75.7	6,482	70.8	69	6,413	447	6.5	2,228
30 to 34 years	10,279	7,671	74.6	7,252	70.6	84	7,168	419	5.5	2,608
35 to 44 years	22,371	17,098	76.4	16,303	72.9	199	16,104	795	4.6	5,273
35 to 39 years	10,867	8,182	75.3	7,763	71.4	98	7,665	419	5.1	2,686
40 to 44 years	11,503	8,916	77.5	8,540	74.2	101	8,439	376	4.2	2,587
45 to 54 years	20,332	15,454	76.0	14,863	73.1	188	14,675	591	3.8	4,878
45 to 49 years	10,784	8,389	77.8	8,064	74.8	103	7,961	325	3.9	2,395

TABLE 3.3

Employment status of the civilian noninstitutional population by age, sex, and race, 2002 [CONTINUED]

(Numbers in thousands)

		2002								
		Civilian labor force								
				Employed				Unemployed		
Age, sex, and race	Civilian noninsti-tutional population	Total	Percent of population	Total	Percent of population	Agri-culture	Nonagri-cultural industries	Number	Percent of labor force	Not in labor force
Women										
50 to 54 years	9,548	7,065	74.0	6,799	71.2	85	6,714	266	3.8	2,483
55 to 64 years	13,703	7,559	55.2	7,296	53.2	115	7,181	263	3.5	6,144
55 to 59 years	7,700	4,913	63.8	4,743	61.6	68	4,676	170	3.5	2,787
60 to 64 years	6,003	2,645	44.1	2,553	42.5	48	2,505	93	3.5	3,357
65 years and over	19,575	1,926	9.8	1,851	9.5	78	1,773	76	3.9	17,649
65 to 69 years	5,104	1,059	20.7	1,013	19.9	36	978	46	4.3	4,045
70 to 74 years	4,735	527	11.1	507	10.7	22	485	20	3.9	4,208
75 years and over	9,736	340	3.5	331	3.4	20	310	10	2.8	9,396
White										
16 years and over	179,783	120,150	66.8	114,013	63.4	3,104	110,909	6,137	5.1	59,633
16 to 19 years	12,596	6,366	50.5	5,441	43.2	202	5,239	925	14.5	6,230
16 to 17 years	6,346	2,445	38.5	2,037	32.1	89	1,948	407	16.7	3,901
18 to 19 years	6,250	3,921	62.7	3,404	54.5	113	3,290	518	13.2	2,328
20 to 24 years	15,360	12,073	78.6	11,096	72.2	339	10,757	977	8.1	3,287
25 to 54 years	99,438	83,599	84.1	80,018	80.5	1,883	78,135	3,581	4.3	15,839
25 to 34 years	30,676	25,908	84.5	24,568	80.1	591	23,977	1,340	5.2	4,768
25 to 29 years	14,472	12,248	84.6	11,567	79.9	279	11,288	681	5.6	2,224
30 to 34 years	16,205	13,660	84.3	13,001	80.2	312	12,690	658	4.8	2,545
35 to 44 years	35,750	30,286	84.7	29,049	81.3	714	28,335	1,237	4.1	5,464
35 to 39 years	17,234	14,500	84.1	13,872	80.5	372	13,500	628	4.3	2,734
40 to 44 years	18,516	15,786	85.3	15,177	82.0	342	14,835	609	3.9	2,730
45 to 54 years	33,012	27,405	83.0	26,401	80.0	578	25,823	1,004	3.7	5,607
45 to 49 years	17,411	14,737	84.6	14,200	81.6	320	13,880	536	3.6	2,675
50 to 54 years	15,600	12,668	81.2	12,201	78.2	258	11,943	468	3.7	2,932
55 to 64 years	22,540	14,148	62.8	13,630	60.5	390	13,240	518	3.7	8,392
55 to 59 years	12,710	9,104	71.6	8,780	69.1	215	8,565	323	3.6	3,606
60 to 64 years	9,830	5,044	51.3	4,849	49.3	175	4,675	194	3.9	4,786
65 years and over	29,849	3,965	13.3	3,828	12.8	289	3,539	137	3.5	25,884
65 to 69 years	8,157	2,156	26.4	2,078	25.5	132	1,946	78	3.6	6,001
70 to 74 years	7,506	1,077	14.4	1,036	13.8	86	950	41	3.8	6,429
75 years and over	14,186	731	5.2	713	5.0	71	642	18	2.5	13,455
Men										
16 years and over	87,361	65,308	74.8	61,849	70.8	2,276	59,573	3,459	5.3	22,053
16 to 19 years	6,439	3,241	50.3	2,725	42.3	155	2,570	516	15.9	3,198
16 to 17 years	3,251	1,215	37.4	987	30.4	70	917	228	18.8	2,035
18 to 19 years	3,189	2,026	63.5	1,738	54.5	85	1,653	288	14.2	1,163
20 to 24 years	7,750	6,444	83.2	5,882	75.9	263	5,619	562	8.7	1,305
25 to 54 years	49,578	45,696	92.2	43,697	88.1	1,365	42,332	1,999	4.4	3,882
25 to 34 years	15,470	14,499	93.7	13,727	88.7	445	13,282	772	5.3	971
25 to 29 years	7,316	6,807	93.0	6,412	87.6	212	6,200	395	5.8	509
30 to 34 years	8,154	7,692	94.3	7,314	89.7	233	7,081	377	4.9	462
35 to 44 years	17,792	16,583	93.2	15,910	89.4	521	15,390	672	4.1	1,209
35 to 39 years	8,586	8,041	93.6	7,708	89.8	277	7,431	332	4.1	546
40 to 44 years	9,206	8,542	92.8	8,202	89.1	244	7,958	340	4.0	663
45 to 54 years	16,317	14,615	89.6	14,060	86.2	400	13,660	554	3.8	1,702
45 to 49 years	8,626	7,862	91.1	7,566	87.7	222	7,344	297	3.8	764
50 to 54 years	7,691	6,752	87.8	6,495	84.4	178	6,316	258	3.8	938
55 to 64 years	10,918	7,665	70.2	7,360	67.4	279	7,082	305	4.0	3,253
55 to 59 years	6,203	4,912	79.2	4,722	76.1	150	4,573	190	3.9	1,291
60 to 64 years	4,715	2,753	58.4	2,638	56.0	129	2,509	115	4.2	1,961
65 years and over	12,676	2,261	17.8	2,184	17.2	214	1,970	77	3.4	10,415
65 to 69 years	3,817	1,237	32.4	1,195	31.3	97	1,098	42	3.4	2,580
70 to 74 years	3,368	600	17.8	575	17.1	65	511	25	4.1	2,768
75 years and over	5,491	423	7.7	414	7.5	52	361	10	2.2	5,068
Women										
16 years and over	92,422	54,842	59.3	52,164	56.4	827	51,336	2,678	4.9	37,581
16 to 19 years	6,157	3,125	50.8	2,716	44.1	47	2,668	409	13.1	3,032
16 to 17 years	3,096	1,229	39.7	1,050	33.9	19	1,031	179	14.6	1,866
18 to 19 years	3,061	1,895	61.9	1,665	54.4	28	1,637	230	12.1	1,166

TABLE 3.3

Employment status of the civilian noninstitutional population by age, sex, and race, 2002 [CONTINUED]

(Numbers in thousands)

		2002								
		Civilian labor force								
				Employed				Unemployed		
Age, sex, and race	Civilian noninstitutional population	Total	Percent of population	Total	Percent of population	Agriculture	Nonagricultural industries	Number	Percent of labor force	Not in labor force
Women										
20 to 24 years	7,611	5,628	74.0	5,214	68.5	76	5,138	415	7.4	1,982
25 to 54 years	49,860	37,902	76.0	36,321	72.8	517	35,804	1,582	4.2	11,958
25 to 34 years	15,207	11,409	75.0	10,842	71.3	146	10,696	567	5.0	3,798
25 to 29 years	7,156	5,441	76.0	5,155	72.0	67	5,087	286	5.3	1,715
30 to 34 years	8,051	5,968	74.1	5,687	70.6	79	5,609	281	4.7	2,083
35 to 44 years	17,958	13,703	76.3	13,138	73.2	193	12,945	565	4.1	4,255
35 to 39 years	8,648	6,459	74.7	6,164	71.3	95	6,068	296	4.6	2,189
40 to 44 years	9,310	7,244	77.8	6,975	74.9	98	6,877	269	3.7	2,066
45 to 54 years	16,695	12,790	76.6	12,341	73.9	178	12,163	449	3.5	3,905
45 to 49 years	8,785	6,874	78.2	6,635	75.5	98	6,537	240	3.5	1,911
50 to 54 years	7,910	5,916	74.8	5,706	72.1	80	5,626	210	3.5	1,994
55 to 64 years	11,622	6,482	55.8	6,269	53.9	111	6,158	213	3.3	5,139
55 to 59 years	6,507	4,192	64.4	4,058	62.4	66	3,993	134	3.2	2,315
60 to 64 years	5,115	2,290	44.8	2,211	43.2	46	2,165	79	3.5	2,825
65 years and over	17,173	1,704	9.9	1,644	9.6	75	1,569	60	3.5	15,469
65 to 69 years	4,340	919	21.2	883	20.4	35	848	35	3.8	3,421
70 to 74 years	4,138	477	11.5	461	11.1	21	440	16	3.4	3,661
75 years and over	8,695	308	3.5	300	3.4	19	281	9	2.8	8,387
Black										
16 years and over	25,578	16,565	64.8	14,872	58.1	131	14,742	1,693	10.2	9,013
16 to 19 years	2,416	870	36.0	611	25.3	7	604	260	29.8	1,546
16 to 17 years	1,235	297	24.0	193	15.6	1	192	103	34.9	939
18 to 19 years	1,181	574	48.6	417	35.3	6	412	156	27.2	608
20 to 24 years	2,779	1,908	68.6	1,543	55.5	16	1,527	365	19.1	871
25 to 54 years	14,988	12,027	80.2	11,055	73.8	82	10,973	972	8.1	2,961
25 to 34 years	5,015	4,134	82.4	3,726	74.3	22	3,705	407	9.9	881
25 to 29 years	2,426	1,963	80.9	1,742	71.8	11	1,730	222	11.3	463
30 to 34 years	2,589	2,171	83.8	1,985	76.7	10	1,975	186	8.6	418
35 to 44 years	5,460	4,458	81.6	4,109	75.2	33	4,075	349	7.8	1,002
35 to 39 years	2,703	2,256	83.5	2,078	76.9	15	2,063	178	7.9	446
40 to 44 years	2,758	2,202	79.8	2,031	73.6	18	2,013	171	7.8	556
45 to 54 years	4,513	3,435	76.1	3,220	71.3	27	3,193	215	6.3	1,078
45 to 49 years	2,462	1,933	78.5	1,795	72.9	14	1,781	137	7.1	529
50 to 54 years	2,051	1,503	73.3	1,425	69.4	12	1,412	78	5.2	549
55 to 64 years	2,571	1,407	54.7	1,332	51.8	16	1,316	76	5.4	1,164
55 to 59 years	1,450	923	63.7	870	60.0	9	860	54	5.8	526
60 to 64 years	1,122	484	43.2	462	41.2	7	455	22	4.5	638
65 years and over	2,823	353	12.5	332	11.8	10	322	21	5.9	2,470
65 to 69 years	934	218	23.3	205	21.9	4	201	13	6.1	716
70 to 74 years	698	80	11.4	75	10.7	3	72	5	6.0	618
75 years and over	1,191	55	4.6	52	4.4	3	49	3	5.3	1,136
Men										
16 years and over	11,391	7,794	68.4	6,959	61.1	117	6,842	835	10.7	3,597
16 to 19 years	1,195	446	37.3	306	25.6	4	302	140	31.3	749
16 to 17 years	615	149	24.2	95	15.4	1	94	54	36.6	466
18 to 19 years	580	297	51.3	212	36.5	4	208	85	28.7	283
20 to 24 years	1,281	906	70.7	725	56.6	14	710	181	20.0	375
25 to 54 years	6,702	5,596	83.5	5,132	76.6	74	5,057	464	8.3	1,106
25 to 34 years	2,223	1,909	85.9	1,729	77.8	20	1,709	180	9.4	314
25 to 29 years	1,074	902	84.0	809	75.4	10	799	93	10.3	171
30 to 34 years	1,149	1,007	87.6	920	80.1	9	911	86	8.6	143
35 to 44 years	2,437	2,064	84.7	1,899	77.9	30	1,869	165	8.0	374
35 to 39 years	1,198	1,037	86.6	955	79.7	14	941	82	7.9	161
40 to 44 years	1,240	1,027	82.8	944	76.2	16	928	83	8.1	213
45 to 54 years	2,042	1,623	79.5	1,503	73.6	24	1,479	120	7.4	419
45 to 49 years	1,114	916	82.3	842	75.6	14	828	74	8.1	197
50 to 54 years	928	707	76.2	661	71.2	10	651	46	6.4	221
55 to 64 years	1,137	664	58.4	624	54.9	15	609	40	6.1	473
55 to 59 years	645	431	66.8	402	62.4	8	394	29	6.6	214
60 to 64 years	492	233	47.4	222	45.0	7	215	12	5.0	259

TABLE 3.3

Employment status of the civilian noninstitutional population by age, sex, and race, 2002 [CONTINUED]

(Numbers in thousands)

Age, sex, and race	Civilian noninsti-tutional population	Civilian labor force								Not in labor force
		Total	Percent of population	Employed				Unemployed		
				Total	Percent of population	Agri-culture	Nonagri-cultural industries	Number	Percent of labor force	
Men										
65 to 69 years	396	115	29.1	110	27.6	4	105	6	5.1	281
70 to 74 years	274	38	13.9	37	13.4	2	34	1	3.8	236
75 years and over	405	28	6.8	26	4 6	2	24	2	(*)	377
Women										
16 years and over	14,187	8,772	61.8	7,914	55.8	14	7,900	858	9.8	5,415
16 to 19 years	1,221	424	34.7	304	24.9	2	302	120	28.3	797
16 to 17 years	620	148	23.8	99	15.9	–	99	49	33.2	472
18 to 19 years	601	276	46.0	205	34.2	2	203	71	25.6	325
20 to 24 years	1,498	1,002	66.9	819	54.6	2	817	183	18.3	496
25 to 54 years	8,286	6,431	77.6	5,923	71.5	7	5,916	508	7.9	1,855
25 to 34 years	2,792	2,225	79.7	1,997	71.5	2	1,995	228	10.2	567
25 to 29 years	1,352	1,061	78.5	932	69.0	1	931	128	12.1	291
30 to 34 years	1,440	1,164	80.9	1,065	73.9	1	1,064	99	8.5	276
35 to 44 years	3,023	2,394	79.2	2,209	73.1	3	2,207	185	7.7	629
35 to 39 years	1,505	1,219	81.0	1,123	74.6	1	1,122	96	7.9	286
40 to 44 years	1,518	1,175	77.4	1,087	71.6	2	1,085	88	7.5	343
45 to 54 years	2,471	1,812	73.3	1,717	69.5	3	1,714	95	5.3	659
45 to 49 years	1,348	1,016	75.4	953	70.7	1	953	63	6.2	332
50 to 54 years	1,123	796	70.9	763	68.0	2	761	32	4.1	327
55 to 64 years	1,434	743	51.8	708	49.4	2	707	35	4.7	691
55 to 59 years	805	492	61.2	467	58.1	1	466	25	5.1	312
60 to 64 years	630	251	39.9	241	38.2	–	240	10	4.1	379
65 years and over	1,747	171	9.8	160	9.1	1	158	12	6.9	1,576
65 to 69 years	537	102	19.1	95	17.7	–	95	7	7.2	435
70 to 74 years	424	42	9.8	38	9.0	–	38	3	8.0	382
75 years and over	787	27	3.5	26	3.4	1	25	1	(*)	759

* Data not shown where base is less than 35,000.

SOURCE: "3. Employment status of the civilian noninstitutional population by age, sex, and race," in *Employment and Earnings,* U.S. Department of Labor, Bureau of Labor Statistics, Washington, DC, June 2003

women who maintained families were unemployed at a rate of 7.0 percent in September 2002 and 8.5 in September 2003. (See Table 3.4.)

Occupations and Industries

Some occupations are more susceptible to unemployment than others. In September 2003 workers in the farming, forestry, and fishing sector had the highest rate of unemployment at 7.4 percent. Those in the management, business, and financial operations occupations had the lowest unemployment rate, at 3.0 percent. Construction laborers also had a high rate of unemployment in September 2003, at 7.0 percent. This high rate reflects the seasonal nature of construction work. (See Table 3.5.)

In 2000 those working in the construction, lumber, and wood products; apparel; and agricultural industries were more likely to find themselves without jobs than those in the primary metal; professional; photographic equipment, paper, and chemicals; communications; finance; insurance and real estate; and professional services industries.

How Long Does Unemployment Last?

In 2002 the average length of unemployment for unemployed workers 16 years of age and over was 16.6 weeks, up from 12.5 weeks in July 2001. On average in 2002, 35.0 percent of the unemployed had been unemployed for less than 5 weeks, more than the 31.0 percent that had been out of work for 5 to 14 weeks in 2001. About 16.0 percent were out of work 15 to 26 weeks and 18.0 percent for more than 27 weeks in 2002, compared to 32.3 percent and 14.0 percent, respectively, the year before.

Because better-paying jobs usually take longer to find, in 2002 men 45 years and older, who were more likely to be seeking higher-paying employment than either women or younger people, remained unemployed longer. Blacks were out of work longer than whites. Widowed, divorced, or separated men and women were unemployed longer than those who had never been married or those who were still living with their spouses. Married men living with their spouses were out of work longer than never-married men.

TABLE 3.4

Selected unemployment indicators, seasonally adjusted, September 2002 and May–September 2003

Characteristic	Number of unemployed persons (in thousands)			Unemployment rates[1]					
	Sept. 2002	Aug. 2003	Sept. 2003	Sept. 2002	May 2003	June 2003	July 2003	Aug. 2003	Sept. 2003
Total, 16 years and over	**8,321**	**8,905**	**8,973**	**5.7**	**6.1**	**6.4**	**6.2**	**6.1**	**6.1**
16 to 19 years	1,243	1,187	1,243	16.2	18.5	19.3	18.4	16.6	17.5
16 to 17 years	568	544	542	19.4	18.5	21.6	20.8	18.7	19.4
18 to 19 years	663	676	687	14.0	19.0	17.9	17.0	15.9	16.1
20 years and over	7,079	7,718	7,729	5.1	5.5	5.7	5.6	5.5	5.5
20 to 24 years	1,433	1,537	1,636	9.6	10.5	10.7	10.3	10.3	10.9
25 years and over	5,632	6,210	6,111	4.6	4.9	5.1	5.0	5.0	4.9
25 to 54 years	4,797	5,252	5,217	4.7	5.0	5.3	5.1	5.1	5.1
25 to 34 years	1,853	2,040	2,042	5.8	6.0	6.5	6.1	6.3	6.3
35 to 44 years	1,677	1,836	1,766	4.6	5.0	5.4	5.2	5.0	4.8
45 to 54 years	1,267	1,375	1,409	3.9	4.1	4.0	4.0	4.1	4.2
55 years and over	819	915	869	3.9	4.5	4.6	4.3	4.1	3.9
Men, 16 years and over	4,610	4,965	5,010	5.9	6.5	6.8	6.6	6.4	6.4
16 to 19 years	716	608	715	18.3	20.8	20.1	20.9	16.9	20.0
16 to 17 years	310	303	312	21.5	21.5	23.8	22.8	20.7	22.6
18 to 19 years	401	328	403	16.3	20.9	17.7	19.5	15.3	18.3
20 years and over	3,895	4,357	4,295	5.3	5.9	6.1	5.9	5.8	5.7
20 to 24 years	827	838	954	10.5	11.4	11.7	11.7	10.8	11.9
25 years and over	3,062	3,530	3,371	4.6	5.2	5.5	5.2	5.3	5.0
25 to 54 years	2,592	3,010	2,878	4.7	5.3	5.5	5.3	5.5	5.2
25 to 34 years	1,000	1,224	1,167	5.7	6.0	6.7	6.4	6.9	6.6
35 to 44 years	887	1,023	967	4.5	5.3	5.6	5.2	5.2	4.9
45 to 54 years	705	762	45	4.1	4.7	4.2	4.4	4.4	4.3
55 years and over	470	520	493	4.1	4.8	5.5	4.6	4.4	4.2
Women, 16 years and over	3,711	3,940	3,962	5.5	5.7	5.9	5.7	5.8	5.8
16 to 19 years	527	579	528	14.0	16.2	18.5	16.0	16.4	15.1
16 to 17 years	258	241	230	17.4	15.8	19.5	18.9	16.7	16.3
18 to 19 years	262	348	285	11.5	17.1	18.0	14.5	16.6	13.7
20 years and over	3,184	3,361	3,434	5.0	5.1	5.2	5.2	5.2	5.3
20 to 24 years	606	699	682	8.7	9.4	9.5	8.9	9.8	9.7
25 years and over	2,570	2,680	2,740	4.5	4.6	4.7	4.7	4.6	4.8
25 to 54 years	2,205	2,242	2,339	4.7	4.7	5.0	4.9	4.7	5.0
25 to 34 years	853	816	875	5.8	5.9	6.2	5.8	5.6	6.0
35 to 44 years	790	813	800	4.6	4.7	5.2	5.2	4.8	4.8
45 to 54 years	562	613	664	3.6	3.4	3.7	3.7	3.8	4.2
55 years and over[2]	350	453	391	3.6	3.6	3.7	4.2	4.5	3.8
Married men, spouse present	1,652	1,785	1,716	3.6	3.9	4.4	3.9	3.8	3.7
Married women, spouse present	1,300	1,383	1,427	3.6	3.7	3.9	3.9	3.8	4.0
Women who maintain families[2]	648	778	775	7.0	8.3	8.7	9.0	8.4	8.5
Full-time workers[3]	6,990	7,530	7,484	5.8	6.3	6.5	6.3	6.2	6.2
Part-time workers[4]	1,336	1,395	1,512	5.3	5.6	5.9	5.5	5.3	5.8

[1] Unemployment as a percent of the civilian labor force.
[2] Not seasonally adjusted.
[3] Full-time workers are unemployed persons who have expressed a desire to work full time (35 hours or more per week) or are on layoff from full-time jobs.
[4] Part-time workers are unemployed persons who have expressed a desire to work part time (less than 35 hours per week) or are on layoff from part-time jobs.

SOURCE: "Table A-7. Selected unemployment indicators, seasonally adjusted, in "The Employment Situation: September 2003," *News,* vol. 03-523, U.S. Department of Labor, Bureau of Labor Statistics, Washington, DC, October 3, 2003

Duration of unemployment can also depend on the type of job held and the time of the year. In 2002 agricultural employees had the least amount of time unemployed (an average of 13.0 weeks). Those employed in manufacturing nondurable goods were unemployed for the longest period of time, an average of 19.9 weeks.

In terms of the median duration of unemployment, agricultural workers fared best in 2002 at 6.8 weeks. The median for those employed in the manufacturing of nondurable goods was 12.4 weeks, the highest median duration of unemployment in 2002.

In 2002, 8.3 million persons 16 years and older were unemployed, up from 6.8 million in 2001. About 1.5 million men and 265,000 women were laid off permanently in 2002. When measured as a percentage of the civilian labor force, blacks had the highest rate of unemployment in 2002, at 5.1 percent, up slightly from 4.0 percent in 2001. Hispanics were unemployed at a rate of 4.1 percent of the civilian labor force in 2002, up from 3.4 percent in 2001. The rate for whites in 2002 was 2.9 percent, up from 2.2 percent in 2001.

Displaced Workers

According to the BLS, between January 1999 and December 2001, 4 million workers were displaced from jobs they had held for a minimum of 3 years. This was an increase of 700,000 workers from the period of January

TABLE 3.5

Employed and unemployed persons by occupation, not seasonally adjusted, September 2002 and September 2003

(Numbers in thousands)

Occupation	Employed		Unemployed		Unemployment rates	
	Sept. 2002	Sept. 2003	Sept. 2002	Sept. 2003	Sept. 2002	Sept. 2003
Total, 16 years and over *	**137,377**	**137,731**	**7,790**	**8,436**	**5.4**	**5.8**
Management, professional, and related occupations	47,735	47,835	1,617	1,602	3.3	3.2
Management, business, and financial operations occupations.	19,807	19,706	705	616	3.4	3.0
Professional and related occupations	27,928	28,129	913	986	3.2	3.4
Service occupations	21,601	21,667	1,436	1,567	6.2	6.7
Sales and office occupations	35,325	35,153	2,020	2,206	5.4	5.9
Sales and related occupations	15,838	15,825	960	1,079	5.7	6.4
Office and administrative support occupations	19,487	19,328	1,059	1,126	5.2	5.5
Natural resources, construction, and maintenance occupations	14,176	15,099	982	1,061	6.5	6.6
Farming, fishing, and forestry occupations	1,133	1,286	95	103	7.7	7.4
Construction and extraction occupations	8,286	8,620	657	651	7.3	7.0
Installation, maintenance, and repair occupations	4,758	5,194	230	307	4.6	5.6
Production, transportation, and material moving occupations	18,540	17,977	1,226	1,333	6.2	6.9
Production occupations	9,923	9,526	659	755	6.2	7.3
Transportation and material moving occupations	8,617	8,451	567	578	6.2	6.4

*Persons with no previous work experience and persons whose last job was in the Armed Forces are included in the unemployed total.

SOURCE: "Table A-10. Employed and unemployed persons by occupation, not seasonally adjusted," in "The Employment Situation: September 2003," *News,* vol. 03-523, U.S. Department of Labor, Bureau of Labor Statistics, Washington, DC, October 3, 2003

1997 to December 1999. A principal factor in the increase of displaced workers was the economic recession that began in March 2001, resulting in plant and company closures and relocations. Sixty-four percent of the 4 million displaced workers were reemployed by January 2002. At that time, whites (64.7 percent) were more likely to be reemployed than blacks (57.7 percent) or Hispanics (55 percent). Men and women had similar reemployment rates, 65.2 percent and 61.6 percent, respectively.

In general, the risk of job loss decreases as the number of years of educational attainment increases. The risk also declines with increasing number of years on the job.

WITHDRAWN FROM THE LABOR FORCE

The labor force includes those working and those unemployed who are still looking for work. By this definition, all others are not in the labor force. In 2002, 72.7 million people were not in the labor force, an increase of over 1 million from 2001. Of those, 54 percent (39.3 million) were aged 55 or older in 2002. Only 4.6 million of those who were not part of the labor force in 2002 still wanted a job, and only 2 million had actually searched for a job during the previous year. Of those who were available for work, some of the reasons they gave for not currently looking were discouragement over job prospects, family responsibilities, and ill health or disability.

HOW MANY HOURS DO AMERICANS WORK?

In 2002 of the 127.7 million nonfarm U.S. workers, 97.5 million worked 35 hours or more per week, while the remain-

ing 30.2 million worked part time (fewer than 35 hours). The average worker labored 39.1 hours per week, while the average full-time employee worked 42.8 hours. (See Table 3.6.)

Who Is Working the Longest Workweeks?

Some occupations required more work time than others. Executive, administrative, and managerial workers averaged 45 hours per week, the second highest rate in 2002. (Transportation and material moving occupations workers logged 45.1 hours per week on average.) The high rate for executive, administrative, and managerial workers may reflect the considerable responsibilities associated with many of these types of jobs. In addition, employers are often not required by law to pay overtime premiums to workers in these occupations, as they must do for most hourly paid workers. These salaried workers tend to be better paid. Handlers, equipment cleaners, helpers, and laborers worked the fewest hours per week, at 40.8 in 2002. (See Table 3.6.)

Americans Work Longer than Workers in Japan and Europe

A September 2003 study by the UN International Labor Organization (ILO) finds that U.S. productivity in 2002 outpaced that of Europe and Japan in terms of annual output per worker for the first substantial period since World War II. Furthermore, the ILO study reveals that the United States widened the productivity gap over the rest of the world. To a significant degree, the output per worker difference was the result of Americans spending more time on the job than their European rivals. Despite spending longer hours on the job, the average number of hours that Americans worked

TABLE 3.6

Persons at work in nonfarm occupations by sex and usual full- or part-time status, 2002

(Numbers in thousands)

Industry and class of worker	Total at work	2002 Worked 1 to 34 hours — Total	For economic reasons	Usually work full time	Usually work part time	Worked 35 hours or more	Average hours — Total at work	Persons who usually work full time
Total, 16 years and over[1]	127,766	30,250	4,018	7,900	18,332	97,516	39.1	42.8
Managerial and professional specialty	40,492	7,393	587	2,733	4,074	33,099	41.5	44.2
Executive, administrative, and managerial	19,884	2,835	230	1,269	1,337	17,049	43.2	45.0
Professional specialty	20,608	4,558	357	1,464	2,737	16,049	39.9	43.3
Technical, sales, and administrative support	37,536	10,287	992	2,354	6,941	27,249	37.5	42.0
Technicians and related support	4,340	941	64	316	560	3,400	38.9	41.7
Sales occupations	15,702	4,486	545	750	3,192	11,216	38.5	44.1
Administrative support, including clerical	17,493	4,860	383	1,288	3,188	12,633	36.3	40.2
Service occupations	18,466	7,146	1,105	935	5,106	11,319	34.6	41.6
Private household	713	406	68	33	305	308	28.8	41.1
Protective service	2,478	395	50	146	199	2,083	42.4	44.7
Service, except private household and protective	15,274	6,345	987	756	4,602	8,929	33.7	41.0
Precision production, craft, and repair	14,179	2,004	540	918	545	12,175	41.4	42.5
Operators, fabricators, and laborers	17,094	3,420	794	960	1,666	13,674	39.9	42.5
Machine operators, assemblers, and inspectors	6,285	908	236	362	310	5,377	40.4	41.7
Transportation and material moving occupations	5,582	1,000	205	293	502	4,582	42.4	45.1
Handlers, equipment cleaners, helpers, and laborers	5,226	1,511	353	304	854	3,715	36.5	40.8
Men, 16 years and over[1]	67,923	11,313	2,032	3,776	5,504	56,610	41.8	44.2
Managerial and professional specialty	20,317	2,530	291	1,172	1,066	17,787	44.4	46.0
Executive, administrative, and managerial	10,799	1,100	129	575	395	9,700	45.7	46.8
Professional specialty	9,517	1,431	162	597	672	8,087	42.9	45.1
Technical, sales, and administrative support	13,865	2,493	291	705	1,498	11,372	41.4	44.4
Technicians and related support	1,998	294	27	148	118	1,704	41.2	42.7
Sales occupations	8,072	1,442	176	325	940	6,630	42.6	46.0
Administrative support, including clerical	3,795	758	87	231	440	3,037	39.0	41.9
Service occupations	7,456	2,165	387	348	1,430	5,291	37.6	43.0
Private household	39	16	3	2	12	22	32.9	(2)
Protective service	1,990	265	34	108	123	1,725	43.6	45.5
Service, except private household and protective	5,427	1,884	350	238	1,296	3,543	35.4	41.8
Precision production, craft, and repair	13,032	1,749	497	840	413	11,283	41.7	42.6
Operators, fabricators, and laborers	13,252	2,375	566	712	1,097	10,877	40.8	43.1
Machine operators, assemblers, and inspectors	4,087	473	124	218	132	3,614	41.4	42.4
Transportation and material moving occupations	5,018	778	172	258	349	4,240	43.3	45.3
Handlers, equipment cleaners, helpers, and laborers	4,147	1,124	271	236	617	3,023	37.1	41.0
Women, 16 years and over[1]	59,843	18,937	1,986	4,124	12,828	40,906	36.1	41.0
Managerial and professional specialty	20,175	4,863	295	1,561	3,007	15,312	38.6	42.1
Executive, administrative, and managerial	9,085	1,736	100	693	942	7,349	40.3	42.7
Professional specialty	11,090	3,128	195	867	2,065	7,962	37.2	41.6
Technical, sales, and administrative support	23,670	7,793	701	1,649	5,443	15,877	35.3	40.3
Technicians and related support	2,343	647	37	168	443	1,696	37.0	40.7
Sales occupations	7,630	3,045	368	425	2,252	4,585	34.3	41.4
Administrative support, including clerical	13,698	4,102	296	1,057	2,749	9,596	35.5	39.7
Service occupations	11,010	4,981	718	587	3,676	6,029	32.6	40.5
Private household	675	389	65	31	294	285	28.6	41.0
Protective service	488	130	16	38	76	357	37.2	41.2
Service, except private household and protective	9,847	4,461	637	518	3,306	5,386	32.7	40.4
Precision production, craft, and repair	1,147	255	43	79	133	892	38.4	41.0
Operators, fabricators, and laborers	3,842	1,044	228	248	569	2,797	36.8	40.2
Machine operators, assemblers, and inspectors	2,198	435	112	145	178	1,763	38.4	40.3
Transportation and material moving occupations	564	222	34	35	153	342	35.1	41.6
Handlers, equipment cleaners, helpers, and laborers	1,079	387	82	68	237	692	34.4	39.5

[1]Excludes farming, forestry, and fishing occupations.
[2]Data not shown where base is less than 35,000.

SOURCE: "23. Persons at work in nonfarm occupations by sex and usual full- or part-time status," in *Employment and Earnings*, U.S. Department of Labor, Bureau of Labor Statistics, Washington, DC, June 2003

decreased from 1,883 hours in 1980 to 1,815 in 2002. For the same period, declines also occurred in Norway (from 1,380 to 1,342), Sweden (from 1,625 to 1,581), France (from 1,587 to 1,545), and Australia (from 1,855 to 1,824). Japan, where workers typically labored longer than Americans, is currently at the same general level as the United

TABLE 3.7

Persons at work 1 to 34 hours in all and nonagricultural industries by reason for working less than 35 hours and usual full- or part-time status, 2002

(Numbers in thousands)

	2002					
	All industries			Nonagricultural industries		
Reason for working less than 35 hours	Total	Usually work full time	Usually work part time	Total	Usually work full time	Usually work part time
Total, 16 years and over	**31,174**	**9,746**	**21,429**	**30,267**	**9,453**	**20,814**
Economic reasons	4,213	1,627	2,586	4,035	1,535	2,500
Slack work or business conditions	2,788	1,380	1,408	2,671	1,314	1,358
Could only find part-time work	1,124	—	1,124	1,100	—	1,100
Seasonal work	165	112	54	132	89	42
Job started or ended during week	135	135	—	132	132	—
Noneconomic reasons	26,961	8,119	18,843	26,232	7,918	18,314
Child-care problems	777	80	697	765	79	686
Other family or personal obligations	5,766	756	5,010	5,621	739	4,882
Health or medical limitations	746	—	746	716	—	716
In school or training	6,177	88	6,089	6,051	85	5,966
Retired or Social Security limit on earnings	1,911	—	1,911	1,809	—	1,809
Vacation or personal day	3,452	3,452	—	3,388	3,388	—
Holiday, legal or religious	597	597	—	590	590	—
Weather-related curtailment	514	514	—	465	465	—
All other reasons	7,022	2,632	4,390	6,828	2,572	4,256
Average hours:						
Economic reasons	23.0	24.1	22.3	23.1	24.2	22.4
Noneconomic reasons	21.4	25.2	19.7	21.4	25.2	19.8

SOURCE: "20. Persons at work 1 to 34 hours in all and nonagricultural industries by reason for working less than 35 hours and usual full- or part-time status," in *Employment and Earnings*, U.S. Department of Labor, Bureau of Labor Statistics, Washington, DC, June 2003

States. This decrease in annual hours worked in the United States is largely attributable to the September 11, 2001, terrorist attacks, when the gross domestic product (GDP; the total value of goods and services produced within the United States) per employed person increased by a meager 0.2 percent in 2001, compared to a 1.2 percent increase in 2000. Although the number of hours worked decreased in 2002, the GDP grew 2.8 percent. The GDP is the most comprehensive measure taken of a country's economic output, and the gross national product per employed person provides a general picture of a nation's overall productivity. The U.S. 2002 GDP per employed person percentage was double the growth rate of 1.2 percent of the European Union and 1.4 percent in Japan. According to the BLS, among the world's 14 largest economies, Korea had the highest GDP per employed person in 2002 (3.5 percent), followed by the United States, Denmark, and Sweden. U.S. worker productivity is not only the result of more hours worked, but also the production and diffusion of information and communication technology in a dynamic capitalist economy, as well as the growth of wholesale and retail trade and financial securities that rely greatly on information and communication technology.

PART-TIME WORK

People work part-time for various reasons. In 2002 there were 31.2 million U.S. part-time workers 16 years

of age and older. About 9.7 million of these workers normally held full-time jobs, but for various reasons now had to work part time. About 17 percent of these part-time workers took part-time work because of economic conditions. These economic reasons, usually caused by employers' circumstances, included slack work, material shortages, or the availability of only part-time work. Most workers who usually worked part time did so for noneconomic reasons: they did not want to work full time or were unavailable for full-time work, perhaps because they were going to school, taking care of children, or had other family or personal obligations. (See Table 3.7.)

MULTIPLE JOBS

In 2002, 5.3 percent of workers (7.3 million) aged 16 years and older held multiple jobs, down slightly from 5.4 percent in 2001. The multiple-job rate among men actually declined from 7 percent in 1970 to 5.1 percent in 2002. The proportion of women holding more than one job increased from 2 percent in 1970 to 5.6 percent in 2002. At a rate of 6.4 percent and 6.7 percent, single (never been married) women and widowed, divorced, or separated women, respectively, were the most likely to have more than one job in 2002. Married women (4.8 percent) and single (never married) men (4.6 percent) were the least likely. (See Table 3.8.) In September 2003 the number of multiple jobholders continued to decline to 7.1 million

TABLE 3.8

Multiple jobholders by selected demographic and economic characteristics, 2001–2002

(Numbers in thousands)

Characteristic	Both sexes				Men				Women			
	Number		Rate[1]		Number		Rate[1]		Number		Rate[1]	
	2001	2002	2001	2002	2001	2002	2001	2002	2001	2002	2001	2002
Age												
Total, 16 years and over[2]	7,357	7,291	5.4	5.3	3,834	3,734	5.2	5.1	3,523	3,557	5.5	5.6
16 to 19 years	303	286	4.5	4.5	124	114	3.6	3.6	179	171	5.4	5.4
20 years and over	7,055	7,006	5.4	5.4	3,711	3,620	5.3	5.2	3,344	3,386	5.5	5.6
20 to 24 years	736	740	5.5	5.5	331	335	4.8	4.8	404	405	6.3	6.4
25 years and over	6,319	6,266	5.4	5.4	3,380	3,285	5.4	5.2	2,940	2,981	5.4	5.5
25 to 54 years	5,453	5,375	5.6	5.6	2,894	2,815	5.5	5.4	2,559	2,560	5.6	5.7
55 years and over	866	891	4.6	4.5	486	470	4.7	4.3	381	421	4.4	4.6
55 to 64 years	716	752	4.9	4.8	391	394	4.9	4.7	326	358	4.8	4.9
65 years and over	150	139	3.5	3.2	95	76	3.9	3.1	55	63	3.0	3.4
Race and Hispanic Origin												
White	6,300	6,270	5.5	5.5	3,298	3,233	5.3	5.2	3,002	3,037	5.7	5.8
Black	747	709	5.0	4.8	380	343	5.5	4.9	367	366	4.5	4.6
Hispanic origin	551	579	3.4	3.5	328	347	3.4	3.5	223	232	3.4	3.4
Marital Status												
Married, spouse present	4,073	3,998	5.2	5.1	2,408	2,362	5.5	5.4	1,665	1,636	4.9	4.8
Widowed, divorced, or separated	1,304	1,313	6.0	6.1	477	452	5.4	5.1	827	861	6.4	6.7
Single (never married)	1,981	1,980	5.4	5.4	950	920	4.7	4.6	1,031	1,060	6.2	6.4
Full- Or Part-Time Status												
Primary job full time, secondary job part time	4,019	3,937	—	—	2,327	2,235	—	—	1,692	1,701	—	—
Primary and secondary jobs both part time	1,578	1,590	—	—	510	493	—	—	1,068	1,097	—	—
Primary and secondary jobs both full time	283	276	—	—	184	186	—	—	100	90	—	—
Hours vary on primary or secondary job	1,437	1,449	—	—	793	801	—	—	644	647	—	—

[1]Multiple jobholders as a percent of all employed persons in specified group.

[2]Includes a small number of persons who work part time on their primary job and full time on their secondary jobs(s), not shown separately.

Note: Detail for the above race and Hispanic-origin groups will not sum to totals because data for the "other races" group are not presented and Hispanics are included in both the white and black population groups.

SOURCE: "36. Multiple jobholders by selected demographic and economic characteristics," in *Employment and Earnings,* U.S. Department of Labor, Bureau of Labor Statistics, Washington, DC, June 2003

persons. The proportion of men holding more than one job at this time fell to 4.9 percent and the rate among women remained constant at 5.6 percent.

STUDENTS WITH JOBS

Of the 22.8 million full-time students over age 15 in 2000, 1.9 million held full-time jobs and 6.9 million held part-time jobs. About 3.6 million out of 5.1 million part-time students held full-time jobs, while 809,000 part-time students worked part-time jobs.

CONTINGENT WORKERS

The BLS defines contingent work as any job in which an individual does not have an explicit or implicit contract for long-term employment. This includes independent contractors, on-call workers, and those working for temporary help services.

As of February 2001 an estimated 1.7 to 4.0 percent of total employment (2.3 to 5.4 million workers) was in contingent jobs. The differences in estimates arise from alternative definitions. The narrowest estimate includes wage and salary workers who held their jobs for one year or less and expected to be employed for an additional year or less.

The middle estimates add the self-employed and independent contractors. The highest estimate drops the time limit on wage and salary workers and includes any worker who believed his or her job was temporary. The 2001 figures showed a decline from 1995, when the broadest figure was 4.9 percent of total employment, to 1999, when the broadest figure was 4.4 percent of the workforce.

Contingent workers were more likely to be in professional specialties, administrative support, and farming occupations and were less likely to be in managerial or sales occupations. It might seem surprising that contingent workers were overrepresented in professional specialty occupations. However, this category includes teachers, who had an above-average rate of contingency employment. Postsecondary teachers represent a substantial part of all contingent workers, reflecting the practice of many colleges and universities using adjunct or temporary teachers with short-term contracts.

Others in the professional category include biological and life scientists, musicians, physicians, and actors and directors. These figures indicate that many contingent workers are highly skilled. The higher proportion of contingent workers in the administrative support occupations, which include clerks, data entry keyers, teachers' aides, and receptionists, comes closer to the stereotypical notion that contingent workers hold jobs that require relatively little formal training.

Although contingent workers were found in every industry, they were much more likely to be concentrated in construction and services industries. Specific industries within the services category that had high contingency rates were personnel supply, private household services, educational services, entertainment and recreation services, and social services. It is important to recognize that although those in the services industry make up a large proportion of contingent workers, most workers in this industry are not contingent.

Over half of all contingency workers reported that they would have preferred to have noncontingent employment.

ALTERNATIVE WORK ARRANGEMENTS

Employees in alternative work arrangements are defined either as individuals whose employment is arranged through an employment intermediary or individuals whose place, time, and quantity of work are potentially unpredictable. These include workers such as independent contractors, on-call workers, workers paid by temporary help firms, and workers whose services are provided through contract firms.

According to the U.S. Census Bureau, as of February 2001 about 9.4 percent of the workforce fell into at least one of these four categories. Of those, 6.4 percent of the total workforce were independent contractors—the largest segment—followed by on-call workers at 1.6 percent, temporary help agency workers at just under 1 percent, and contract company employees at about 0.5 percent. These figures remained fairly steady over the preceding six years, with independent contractors dropping slightly from 6.7 percent in 1995 and 1997, and on-call, temporary help agency, and contract company workers remaining within one-tenth of 1 percent of the 1995 and 1997 totals.

These workers were less likely to prefer traditional work arrangements than contingent workers in 2000; about 44.4 percent of temporary help agency workers said they would prefer traditional work arrangements, compared to 43.4 percent of on-call workers and 8.8 percent of independent contractors.

OCCUPATIONAL INJURIES, ILLNESSES, AND FATALITIES

The rate of occupational injury and illness for full-time workers increased during the 1980s but steadily decreased after the mid-1990s. The BLS estimates that there were 6.3 cases of injury and illness per 100 workers in private industry workplaces in 1999, down from 6.7 in 1998 and 8.4 in 1994. In 2001 the bureau reported 5.2 million injuries and illnesses in the private sector, a rate of 5.7 cases per 100 workers. This rate is the lowest since the bureau began compiling this information in the early 1970s. In 2001, among goods-producing industries, manufacturing had the highest rate of injuries and illnesses at 8.1 per 100 workers. Transportation and public utilities workers had a rate of 6.9 in 2001, the highest in the service-producing sector.

In 2002 there were a total of 5,524 fatal work injuries recorded, a 6.6 percent decrease from 2001. The 2002 count is the lowest ever recorded by BLS's Census of Fatal Occupational Injuries. Operators, fabricators, and laborers incurred the highest number of fatal on-the-job injuries at 1,895, the most of any major occupational group, and nearly 33 percent of all the fatal work injuries reported that year. Nevertheless, the number of fatalities incurred by this occupational group declined for the third straight year to about 7 percent lower than in 2001. In 2002 fatal injuries suffered by construction laborers also declined, from a high of 350 in 2001 to 302, a 14 percent drop. Truck drivers experienced the most fatal injuries (808) than any other individual occupation. Highway crashes were the leading cause of on-the-job deaths (1,372, or 25 percent of all fatal occupational injuries), followed by contact with objects and equipment (873), and assaults and violent acts (840).

UNION AFFILIATION

Union membership has decreased dramatically over the last two decades of the 20th century. In 1975, 28.9 percent of the nation's workers were union members. This proportion dropped to 21.9 percent in 1982, 15.8 percent in 1992, and just 13.9 percent in both 1998 and 1999. A total of 13.2 percent of the employed workforce were union members in 2002. The recession of the early 1980s, the movement of jobs overseas, the decline in traditionally unionized heavy industry, management's desire to eliminate union power, the threat of job loss, unimaginative union leadership, and vastly improved working conditions and benefits all contributed to the decline in union membership. (See Table 3.9.)

Instead of demanding better hours, more pay, and improved working conditions—the traditional union demands—most unions agreed to "give-backs" (surrendering existing benefits) and lower salaries in exchange for job guarantees during the 1980s. However, many companies have continued to develop factories overseas or to purchase heavily from foreign producers, which has resulted in fewer jobs for U.S. workers and more plant shutdowns.

In the mid-1990s, concerned about their declining membership, unions became more aggressive in recruiting members. Although concerned about eroding benefits,

TABLE 3.9

Union affiliation of employed wage and salary workers by selected characteristics, 2001–2002

(Numbers in thousands)

	2001					2002				
		Members of unions[1]		Represented by unions[2]			Members unions[1]		Represented by unions[2]	
Characteristic	Total em-ployed	Total	Percent of em-ployed	Total	Percent of em-ployed	Total em-ployed	Total	Percent of em-ployed	Total	Percent of em-ployed
Sex and age										
Total, 16 years and over	122,482	16,387	13.4	18,114	14.8	122,009	16,108	13.2	17,772	14.6
16 to 24 years	19,698	1,015	5.2	1,184	6.0	19,258	985	5.1	1,132	5.9
25 years and over	102,784	15,372	15.0	16,930	16.5	102,751	15,123	14.7	16,640	16.2
25 to 34 years	28,809	3,264	11.3	3,659	12.7	28,253	3,164	11.2	3,541	12.5
35 to 44 years	31,962	4,733	14.8	5,191	16.2	31,296	4,442	14.2	4,876	15.6
45 to 54 years	26,909	5,068	18.8	5,543	20.6	27,086	5,011	18.5	5,470	20.2
55 to 64 years	12,032	2,063	17.1	2,265	18.8	12,982	2,257	17.4	2,469	19.0
65 years and over	3,072	243	7.9	272	8.9	3,133	247	7.9	284	9.1
Men, 16 years and over	63,756	9,578	15.0	10,410	16.3	63,384	9,335	14.7	10,135	16.0
16 to 24 years	10,137	607	6.0	704	6.9	9,862	610	6.2	691	7.0
25 years and over	53,619	8,971	16.7	9,706	18.1	53,522	8,725	16.3	9,444	17.6
25 to 34 years	15,627	1,983	12.7	2,169	13.9	15,297	1,879	12.3	2,075	13.6
35 to 44 years	16,657	2,821	16.9	3,028	18.2	16,390	2,632	16.1	2,821	17.2
45 to 54 years	13,561	2,840	20.9	3,070	22.6	13,611	2,793	20.5	3,006	22.1
55 to 64 years	6,168	1,195	19.4	1,292	20.9	6,593	1,285	19.5	1,386	21.0
65 years and over	1,605	131	8.1	148	9.2	1,630	136	8.3	156	9.5
Women, 16 years and over	58,726	6,809	11.6	7,704	13.1	58,625	6,772	11.6	7,636	13.0
16 to 24 years	9,561	409	4.3	480	5.0	9,397	375	4.0	441	4.7
25 years and over	49,166	6,400	13.0	7,224	14.7	49,229	6,398	13.0	7,195	14.6
25 to 34 years	13,181	1,281	9.7	1,490	11.3	12,956	1,285	9.9	1,465	11.3
35 to 44 years	15,305	1,912	12.5	2,163	14.1	14,906	1,810	12.1	2,055	13.8
45 to 54 years	13,349	2,227	16.7	2,474	18.5	13,474	2,218	16.5	2,464	18.3
55 to 64 years	5,864	868	14.8	973	16.6	6,390	972	15.2	1,083	17.0
65 years and over	1,467	113	7.7	124	8.5	1,503	112	7.4	128	8.5
Race, Hispanic origin, and sex										
White, 16 years and over	101,546	13,209	13.0	14,574	14.4	101,082	12,930	12.8	14,228	14.1
Men	53,731	7,909	14.7	8,585	16.0	53,305	7,700	14.4	8,335	15.6
Women	47,815	5,300	11.1	5,989	12.5	47,777	5,230	10.9	5,893	12.3
Black, 16 years and over	14,261	2,409	16.9	2,668	18.7	14,127	2,383	16.9	2,648	18.7
Men	6,488	1,221	18.8	1,330	20.5	6,499	1,184	18.2	1,297	20.0
Women	7,773	1,188	15.3	1,338	17.2	7,628	1,198	15.7	1,351	17.7
Hispanic origin, 16 years and over	15,174	1,679	11.1	1,876	12.4	15,523	1,638	10.5	1,823	11.7
Men	8,997	1,032	11.5	1,136	12.6	9,131	1,012	11.1	1,114	12.2
Women	6,177	647	10.5	740	12.0	6,392	625	9.8	709	11.1
Full- or part-time status[3]										
Full-time workers	101,187	14,921	14.7	16,445	16.3	100,204	14,592	14.6	16,078	16.0
Part-time workers	21,057	1,437	6.8	1,637	7.8	21,573	1,484	6.9	1,658	7.7

[1]Data refer to members of a labor union or an employee association similar to a union.
[2]Data refer to members of a labor union or an employee association similar to a union as well as workers who report no union affiliation but whose jobs are covered by a union or an employee association contract.
[3]The distinction between full- and part-time workers is based on hours usually worked. Beginning in 1994, these data will not sum to totals because full- or part-time status on the principal job is not identifiable for a small number of multiple jobholders. Data refer to the sole or principal job of full- and part-time workers. Excluded are all self-employed workers regardless of whether or not their businesses are incorporated. Detail for the above race and Hispanic-origin groups will not sum to totals because data for the "other races" group are not presented and Hispanics are included in both the white and black population groups.

SOURCE: "40. Union affiliation of employed wage and salary workers by selected characteristics," in *Employment and Earnings*, U.S. Department of Labor, Bureau of Labor Statistics, Washington, DC, June 2003

wages, and jobs, many workers were still wary of unions. The reputation of some union leaders, both past and present, disturbed them, and many workers feared losing their jobs if they became involved in union activities. The 1997 United Parcel Service nationwide strike, in which the union negotiated a five-year $9.3 billion contract, promoted a more positive public view of unions.

In 2002 men (16.0 percent) were more likely to be union members than women (13.0 percent), and blacks (18.7 percent) were more likely to be unionized than whites (14.1 percent) or Hispanics (11.7 percent). Blacks were more likely to be union members because they were more likely to work in blue-collar or government jobs, while whites were more likely to work in professional and managerial jobs. (See Table 3.9.)

TABLE 3.10

Union affiliation of employed wage and salary workers by occupation and industry, 2001–2002

(Numbers in thousands)

Occupation and industry	2001 Total employed	2001 Members of unions[1] Total	2001 Members of unions[1] Percent of employed	2001 Represented by unions[2] Total	2001 Represented by unions[2] Percent of employed	2002 Total employed	2002 Members of unions[1] Total	2002 Members of unions[1] Percent of employed	2002 Represented by unions[2] Total	2002 Represented by unions[2] Percent of employed
Occupation										
Managerial and professional specialty	36,660	4,665	12.7	5,417	14.8	36,969	4,788	13.0	5,534	15.0
Executive, administrative, and managerial	17,075	945	5.5	1,148	6.7	17,296	1,005	5.8	1,223	7.1
Professional specialty	19,585	3,720	19.0	4,269	21.8	19,674	3,783	19.2	4,310	21.9
Technical, sales, and administrative support	36,335	3,208	8.8	3,632	10.0	35,770	3,176	8.9	3,552	9.9
Technicians and related support	4,448	474	10.7	537	12.1	4,349	469	10.8	524	12.0
Sales occupations	13,749	480	3.5	549	4.0	13,810	496	3.6	559	4.0
Administrative support, including clerical	18,138	2,253	12.4	2,545	14.0	17,610	2,210	12.6	2,470	14.0
Service occupations	17,434	2,296	13.2	2,504	14.4	17,898	2,249	12.6	2,473	13.8
Protective service	2,482	936	37.7	1,004	40.5	2,584	957	37.0	1,021	39.5
Service, except protective service	14,952	1,360	9.1	1,500	10.0	15,314	1,293	8.4	1,452	9.5
Precision production, craft, and repair	12,886	2,740	21.3	2,874	22.3	12,413	2,570	20.7	2,686	21.6
Operators, fabricators, and laborers	17,250	3,394	19.7	3,590	20.8	16,901	3,235	19.1	3,422	20.3
Machine operators, assemblers, and inspectors	6,676	1,338	20.0	1,413	21.2	6,269	1,184	18.9	1,244	19.8
Transportation and material moving occupations	5,226	1,215	23.2	1,292	24.7	5,294	1,163	22.0	1,241	23.4
Handlers, equipment cleaners, helpers, and laborers	5,347	841	15.7	885	16.6	5,338	888	16.6	938	17.6
Farming, forestry, and fishing	1,917	83	4.3	98	5.1	2,058	89	4.3	104	5.1
Industry										
Private wage and salary workers	103,142	9,201	8.9	10,028	9.7	102,420	8,756	8.5	9,548	9.3
Agriculture	1,725	27	1.6	36	2.1	1,819	42	2.3	48	2.6
Nonagricultural industries	101,417	9,174	9.0	9,993	9.9	100,600	8,714	8.7	9,501	9.4
Mining	531	66	12.4	70	13.1	458	39	8.5	46	10.0
Construction	7,054	1,275	18.1	1,321	18.7	6,883	1,184	17.2	1,228	17.8
Manufacturing	18,501	2,697	14.6	2,861	15.5	17,324	2,484	14.3	2,621	15.1
Durable goods	11,252	1,690	15.0	1,787	15.9	10,344	1,612	15.6	1,687	16.3
Nondurable goods	7,249	1,008	13.9	1,073	14.8	6,979	872	12.5	935	13.4
Transportation and public utilities	7,502	1,752	23.4	1,851	24.7	7,433	1,712	23.0	1,810	24.3
Transportation	4,501	1,077	23.9	1,140	25.3	4,525	1,078	23.8	1,133	25.0
Communications and public utilities	3,001	675	22.5	711	23.7	2,908	634	21.8	677	23.3
Wholesale and retail trade	25,354	1,182	4.7	1,298	5.1	25,475	1,134	4.5	1,256	4.9
Wholesale trade	4,615	254	5.5	273	5.9	4,514	220	4.9	238	5.3
Retail trade	20,740	928	4.5	1,025	4.9	20,961	914	4.4	1,018	4.9
Finance, insurance, and real estate	7,742	156	2.0	217	2.8	7,849	151	1.9	196	2.5
Services	34,733	2,046	5.9	2,376	6.8	35,179	2,011	5.7	2,344	6.7
Government workers	19,340	7,186	37.2	8,086	41.8	19,589	7,352	37.5	8,223	42.0
Federal	3,324	1,046	31.5	1,221	36.8	3,297	1,064	32.3	1,244	37.7
State	5,729	1,737	30.3	1,980	34.6	5,706	1,758	30.8	2,005	35.1
Local	10,287	4,403	42.8	4,885	47.5	10,585	4,530	42.8	4,974	47.0

[1]Data refer to members of a labor union or an employee association similar to a union.
[2]Data refer to members of a labor union or an employee association similar to a union as well as workers who report no union affiliation but whose jobs are covered by a union or an employee association contract.
Data refer to the sole or principal job of full- and part-time workers. Excluded are all self-employed workers regardless of whether or not their businesses are incorporated.

SOURCE: "42. Union affiliation of employed wage and salary workers by occupation and industry," in *Employment and Earnings,* U.S. Department of Labor, Bureau of Labor Statistics, Washington, DC, June 2003

Not surprisingly, in 2002 more blue-collar workers were unionized than managers. By occupation, protective service workers (police and firefighters) were most likely to be members of unions (37.0 percent) or represented by unions (39.5 percent). (There are instances where nonunion members are represented by unions.) Within industry, government workers had high membership in unions, at 37.5 percent, with 42 percent represented by unions. They were followed by transportation and public utilities workers, of whom 22.0 percent were union members and 23.4 percent were represented by unions in 2002. (See Table 3.10.)

Union workers are generally better paid than nonunion workers, a statistic that holds true across gender and ethnic lines. In 2002 the median earnings for a union member was $740 per week, up from $717 in 2001, compared to a nonunion worker who earned $587 in 2002, up from $573 in 2001.

WORK STOPPAGES

The number of work stoppages (strikes) has decreased dramatically over the past several decades. In 1974 there

TABLE 3.11

Percent of workers participating in health care and retirement benefits, by selected characteristics,[1] March 2003

Characteristics	Retirement benefits			Health care benefits			
	All plans[2]	Defined benefit	Defined contribution	Medical care	Dental care	Vision care	Plan type not available
All employees	49	20	40	45	32	19	8
Worker characteristics:[3]							
White-collar occupations[4]	59	22	51	50	37	21	8
Blue-collar occupations[4]	50	24	38	51	33	20	10
Service occupations[4]	21	7	16	22	15	9	3
Full time	58	24	48	56	40	23	9
Part time	18	8	14	9	6	5	3
Union	83	72	39	60	51	37	23
Nonunion	45	15	40	44	30	17	7
Average wage less than $15 per hour	35	11	29	35	22	12	6
Average wage $15 per hour or higher	70	33	57	61	47	28	12
Establishment characteristics:							
Goods-producing	63	31	49	57	42	25	12
Service-producing	45	16	37	42	29	17	7
1-99 workers	35	8	31	36	21	11	6
100 workers or more	65	33	51	55	44	27	10
Geographic areas:[5]							
Metropolitan areas	50	21	41	45	33	19	9
Nonmetropolitan areas	42	14	36	44	27	17	4
New England	44	15	37	43	31	14	9
Middle Atlantic	56	30	43	47	32	24	9
East North Central	56	23	46	47	34	17	10
West North Central	48	21	37	43	31	17	5
South Atlantic	46	16	40	44	30	14	7
East South Central	51	14	46	53	37	28	6
West South Central	42	18	35	47	30	17	4
Mountain	38	10	34	34	28	17	6
Pacific	46	20	37	45	33	24	10

[1]Covers all 50 States and the District of Columbia.
[2]Includes defined benefit pension plans and defined contribution retirement plans. The total is less than the sum of the individual items because many employees participated in both types of plans.
[3]Employees are classified as working either a full-time or part-time schedule based on the definition used by each establishment. Union workers are those whose wages are determined through collective bargaining.
[4]A classification system including about 480 individual occupations is used to cover all workers in the civilian economy.
[5]Data are presented for metropolitan and nonmetropolitan area divisions as well as nine census divisions.
Note: Because of rounding, sums of individual items may not equal totals. Where applicable, dash indicates no employees in this category or data do not meet publication criteria.

SOURCE: "Table 1. Percent of workers participating in health care and retirement benefits, by selected characteristics, private industry, National Compensation Survey, March 2003" in "Employee Benefits in Private Industry, 2003," *News*, vol. 03-489, U.S. Department of Labor, Bureau of Labor Statistics, Washington, DC, September 17, 2003

were 424 work stoppages resulting in 31.8 million days idle. (This figure is calculated by multiplying the number of workers by the number of days they were on strike.) For most of the remainder of the 1970s, there were 200 to 300 work stoppages a year.

This changed dramatically during the 1980s. The number fell from 187 in 1980 to only 40 in 1988, rising slightly to 44 in 1990, with just 5.9 million days idle. In 1992 the number of work stoppages decreased to 35, involving nearly 4 million days. In 1994 the number of stoppages rose to 45, involving 5 million days. This dropped again to 37 stoppages in 1996 (with 4.9 million lost workdays), then 34 work stoppages in 1998 (with 5.1 million lost workdays), and reached a low of 17 stoppages in 1999. In 2002 major work stoppages rose slightly to a total of 19, idling some 45,900 workers and accounting for 659,600 lost workdays. The decrease in the number of

strikes is tied to the decline in union membership, better working conditions, and the relatively strong economy.

EMPLOYEE BENEFIT PLANS

Throughout the 1990s those working for medium and large companies were most likely to be participants in medical care plans, but the rates for medical benefits for most workers in all sectors were cut back during this time. Ninety-six percent of those working for medium and large private-sector companies participated in health insurance plans in 1984. By 1989, 92 percent of medium and large private-sector companies had participants in medical care plans, and by 1997 only 76 percent of the workers in these companies were participating in medical care plans. For those in state and local governments, the rates dropped from 93 percent in 1990 to 86 percent in 1998, the most recent data. The benefits for small private-sector companies rose slightly from 69 percent in 1990 to 71 percent in 1992 before dropping to 64 percent in 1996. In March 2003, 45 percent of all employees were covered by employer-sponsored medical care plans, down from 63 percent in the 1992–1993 period. (See Table 3.11.) The vast majority of these employees were in medical plans requiring employee contributions for both family and single coverage. In the first quarter of 2003, employee contributions to medical care premiums averaged $228.98 per month for family coverage and $60.24 per month for single coverage. The average monthly contribution required of employees has soared almost 75 percent for both family and single coverage since the 1992–1993 period.

The rate of paid vacations changed little for workers during the 1990s, though the rate at medium and large private establishments dropped from around 100 percent in the 1980s to 95 percent in 1997. Despite this change, these workers were still most likely to have paid vacations. In 1996, 86 percent of employees in small private firms had paid vacations, and in 1998 (the most recent data) only two-thirds of state and local government workers (67 percent) received paid vacations. In 2000, 80 percent of all workers in the private sector received paid vacations and 77 percent of these employees received paid holidays.

Defined-benefit pension plans (i.e., a pension plan that pays a specified amount to retirees) were one of the only benefits that were more likely to be offered to state and local government workers (90 percent in 1998) than to those working in either medium and large firms (50 percent in 1997) or small private-sector firms (15 percent in 1996), according to the most recent statistics available.

CHAPTER 4
INCOME AND POVERTY

The federal government measures family and household income in a number of ways. While the U.S. Census Bureau conducts most of the surveys, small differences can result from surveys being taken at different times of the year or with a slightly different focus. In many cases, the person being interviewed may not answer all the questions, therefore, the figures may vary from category to category. Furthermore, none of these statistics are absolutely accurate—they are all estimates based on the best current survey methods.

All demographic surveys suffer from undercoverage of the population resulting from missed housing units and missed persons within sample households. Weighting procedures that account for missing persons try to correct the undercoverage, but its final impact on estimates is unknown. In addition, most of the statistics try to consider inflation. To do this, the researchers usually select a base year and then present their findings in the dollars of that year.

AVERAGE PAY

Overall, in 2001 the level of average annual pay for all Americans was $36,214, up by 2.5 percent ($35,320) from 2000, the third lowest pay growth in 10 years. The metropolitan area with the highest average annual pay was San Jose, California ($65,926), a position it has held since 1997. San Jose retained its position even though it experienced the largest decline (13.5 percent) in average annual pay among the 10 metropolitan areas with decreases in 2001. The second highest average annual pay metropolitan area was San Francisco ($59,761), followed by New York City ($58,963), New Haven–Bridgeport–Stamford–Waterbury–Danbury, Connecticut ($52,177), and Middlesex–Somerset–Hunterdon, New Jersey ($49,830). The average pay level in these five metropolitan areas ranged from 31 to 74 percent above the average for all U.S. metropolitan areas. Of the 318 metropolitan areas in the United States, the annual pay level averaged $37,897 in 2001, an increase of $880 from 2000.

In 2001 the average annual pay increased at a higher rate in nonmetropolitan areas (3.3 percent) than in metropolitan areas (2.4 percent). The average annual pay in nonmetropolitan areas in 2001 was $28,190, up from $27,303 in 2000. This was the first time since 1994 that growth in total nonmetropolitan average annual pay exceeded that of metropolitan area average annual pay. Nevertheless, nonmetropolitan average annual pay in 2001 was 26 percent less than its metropolitan counterpart, a difference of $9,707.

HOUSEHOLDS AND FAMILIES

This section presents the results of surveys on both households and families and is based on several Current Population Reports prepared by the Census Bureau in Washington, D.C., including *Income in the United States: 2002* (2003), *Poverty in the United States: 2002* (2003), and *Household Net Worth and Asset Ownership: 1998 and 2000* (2003). Households include family and nonfamily households. A nonfamily household is one in which a person maintaining the household lives either alone or with nonrelatives only, such as roommates or boarders. A family is a group of two or more persons related by birth, marriage, or adoption and living together.

MEDIAN INCOMES

Households and Family

The Census Bureau measures both the median income (one-half earn more than this figure, and one-half earn less) and the mean (average) income, although more frequently it focuses on the median income. In 2002 the median income for all U.S. households was $42,409, down from $42,900 in 2001 and up from $42,148 in 2000 (as measured in 2002 dollars). This amounts to a 1.1 percent decrease in real income from 2001 to 2002.

The working wife has become an essential feature of the U.S. economy and an important influence on the economic level of the family. In 2002 about 63.6 million women 20 years of age and older were in the civilian labor force, and about 41.8 million were counted as full-time, year-round workers, compared to 58.7 million males. The number of wives in the paid labor force in 1968 was 15.8 million (36.6 percent of all married couple families). In 1977 wives were working in 55 percent of all married-couple families. By 1997 this number was 66 percent, dropping slightly in 1998 to 61 percent and rising again in 1999 to 61.9 percent of all married-couple families, or about 34.2 million women. In 1977 both spouses worked in 50 percent of all married-couple families, and by 1997 this had risen to 61 percent of all married-couple families. In 1997 the percent of married couples with children who had dual incomes was 71.1 percent.

Regions and States

Between 2001 and 2002 median household income levels in only one of the four national regions declined to any statistical significance. The Midwest showed a 2.0 percent decline in median household income to $43,622. In 2002 the median income of households in the Northeast was $45,862, in the West $45,143, and $39,522 in the South.

When comparing the relative ranking of states, the Census Bureau considers three-year averages a more accurate indicator. For 2000 through 2002 average median incomes were highest in Maryland ($55,912), Alaska ($55,412), and Minnesota ($54,931). Average median incomes from 2000 to 2002 were lowest in West Virginia ($30,072), Arkansas ($32,423), and Mississippi ($32,447).

Residence

In 2002 households located inside central cities in large metropolitan areas (1 million or more population) had a median income of $36,863, compared to a median income of $50,717 for households located in the suburbs of large metropolitan areas. The median income in households outside metropolitan areas was $34,654 in 2002.

Race and Hispanic Origin

The median income of all households in the United States was $42,409 in 2002. Asians had the highest median household income ($52,626) among the racial and Hispanic-origin groups. Non-Hispanic white households ($45,086) had the second highest, followed by Hispanic-origin households ($33,103) and black households ($29,026).

Although Asians and Pacific Islanders as a group had the highest median household income in 1999, their income per household member was lower than the income per household member of non-Hispanic white households. (The income per household member measure represents the average amount of income available to each household member.) The larger average size of Asian and Pacific

Islander households (3.15 persons compared to 2.47 for non-Hispanic white households) produced an average income per household member of $21,134 in 1999, less than the $24,109 for non-Hispanic white households. The income per household member for black households was $14,397, and for Hispanics, $11,621, based on average household sizes of 2.75 and 3.46, respectively.

Per Capita Income

The Census Bureau defines per capita income as "the average income computed for every man, woman, and child in a particular group." This number is gathered by dividing the total income of a particular group by the total population in that group. In *Income in the United States: 2002,* the per capita income for the total population in 2002 was estimated at $22,794, a 1.8 percent decrease in real dollars from 2001, when it was $23,214. This was the first annual decline in overall per capita income since 1991. Real per capita income by race declined by 1.5 percent for whites (to $24,142), rose by 1.6 percent for blacks (to $15,441), declined by 2.2 percent for Asians (to $24,131), and increased by 2.1 percent for Hispanics (to $13,487).

Gender

In the third quarter of 2003, among year-round, usually full-time workers, the median earnings for females 16 years of age and over was $550 per week, or 80 percent of the $689 median for men of the same group. The proportion of women's earnings relative to men's has increased steadily for almost 25 years. From 1979, when the Bureau of Labor Statistics (BLS) began to regularly compile weekly earning statistics, to the third quarter of 2003 the ratio of women's to men's earnings has increased by 16 percentage points. The female-to-male earnings ratios among whites was 80.4 percent. In comparison, the female-to-male earnings ratios were higher among blacks (84.2 percent) and Hispanics (89.4 percent), but lower among Asians (77.7 percent).

Recent increases in the female-to-male earnings ratio have been due more to declines in the earnings of men than to increases in the earnings of women. Since 1989 the earnings of men have declined slightly or remained stagnant, while the earnings of women have increased by 4.6 percent. According to some observers, factors that contribute to the gender wage gap include differences in education, years and continuity of work experience, types of occupations or industries traditionally chosen by women workers, and union status. According to the BLS, in the third quarter of 2003 among college graduates with professional or master's degrees, the highest earning 10 percent of female workers made $1,812 or more per week, compared to $2,495 or more for their male counterparts.

Compared to men with the same educational attainment, in the third quarter of 2003 the lowest earning 10 percent of women with less than a high school education earned $213 per week, compared to $269 for their male counterparts. Women who graduated from high school but did not go to college earned $276 per week, compared to $344 of their male counterparts. Women with a bachelor's degree earned $433 per week, compared to $524 for their male counterparts.

Education

Education is a very important factor influencing income. Median earnings increase sharply as educational attainment increases. The 1999 median earnings of those households whose householders had a 9th- to 12th-grade education (no diploma) were $21,737; for high school graduates, $35,744; for those with an associate's degree, $49,279; and for those with a bachelor's degree or post-graduate degree, such as a master's, $69,804.

MONEY INCOME DISTRIBUTION

Of the 111.2 million U.S. households in 2002, 16.1 percent earned less than $15,000, while 40.6 percent made between $15,000 and $50,000. Just over 43 percent earned $50,000 or more. The proportions have changed somewhat over the past 35 years. In 1967, after adjusting for inflation, 55 percent of U.S. households made $15,000 to $49,999; 22.3 percent earned less than $15,000; and 22.6 percent made more than $50,000. The proportion making $100,000 or more rose from 2.9 percent in 1967, to 8.1 percent in 1993, and to 14.1 percent in 2002. While 15.0 percent of white households in 2002 made $100,000 or more, only 7.2 percent of Hispanic and 6.4 percent of black households earned that much.

Income Inequality

Another, more significant, way to show how income is divided in the United States is to determine how much of the nation's total income is earned by each economic quintile (one-fifth) of the population. From 1967 to 2002 the proportion of income made by the highest earning 20 percent of the population increased by 5.9 percent, from 43.8 percent to 49.7 percent, and the proportion of income made by the top 5 percent increased by 4.2 percent from 17.5 percent to 21.7 percent. Meanwhile, each of the remaining economic quintiles lost ground. The first 20 percent of household incomes declined from 4.0 percent in 1967 to 3.5 percent in 2002; the second quintile declined from 10.8 percent in 1967 to 8.8 percent in 2002; the third quintile declined from 17.3 percent in 1967 to 14.8 percent in 2002; and the fourth quintile declined from 24.2 percent in 1967 to 23.3 percent in 2002. The declines in the second, third, and fourth quintiles indicate that the middle class is shrinking in the United States.

Another way to look at the growth in inequality over time is to compare incomes at selected positions in the income distribution. A household at the 95th percentile in 2002 (top 5 percent) had $132,086 more in income, which is at least 8.3 times that of a household at the 20th percentile ($17,916). Three decades before, in 1967, a household at the 95th percentile had at least 6.3 times the income as that of a household at the 20th percentile.

Examining the change in average (mean) real household income for each quintile is still another way to consider growth in inequality. The average income of households in the top quintile grew 57 percent, from $81,883 (in 2002 dollars) in 1967 to $143,743 in 2002, and the fourth quintile increased 33.5 percent, from $45,185 to $67,326. During the same period, the average income in the lowest quintile grew from $7,419 to $9,990 (in 2002 dollars), an increase of 33.5 percent, and that in the second lowest quintile grew by only 25 percent, from $20,227 to $25,400.

Ratio of Family Income to Poverty Threshold

Studying the changes in the ratio of family income to poverty thresholds is also a way to look at the changes in income distribution. Poverty thresholds (levels) represent the amounts of annual income, depending on family size and composition, below which a family or individual is considered poor. For example, in 2002 the poverty threshold for one person under the age of 65 years was $9,359, while the threshold for four persons was $18,556.

A ratio of 1.00 indicates that the family has an income equal to the poverty threshold for its size and composition. The average ratio in the bottom quintile in 1967 was 0.97, while the average in the top quintile was 6.06. By 2002, of 285.3 million people, about 14.0 million (4.9 percent) had a ratio of under 0.50, well below the poverty level. This figure had risen from 4.4 percent in 2000. Another 20.5 million (about 7.2 percent) were above 0.50 percent in 2002, but still had a ratio under 1.00, making a total of about 34.5 million people (or 12.1 percent) of all Americans below the poverty threshold. In 2000, 11.3 percent of people lived below the poverty threshold.

The "near poor," whose family income was at least as much as their poverty threshold (but not by more than 1.25 times), comprised 4.4 percent of the population in 2002, a slight change from 4.5 in 2000.

The income deficit for families in poverty—the difference in dollars between a family's actual income and the poverty threshold for a family of that size—averaged $7,205 in 2002, up from $6,800 in 2002. The per capita income deficit in families was $2,123 in 2002, up from $1,922 in 2000.

Reasons for Income Inequality

Several factors contribute to the growing inequality of income between the lowest and highest quintiles. The elderly population, which generally earns less than the average, is growing. An increasing number of people are living in nonfamily situations (mainly those who live alone or with nonrelatives), a category of people who usually make less money than the traditional family. The proportion of families headed by a female householder with no husband present has also increased, from 11.6 percent of all households in 1990 to 12.2 percent in 2000.

Other factors that the Census Bureau believes may contribute to the growing inequality of income distribution include the aging of the baby boom generation, which is earning more, and a greater number of women working outside the home and contributing to family income. The increasing tendency over this period for men with higher-than-average earnings to marry women with higher-than-average earnings has also contributed to widening the gap between high-income and low-income households.

In addition, the wage distribution has become considerably more unequal. The highly skilled, trained, and educated workers at the top have experienced real wage gains, while those at the bottom have suffered real wage losses. One factor is the shift in employment from goods-producing industries—which generally provided high-wage opportunities for low-skilled workers—toward services and other low-wage sectors such as retail trade, which generally pay less. Other factors that tend to lead to lower wages for less educated workers are intense global competition and immigration, the decline of the proportion of workers belonging to unions, and the drop in the real value of the minimum wage. Still others are the increasing need for computer skills and the growing use of temporary workers.

Fluctuations in Income

Most Americans experience significant fluctuations in their economic well-being from year to year. About three-fourths of the population see their economic well-being go either up or down by at least 5 percent from one year to the next as a result of changes in living arrangements, program participation, work status, or other circumstances.

One measure of economic well-being is the income-to-poverty ratio, or income ratio, the ratio of a person's annual family income to the family's poverty threshold or level. The proportion of persons whose income ratios rose from one year to the next was smaller in the 1990s than in the 1980s, reaching its minimum during the 1990–91 recession (downturn in the economy). Conversely, the percentage of people who experienced declines in their income ratios yearly grew larger from the 1980s to the 1990s.

Although statistics such as median income do not change much in real terms from one year to the next, income ratios do shift for most Americans. From one year to the next, about one-fourth of all Americans had stable income ratios. Therefore, the large majority (about three-fourths) were subject to considerable changes from year to year, regardless of the status of the business cycle (ups and downs in the economy from times of prosperity to times of recession). Over the course of a lifetime, the average American will likely experience a number of these shifts.

While the state of the economy is an important factor in determining which way these fluctuations go, it is not the only factor. People had an even (50-50) chance or better to have an income-ratio rise of 5 percent or more from one year to the next if, over the course of two years:

- They began to work year-round, full-time

- The number of workers in the household increased

- They married or otherwise became part of a married-couple family

- The number of adults in their household increased or the number of dependent children decreased

Conversely, most people saw their income ratios decline significantly when they ceased to:

- Be married

- Work year-round, full-time

The lower a person's current annual income is, the more likely it will rise the following year, and the less likely it will fall. For instance, among those whose 1993 family income was below the poverty level, 53 percent saw their income ratios rise 5 percent or more the following year, while 26 percent experienced drops. On the other hand, among those at the top of the ladder (families with incomes four or more times the 1993 poverty level), 45 percent experienced declines, while 31 percent posted gains.

HOW MUCH IS A PERSON WORTH?

"How much is a person worth?" is normally asked as an economic question, not a moral or social one. In *Net Worth and Asset Ownership of Households: 1998 and 2000* (Washington, D.C., 2003), the Census Bureau finds that the median household net worth—the value of assets (what you own) less any debts (what you owe)—increased from $49,932 in 1998 to $55,000 in 2000, after adjusting for inflation. (The Census Bureau cautions that financial holdings of certain types of wealth tend to be underreported, so these figures might be somewhat low.)

Households with considerable net worth generally have the chance to offer their members greater opportunities. They are better able to buy the things they want, to feel more secure, to travel, to send their children to college, and to help their grown children get started. Greater net worth can buy political influence and power or at least present the opportunity to meet those who have that

TABLE 4.1

Family holdings of debt, by selected characteristics of families and type of debt, 1998 and 2001

A. 1998 SURVEY OF CONSUMER FINANCES

Family characteristic	Home-secured	Other residential property	Installment loans	Credit card balances	Other lines of credit	Other	Any debt
			Percentage of families holding debt				
All families	**43.1**	**5.1**	**43.7**	**44.1**	**2.3**	**8.8**	**74.1**
Percentile of income							
Less than 20	11.2	*	27.3	24.5	*	5.5	47.3
20–39.9	23.9	2.0	36.7	40.9	1.7	6.2	66.8
40–59.9	43.7	4.3	51.2	50.1	2.7	7.8	79.9
60–79.9	63.5	7.0	51.6	57.4	2.9	11.3	87.3
80–89.9	73.6	7.8	58.4	53.1	4.5	12.1	89.6
90–100	73.0	15.3	45.4	42.1	2.5	13.9	88.1
Age of head (years)							
Less than 35	33.2	2.0	60.0	50.7	2.4	9.6	81.2
35–44	58.7	6.7	53.3	51.3	3.6	11.4	87.6
45–54	58.8	7.0	51.2	52.5	3.6	11.1	87.0
55–64	49.4	7.8	37.9	45.7	1.6	8.3	76.4
65–74	26.0	5.3	20.2	29.2	*	4.1	51.4
75 or more	11.5	1.8	4.2	11.2	*	2.0	24.6
Race or ethnicity of respondent							
White non-Hispanic	46.7	5.5	44.3	44.4	2.4	8.8	74.9
Nonwhite or Hispanic	30.7	4.0	41.6	43.3	1.9	8.8	71.1
Current work status of head							
Working for someone else	50.8	5.3	55.2	53.5	2.7	10.8	86.8
Self-employed	63.1	10.9	46.3	47.5	3.7	10.7	84.6
Retired	18.6	3.1	15.8	20.9	*	3.3	39.9
Other not working	26.8	*	39.0	39.0	*	7.5	65.7
Housing status							
Owner	65.1	6.3	44.3	46.2	1.8	9.3	79.4
Renter or other	...	2.9	42.6	40.0	3.4	7.8	63.5
Percentile of net worth							
Less than 25	11.2	*	47.2	39.5	2.8	9.3	65.6
25–49.9	47.4	3.3	49.9	54.9	2.5	9.3	81.4
50–74.9	56.2	4.9	46.3	48.7	1.7	7.6	76.8
75–89.9	56.8	9.0	34.4	36.7	2.0	7.6	70.2
90–100	59.0	14.9	27.3	28.4	2.6	10.8	75.9
			Median value of holdings for families holding debt (thousands of 2001 dollars)				
All families	**67.5**	**43.5**	**9.5**	**1.9**	**2.7**	**3.3**	**35.4**
Percentile of income							
Less than 20	27.2	*	4.4	1.0	*	1.1	4.8
20–39.9	40.3	35.9	6.7	1.3	1.2	1.9	11.0
40–59.9	47.9	20.7	8.7	2.1	1.6	2.2	27.8
60–79.9	70.8	31.1	13.0	2.4	3.0	3.3	62.9
80–89.9	87.6	46.4	12.5	2.2	3.3	5.4	92.9
90–100	127.4	76.2	15.8	3.3	7.0	10.9	137.3
Age of head (years)							
Less than 35	77.3	59.9	9.9	1.6	1.1	1.9	20.9
35–44	76.2	43.5	8.3	2.2	1.5	3.3	60.6
45–54	74.0	43.5	10.9	2.0	3.3	5.4	52.2
55–64	52.2	44.6	9.0	2.2	5.3	5.4	37.2
65–74	28.3	27.4	7.0	1.2	*	4.9	13.0
75 or more	23.1	32.4	9.7	.8	*	1.9	8.8
Race or ethnicity of respondent							
White non-Hispanic	67.5	46.4	9.8	2.2	3.0	3.6	43.2
Nonwhite or Hispanic	67.5	32.7	7.8	1.2	.8	1.9	16.9
Current work status of head							
Working for someone else	71.8	38.5	9.6	2.1	3.0	3.3	38.2
Self-employed	80.4	59.7	12.0	2.2	4.1	7.1	70.1
Retired	40.3	37.0	6.3	1.1	*	2.1	11.1
Other not working	62.0	*	7.3	1.3	*	1.2	13.7
Housing status							
Owner	67.5	45.7	10.4	2.2	2.4	4.4	65.9
Renter or other	...	29.9	8.3	1.4	3.0	1.4	6.5

TABLE 4.1

Family holdings of debt, by selected characteristics of families and type of debt, 1998 and 2001 [CONTINUED]

A. 1998 SURVEY OF CONSUMER FINANCES

Family characteristic	Home-secured	Other residential property	Installment loans	Credit card balances	Other lines of credit	Other	Any debt
	Median value of holdings for families holding debt (thousands of 2001 dollars)						
Percentile of net worth							
Less than 25	61.5	*	8.6	1.7	1.1	1.6	9.1
25–49.9	60.0	31.6	8.5	2.0	3.3	2.2	31.3
50–74.9	64.2	23.9	9.7	2.0	3.3	5.4	50.1
75–89.9	76.2	58.8	11.1	1.6	1.4	6.5	70.8
90–100	108.8	78.4	16.0	2.0	10.9	21.8	105.5

B. 2001 SURVEY OF CONSUMER FINANCES

Percentage of families holding debt

Family characteristic	Home-secured	Other residential property	Installment loans	Credit card balances	Other lines of credit	Other	Any debt
All families	**44.6**	**4.7**	**45.2**	**44.4**	**1.5**	**7.2**	**75.1**
Percentile of income							
Less than 20	13.8	*	25.5	30.3	1.3	5.9	49.3
20–39.9	27.0	1.8	43.2	44.5	1.5	5.6	70.2
40–59.9	44.4	3.2	51.9	52.8	1.5	7.7	82.1
60–79.9	61.8	5.4	56.7	52.6	1.5	7.7	85.6
80–89.9	76.9	10.3	55.7	50.3	2.6	9.3	91.4
90–100	75.4	14.9	41.2	33.1	1.4	8.8	85.3
Age of head (years)							
Less than 35	35.7	2.7	63.8	49.6	1.7	8.8	82.7
35–44	59.6	4.9	57.1	54.1	1.7	8.0	88.6
45–54	59.8	6.5	45.9	50.4	1.5	7.4	84.6
55–64	49.0	8.0	39.3	41.6	3.1	7.4	75.4
65–74	32.0	3.4	21.1	30.0	*	5.0	56.8
75 or more	9.5	2.0	9.5	18.4	*	3.6	29.2
Race or ethnicity of respondent							
White non-Hispanic	47.6	5.4	45.3	43.3	1.7	7.4	75.8
Nonwhite or Hispanic	35.1	2.5	44.6	47.7	1.1	6.5	72.9
Current work status of head							
Working for someone else	52.5	5.3	57.0	53.2	1.4	8.2	86.5
Self-employed	59.1	7.4	39.8	42.8	3.5	8.1	81.7
Retired	19.6	2.2	17.2	24.0	*	4.4	44.3
Other not working	27.9	*	41.2	32.2	*	6.1	61.5
Housing status							
Owner	66.0	6.0	45.5	44.4	1.0	6.9	79.9
Renter or other	…	2.0	44.5	44.3	2.8	7.8	65.0
Percentile of net worth							
Less than 25	11.2	*	48.9	45.5	2.4	8.3	68.7
25–49.9	49.4	2.0	51.0	55.1	1.3	7.2	80.8
50–74.9	59.1	5.4	48.1	44.6	*	7.1	77.9
75–89.9	61.2	7.9	37.2	38.9	*	4.9	74.9
90–100	55.5	15.0	25.6	22.4	2.1	8.2	70.2
	Median value of holdings for families holding debt (thousands of 2001 dollars)						
All families	**70.0**	**40.0**	**9.7**	**1.9**	**3.9**	**3.0**	**38.8**
Percentile of income							
Less than 20	28.0	*	4.6	1.0	.5	1.0	5.2
20–39.9	40.0	30.0	6.6	1.2	1.1	3.0	11.5
40–59.9	56.1	38.8	9.7	2.0	.7	2.0	29.1
60–79.9	75.6	41.9	11.9	2.3	4.0	3.0	62.3
80–89.9	91.0	31.2	14.5	3.8	7.8	4.0	96.8
90–100	134.0	77.0	13.4	2.8	10.0	21.0	146.4
Age of head (years)							
Less than 35	77.0	52.0	9.5	2.0	.5	2.0	24.9
35–44	80.0	45.5	11.1	2.0	.7	3.1	61.5
45–54	75.0	33.5	9.6	2.3	5.3	5.0	54.3
55–64	55.0	40.0	9.0	1.9	20.5	5.0	34.6
65–74	39.0	77.0	7.0	1.0	*	2.5	13.1
75 or more	44.8	42.0	5.8	.7	*	2.5	5.0
Race or ethnicity of respondent							
White non-Hispanic	74.0	40.0	10.0	2.0	4.0	3.6	44.5
Nonwhite or Hispanic	61.0	40.0	8.1	1.5	1.0	2.0	20.0

TABLE 4.1

Family holdings of debt, by selected characteristics of families and type of debt, 1998 and 2001 [CONTINUED]

B. 2001 SURVEY OF CONSUMER FINANCES

Family characteristic	Home-secured	Other residential property	Installment loans	Credit card balances	Other lines of credit	Other	Any debt
	Median value of holdings for families holding debt (thousands of 2001 dollars)						
Current work status of head							
Working for someone else	74.0	37.5	10.0	2.0	3.0	2.1	42.5
Self-employed	100.0	87.5	10.2	2.5	15.0	11.9	77.8
Retired	31.5	45.9	6.9	.9	*	3.3	9.8
Other not working	72.0	*	9.8	2.0	*	2.5	33.8
Housing status							
Owner	70.0	41.0	10.4	2.1	15.0	4.0	69.4
Renter or other	...	37.6	7.0	1.2	1.0	2.0	6.0
Percentile of net worth							
Less than 25	57.0	*	8.3	1.6	.5	2.0	8.8
25–49.9	56.5	20.0	9.4	1.9	1.8	1.2	38.5
50–74.9	69.0	47.0	10.0	2.0	*	4.0	60.0
75–89.9	86.0	30.0	11.7	2.1	*	7.0	80.3
90–100	135.0	77.0	11.3	2.0	20.5	30.0	126.0

Note: . . .Not applicable.
*Ten or fewer observations.

SOURCE: Ana M. Aizcorbe, Arthur B. Kennickell, and Kevin B. Moore, "11. Family holdings of debt, by selected characteristics of families and type of debt, 1998 and 2001 surveys," in "Recent Changes in U.S. Family Finances: Evidence from the 1998 and 2001 Survey of Consumer Finances," *Federal Reserve Bulletin,* January 2003

power. Net worth is a major factor in determining a household's position and power in U.S. society.

Net Worth

The Census Bureau finds huge disparities in net worth among the various sectors of society. As was the case with income, in 2000 households in the highest quintile (the upper one-fifth) had a net worth of $185,500, up significantly from $161,174 in 1998. The lowest quintile showed a net worth of $7,396 in 2000, a slight increase from $6,073 in 1998. Households in the second and third quintiles remained fairly stable from 1998 to 2000, with the fourth quintile showed sizable gains in median net worth.

In 2000 the ownership rate of home equity varied significantly with income, from 46.2 percent for the lowest income group to 87.1 percent for the wealthiest group. As might be expected, rates also varied substantially between the lowest and wealthiest groups in terms of ownership of stocks and mutual fund shares (9.2 percent compared to 51.6 percent), retirement accounts such as IRA or Keogh accounts (8.6 percent compared to 42.6 percent), and interest-earning assets at financial institutions (39.2 percent compared to 86.3 percent).

Race, Age, and Households

In 2000 the median net worth of black households was $7,500, or less than 10 percent of that of white households ($79,454). The median net worth of Hispanic households was higher than that of blacks, at $9,750.

Married-couple households in 2000 had a median net worth of $91,218, considerably more than those of male householders ($24,659) and female householders ($23,028). When net worth levels were compared within age groups, households maintained by women younger than 55 years of age had a much lower median net worth than those of their male counterparts. Not surprisingly, those who had been working for the full year, those owning their own homes, and those who earned higher incomes tended to have a greater net financial worth.

Assets

In the 2000 study on net worth, the Census Bureau asked the respondents what type of financial assets they owned.

- 85.8 percent owned their own cars

- 67.2 percent owned their own homes

- 65.0 percent had some type of interest-earning asset at financial institutions

- 37.5 percent had a checking account

- 27.1 percent held either stocks or mutual fund shares (which invest in stocks and bonds)

- 23.1 percent had an IRA or Keogh account for retirement

- 14.7 percent had bought U.S. savings bonds

- 4.9 percent held rental property

In 2000 home ownership accounted for 32.3 percent of total net worth, compared to 33.7 percent in 1998.

FIGURE 4.1

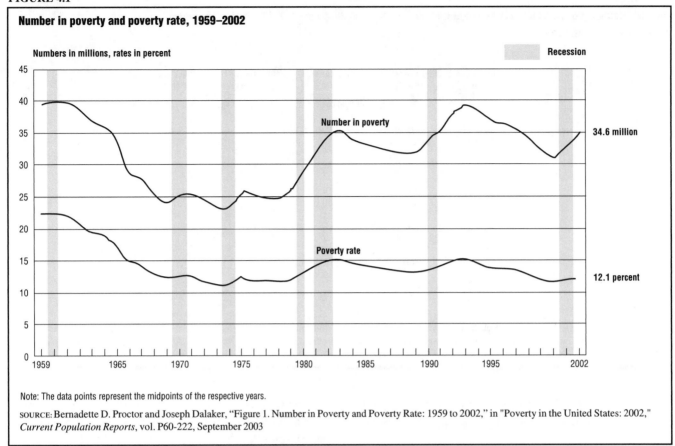

Number in poverty and poverty rate, 1959–2002

Numbers in millions, rates in percent

Recession

Number in poverty

34.6 million

Poverty rate

12.1 percent

Note: The data points represent the midpoints of the respective years.

SOURCE: Bernadette D. Proctor and Joseph Dalaker, "Figure 1. Number in Poverty and Poverty Rate: 1959 to 2002," in "Poverty in the United States: 2002," *Current Population Reports*, vol. P60-222, September 2003

Stocks and mutual fund shares made up the next largest share of net worth at 15.6 percent in 2000, compared to 18.8 percent four years earlier. Interest-earning assets at financial institutions accounted for 8.9 percent in 2002, compared to 8.1 percent in 1998.

DEBT

The Federal Reserve Board's 2001 Survey of Consumer Finances provides information on family debt. Most families (75.1 percent) had some type of debt (including mortgage debt) in 2001. (See Table 4.1.)

The median amount of debt tends to increase with family income, likely because of borrowing associated with the acquisition of nonfinancial assets (homes, cars, and so on). In 2001 indebted households with the lowest earning capacity typically owed $5,200, but those with the highest incomes typically owed over $146,400. (See Table 4.1.)

By age group, the proportion of families borrowing varies only a little for the groups with heads younger than 65, but it falls off quickly for those 65 years and over. The drop-off in median borrowing in these older groups is even sharper. The age pattern is largely explained by the paying off of mortgages on homes.

Among home owners, 79.9 percent had debt in 2001, compared to 65.0 percent of renters—nearly all the differ-ence was attributable to mortgage debt. The differences in the proportions for non-Hispanic whites and Hispanics were small.

POVERTY

In 2002 poverty thresholds varied from $9,359 for a person under 65 years of age living alone, to $18,556 for a family of four, to $39,843 for a family of nine or more members. In 2002 for the second consecutive year the poverty rate and the number in poverty both increased from the previous year. An estimated 12.1 percent of all Americans (34.6 million) were living in poverty in 2002, up from 11.7 percent (32.9 million) in 2001. According to the Census Bureau, the poverty rate for 2002 was not sta-tistically very different from the record low of 11.1 per-cent set in 1973. The poverty rate declined from a high of 22.4 percent in 1959, when data on poverty were first offi-cially tabulated, to about 11 percent for most of the 1970s. It began rising in 1980, reaching 15.2 percent in 1983. Since then, it declined to 13.1 percent in 1989, increased to 15.1 percent in 1993, and then declined to 11.3 in 2000 before rising again. (See Figure 4.1.)

Characteristics of the Poor

AGE. In 2002, 16.7 percent of the nation's poor were people under 18 years of age, up from 16.2 percent in

FIGURE 4.2

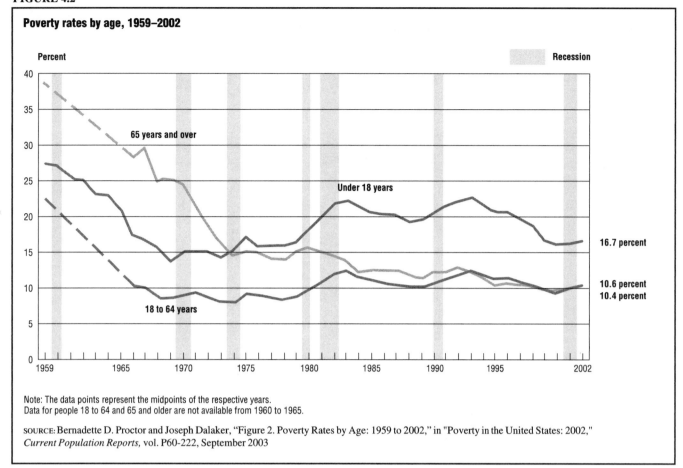

Poverty rates by age, 1959–2002

Note: The data points represent the midpoints of the respective years.
Data for people 18 to 64 and 65 and older are not available from 1960 to 1965.

SOURCE: Bernadette D. Proctor and Joseph Dalaker, "Figure 2. Poverty Rates by Age: 1959 to 2002," in "Poverty in the United States: 2002," *Current Population Reports,* vol. P60-222, September 2003

2000—the lowest poverty rate for this age group since 1979. (See Figure 4.2.) The poverty rate for children living in female-householder families (no spouse present) has fluctuated since 1980, but has undergone a steeper decline between 1993 and 2000 than did the rate for all children. In 1993, 54 percent of children living in female-householder families were living in poverty; by 2001 this proportion had decreased to 39 percent. Children in married-couple families were much less likely to be living in poverty than children living only with their mothers. In 2001, 8 percent of children in married-couple families were living in poverty, compared to 39 percent in female-householder families. (See Figure 4.3.)

In 2002 the poverty rate for people 18 to 64 years of age was 10.6 percent, compared to 10.1 percent in 2001. The poverty rate for people under 18 years of age in 2002 was 16.7 percent, compared to 16.3 percent in 2001. For people 65 years of age and older, the poverty rate in 2002 was 10.4, compared to 10.1 the year prior. Prior to 1974 the poverty rate for children was less than that of the elderly. Since 1974 it has been higher than the rates of other age groups.

RACE AND NATIVITY. Blacks (24.1 percent) and Hispanics (21.8 percent) were the most likely to live in poverty in 2002. That year both groups were almost three times as like- ly as white non-Hispanics (8.0 percent) and twice as likely as Asians and Pacific Islanders (10.2) to live in poverty. These numbers changed very little in 2001: the poverty rate for non-Hispanic whites was 7.8 percent; for blacks, 22.7 percent; and for Asians and Pacific Islanders, 10.2 percent. The poverty rate for persons of Hispanic origin was 21.4 percent.

These disparities are borne out in the three-year average poverty rates. From 2000 to 2002 the three-year average poverty rate for all races was 12.1 percent. During that period, the average poverty rate was 7.7 for non-Hispanic whites, 21.5 for Hispanics, 23.1 for blacks, and 10.0 percent for Asians and Pacific Islanders.

According to the Census Bureau, although blacks remained disproportionately poor in 2002, the difference in poverty rates between blacks and white non-Hispanics has narrowed since its peak in 1993, when the poverty rate for blacks was 23.2 percentage points higher than that for white non-Hispanics. In 2002 the difference was 16.1 percentage points.

In 2002 the poverty rate for the foreign born—which includes naturalized citizens and noncitizens—was 16.6 percent, compared to 11.5 percent for the native born. Of the foreign-born population who were not naturalized citizens, 20.7 percent were poor in 2002, compared to 10 percent for naturalized citizens.

FIGURE 4.3

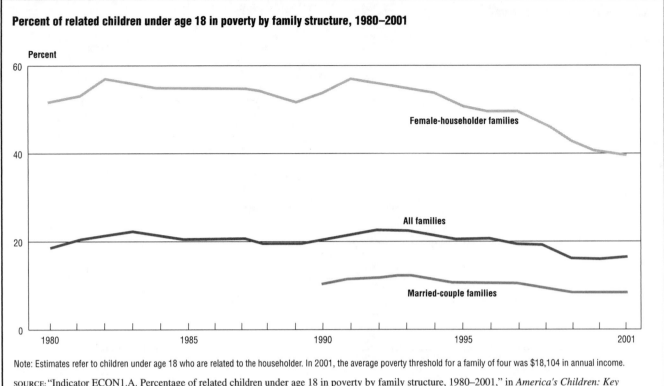

Percent of related children under age 18 in poverty by family structure, 1980–2001

Note: Estimates refer to children under age 18 who are related to the householder. In 2001, the average poverty threshold for a family of four was $18,104 in annual income.

SOURCE: "Indicator ECON1.A. Percentage of related children under age 18 in poverty by family structure, 1980–2001," in *America's Children: Key National Indicators of Well-Being 2003,* Federal Interagency Forum on Child and Family Statistics, Washington, DC, July 2003

Families in Poverty

In 2002, 9.6 percent of all families of all races were below the poverty level. Married-couple families had a poverty rate of 5.3 percent. For families with a male householder with no spouse present, the rate was 12.1 percent, in comparison to 26.5 percent of families with female householders without a spouse present. This number was down from 27.8 percent in 1999 and 32.6 percent in 1996. Although still high, this rate has generally declined since 1959, when 42.6 percent of female householders with no spouse percent were below the poverty level. (See Table 4.2.)

In 2002 white families had a far lower poverty rate (8.0 percent) than black families (24.1 percent) or families with a householder of Hispanic origin (21.8 percent). The poverty rate for white families with a female householder and no husband present was 20.0 percent; blacks, 38.2 percent; Hispanics, 36.4 percent; and Asians and Pacific Islanders, 15.3 percent.

In 2000 black families headed by males with no spouse present had a poverty rate of 20.3 percent. Hispanic families headed by males with no spouse present had a poverty rate of 19.6 percent, while similar white families had a poverty rate of 9.9 percent. Female-householder families made up 79 percent of all poor black families, compared to 46 percent of poor Hispanic-origin families and 44 percent of poor white families.

FAMILIES WITH CHILDREN. In 2002 families with children were more likely to be in poverty than families without children because family income had to be stretched further to support additional persons. Among the general population, 16.3 percent of families with children under age 18 lived in poverty, compared to 15.8 percent the year before. Married couples with children were far less likely to live below the poverty level than families with children in which only one spouse was present. (See Table 4.3.)

FEMALE-HEADED FAMILIES. In all instances, a far greater percentage of female-headed families lived below the poverty line than male-headed families, and a greater percentage of both lived in poverty than did married couples. (See Table 4.3.) Families headed by females have been a growing proportion of all poor families. In 1959 such families accounted for about one-fourth (23 percent) of all the families living in poverty. By 1986 female-headed families accounted for half (51 percent) of all families living in poverty. In 2002, 70.8 percent of female-headed households with no workers were below the poverty level, demonstrating the vulnerability of such households when compared to the 17.0 percent poverty rate of married-couple families with no workers.

On the other hand, the proportion of female-headed families living in poverty has dropped over the past several decades. In 1959 almost 43 percent of all female-

TABLE 4.2

Poverty status of families by type of family, 1959–2002

[Numbers in thousands. Families as of March of the following year]

Year and characteristic	All families			Married-couple families			Male householder, no wife present			Female householder, no husband present		
		Below poverty level			Below poverty level			Below poverty level			Below poverty level	
	Total	Number	Percent	Total	Number	Percent	Total	Number	Percent	Total	Number	Percent
All races												
2002	75,616	7,229	9.6	57,327	3,052	5.3	4,663	564	12.1	13,626	3,613	26.5
2001	74,340	6,813	9.2	56,755	2,760	4.9	4,440	583	13.1	13,146	3,470	26.4
2000	73,778	6,400	8.7	56,598	2,636	4.7	4,277	485	11.3	12,903	3,278	25.4
1999	73,206	6,792	9.3	56,290	2,748	4.9	4,099	485	11.8	12,818	3,559	27.8
1998	71,551	7,186	10.0	54,778	2,879	5.3	3,977	476	12.0	12,796	3,831	29.9
1997	70,884	7,324	10.3	54,321	2,821	5.2	3,911	508	13.0	12,652	3,995	31.6
1996	70,241	7,708	11.0	53,604	3,010	5.6	3,847	531	13.8	12,790	4,167	32.6
1995	69,597	7,532	10.8	53,570	2,982	5.6	3,513	493	14.0	12,514	4,057	32.4
1994	69,313	8,053	11.6	53,865	3,272	6.1	3,228	549	17.0	12,220	4,232	34.6
1993	68,506	8,393	12.3	53,181	3,481	6.5	2,914	488	16.8	12,411	4,424	35.6
1992	68,216	8,144	11.9	53,090	3,385	6.4	3,065	484	15.8	12,061	4,275	35.4
1991	67,175	7,712	11.5	52,457	3,158	6.0	3,025	392	13.0	11,693	4,161	35.6
1990	66,322	7,098	10.7	52,147	2,981	5.7	2,907	349	12.0	11,268	3,768	33.4
1989	66,090	6,784	10.3	52,137	2,931	5.6	2,884	348	12.1	10,890	3,504	32.2
1988	65,837	6,874	10.4	52,100	2,897	5.6	2,847	336	11.8	10,890	3,642	33.4
1987	65,204	7,005	10.7	51,675	3,011	5.8	2,833	340	12.0	10,696	3,654	34.2
1986	64,491	7,023	10.9	51,537	3,123	6.1	2,510	287	11.4	10,445	3,613	34.6
1985	63,558	7,223	11.4	50,933	3,438	6.7	2,414	311	12.9	10,211	3,474	34.0
1984	62,706	7,277	11.6	50,350	3,488	6.9	2,228	292	13.1	10,129	3,498	34.5
1983	62,015	7,647	12.3	50,081	3,815	7.6	2,038	268	13.2	9,896	3,564	36.0
1982	61,393	7,512	12.2	49,908	3,789	7.6	2,016	290	14.4	9,469	3,434	36.3
1981	61,019	6,851	11.2	49,630	3,394	6.8	1,986	205	10.3	9,403	3,252	34.6
1980	60,309	6,217	10.3	49,294	3,032	6.2	1,933	213	11.0	9,082	2,972	32.7
1979	59,550	5,461	9.2	49,112	2,640	5.4	1,733	176	10.2	8,705	2,645	30.4
1978	57,804	5,280	9.1	47,692	2,474	5.2	1,654	152	9.2	8,458	2,654	31.4
1977	57,215	5,311	9.3	47,385	2,524	5.3	1,594	177	11.1	8,236	2,610	31.7
1976	56,710	5,311	9.4	47,497	2,606	5.5	1,500	162	10.8	7,713	2,543	33.0
1975	56,245	5,450	9.7	47,318	2,904	6.1	1,445	116	8.0	7,482	2,430	32.5
1974	55,698	4,922	8.8	47,069	2,474	5.3	1,399	125	8.9	7,230	2,324	32.1
1973	55,053	4,828	8.8	46,812	2,482	5.3	1,438	154	10.7	6,804	2,193	32.2
1972	54,373	5,075	9.3	46,314	(NA)	(NA)	1,452	(NA)	(NA)	6,607	2,158	32.7
1971	53,296	5,303	10.0	45,752	(NA)	(NA)	1,353	(NA)	(NA)	6,191	2,100	33.9
1970	52,227	5,260	10.1	44,739	(NA)	(NA)	1,487	(NA)	(NA)	6,001	1,952	32.5
1969	51,586	5,008	9.7	44,436	(NA)	(NA)	1,559	(NA)	(NA)	5,591	1,827	32.7
1968	50,511	5,047	10.0	43,842	(NA)	(NA)	1,228	(NA)	(NA)	5,441	1,755	32.3
1967	49,835	5,667	11.4	43,292	(NA)	(NA)	1,210	(NA)	(NA)	5,333	1,774	33.3
1966	48,921	5,784	11.8	42,553	(NA)	(NA)	1,197	(NA)	(NA)	5,171	1,721	33.1
1965	48,278	6,721	13.9	42,107	(NA)	(NA)	1,179	(NA)	(NA)	4,992	1,916	38.4
1964	47,836	7,160	15.0	41,648	(NA)	(NA)	1,182	(NA)	(NA)	5,006	1,822	36.4
1963	47,436	7,554	15.9	41,311	(NA)	(NA)	1,243	(NA)	(NA)	4,882	1,972	40.4
1962	46,998	8,077	17.2	40,923	(NA)	(NA)	1,334	(NA)	(NA)	4,741	2,034	42.9
1961	46,341	8,391	18.1	40,405	(NA)	(NA)	1,293	(NA)	(NA)	4,643	1,954	42.1
1960	45,435	8,243	18.1	39,624	(NA)	(NA)	1,202	(NA)	(NA)	4,609	1,955	42.4
1959	45,054	8,320	18.5	39,335	(NA)	(NA)	1,226	(NA)	(NA)	4,493	1,916	42.6

Note: NA Not available. Before 1979, unrelated subfamilies were included in all families. Beginning in 1979, unrelated subfamilies are excluded from all families.

SOURCE: Bernadette D. Proctor and Joseph Dalaker, "Table A-3. Poverty Status of Families by Type of Family, 1959 to 2002," in "Poverty in the United States: 2002," *Current Population Reports*, vol. P60–222, September 2003

headed families were living in poverty. By 1979 the proportion had dropped to 30 percent. By 1993 it had risen to about 36 percent. In 1998, 30 percent of female-headed families were poor, and by 2002 that figure had dropped even further to 26.5 percent, up 1.8 percent from 2000.

Poverty in Geographic Regions

In 2002 the Midwest was the only region in the nation where both the number in poverty and poverty rate increased, to 6.6 million (10.3 percent) from 6.0 million (9.4 percent) in 2001. The poverty rate was still the highest in the South (13.8 percent), which was only a slight change from 2001. The poverty rates in the Northeast and West in 2002 remained almost unchanged at 10.9 percent and 12.4 percent, respectively. (See Table 4.3.)

Who Stays Poor?

The Census Bureau studied poor Americans over a two-year period in 1993 and 1994. The Census Bureau found that only about one-third of those who were poor in an average month in 1994 were poor in all of 1993 and 1994. Blacks and Hispanics were less likely to get out of

TABLE 4.3

People and families in poverty by selected characteristics, 2001–02

(Numbers in thousands, confidence intervals (C.I.) in thousands or percentage points as appropriate)

Characteristic	2001 below poverty level				2002 below poverty level				Change in poverty (2002 less 2001)[1]			
	Number	90-percent C.I. (±)	Percent	90-percent C.I. (±)	Number	90-percent C.I. (±)	Percent	90-percent C.I. (±)	Number	90-percent C.I. (±)	Percent	90-percent C.I. (±)
People												
Total	32,907	644	11.7	0.2	34,570	658	12.1	0.2	[2]1,663	683	[2]0.4	0.2
Family status												
In families	23,215	551	9.9	0.2	24,534	566	10.4	0.2	[2]1,319	586	[2]0.4	0.3
Householder	6,813	172	9.2	0.2	7,229	178	9.6	0.2	[2]416	199	[2]0.4	0.3
Related children under 18	11,175	323	15.8	0.5	11,646	332	16.3	0.5	[2]472	344	[2]0.5	0.5
Related children under 6	4,188	207	18.2	1.0	4,296	211	18.5	1.0	108	219	0.3	1.0
In unrelated subfamilies	466	82	39.8	7.6	417	77	33.7	6.7	−48	84	−6.1	7.6
Reference person	172	50	36.4	11.4	167	49	31.7	10.0	−6	51	−4.6	11.4
Children under 18	292	56	44.6	9.9	241	51	35.4	8.4	−51	58	−9.2	9.7
Unrelated individual	9,226	207	19.9	0.5	9,618	212	20.4	0.5	[2]392	240	0.5	0.5
Male	3,833	122	17.3	0.6	4,023	125	17.7	0.7	[2]190	141	0.4	0.7
Female	5,393	149	22.3	0.7	5,595	153	22.9	0.7	[2]203	171	0.6	0.8
Age												
Under 18 years	11,733	329	16.3	0.5	12,133	337	16.7	0.5	[2]400	350	0.4	0.5
18 to 64 years	17,760	483	10.1	0.3	18,861	498	10.6	0.3	[2]1,101	515	[2]0.5	0.3
65 years and over	3,414	129	10.1	0.4	3,576	132	10.4	0.4	[2]163	137	0.3	0.3
Nativity												
Native	27,698	597	11.1	0.2	29,012	609	11.5	0.2	[2]1,314	633	[2]0.4	0.3
Foreign born	5,209	308	16.1	1.0	5,558	317	16.6	1.0	[2]349	329	0.6	1.0
Naturalized citizen	1,186	148	9.9	1.2	1,285	154	10.0	1.1	99	158	0.1	1.3
Not a citizen	4,023	271	19.7	1.3	4,273	280	20.7	1.3	250	290	1.1	1.5
Region												
Northeast	5,687	266	10.7	0.5	5,871	270	10.9	0.5	184	281	0.2	0.5
Midwest	5,966	278	9.4	0.4	6,616	293	10.3	0.5	[2]650	299	[2]0.9	0.5
South	13,515	458	13.5	0.5	14,019	466	13.8	0.5	[2]505	484	0.3	0.5
West	7,739	364	12.1	0.6	8,064	372	12.4	0.7	325	385	0.3	0.7
Residence												
Inside metropolitan areas	25,446	575	11.1	0.3	27,096	591	11.6	0.3	[2]1,649	612	[2]0.5	0.3
Inside central cities	13,394	427	16.5	0.5	13,784	433	16.7	0.5	390	451	0.2	0.5
Outside central cities	12,052	406	8.2	0.3	13,311	426	8.9	0.3	[2]1,259	436	[2]0.7	0.3
Outside metropolitan areas	7,460	394	14.2	0.8	7,474	395	14.2	0.8	14	415	—	0.8
Families												
Total	6,813	172	9.2	0.2	7,229	178	9.6	0.2	[2]416	199	[2]0.4	0.3
Type of family												
Married-couple	2,760	102	4.9	0.2	3,052	107	5.3	0.2	[2]292	120	[2]0.5	0.2
Female householder, no husband present	3,470	116	26.4	1.0	3,613	118	26.5	1.0	[2]143	133	0.1	1.2
Male householder, no spouse present	583	45	13.1	1.1	564	44	12.1	1.0	−20	51	−1.1	1.2

Note: — Represents zero.
[1]Details may not sum to totals because of rounding.
[2]Statistically different from zero at the 90-percent confidence level.

SOURCE: Bernadette D. Proctor and Joseph Dalaker, "Table 2. People and Families in Poverty by Selected Characteristics: 2001 and 2002," in "Poverty in the United States: 2002," *Current Population Reports*, vol. P60–222, September 2003

poverty, as were children, people in female-headed households, and those not working. A noticeable proportion of the population was chronically poor—5.3 percent were poor all 24 months of 1993 and 1994. One-half of all poverty spells lasted 4.5 months or longer, and blacks had significantly longer poverty spells than whites. One-half of all poverty spells experienced by blacks lasted longer than 6.8 months, compared with 4.2 months for whites and 5 months for Hispanics.

Who Gets Assistance?

In 1998 over $392 billion was paid out in total cash and noncash benefits for persons on limited incomes. Of that, about $277 billion came from federal sources, and the remaining $114 billion came from states. Medicaid accounted for the largest payout of benefits, at $177 billion; the second largest was supplemental security income, at $33.6 billion. The refunded portion of the earned income tax credit (a tax credit for working families with

TABLE 4.4

Households experiencing difficulty meeting basic needs in past 12 months, 1998

(In percent)

Item	Any difficulty	Did not pay utility bills	Food insecurity	Needed to visit dentist	Needed to visit doctor	Did not pay rent or mortgage
Total	**21.2**	**9.2**	**9.1**	**7.9**	**6.1**	**5.4**
Age of householder						
15 to 29 years	30.8	13.9	12.7	11.8	7.9	8.3
30 to 44 years	26.3	12.4	10.8	9.9	7.4	7.8
45 to 64 years	19.6	8.0	8.4	7.4	6.4	4.6
65 years and older	9.9	3.0	5.3	3.2	2.7	1.1
Sex of householder						
Male	17.5	6.9	7.1	6.8	5.1	4.5
Female	25.7	11.8	11.5	9.2	7.4	6.5
Race/ethnicity of householder						
White	19.0	7.6	7.6	7.5	5.6	4.7
Non-Hispanic	17.7	7.1	6.4	7.2	5.4	4.1
Black	36.4	20.0	18.2	10.8	9.5	10.4
Other race	20.5	7.8	13.6	7.8	6.5	5.5
Hispanic (of any race)	32.8	13.8	19.3	10.9	8.9	10.3
Household income quintile						
Lowest quintile	33.9	14.7	20.2	11.8	11.2	9.3
2nd quintile	27.0	12.8	12.0	11.0	8.3	7.4
3rd quintile	22.3	9.6	7.5	8.6	5.9	5.2
4th quintile	14.9	6.1	4.0	5.4	3.6	3.3
Highest quintile	7.9	2.6	1.7	2.7	1.7	1.6
Education of householder						
Less than high school graduate	29.4	12.4	17.0	10.1	9.5	7.1
High school graduate	23.0	10.8	9.6	8.4	6.3	6.3
Some college	23.1	10.1	8.5	9.1	6.7	6.0
Bachelor's or higher	10.8	3.7	3.3	4.4	2.9	2.2
Householder disability						
Disabled	42.5	19.2	24.8	16.5	16.2	11.8
Not disabled	19.0	8.1	7.4	7.0	5.1	4.7
Household structure						
Nonfamily household						
Lives alone	20.1	7.2	9.6	7.7	6.7	4.5
Lives with others	24.4	7.6	9.0	11.7	9.1	4.9
Family household						
Married, no children	10.8	3.8	3.8	4.2	3.3	2.2
Married, children	21.4	10.0	7.6	8.0	5.6	5.7
Unmarried, no children	24.2	9.8	10.8	9.4	8.1	5.8
Unmarried, children	46.7	25.8	23.6	15.5	11.3	14.7
Tenure						
Owner	14.9	6.1	5.2	5.5	4.3	3.2
Renter	33.9	15.3	16.8	12.8	10.0	9.8
Region						
Northeast	19.6	9.2	8.5	6.8	4.4	5.0
Midwest	20.1	9.4	8.1	6.9	5.8	5.1
South	21.8	9.0	9.2	8.6	7.0	5.2
West	22.9	9.2	10.5	9.0	6.6	6.3
Metropolitan status						
Central city	30.9	14.0	14.3	11.7	9.2	9.1
Metropolitan, outside central city	19.7	8.5	8.3	7.3	5.5	5.0
Nonmetropolitan	20.3	8.3	8.3	7.6	6.4	4.4

SOURCE: Kurt J. Bauman, "Table D. Households Experiencing Difficulties Meeting Basic Needs in Past 12 Months: 1998," in "Extended Measures of Well-Being: Living Conditions in the United States: 1998," *Current Population Reports*, vol. P70–87, March 2003

incomes under $31,152) was next, accounting for $25.3 billion, followed by food stamps at $22.3 billion.

Millions of Americans received some sort of aid from the government each month in 1998: people living in poverty, veterans, the elderly, disadvantaged youths, foster children, Native Americans, and college students were some of the people assisted in various ways by federal and state monies. In each month in 1998, on average there were 58.2 million who received a refunded portion of the earned income tax credit, 41.3 million recipients of Medicaid, and 21 million recipients of food stamps. Furthermore, 21.4 million meals were served each month to children who took part in school lunch and breakfast programs.

Basic Needs

In 1998 about one of every five Americans lived in a household that had at least one problem meeting basic needs. Almost 34 percent of the poor, those in the lowest income quintile, could not meet essential expenses at some time during 1998. Almost 15 percent of these households did not pay their full gas, electric, or oil bill, and 9.3 percent did not pay their full rent or mortgage. Nearly every type of difficulty was more common among female-headed households and those containing children. Blacks and Hispanics were more likely than whites to have difficulty meeting basic needs. (See Table 4.4.)

Health and Nutrition

In 1998 those at or below the poverty level were more than twice as likely as those above the poverty level to live in households reporting that a member did not see a doctor or dentist when needed. People without insurance were about four times more likely to report not seeing a doctor or dentist than those who had insurance coverage. The poor were far more likely to report not having enough food to eat, as were children, blacks, Hispanics, and female householders.

In 2000 about 7.3 million households participated in the Food Stamp Program. Of those, 53.9 percent were households with children, followed by 27.5 percent of households with a disabled person and 21.0 percent of households with the elderly.

In 2000 some 40 percent of those who participated in the Food Stamp Program were non-Hispanic whites, followed by blacks (35.8 percent), Hispanics (18.5 percent), and Asians (3.5 percent). Females accounted for well over half (59.7 percent) of food stamp recipients. In 2000, 36.9 percent of households receiving food stamps were single-parent households, compared to 7.8 percent of married-couple households.

CHAPTER 5

HEALTH

Health care expenditures by Americans soared from $73.1 billion in 1970, to $245.8 billion in 1980, to $695.6 billion in 1990, and to $1.4 trillion in 2001. From 2001 to 2002 these expenditures have increased 8.7 percent, compared to a 7.4 percent increase in 2000. To examine the rapid escalation of national health care expenditures in another way, per capita spending in the United States was $5,035 in 2001 compared to $2,738 in 1990 and $143 in 1960.

This high rate of growth in health care expenditures, combined with the underperforming economy in much of the new millennium, has resulted in expenditures claiming a bigger piece of the gross domestic product (GDP; the total value of goods and services produced within the United States). More than any other industrialized country in the world, the United States continues to spend more on health care. In 1970, 7.0 percent of the GDP went to health care; by 2000 the percentage had nearly doubled to 13.3 percent. In comparison, Canada and France, the countries with the next highest shares, expended between 9.1 and 9.5 percent, respectively, while Germany and Switzerland expended between 10.6 and 10.7 percent, respectively. (See Table 5.1.)

In 2001 national health expenditures grew 8.7 percent, compared to the 1990 growth rate of 11.0 percent, partly because of lower inflation and partly because of slower growth in health care use. Slower growth in the use of health care and in health care costs are also a result of the rise of health maintenance organizations and managed care, both of which attempt to control costs and profitably deliver health care.

WHERE DOES THE SPENDING GO?

In 2001, 86.5 percent, or over $1.2 trillion, of total health care spending went for personal health care. The remaining 13.5 percent was spent mainly on program administration, government public health activities, research, and buildings.

Of the revenue devoted to personal health care in 2001, about $451.2 billion (32 percent) was spent on hospital care, while physician services accounted for $313.6 billion (22 percent). Physicians influenced other spending, since they usually determine who will be hospitalized, what type and quantity of services the hospital patient will receive, and what type of drugs will be administered. Insurance programs, however, are playing an ever greater role in making these decisions. Retail outlet sales of medical products (13 percent), nursing home and home health care (9 percent), and dentists' services (4.6 percent) accounted for much of the remaining personal health care expenditures in 2001.

While general inflation has played a role in the increase in the cost of health care, health care costs have generally run well ahead of inflation. The average annual percent of change per year in the medical care component of the Consumer Price Index (which measures the rate of inflation) was 4.7 percent in 2002 and 4.6 percent the year before, compared to 3.4 percent per year from 1995 to 2000. In comparison, the overall inflation rate dropped from 4.7 percent in 1990, to 3.4 percent in 2000, to 1.6 percent in 2002.

WHO PAYS FOR IT?

All Americans pay for the nation's health care system—whether directly out of pocket, through health insurance premiums, or indirectly through taxes that help support government payments. In 2001 direct out-of-pocket payments (e.g., the money paid directly to the doctor, dentist, or pharmacy and not later reimbursed by an insurance company) accounted for 16.6 percent of all personal health care expenditures, down significantly from 27.1 percent in 1980. (See Table 5.2.)

Private health insurance companies and the government are the major third-party payers of health

TABLE 5.1

Total health expenditures as a percent of gross domestic product and per capita health expenditures in dollars, selected countries and years, 1960–2000

Country	1960	1970	1980	1990	1995	1996	1997	1998	1999	2000[1]

Health expenditures as a percent of gross domestic product

Country	1960	1970	1980	1990	1995	1996	1997	1998	1999	2000[1]
Australia	4.3	- - -	7.0	7.8	8.2	8.3	8.4	8.5	8.4	8.3
Austria	4.3	5.3	7.6	7.1	8.6	8.7	8.0	8.0	8.1	8.0
Belgium	- - -	4.0	6.4	7.4	8.7	8.8	8.5	8.5	8.7	8.7
Canada	5.4	7.0	7.1	9.0	9.1	8.9	8.9	9.1	9.2	9.1
Czech Republic	- - -	- - -	- - -	5.0	7.3	7.1	7.1	7.1	7.2	7.2
Denmark	- - -	- - -	9.1	8.5	8.2	8.3	8.2	8.4	8.5	8.3
Finland	3.9	5.6	6.4	7.9	7.5	7.7	7.3	6.9	6.9	6.6
France	- - -	- - -	- - -	8.6	9.6	9.6	9.4	9.3	9.4	9.5
Germany	4.8	6.3	8.8	8.7	10.6	10.9	10.7	10.6	10.7	10.6
Greece	- - -	6.1	6.6	7.5	8.9	8.9	8.7	8.7	8.7	8.3
Hungary	- - -	- - -	- - -	- - -	7.5	7.2	7.0	6.9	6.8	6.8
Iceland	3.3	4.9	6.1	7.9	8.2	8.2	8.0	8.3	8.7	8.9
Ireland	3.6	5.1	8.4	6.6	7.2	7.0	6.9	6.8	6.8	6.7
Italy	3.6	5.1	- - -	8.0	7.4	7.5	7.7	7.7	7.8	8.1
Japan	3.0	4.5	6.4	5.9	7.0	7.0	7.2	7.1	7.4	7.8
Korea	- - -	- - -	- - -	4.8	4.7	4.9	5.0	5.1	5.6	5.9
Luxembourg	- - -	3.6	5.9	6.1	6.4	6.4	5.9	5.8	6.0	- - -
Mexico	- - -	- - -	- - -	4.4	5.6	5.3	5.3	5.3	5.4	5.4
Netherlands	- - -	- - -	7.5	8.0	8.4	8.3	8.2	8.1	8.2	8.1
New Zealand	- - -	5.1	5.9	6.9	7.2	7.2	7.5	7.9	7.9	8.0
Norway	2.9	4.4	7.0	7.8	8.0	8.0	7.9	8.6	8.8	7.8
Poland	- - -	- - -	- - -	5.3	6.0	6.4	6.1	6.4	6.2	- - -
Portugal	- - -	2.6	5.6	6.2	8.3	8.5	8.6	8.3	8.4	8.2
Slovak Republic	- - -	- - -	- - -	- - -	- - -	- - -	6.1	5.9	5.8	5.9
Spain	1.5	3.6	5.4	6.6	7.7	7.7	7.6	7.6	7.7	7.7
Sweden	4.5	6.9	9.1	8.5	8.1	8.4	8.1	7.9	- - -	- - -
Switzerland	4.9	5.6	7.6	8.5	10.0	10.4	10.4	10.6	10.7	10.7
Turkey	- - -	2.4	3.3	3.6	3.4	3.9	4.2	4.8	- - -	- - -
United Kingdom	3.9	4.5	5.6	6.0	7.0	7.0	6.8	6.8	7.1	7.3
United States	5.1	7.0	8.8	12.0	13.4	13.3	13.1	13.1	13.2	13.3

Per capita health expenditures[2]

Country	1960	1970	1980	1990	1995	1996	1997	1998	1999	2000[1]
Australia	$ 87	- - -	$ 658	$1,300	$1,765	$1,854	$1,950	$2,058	$2,141	$2,211
Austria	64	$159	662	1,206	1,831	1,940	1,873	1,968	2,061	2,162
Belgium	- - -	130	577	1,245	1,896	1,982	2,013	2,008	2,144	2,269
Canada	109	260	710	1,676	2,114	2,091	2,181	2,285	2,428	2,535
Czech Republic	- - -	- - -	- - -	576	902	917	930	944	972	1,031
Denmark	- - -	- - -	819	1,453	1,882	2,004	2,100	2,241	2,358	2,420
Finland	54	161	509	1,295	1,415	1,487	1,550	1,529	1,605	1,664
France	- - -	- - -	- - -	1,517	1,980	1,997	2,046	2,109	2,226	2,349
Germany	90	223	824	1,600	2,164	2,341	2,465	2,520	2,616	2,748
Greece	- - -	98	348	712	1,131	1,179	1,224	1,307	1,375	1,399
Hungary	- - -	- - -	- - -	- - -	677	671	693	751	787	841
Iceland	50	137	576	1,376	1,823	1,911	1,988	2,204	2,409	2,608
Ireland	36	99	454	777	1,300	1,318	1,526	1,576	1,752	1,953
Italy	48	151	- - -	1,321	1,486	1,566	1,684	1,774	1,882	2,032
Japan	26	130	522	1,083	1,631	1,699	1,831	1,735	1,852	2,012
Korea	- - -	- - -	- - -	355	535	611	657	630	758	893
Luxembourg	- - -	148	605	1,492	2,122	2,192	2,204	2,361	2,613	- - -
Mexico	- - -	- - -	- - -	260	388	381	411	431	452	490
Netherlands	- - -	- - -	668	1,333	1,787	1,818	1,958	2,040	2,172	2,246
New Zealand	- - -	174	458	937	1,244	1,267	1,364	1,450	1,526	1,623
Norway	46	131	632	1,363	1,865	2,026	2,193	2,439	2,550	2,362
Poland	- - -	- - -	- - -	258	420	469	461	543	558	- - -
Portugal	- - -	40	265	611	1,146	1,211	1,360	1,345	1,402	1,441
Slovak Republic	- - -	- - -	- - -	- - -	- - -	- - -	608	641	649	690
Spain	14	83	328	813	1,184	1,238	1,294	1,384	1,469	1,556
Sweden	89	270	850	1,492	1,622	1,716	1,770	1,748	- - -	- - -
Switzerland	136	288	881	1,836	2,555	2,615	2,841	2,952	3,080	3,222
Turkey	- - -	23	75	171	190	234	272	303	- - -	- - -
United Kingdom	74	144	444	972	1,315	1,422	1,481	1,527	1,666	1,763
United States	143	348	1,067	2,738	3,688	3,847	4,007	4,178	4,392	4,672

Note: - - - Data not available.
[1]Preliminary figures.
[2]Per capita health expenditures for each country have been adjusted to U.S. dollars using gross domestic product purchasing power parities for each year.

SOURCE: V.M. Freid, K. Prager, A.P. MacKay, H. Xia, "Table 127. "Table 111. Total health expenditures as a percent of gross domestic product and per capita health expenditures in dollars: Selected countries and years, 1960–2000," in *Health, United States, 2003, with Chartbook on Trends in the Health of Americans,* Centers for Disease Control and Prevention, National Center for Health Statistics, Hyattsville, MD, September 2003

TABLE 5.2

Personal health care expenditures, according to type of expenditure and source of funds, selected years 1960–2001

Type of personal health care expenditures and source of funds	1960	1970	1980	1990	1995	1998	1999	2000	2001
					Amount				
Per capita	$ 126	$ 301	$ 931	$2,398	$3,233	$ 3,668	$3,833	$4,057	$4,370
					Amount in billions				
All personal health care expenditures[1]	$ 23.4	$ 63.2	$ 214.6	$ 609.4	$ 865.7	$ 1,009.4	$1,064.6	$1,137.6	$1,236.4
					Percent distribution				
All sources of funds	100.0	100.0	100.0	100.0	100.0	100.0	100.0	100.0	100.0
Out-of-pocket payments	55.2	39.7	27.1	22.5	16.9	17.4	17.3	17.1	16.6
Private health insurance	21.4	22.3	28.3	33.4	33.3	33.8	34.4	34.9	35.4
Other private funds	2.0	2.8	4.3	5.0	5.1	5.4	5.3	4.9	4.6
Government	21.4	35.2	40.3	39.0	44.7	43.4	43.0	43.0	43.4
Federal	8.7	22.9	29.3	28.6	34.2	33.2	32.6	32.6	32.9
State and local	12.6	12.3	11.1	10.5	10.5	10.2	10.3	10.4	10.6
					Amount in billions				
Hospital care expenditures[2]	$ 9.2	$ 27.6	$ 101.5	$ 253.9	$ 343.6	$ 378.4	$ 393.7	$ 416.5	$ 451.2
					Percent distribution				
All sources of funds	100.0	100.0	100.0	100.0	100.0	100.0	100.0	100.0	100.0
Out-of-pocket payments	20.8	9.1	5.2	4.4	3.0	3.1	3.2	3.2	3.1
Private health insurance	35.8	32.6	35.6	38.3	32.3	31.9	32.7	33.4	33.7
Other private funds	1.2	3.3	4.9	4.1	4.3	5.2	5.2	5.3	4.9
Government[3]	42.2	55.1	54.3	53.2	60.3	59.7	58.9	58.1	58.3
Medicaid[4]	…	9.6	10.4	10.9	15.9	16.1	16.8	16.8	17.1
Medicare	…	19.4	26.0	26.7	31.4	32.1	31.0	30.2	29.9
					Amount in billions				
Physician services expenditures	$ 5.4	$ 14.0	$ 47.1	$ 157.5	$ 220.5	$ 256.8	$ 270.2	$ 288.8	$ 313.6
					Percent distribution				
All sources of funds	100.0	100.0	100.0	100.0	100.0	100.0	100.0	100.0	100.0
Out-of-pocket payments	61.6	46.1	30.2	19.3	11.9	12.0	11.6	11.6	11.2
Private health insurance	29.8	30.1	35.3	43.0	48.6	47.8	47.2	47.6	48.1
Other private funds	1.4	1.6	3.9	7.2	8.0	8.6	8.5	7.5	7.1
Government[3]	7.2	22.2	30.5	30.6	31.5	31.7	32.7	33.3	33.6
Medicaid[4]	…	4.6	5.2	4.5	6.7	6.5	6.5	6.6	6.8
Medicare	…	11.8	17.4	19.1	18.9	19.9	20.4	20.6	20.4
					Amount in billions				
Nursing home expenditures[5]	$ 0.8	$ 4.2	$ 17.7	$ 52.7	$ 74.6	$ 89.1	$ 89.6	$ 93.8	$ 98.9
					Percent distribution				
All sources of funds	100.0	100.0	100.0	100.0	100.0	100.0	100.0	100.0	100.0
Out-of-pocket payments	77.9	53.6	40.0	37.5	26.7	28.0	28.3	27.9	27.2
Private health insurance	0.0	0.2	1.2	5.8	7.5	8.3	8.4	7.8	7.6
Other private funds	6.3	4.9	4.5	7.5	6.4	5.1	5.1	4.4	3.7
Government[3]	15.7	41.2	54.2	49.2	59.5	58.7	58.2	59.9	61.5
Medicaid[4]	…	22.3	50.2	43.9	47.5	45.0	46.7	47.6	47.5
Medicare	…	3.4	1.7	3.2	9.7	11.5	9.3	10.1	11.7

expenditures. (The patient is the first party and the doctor, pharmacist, or hospital is the second party.) The federal, state, and local governments (43.4 percent), private health insurance (35.4 percent), and other private sources (4.6 percent), such as charities and philanthropy, paid for over 83 percent of the nation's personal health care bill in 2001. (See Table 5.2.)

Most observers believe that the major reason medical costs have increased so rapidly is the high proportion paid by third parties. They believe that patients are much less apt to be thrifty, discerning consumers if their employer or the government is paying the bills. In 2001 third-party sources paid $437.6 billion, or 96.9 percent, of the cost of hospital bills, 88.8 percent ($279 billion) of doctors' bills, 72.8 percent ($72 billion) of nursing home

costs, and 69.3 percent ($97 billion) of prescription drug expenditures. (See Table 5.2.)

Medicare and Medicaid

Medicare is the largest federal program designed to help persons age 65 years and older with their medical bills. In 2001 it paid for 29.9 percent ($135.3 billion) of the nation's hospital care expenditures, 20.4 percent (62.7 billion) of physician services expenditures, and 11.7 percent (11.8 billion) of nursing home expenditures. From 1990 to 2001 Medicare expenditures in hospital care, physician services, and nursing home care more than doubled from $99.6 billion to $210.5 billion. (See Table 5.2.)

In 2001 Medicaid, a health insurance program for certain low-income and needy individuals, covered 17.1

TABLE 5.2

Personal health care expenditures, according to type of expenditure and source of funds, selected years 1960–2001 [CONTINUED]

Type of personal health care expenditures and source of funds	1960	1970	1980	1990	1995	1998	1999	2000	2001
					Amount in billions				
Prescription drug expenditures	$ 2.7	$ 5.5	$ 12.0	$ 40.3	$ 60.8	$ 87.3	$ 104.4	$ 121.5	$ 140.6
					Percent distribution				
All sources of funds	100.0	100.0	100.0	100.0	100.0	100.0	100.0	100.0	100.0
Out-of-pocket payments	96.0	82.4	69.4	59.1	42.7	34.9	32.9	31.4	30.7
Private health insurance	1.3	8.8	16.7	24.4	37.1	43.9	45.8	46.6	47.4
Other private funds	0.0	0.0	0.0	0.0	0.0	0.0	0.0	0.0	0.0
Government[3]	2.7	8.8	13.9	16.6	20.1	21.1	21.3	22.0	21.9
Medicaid[4]	...	7.6	11.7	12.6	16.0	16.5	16.5	17.1	17.1
Medicare	...	0.0	0.0	0.5	1.3	2.0	2.0	1.9	1.7
					Amount in billions				
All other personal health care expenditures[6]	$ 5.3	$ 11.9	$ 36.3	$ 104.9	$ 166.2	$ 197.9	$ 206.6	$ 216.9	$ 232.1
					Percent distribution				
All sources of funds	100.0	100.0	100.0	100.0	100.0	100.0	100.0	100.0	100.0
Out-of-pocket payments	84.2	78.6	64.3	49.6	38.3	39.0	39.1	38.6	37.4
Private health insurance	1.6	3.3	15.5	24.7	25.1	26.3	26.2	25.9	25.8
Other private funds	4.2	3.6	4.3	4.7	4.3	4.3	4.2	3.9	3.7
Government[3]	10.1	14.5	16.0	20.9	32.3	30.4	30.5	31.5	33.1
Medicaid[4]	...	3.3	3.9	6.5	12.5	14.0	14.9	15.6	16.8
Medicare	...	1.1	3.8	7.1	13.3	10.0	9.0	9.0	9.3

Note: . . . Category not applicable.

[1]Includes all expenditures for specified health services and supplies other than expenses for program administration, net cost of private health insurance, and government public health activities.

[2]Includes expenditures for hospital-based nursing home care and home health agency care.

[3]Includes other government expenditures for these health care services, for example, Medicaid State Children's Health Insurance Program (SCHIP) expansion and SCHIP, care funded by the Department of Veterans Affairs, and State and locally financed subsidies to hospitals.

[4]Excludes Medicaid SCHIP expansion and SCHIP.

[5]Includes expenditures for care in freestanding nursing homes. Expenditures for care in facility-based nursing homes are included with hospital care.

[6]Includes expenditures for dental services, other professional services, home health care, nonprescription drugs and other medical nondurables, vision products and other medical durables, and other personal health care, not shown separately.

SOURCE: V.M. Freid, K. Prager, A.P. MacKay, H. Xia, "Table 116. Personal health care expenditures, according to type of expenditure and source of funds: United States, selected years 1960–2001," in *Health, United States, 2003, with Chartbook on Trends in the Health of Americans,* Centers for Disease Control and Prevention, National Center for Health Statistics, Hyattsville, MD, September 2003

percent ($76.7 billion) of all hospital care expenditures, 6.8 percent ($219.5 billion) of all physician services expenditures, 47.5 percent ($46.8 billion) of all nursing home expenditures, and 17.1 percent ($23.9 billion) of all prescription drug expenditures. Federal, state, and local governments jointly fund this program, which is heavily weighted toward institutional services. (See Table 5.2.)

INSURANCE COVERAGE

Over the past 20 years, Americans have changed the way they insure themselves. In 1965 almost all insured people were covered either by insurance companies or the Federal Employee Program. While these two categories still remain the major private insurers, an increasing number of Americans are being covered by self-insured plans in which a large company, government authority, or perhaps a school district insures itself. The institution may administer the plan itself or hire a company to do it. In addition, a growing number of companies are turning to health maintenance organizations (HMOs) in an attempt to control increasing medical costs.

Between 1995 and 2001 the proportion of the population under 65 years of age with private health insurance remained stable, between 71 percent and 73 percent, after declining from 77 percent in 1984. In 2001 more than 90 percent of private coverage was received through a past or present employer or union. Changes in Medicaid eligibility rules increased the proportion of the population covered by Medicaid from 6.7 percent in 1984 to 10.3 percent in 2001. (See Table 5.3.) The proportion of the population under 65 years of age without any health care coverage increased from 14.3 percent in 1984 to 16.2 percent in 2001. (See Table 5.4.)

In 2001, 90 percent of people over 65 years of age who had private health insurance were also covered by Medicare. Of people 65 to 74 years of age in 2001, 17.4 percent were covered by Medicare alone, and of those over age 75, 18.4 percent were covered by Medicare alone. (See Table 5.5.)

Statistics released by the Department of Health and Human Services from 1984 to 2001 show an increase in the number of Americans under the age of 65 covered by

TABLE 5.3

Medicaid coverage among persons under 65 years of age, according to selected characteristics, selected years 1984–2001

Characteristic	1984	1989	1995	1996	1997	1998	1999	2000	2001
					Number in millions				
Total[1]	14.0	15.4	26.6	25.8	22.9	21.1	21.9	22.9	25.2
					Percent of population				
Total, age adjusted[1,2]	6.7	7.1	11.3	10.9	9.6	8.8	9.0	9.4	10.3
Total, crude[2]	6.8	7.2	11.5	11.1	9.7	8.9	9.1	9.5	10.4
Age									
Under 18 years	11.9	12.6	21.5	20.7	18.4	17.1	18.1	19.4	21.2
Under 6 years	15.5	15.7	29.3	28.2	24.7	22.4	23.5	24.3	25.8
6–17 years	10.1	10.9	17.4	16.9	15.2	14.5	15.5	17.0	19.0
18–44 years	5.1	5.2	7.8	7.6	6.6	5.8	5.7	5.6	6.3
18–24 years	6.4	6.8	10.4	9.7	8.8	8.0	8.1	8.1	8.4
25–34 years	5.3	5.2	8.2	7.8	6.8	5.7	5.7	5.5	6.2
35–44 years	3.5	4.0	5.9	6.2	5.2	4.6	4.3	4.3	5.1
45–64 years	3.4	4.3	5.6	5.3	4.6	4.5	4.4	4.5	4.7
45–54 years	3.2	3.8	5.1	4.9	4.0	4.1	3.9	4.2	4.4
55–64 years	3.6	4.9	6.4	5.9	5.6	5.0	5.3	4.9	5.2
Sex[2]									
Male	5.2	5.6	9.2	8.9	8.1	7.5	7.7	8.0	8.9
Female	8.0	8.6	13.3	12.8	11.0	10.1	10.4	10.8	11.6
Race[2,3]									
White only	4.6	5.1	8.8	8.7	7.5	6.7	6.9	7.2	8.1
Black or African American only	18.9	17.8	26.0	23.0	20.5	19.6	18.7	19.4	20.4
American Indian and Alaska Native only	#	#	#	#	#	#	41.3	44.2	15.5
Asian only	9.1	11.3	10.7	*11.5	9.4	6.7	8.4	7.8	8.8
Native Hawaiian and Other Pacific Islander only	---	---	---	---	---	---	*	*	*
2 or more races	---	---	---	---	---	---	15.8	15.6	14.6
Hispanic origin and race[2,3]									
Hispanic or Latino	12.2	12.7	19.8	18.5	16.0	14.1	14.1	14.2	16.0
Mexican	11.1	11.5	18.8	17.6	15.3	12.6	12.4	12.5	14.6
Puerto Rican	28.6	26.9	31.1	31.3	28.9	24.5	27.0	27.6	28.5
Cuban	4.8	7.8	13.8	*13.1	8.2	*9.1	8.3	9.7	12.2
Other Hispanic or Latino	7.4	10.4	16.9	15.0	13.9	13.9	13.8	14.1	15.0
Not Hispanic or Latino	6.2	6.6	10.2	9.7	8.7	8.0	8.2	8.6	9.3
White only	3.7	4.2	7.1	7.0	6.2	5.7	6.0	6.3	7.0
Black or African American only	19.1	17.8	25.6	22.7	20.3	19.4	18.7	19.3	20.3
Age and percent of poverty level[4]									
All ages:[2]									
Below 100 percent	30.5	35.3	44.7	42.9	38.8	37.9	36.8	37.2	39.0
100–149 percent	7.5	11.0	18.0	17.4	17.5	16.0	18.6	20.3	23.5
150–199 percent	3.1	5.0	7.9	8.0	7.4	7.2	9.8	10.8	13.3
200 percent or more	0.6	1.1	1.8	1.7	1.7	1.8	2.0	2.3	2.6
Under 18 years:									
Below 100 percent	43.1	47.8	66.0	65.2	59.7	58.7	59.9	60.9	64.3
100–149 percent	9.0	12.3	27.2	26.6	30.2	25.9	33.5	37.1	41.4
150–199 percent	4.4	6.1	13.1	12.2	12.2	12.8	18.0	21.5	26.5
200 percent or more	0.8	1.6	3.3	2.8	2.9	3.2	3.7	4.7	5.3

Medicaid and private health insurance from 155.8 million to 188.3 million. However, for the same period the percentage of people under the age of 65 with health care declined from 83.8 percent to 81.8 percent, respectively. More than 83 percent of whites under the age of 65 were covered by some type of health insurance plan in 2001, compared to 77.9 percent of blacks and 63.6 percent of Hispanics.

Lack of Health Care Coverage

In 2002, 15.2 percent (43.5 million) of people in the United States were without health insurance coverage, up from 14.6 percent in 2001, an increase of 2.3 million people. (The percentages shown by type of health insurance coverage are not mutually exclusive; persons can be cov-ered by more than one type of health insurance.) Despite programs such as Medicaid and Medicare, 30.4 percent of those below the poverty level had no health insurance in 2002. Of those with a household income of less than $25,000, 23.5 percent (62.9 million) were uninsured. People with low incomes, young people, blacks, and persons of Hispanic origin were more likely not to have health insurance. Males were more likely than females to be uninsured. (See Table 5.6.)

Among all age groups, young adults between 18 and 24 were less likely than other age groups to have health insurance in 2001 and 2002. In 2002, 29.6 percent of this age group lacked coverage. For those in poverty, 48.6 percent of adults between 25 and 34 lacked health insurance

TABLE 5.3

Medicaid coverage among persons under 65 years of age, according to selected characteristics, selected years 1984–2001 [CONTINUED]

Characteristic	1984	1989	1995	1996	1997[1]	1998	1999	2000	2001
Geographic region[2]					Percent of population				
Northeast	8.5	6.8	11.7	11.5	11.2	9.8	10.1	10.5	10.8
Midwest	7.2	7.5	10.3	8.7	8.2	7.5	7.3	7.9	9.0
South	5.0	6.4	11.1	11.1	8.6	8.6	8.9	9.4	10.7
West	6.9	8.2	12.4	12.4	11.4	9.7	10.3	10.2	10.6
Location of residence[2]									
Within MSA[5]	7.1	7.0	11.1	10.4	9.5	8.5	8.4	8.8	9.8
Outside MSA[5]	5.9	7.8	12.0	12.7	9.9	9.8	11.5	11.9	12.4

[1]Includes all other races not shown separately and unknown poverty level.
[2]Estimates are for persons under 65 years of age and are age adjusted to the year 2000 standard using three age groups: under 18 years, 18–44 years, and 45–64 years.
[3]The race groups, white, black, American Indian and Alaska Native (AI/AN), Asian, Native Hawaiian and Other Pacific Islander, and 2 or more races, include persons of Hispanic and non-Hispanic origin. Persons of Hispanic origin may be of any race. Starting with data year 1999 race-specific estimates are tabulated according to 1997 Standards for Federal data on Race and Ethnicity and are not strictly comparable with estimates for earlier years. The five single race categories plus multiple race categories shown in the table conform to 1997 Standards. The 1999 and later race-specific estimates are for persons who reported only one racial group; the category "2 or more races" includes persons who reported more than one racial group. Prior to data year 1999, data were tabulated according to 1977 Standards with four racial groups and the category "Asian only" included Native Hawaiian and Other Pacific Islander. Estimates for single race categories prior to 1999 included persons who reported one race or, if they reported more than one race, identified one race as best representing their race.
[4]Missing family income data were imputed for 15–17 percent of the sample under 65 years of age in 1994–96. Percent of poverty level was unknown for 19 percent of sample persons under 65 in 1997, 24 percent in 1998, 27 percent in 1999, and 26 percent in 2000 and 2001.
[5]MSA is metropolitan statistical area.
Notes: # Estimates calculated upon request.
*Estimates are considered unreliable. Data preceded by an asterisk have a relative standard error of 20–30 percent. Data not shown have a relative standard error of greater than 30 percent.
- - - Data not available.
Medicaid includes other public assistance through 1996. Starting in 1997 includes state-sponsored health plans. Starting in 1999 includes State Children's Health Insurance Program (SCHIP). In 2001, 7.9 percent were covered by Medicaid, 1.2 percent by state-sponsored health plans, and 1.2 percent by SCHIP.

SOURCE: V.M. Freid, K. Prager, A.P. MacKay, H. Xia, "Table 128. Medicaid coverage among persons under 65 years of age, according to selected characteristics: United States, selected years 1984–2001," in *Health, United States, 2003, with Chartbook on Trends in the Health of Americans,* Centers for Disease Control and Prevention, National Center for Health Statistics, Hyattsville, MD, September 2003

in 2002. Because of Medicare, the elderly were most likely to be covered—only 0.8 percent lacked coverage. However, that rate was higher among the poor elderly, 1.9 percent of whom lacked any type of health care coverage. Almost 11.6 percent of uninsured children under 18 years of age lacked health insurance, but among poor children the rate of uninsured was 20.1 percent.

In 2002, 32.4 percent of all Hispanics and over two-fifths of poor Hispanics (42.8 percent) lacked health insurance. Some 20.2 percent of blacks lacked health insurance. The rate among poor blacks was slightly higher, at 26.4 percent. Among whites in 2002, 14.2 percent had no health coverage, but among poor whites that rate more than doubled to 31.4 percent.

Noncoverage rates fall as household income rises. In 2002 the percentage of persons without health insurance ranged from 8.2 percent among those in households with incomes of $75,000 or more to 19.3 percent among those in households with incomes between $25,000 and $49,999. Nearly 12 percent of those earning $50,000 to $74,999 were not covered.

Geographically, the highest rates for persons under 65 years of age without health insurance in 2001 occurred in the West. Texas led the nation with 25.9 percent of its population without health insurance, followed by New Mexico (23.9 percent), Louisiana (21.7 percent), and Cal-

ifornia (21.3 percent). Iowa had the lowest rate of uninsured at 8.7 percent, followed by Wisconsin and Minnesota at 8.8 percent, Rhode Island at 9.0 percent, and Massachusetts at 9.3 percent. (See Table 5.7.)

HEALTH MAINTENANCE ORGANIZATIONS

HMOs are group practices organized to provide complete coverage for subscribers' health needs at preestablished prices. The number of HMOs more than tripled from 174 in 1976, to 652 in 1997, then dropped to 500 in 2002. (See Table 5.8.)

As an alternative to traditional health insurance coverage, many major companies have turned to HMOs in an attempt to lower health-coverage costs. While this has increased the number of people using HMOs, it has also meant that HMOs can no longer be as selective in their membership. This has exposed HMOs to higher-risk individuals who in general would otherwise be served by traditional health insurance companies. This wider mix of clients has made it more difficult for many HMOs to be profitable.

The number of people enrolled in HMOs increased dramatically from 6 million in 1976 to 76.1 million or 26.4 percent of the U.S. population in 2002. HMOs are most popular in the West (the home of Kaiser Permanente, the largest nonprofit HMO), where 38.2 percent of all

TABLE 5.4

People without health insurance coverage by selected characteristics, selected years 1984–2001

Characteristic	1984	1989	1995	1996	1997	1998	1999	2000	2001
					Number in millions				
Total[1]	29.8	33.4	37.1	38.6	41.0	39.2	38.5	40.5	39.2
					Percent of population				
Total, age adjusted[1,2]	14.3	15.3	15.9	16.5	17.4	16.5	16.1	16.8	16.2
Total, crude[2]	14.5	15.6	16.1	16.6	17.5	16.6	16.1	16.8	16.1
Age									
Under 18 years	13.9	14.7	13.4	13.2	14.0	12.7	11.9	12.4	11.0
Under 6 years	14.9	15.1	11.8	11.7	12.5	11.5	11.0	11.7	9.7
6–17 years	13.4	14.5	14.3	13.9	14.7	13.3	12.3	12.8	11.7
18–44 years	17.1	18.4	20.4	21.1	22.4	21.4	21.0	22.0	21.7
18–24 years	25.0	27.1	28.0	29.3	30.1	29.0	27.4	29.7	29.3
25–34 years	16.2	18.3	21.1	22.4	23.8	22.2	22.1	22.7	22.3
35–44 years	11.2	12.3	15.1	15.2	16.7	16.4	16.3	16.8	16.7
45–64 years	9.6	10.5	10.9	12.1	12.4	12.2	12.2	12.7	12.3
45–54 years	10.5	11.0	11.6	12.4	12.8	12.6	12.8	12.8	13.0
55–64 years	8.7	10.0	9.9	11.6	11.8	11.4	11.4	12.5	11.0
Sex[2]									
Male	15.0	16.4	17.2	17.8	18.5	17.5	17.2	17.8	17.2
Female	13.6	14.3	14.6	15.2	16.2	15.5	15.0	15.8	15.1
Race[2,3]									
White only	13.4	14.2	15.3	15.8	16.3	15.2	14.6	15.2	14.7
Black or African American only	20.0	21.4	18.2	19.6	20.2	20.7	19.5	20.0	19.3
American Indian and Alaska Native only	#	#	#	#	#	#	38.3	38.2	33.4
Asian only	18.0	18.5	18.2	19.0	19.3	18.1	16.4	17.3	17.1
Native Hawaiian and Other Pacific Islander only	---	---	---	---	---	---	*	*	*
2 or more races	---	---	---	---	---	---	16.8	18.4	18.6
Hispanic origin and race[2,3]									
Hispanic or Latino	29.1	32.4	31.5	32.4	34.3	34.0	33.9	35.4	34.8
Mexican	33.2	38.8	36.2	37.5	39.2	40.0	38.0	39.9	39.0
Puerto Rican	18.1	23.3	18.3	15.1	19.4	19.4	19.8	16.4	16.0
Cuban	21.6	20.9	22.1	18.8	20.5	18.4	19.7	25.2	19.2
Other Hispanic or Latino	27.5	25.2	29.7	30.5	32.9	31.1	30.8	32.7	33.1
Not Hispanic or Latino	13.0	13.5	14.0	14.5	15.1	14.1	13.5	14.1	13.4
White only	11.8	11.9	12.9	13.3	13.7	12.5	12.1	12.5	11.9
Black or African American only	19.7	21.3	18.1	19.5	20.1	20.7	19.4	20.0	19.2
Age and percent of poverty level[4]									
All ages:[2]									
Below 100 percent	34.7	35.8	31.7	34.5	34.4	34.6	34.4	34.2	33.3
100–149 percent	27.0	31.3	31.7	33.3	36.1	36.5	35.8	36.5	32.4
150–199 percent	17.4	21.8	24.0	24.3	25.9	26.7	27.7	27.3	26.4
200 percent or more	5.8	6.8	8.6	8.6	8.8	8.0	7.7	8.7	8.4
Under 18 years:									
Below 100 percent	28.9	31.6	20.0	21.0	22.4	21.5	21.6	20.4	19.8
100–149 percent	22.8	26.1	24.8	25.0	26.1	28.0	24.9	25.6	18.5
150–199 percent	12.7	15.8	18.0	16.0	19.7	17.3	18.8	16.8	16.1
200 percent or more	4.2	4.4	6.4	6.1	6.1	5.0	4.4	5.5	4.5

people are enrolled in an HMO. They are least preferred in the South (19.8 percent) and Midwest (20.6 percent). (See Table 5.8.)

HOSPITAL CARE

Responses to Rising Hospital Costs

In the mid-1970s growth in health care spending greatly exceeded growth in the overall economy. This led to the first cost-containment effort focused on health care costs. In 1977 the government asked hospitals to voluntarily control rising costs. This voluntary effort met with initial success in controlling hospital costs, and growth rates from 1977 through 1979 were lower than in the mid-1970s. However, by 1980 hospital costs were again grow-

ing rapidly, and economists predicted the exhaustion of Medicare's Hospital Insurance Fund by the early 1990s.

In response, Congress passed several provisions in the Tax Equity and Fiscal Responsibility Act of 1982 (PL 97-248) intended to reduce the rate of increase per case that Medicare paid to hospitals. Hospitals were to be paid on a per-case rather than per-day basis. To implement this, Congress passed the preadmission payment system in 1983, which established average costs per case for 467 medical procedures for which Medicare would pay. In addition to Medicare, other third-party payers have made changes to control costs, such as preadmission review and mandatory second opinions. Also, to keep down costs, insurance companies, through managed care, negotiate

TABLE 5.4

People without health insurance coverage by selected characteristics, selected years 1984–2001 [CONTINUED]

Characteristic	1984	1989	1995	1996	1997	1998	1999	2000	2001
					Percent of population				
Geographic region[2]									
Northeast	11.1	10.5	12.1	12.2	13.1	11.9	11.5	12.3	11.7
South	17.4	19.4	19.2	20.0	20.7	20.0	19.8	20.4	20.0
West	17.8	18.4	17.7	18.6	20.4	19.9	18.6	20.2	18.6
Location of residence[2]									
Within MSA[5]	13.3	14.9	15.2	15.6	16.7	15.8	15.3	16.3	15.6
Outside MSA[5]	16.4	16.9	18.7	19.7	19.9	19.2	18.9	18.8	18.5

[1]Includes all other races not shown separately and unknown poverty level.
[2]Estimates are for persons under 65 years of age and are age adjusted to the year 2000 standard using three age groups: under 18 years, 18–44 years, and 45–64 years.
[3]The race groups, white, black, American Indian and Alaska Native (AI/AN), Asian, Native Hawaiian and Other Pacific Islander, and 2 or more races, include persons of Hispanic and non-Hispanic origin. Persons of Hispanic origin may be of any race. Starting with data year 1999 race-specific estimates are tabulated according to 1997 Standards for Federal data on Race and Ethnicity and are not strictly comparable with estimates for earlier years. The five single race categories plus multiple race categories shown in the table conform to 1997 Standards. The 1999 and later race-specific estimates are for persons who reported only one racial group; the category "2 or more races" includes persons who reported more than one racial group. Prior to data year 1999, data were tabulated according to 1977 Standards with four racial groups and the category "Asian only" included Native Hawaiian and Other Pacific Islander. Estimates for single race categories prior to 1999 included persons who reported one race or, if they reported more than one race, identified one race as best representing their race.
[4]Missing family income data were imputed for 15–17 percent of the sample under 65 years of age in 1994–96. Percent of poverty level was unknown for 19 percent of sample persons under 65 in 1997, 24 percent in 1998, 27 percent in 1999, and 26 percent in 2000 and 2001.
[5]MSA is metropolitan statistical area.
Notes: #Estimates calculated upon request.
* Estimates are considered unreliable. Data not shown have a relative standard error of greater than 30 percent.
- - - Data not available.
Persons not covered by private insurance, Medicaid, State Children's Health Insurance Program (SCHIP), public assistance (through 1996), state-sponsored or other government-sponsored health plans (starting in 1997), Medicare, or military plans are included.

SOURCE: V.M. Fried, K. Prager, A.P. MacKay, H. Xia, "Table 129. No health coverage among persons under 65 years of age, according to selected characteristics: United States, selected years 1984–2001," in *Health, United States, 2003, with Chartbook on Trends in the Health of Americans*, Centers for Disease Control and Prevention, National Center for Health Statistics, Hyattsville, MD, September 2003

with hospitals and doctors on how much the insurance companies will pay for services.

Uncompensated Care

Rising costs have forced some people to forgo insurance coverage. People who are uninsured frequently rely on hospitals for their primary care and often do not seek care until their illnesses require hospitalization. In many cases, these persons cannot afford to pay their hospital bills, resulting in hospitals delivering care for which they are not compensated (paid). Uncompensated care is a concern for hospitals because revenues must cover expenses so that facilities can maintain operations. Hospitals set charges, such as room rates and operating room fees, anticipating that a certain portion of billed amounts will not be paid.

Delivery of Care

The cost-containment efforts of the federal government and insurance companies have changed the methods of health care. Preadmission testing in outpatient departments and physicians' offices has replaced early admission to the hospital and reduced the length of hospital stays. The delivery of hospital care has shifted from more costly inpatient care to less costly outpatient care. Medical procedures that were once performed on an inpatient basis are now being done either in a doctor's office or outpatient departments located in hospitals, thus not requiring the individual to spend the night.

In 1980, 16.3 percent of surgeries in community hospitals were done on an outpatient basis; by 2001 this proportion had risen to 63.0 percent. Between 1975 and 2001, the number of inpatient admissions to all hospitals fell from 36.1 million to 35.6 million. During the same time period, outpatient visits in all hospitals more than doubled, from 245.8 million to 612.2 million.

Technological Advances

Since 1980 technological advances have allowed more patients to be treated on an outpatient basis. Less invasive techniques (often nonsurgical treatments) have made less traumatic treatments possible so that patients are able to return home sooner. For example, extracorporeal shock wave lithotripsy is a noninvasive procedure that pulverizes kidney stones, eliminating the need for surgery. Magnetic resonance imaging machines allow diagnosis without surgery. New anesthetics wear off more quickly, allowing surgery patients to go home the same day. On the other hand, new technology contributes to higher costs for outpatient care.

Other Changes

Hospitals have reduced the number of beds to accommodate the lower number of admissions and shorter lengths of stay. From 1975 to 2001 the number of beds for use in all hospitals fell 33 percent from 1,465,828 to 987,440. However, these reductions still have not kept up with reduced inpatient use. In 1975 an average of 76.7

TABLE 5.5

Health insurance coverage for persons 65 years of age and over, by type of coverage and selected characteristics, selected years 1989–2001

Characteristic	Private insurance[1]						Private insurance obtained through workplace[1,2]					
	1989	1995	1998	1999	2000	2001	1989	1995	1998	1999	2000	2001
						Number in millions						
Total[3]	22.4	23.5	21.5	20.8	20.6	20.6	11.2	12.4	12.0	11.3	11.7	11.9
						Percent of population						
Total, age adjusted[3,4]	76.1	74.5	66.7	64.0	63.1	62.7	37.3	38.9	37.1	34.6	35.6	36.0
Total, crude[3]	76.5	74.6	66.7	64.1	63.1	62.7	38.4	39.5	37.3	34.9	35.8	36.1
Age												
65–74 years	78.2	75.1	66.6	64.5	62.7	63.0	43.7	43.3	40.4	38.6	39.4	39.7
75 years and over	73.9	73.9	66.8	63.5	63.6	62.4	30.2	34.1	33.5	30.3	31.4	31.9
75–84 years	75.9	75.7	68.1	64.6	64.6	63.9	32.0	36.0	35.7	32.3	33.1	33.3
85 years and over	65.5	67.3	61.8	59.6	59.5	57.0	22.8	27.3	25.3	23.2	24.7	26.7
Sex[4]												
Male	77.4	76.6	68.5	64.5	64.3	63.8	42.1	43.3	41.4	38.6	39.7	40.1
Female	75.4	73.2	65.5	63.8	62.2	61.9	34.0	35.8	34.0	31.8	32.5	33.0
Race[4,5]												
White only	79.8	78.3	70.3	67.6	66.9	66.4	38.7	40.4	38.5	35.8	37.2	37.4
Black or African American only	42.3	40.3	40.3	39.9	35.6	37.6	23.7	24.6	27.4	27.5	25.0	27.9
American Indian and Alaska Native only	*	*	*37.9	*35.2	*	*31.8	*	*	*	*33.3	*	*
Asian only	#	#	40.8	33.1	43.3	40.9	#	#	28.3	21.4	23.2	23.5
Native Hawaiian and Other Pacific Islander only	---	---	---	*	*	*	---	---	---	*	*	*
2 or more races	---	---	---	56.0	63.1	50.0	---	---	---	*26.9	48.4	32.3
Hispanic origin and race[4,5]												
Hispanic or Latino	42.3	39.8	29.1	26.9	23.4	24.0	22.2	18.4	17.9	17.4	15.1	16.2
Mexican	33.5	31.8	26.5	27.4	20.3	24.8	20.2	15.9	17.5	16.9	12.8	16.8
Not Hispanic or Latino	77.2	76.2	68.7	66.2	65.5	65.2	37.7	39.9	38.2	35.7	36.8	37.2
White only	81.0	80.3	72.3	69.7	69.1	68.8	39.3	41.7	39.5	36.8	38.3	38.6
Black or African American only	42.4	40.1	40.5	40.1	35.6	37.6	23.7	24.4	27.6	27.6	25.0	28.0
Percent of poverty level[4,6]												
Below 100 percent	46.1	40.0	32.8	28.3	29.9	27.8	11.6	13.8	10.2	8.8	10.8	11.9
100–149 percent	67.7	67.6	48.7	44.6	44.2	45.7	22.2	26.7	19.3	14.7	16.1	20.6
150–199 percent	81.1	76.0	65.6	62.0	63.1	63.1	39.0	38.7	31.4	27.2	29.8	28.1
200 percent or more	85.5	85.3	78.6	75.5	74.4	74.2	49.4	49.3	49.8	45.4	47.3	46.8
Geographic region[4]												
Northeast	76.1	76.2	72.0	66.0	66.7	66.1	42.2	44.6	43.9	39.7	38.7	38.8
Midwest	81.9	82.3	78.3	77.0	75.9	72.4	40.0	44.7	41.6	38.5	41.2	40.5
South	73.0	70.7	62.0	60.2	58.4	60.2	32.0	33.7	33.3	31.0	31.9	34.1
West	74.7	68.8	54.9	51.5	51.5	51.7	37.1	33.6	30.9	30.6	31.7	30.6
Location of residence[4]												
Within MSA[7]	76.6	74.7	65.5	62.8	61.4	61.2	39.9	40.9	38.7	36.0	36.9	36.5
Outside MSA[7]	74.8	73.9	70.6	68.2	68.5	68.1	30.2	32.2	31.8	30.0	31.5	34.1

percent of these beds were filled; in 2001 this proportion had dropped to 66.7 percent.

Hospitals have been forced to run their operations in a more competitive manner, seeking cost-saving measures, advertising, and specializing in certain services. Less competitive hospitals have closed, merged, or been acquired by other hospitals. Between 1975 and 2001 the number of hospitals dropped from 7,156 to 5,801, a decline of 18.5 percent.

HOSPITAL STAYS. Because of these changes, the number of admissions, the days of care, and the length of stay in the nation's hospitals have been dropping. However, from 1999 to 2001 the rate of hospital discharges per 1,000 population increased from 119.7 to 122.0, which is still lower than it was at 124.3 in 1997. The average stay decreased, down from 4.8 days in 1997 to 4.5 days in 2001.

Blacks and the poor were more likely to be admitted to a hospital and more likely to stay longer. In 2001 hospital stays among blacks averaged 5.0 days, compared to 4.0 days for both whites and Hispanics. Average hospital stays for the poor (5.1 days) and the near poor (4.7 days) were markedly longer than for the nonpoor (3.7 days). In 2001 the average hospital stay for the insured (4.2 days) was the same as for the uninsured (4.2 days).

VISITING THE DOCTOR

Americans generally visit the doctor quite regularly. In 2001 only 16.5 percent of Americans had not seen their

TABLE 5.5

Health insurance coverage for persons 65 years of age and over, by type of coverage and selected characteristics, selected years 1989–2001 [CONTINUED]

Characteristic	Medicare fee-for-service only[1,8]						Medicare health maintenance organization[1,9]					
	1989	1995	1998	1999	2000	2001	1989	1995	1998	1999	2000	2001
	Number in millions											
Total[3]	4.5	4.6	4.7	5.1	5.5	5.9	---	---	4.7	5.2	5.0	4.2
	Percent of population											
Total, age adjusted[3,4]	15.7	14.8	14.5	15.8	16.8	17.9	---	---	14.4	16.0	15.2	12.9
Total, crude[3]	15.4	14.7	14.5	15.8	16.8	17.9	---	---	14.5	16.0	15.2	12.9
Age												
65–74 years	13.8	14.4	13.7	15.6	16.4	17.4	---	---	15.3	16.1	15.8	12.8
75 years and over	17.8	15.2	15.4	15.9	17.4	18.4	---	---	13.5	15.9	14.6	13.1
75–84 years	16.2	14.1	14.2	15.2	16.0	17.0	---	---	13.7	16.5	15.5	13.4
85 years and over	24.9	19.2	19.7	18.4	22.7	23.7	---	---	12.8	13.7	11.1	11.9
Sex[4]												
Male	14.9	14.3	13.2	15.4	16.1	17.4	---	---	14.7	16.5	15.6	12.5
Female	16.2	15.0	15.4	16.0	17.4	18.2	---	---	14.2	15.6	15.0	13.3
Race[4,5]												
White only	13.9	13.5	13.3	14.4	15.5	16.5	---	---	14.0	15.8	15.2	13.0
Black or African American only	34.9	29.0	26.7	28.0	29.6	30.5	---	---	17.6	16.5	14.7	11.2
American Indian and Alaska Native only	*	*	*26.6	*39.1	*	*37.9	---	---	*	*	*	*
Asian only	#	#	*12.6	22.0	21.4	19.8	---	---	17.0	18.9	16.0	13.4
Native Hawaiian and Other Pacific Islander only	---	---	---	*	*	*	---	---	---	*	*	*
2 or more races	---	---	---	*19.1	*	*21.7	---	---	---	*21.8	*29.8	*16.3
Hispanic origin and race[4,5]												
Hispanic or Latino	22.7	23.6	20.6	22.8	20.8	23.9	---	---	24.4	25.7	25.0	20.1
Mexican	#	#	21.5	26.3	22.7	29.3	---	---	23.3	26.0	24.5	18.9
Not Hispanic or Latino	15.5	14.3	14.2	15.3	16.6	17.5	---	---	13.9	15.4	14.6	12.5
White only	13.6	12.9	12.9	13.9	15.3	16.1	---	---	13.5	15.2	14.5	12.5
Black or African American only	34.9	29.1	26.7	28.0	29.6	30.5	---	---	17.5	16.5	14.7	11.2
Percent of poverty level[4,6]												
Below 100 percent	26.4	23.4	21.9	24.8	23.6	23.3	---	---	11.0	13.8	14.4	8.6
100–149 percent	20.7	18.6	22.2	23.1	22.0	24.5	---	---	16.6	17.7	17.0	12.5
150–199 percent	13.6	16.8	14.3	17.1	16.6	16.6	---	---	18.6	20.4	16.0	15.0
200 percent or more	11.0	10.8	8.0	10.3	11.4	11.5	---	---	15.2	15.7	16.7	14.5
Geographic region[4]												
Northeast	17.4	15.3	12.3	13.8	17.1	17.6	---	---	12.7	17.5	12.5	13.5
Midwest	13.8	11.0	12.9	11.7	13.5	16.1	---	---	7.7	9.0	8.4	7.5
South	16.6	15.9	17.5	20.3	19.6	19.7	---	---	12.5	12.2	13.2	10.2
West	14.4	17.2	13.7	14.9	15.7	17.3	---	---	28.2	31.0	30.6	23.8
Location of residence[4]												
Within MSA[7]	15.9	14.9	13.4	14.9	16.4	17.6	---	---	17.7	19.7	18.7	15.8
Outside MSA[7]	15.5	14.2	18.2	18.7	18.2	19.0	---	---	3.5	3.4	4.4	3.1

physicians or been to an emergency department for treatment within the previous 12 months. Almost 46 percent of Americans reported seeing their doctor or going to an emergency department for treatment between 1 and 3 times within the previous 12 months, while 24.4 percent had done so from 4 to 9 times.

Children under six years of age were the most likely to have seen a doctor or been to the emergency room; only 5.5 percent were reported not to have seen a doctor within the year. People over the age of 75 were also likely to have been to the doctor more than the rest of the population, with only 5.8 reporting not having seen a doctor. In 2001, 45.1 percent of women and 46.5 percent of men had seen their doctor or been treated in an emergency department 1 to 3 times within the previous 12 months.

VISITING THE DENTIST

In 2001, 65.6 percent of the population two years of age and older visited a dentist. Females (68.5 percent) were more likely to go to the dentist than males (62.6 percent). Of all age groups, children 2 to 17 years old had the highest rate of visits (73.3 percent); the lowest rate of visits was by people 65 years of age or older (56.3 percent). Whites 2 years of age and older visited the dentist more often in 2001 (67.4 percent) than Asians (64.9 percent), blacks (56.9 percent), Native Americans or Alaskan Natives (53.9 percent), or Hispanics (51.2 percent). By geographical region, people 2 years of age and over in the South (60.2 percent) were least likely to visit a dentist in the past year, with those in the Northeast (72.2 percent) being most likely except for the age group of people over 65, who were more likely to visit a dentist if they were living in the West.

TABLE 5.5

Health insurance coverage for persons 65 years of age and over, by type of coverage and selected characteristics, selected years 1989–2001 [CONTINUED]

Characteristic	Medicaid[1,10]					
	1989	1995	1998	1999	2000	2001
	Number in millions					
Total[3]	2.0	3.0	2.6	2.4	2.5	2.7
	Percent of population					
Total, age adjusted[3,4]	7.2	9.6	8.1	7.4	7.6	8.1
Total, crude[3]	7.0	9.4	8.1	7.3	7.6	8.1
Age						
65–74 years	6.3	8.4	7.8	6.6	7.7	7.8
75 years and over	8.2	10.9	8.4	8.1	7.5	8.5
75–84 years	7.9	9.9	7.8	7.2	7.2	8.1
85 years and over	9.7	14.3	10.5	11.4	8.6	10.3
Sex[4]						
Male	5.2	5.8	6.2	5.3	5.5	6.1
Female	8.6	12.2	9.5	8.8	9.2	9.7
Race[4,5]						
White only	5.6	7.4	6.4	5.6	5.6	6.2
Black or African American only	21.2	28.4	18.0	18.2	19.6	20.0
American Indian and Alaska Native only	*	*	*	*	*35.8	*
Asian only	#	#	33.4	28.2	21.3	23.7
Native Hawaiian and Other Pacific Islander only	- - -	- - -	- - -	*	*	*
2 or more races	- - -	- - -	- - -	*	*	*19.9
Hispanic origin and race[4,5]						
Hispanic or Latino	26.4	32.7	27.2	24.0	29.6	30.1
Mexican	#	#	29.0	17.5	28.1	25.6
Not Hispanic or Latino	6.6	8.5	7.1	6.4	6.3	6.8
White only	4.9	6.1	5.4	4.7	4.6	4.9
Black or African American only	21.1	28.5	18.0	18.1	19.5	20.0
Percent of poverty level[4,6]						
Below 100 percent	28.2	36.4	36.7	35.7	35.0	38.8
100–149 percent	9.0	12.8	14.1	15.3	16.2	18.6
150–199 percent	4.7	5.9	6.1	4.2	4.7	7.1
200 percent or more	2.4	2.4	3.5	2.9	2.8	3.1
Geographic region[4]						
Northeast	5.4	8.9	7.5	7.3	7.4	7.9
Midwest	3.7	5.8	4.9	5.7	4.5	5.1
South	9.7	11.8	9.6	8.2	9.4	9.3
West	9.4	11.5	10.2	8.2	8.6	10.0
Location of residence[4]						
Within MSA[7]	6.5	8.9	8.0	6.9	7.2	8.1
Outside MSA[7]	8.8	11.7	8.4	8.8	9.0	8.3

[1]Almost all persons 65 years of age and over are covered by Medicare also. In 2001, 90 percent of older persons with private insurance also had Medicare.
[2]Private insurance originally obtained through a present or former employer or union. Starting in 1997 also includes private insurance obtained through workplace, self-employed, or professional association.
[3]Includes all other races not shown separately and unknown poverty level.
[4]Estimates are for persons 65 years of age and older and are age adjusted to the year 2000 standard using two age groups: 65–74 years and 75 years and over.
[5]The race groups, white, black, American Indian and Alaska Native (AI/AN), Asian, Native Hawaiian and Other Pacific Islander, and 2 or more races, include persons of Hispanic and non-Hispanic origin. Persons of Hispanic origin may be of any race. Starting with data year 1999 race-specific estimates are tabulated according to 1997 Standards for Federal data on Race and Ethnicity and are not strictly comparable with estimates for earlier years. The five single race categories plus multiple race categories shown in the table conform to 1997 Standards. The 1999 and later race-specific estimates are for persons who reported only one racial group; the category "2 or more races'" includes persons who reported more than one racial group. Prior to data year 1999, data were tabulated according to 1977 Standards with four racial groups and the category "Asian only" included Native Hawaiian and Other Pacific Islander. Estimates for single race categories prior to 1999 included persons who reported one race or, if they reported more than one race, identified one race as best representing their race.
[6]Missing family income data were imputed for 22–25 percent of the sample 65 years of age and over in 1994–96. Percent of poverty level was unknown for 29 percent of sample persons 65 or older in 1997, 34 percent in 1998, 38 percent in 1999, 39 percent in 2000, and 40 percent in 2001.
[7]MSA is metropolitan statistical area.
[8]Medicare fee-for-service only includes persons who are not covered by private health insurance, Medicaid, or a Medicare health maintenance organization.
[9]Persons reporting Medicare coverage are considered to have HMO coverage if they responded yes when asked if they were under a Medicare managed care arrangement such as an HMO.
[10]Includes public assistance through 1996. Starting in 1997 includes State-sponsored health plans. In 2001 the age-adjusted percent of the population 65 years of age and over covered by Medicaid was 7.6 percent, and 0.5 percent were covered by State-sponsored health plans.
Note: * Estimates are considered unreliable. Data preceded by an asterisk have a relative standard error of 20–30 percent. Data not shown have a relative standard error of greater than 30 percent.
Estimates calculated upon request.
- - - Data not available.
Percents do not add to 100 because elderly persons with more than one type of insurance in addition to Medicare appear in more than one column, and because the percent of elderly persons without health insurance (1.3 percent in 2001) is not shown.

SOURCE: V.M. Freid, K. Prager, A.P. MacKay, H. Xia, "Table 130. Health insurance coverage for persons 65 years of age and over, according to type of coverage and selected characteristics: United States, selected years 1989–2001," in *Health, United States, 2003, with Chartbook on Trends in the Health of Americans*, Centers for Disease Control and Prevention, National Center for Health Statistics, Hyattsville, MD, September 2003

TABLE 5.6

People without health insurance coverage for the entire year by selected characteristics, 2001–02

(Numbers in thousands.)

Characteristic	2001	Uninsured			2002	Uninsured			Change 2002 less 2001[1]	Uninsured	
	Total	Number	Percent[1]	Percent 90-percent confidence interval (±)	Total	Number	Percent[1]	Percent 90-percent confidence interval (±)	Number	Percent	Percent 90-percent confidence interval (±)
People											
Total	282,082	41,207	14.6	0.2	285,933	43,574	15.2	0.2	*2,367	*0.6	0.2
Sex											
Male	137,871	21,722	15.8	0.3	139,876	23,327	16.7	0.3	*1,606	*0.9	0.3
Female	144,211	19,485	13.5	0.2	146,057	20,246	13.9	0.2	*761	*0.4	0.3
Age											
Under 18 years	72,628	8,509	11.7	0.3	73,312	8,531	11.6	0.3	22	20.1	0.4
18 to 24 years	27,312	7,673	28.1	0.7	27,438	8,128	29.6	0.7	*456	*1.5	0.9
25 to 34 years	38,670	9,051	23.4	0.7	39,243	9,769	24.9	0.7	718	*1.5	0.7
35 to 44 years	44,284	7,131	16.1	0.5	44,074	7,781	17.7	0.5	*650	*1.6	0.6
45 to 64 years	65,419	8,571	13.1	0.3	67,633	9,106	13.5	0.3	*535	0.4	0.4
65 years and over	33,769	272	0.8	0.2	34,234	258	0.8	0.2	214	20.1	0.2
Nativity											
Native	249,629	30,364	12.2	0.2	252,463	32,388	12.8	0.2	*2,023	*0.7	0.2
Foreign born	32,453	10,843	33.4	0.8	33,471	11,186	33.4	0.8	343	–	0.9
Naturalized citizen	11,962	2,060	17.2	1.0	12,837	2,251	17.5	1.0	*191	0.3	1.2
Not a citizen	20,491	8,782	42.9	1.0	20,634	8,935	43.3	1.0	153	0.4	1.2
Region											
Northeast	53,300	6,399	12.0	0.3	54,139	7,057	13.0	0.3	*658	*1.0	0.4
Midwest	63,779	6,840	10.7	0.3	64,581	7,533	11.7	0.3	*694	*0.9	0.4
South	100,652	16,712	16.6	0.3	101,800	17,773	17.5	0.3	*1,061	*0.9	0.4
West	64,351	11,257	17.5	0.5	65,413	11,210	17.1	0.5	246	20.4	0.5
Household Income											
Less than $25,000	62,209	14,474	23.3	0.5	62,979	14,776	23.5	0.5	302	0.2	0.5
$25,000 to $49,999	76,226	13,516	17.7	0.3	75,927	14,638	19.3	0.3	*1,122	*1.5	0.4
$50,000 to $74,999	58,114	6,595	11.3	0.3	58,622	6,904	11.8	0.3	*309	*0.4	0.4
$75,000 or more	85,532	6,623	7.7	0.2	88,406	7,256	8.2	0.3	*633	*0.5	0.3
Education (18 years and older)											
Total	209,454	32,698	15.6	0.2	212,622	35,042	16.5	0.2	*2,344	*0.9	0.3
No high school diploma	35,423	9,776	27.6	0.7	34,829	9,768	28.0	0.7	28	0.4	0.8
High school graduate only	66,682	11,618	17.4	0.3	67,512	12,671	18.8	0.3	*1,053	*1.3	0.5
Some college, no degree	40,282	5,815	14.4	0.5	41,319	6,214	15.0	0.5	*398	*0.6	0.6
Associate degree	16,183	1,754	10.8	0.7	16,350	1,981	12.1	0.7	*226	*1.3	0.8
Bachelor's degree or higher	50,884	3,734	7.3	0.3	52,612	4,408	8.4	0.3	*674	*1.0	0.4
Work Experience (18 to 64 years old)											
Total	175,685	32,426	18.5	0.3	178,388	34,785	19.5	0.3	*2,359	*1.0	0.3
Worked during year	142,474	24,230	17.0	0.3	142,918	25,679	18.0	0.3	*1,449	*1.0	0.3
Worked full-time	118,776	19,014	16.0	0.3	118,411	19,911	16.8	0.3	*897	*0.8	0.3
Worked part-time	23,698	5,216	22.0	0.7	24,506	5,767	23.5	0.7	*552	*1.5	0.9
Did not work	33,211	8,197	24.7	0.7	35,470	9,106	25.7	0.7	*909	*1.0	0.7

Note: – Represents zero or rounds to zero.
*Statistically different from zero at the 90-percent confidence level.
[1]Details may not sum to totals because of rounding.

SOURCE: Robert J. Mills and Shailesh Bhandari, "Table 1. People Without Health Insurance for the Entire Year by Selected Characteristics: 2001 and 2002," in " Health Insurance Coverage 2002," *Current Population Reports*, vol. P60-223, September 2003

MAMMOGRAPHY

During the 1990s, among women 40 years of age and older, there was a dramatic rise in the use of mammography (an X-ray examination of the breast that can detect abnormalities, such as tumors). In 1987 only 29.0 percent of all women 40 years and older reported having a mammogram within the previous two years, compared to 70.3 percent of women in 2000. In 2000 more than three-fourths (78.6 percent) of women between 50 and 64 years of age reported having had a mammogram within the past

TABLE 5.7

Persons under 65 years of age without health insurance coverage by state, selected years, 1987–2001

Geographic region and State	2001	1987	1990	1995	1996	1997[1]	1998	1999[2]	2000	2001
	Number in thousands					Percent of population				
United States	40,935	14.4	15.7	17.3	17.6	18.2	18.4	16.2	16.1	16.5
New England:										
Connecticut	342	7.4	8.0	10.3	12.4	13.8	14.3	10.4	11.3	11.7
Maine	132	9.9	12.6	15.4	13.9	17.1	14.6	12.4	12.8	12.3
Massachusetts	515	7.0	10.2	12.5	14.1	14.3	11.6	10.4	9.9	9.3
New Hampshire	119	11.4	11.1	11.4	10.9	13.3	12.5	10.3	9.6	11.0
Rhode Island	79	7.8	13.1	15.4	12.0	12.3	7.6	7.1	8.7	9.0
Vermont	58	11.1	10.5	14.5	12.4	10.8	11.0	12.3	9.9	10.8
Mideast:										
Delaware	73	11.9	15.6	17.2	14.8	15.1	17.1	11.1	10.6	10.5
District of Columbia	70	17.1	21.3	19.3	16.8	18.3	19.2	15.7	16.0	14.2
Maryland	650	10.9	14.2	17.2	12.8	14.9	18.9	12.5	11.8	13.8
New Jersey	1,100	9.0	11.3	16.2	19.1	18.4	18.0	13.3	14.0	15.1
New York	2,898	13.1	13.6	17.2	19.1	20.0	19.7	17.1	18.5	17.7
Pennsylvania	1,109	8.4	11.8	11.6	11.1	11.7	12.1	9.7	10.0	10.6
Great Lakes:										
Illinois	1,669	10.9	12.2	12.3	12.5	13.9	16.6	14.5	15.5	15.3
Indiana	708	15.2	12.3	14.6	12.2	12.8	16.1	10.6	12.8	13.6
Michigan	1,022	9.4	10.4	11.0	10.1	13.2	14.9	11.2	10.3	11.7
Ohio	1,248	10.3	11.7	13.5	13.1	13.1	11.7	11.6	12.8	12.8
Wisconsin	406	7.4	7.8	8.1	9.5	9.1	13.2	11.0	8.5	8.8
Plains:										
Iowa	215	8.3	9.4	12.9	13.1	13.6	10.9	8.7	10.3	8.7
Kansas	301	11.6	12.3	14.2	13.1	13.6	12.2	13.3	12.6	13.5
Minnesota	391	7.4	9.9	9.0	11.2	10.2	10.3	8.1	9.0	8.8
Missouri	564	11.8	14.2	16.7	15.3	14.7	12.1	7.8	10.7	11.6
Nebraska	160	11.0	9.6	10.3	12.9	12.2	10.2	11.5	10.3	10.8
North Dakota	60	8.7	7.2	9.4	11.2	11.7	16.5	13.4	13.2	11.2
South Dakota	69	15.4	13.5	10.8	11.1	13.7	16.3	12.3	12.9	10.9
Southeast:										
Alabama	573	17.9	19.3	15.7	14.9	18.0	19.5	15.1	14.9	14.9
Arkansas	425	23.5	20.1	20.5	24.8	28.1	21.7	16.6	16.7	18.8
Florida	2,822	20.5	21.5	21.7	22.7	23.6	21.1	21.5	21.1	20.6
Georgia	1,371	14.5	17.1	20.0	19.6	19.3	19.4	16.5	15.7	18.1
Kentucky	491	16.8	15.1	16.8	17.6	16.9	16.0	14.9	15.3	14.1
Louisiana	839	18.9	22.1	22.9	23.2	22.0	21.3	24.1	20.4	21.7
Mississippi	458	19.3	22.1	22.3	20.5	22.6	22.9	17.9	15.5	18.4
North Carolina	1,163	15.0	15.6	16.4	18.0	17.6	17.0	16.2	15.3	16.3
South Carolina	491	12.4	18.1	16.0	18.7	18.7	17.4	18.0	13.7	14.1
Tennessee	640	16.6	15.4	16.4	17.1	15.2	14.3	11.4	12.2	12.6
Virginia	765	11.4	17.3	15.2	13.8	14.1	15.8	14.8	13.0	12.2
West Virginia	233	15.9	16.0	18.3	17.9	20.5	20.8	18.7	16.5	15.8
Southwest:										
Arizona	943	20.4	18.1	23.2	27.5	27.7	26.9	22.7	18.7	20.0
New Mexico	372	25.3	24.6	28.3	24.7	25.2	24.0	27.6	27.2	23.9
Oklahoma	619	20.4	21.2	22.1	19.6	20.2	21.2	19.1	21.9	20.9
Texas	4,920	23.0	23.2	27.0	26.7	26.7	26.9	24.4	25.4	25.9
Rocky Mountains:										
Colorado	687	15.6	16.3	15.9	17.8	16.4	16.4	16.6	15.8	17.2
Idaho	209	17.2	16.9	15.9	18.6	19.9	19.7	20.6	17.3	17.9
Montana	121	17.3	15.7	14.8	15.4	22.0	21.9	20.1	19.2	15.9
Utah	335	13.4	9.8	13.0	13.3	14.8	15.1	14.2	13.6	16.0
Wyoming	77	12.7	13.7	17.6	15.0	17.4	18.8	17.0	17.8	18.1
Far West:										
Alaska	99	17.0	16.1	12.9	13.8	18.9	17.9	19.2	20.0	16.6
California	6,659	18.5	21.1	22.6	22.2	23.7	24.4	21.0	20.4	21.3
Hawaii	114	8.5	7.8	9.9	9.7	8.7	11.3	11.4	10.6	10.8
Nevada	341	17.4	18.3	21.1	17.6	19.9	23.7	20.2	18.8	17.9
Oregon	442	17.2	14.6	13.9	17.4	14.8	16.0	15.6	14.4	14.2
Washington	772	14.4	12.7	13.7	14.8	12.4	13.4	15.3	15.3	14.8

[1]Beginning with data for 1997, people with no coverage other than access to the Indian Health Service are no longer considered covered by health insurance. The effect of this change on the number uninsured is negligible.
[2]Starting in 1999 estimates reflect the results of follow-up verification questions. In 1999 the use of verification questions decreased the percent uninsured by 1.2 percentage points.

SOURCE: V.M. Freid, K. Prager, A.P. MacKay, H. Xia, "Table 151. Persons under 65 years of age without health insurance coverage by State: United States, selected years 1987–2001," in *Health, United States, 2003, with Chartbook on Trends in the Health of Americans,* Centers for Disease Control and Prevention, National Center for Health Statistics, Hyattsville, MD, September 2003

TABLE 5.8

Health maintenance organizations (HMOs) and enrollment, according to model type, geographic region, and federal program, selected years 1976–2002

Plans and enrollment	1976	1980	1990	1995	1997	1998	1999	2000	2001	2002
Plans					**Number**					
All plans	174	235	572	562	652	651	643	568	541	500
Model type:[1]										
Individual practice association[2]	41	97	360	332	284	317	309	278	257	229
Group[3]	122	138	212	108	98	116	123	101	104	100
Mixed	- - -	- - -	- - -	122	258	212	208	188	180	171
Geographic region:										
Northeast	29	55	115	100	110	107	110	98	96	87
Midwest	52	72	160	157	184	185	179	161	190	140
South	23	45	176	196	236	237	239	203	158	178
West	70	63	121	109	121	122	115	106	97	95
Enrollment[1]					**Number of persons in millions**					
Total	**6.0**	**9.1**	**33.0**	**50.9**	**66.8**	**76.6**	**81.3**	**80.9**	**79.5**	**76.1**
Model type:[1]										
Individual practice association[2]	0.4	1.7	13.7	20.1	26.7	32.6	32.8	33.4	33.1	31.6
Group[3]	5.6	7.4	19.3	13.3	11.0	13.8	15.9	15.2	15.6	15.0
Mixed	- - -	- - -	- - -	17.6	29.0	30.1	32.6	32.3	30.9	29.6
Federal program:[4]										
Medicaid[5]	- - -	0.3	1.2	3.5	5.6	7.8	10.4	10.8	11.4	12.8
Medicare	- - -	0.4	1.8	2.9	4.8	5.7	6.5	6.6	6.1	5.4
					Percent of HMO enrollees					
Model type										
Individual practice association[2]	6.6	18.7	41.6	39.4	39.9	42.6	40.3	41.3	41.6	41.5
Group[3]	93.4	81.3	58.4	26.0	16.5	18.0	19.6	18.9	19.5	19.4
Mixed	- - -	- - -	- - -	34.5	43.4	39.2	40.1	39.9	38.8	38.8
Federal program:[4]										
Medicaid[5]	- - -	2.9	3.5	6.9	8.2	10.2	12.7	13.3	14.3	16.9
Medicare	- - -	4.3	5.4	5.7	7.2	7.4	8.0	8.1	7.7	7.1
					Percent of population enrolled in HMOs					
Total	**2.8**	**4.0**	**13.4**	**19.4**	**25.2**	**28.6**	**30.1**	**30.0**	**28.3**	**26.4**
Geographic region:										
Northeast	2.0	3.1	14.6	24.4	32.4	37.8	36.7	36.5	35.1	33.4
Midwest	1.5	2.8	12.6	16.4	19.5	22.7	23.3	23.2	21.7	20.6
South	0.4	0.8	7.1	12.4	17.9	21.0	23.9	22.6	21.0	19.8
West	9.7	12.2	23.2	28.6	36.4	39.1	41.4	41.7	40.7	38.2

Note: - - - Data not available.

[1]Enrollment or number of plans may not equal total because some plans did not report these characteristics.

[2]An HMO operating under an individual practice association model contracts with an association of physicians from various settings (a mixture of solo and group practices) to provide health services.

[3]Group includes staff, group, and network model types.

[4]Federal program enrollment in HMOs refers to enrollment by Medicaid or Medicare beneficiaries, where the Medicaid or Medicare program contracts directly with the HMO to pay the appropriate annual premium.

[5]Data for 1990 and later include enrollment in managed care health insuring organizations.

SOURCE: V.M. Freid, K. Prager, A.P. MacKay, H. Xia, "Table 132. Health maintenance organizations (HMOs) and enrollment, according to model type, geographic region, and Federal program: United States, selected years 1976–2002," in *Health, United States, 2003, with Chartbook on Trends in the Health of Americans,* Centers for Disease Control and Prevention, National Center for Health Statistics, Hyattsville, MD, September 2003

two years. Among women 40 to 49 years of age, the rate was 64.2 percent.

Although the rate is lower among poor women, that rate has also increased since 1987, when only 16.4 percent of women over the age of 40 who were below the poverty line had a mammogram within the previous two years, compared to 55.2 percent in 2000. Hispanic women over the age of 40 (61.4 percent) were less likely to have had a mammogram within the previous two years in 2000 than black women (67.8 percent) or white women (71.4 percent).

HOW DO AMERICANS FEEL?

In 2001 only 9.2 percent of Americans responded that they felt in only fair or poor health, a decrease from 10.4 in 1991, as reported in *Health, United States, 2003* by the National Center for Health Statistics. The older the person, the more likely he or she was to admit to not feeling very well. Blacks, Native Americans or Alaska Natives, and poor Americans were far more likely than the general population to feel their health was not up to par.

AIDS AND HIV

In 2002, 31,644 men and 10,951 women, 13 years of age and over, had been diagnosed with acquired immunodeficiency syndrome (AIDS). In 1999 for men, the highest rate of infection occurred in those who had sex with other men (57.3 percent), whereas in women the highest

TABLE 5.9

Leading causes of death and numbers of deaths, according to age, 1980 and 2000

Age and rank order	1980		2000	
	Cause of death	Deaths	Cause of death	Deaths
Under 1 year				
. . .	All causes	45,526	All causes	28,035
1	Congenital anomalies	9,220	Congenital malformations, deformations and chromosomal abnormalities	5,743
2	Sudden infant death syndrome	5,510	Disorders related to short gestation and low birthweight, not elsewhere classified	4,397
3	Respiratory distress syndrome	4,989	Sudden infant death syndrome	2,523
4	Disorders relating to short gestation and unspecified low birthweight	3,648	Newborn affected by maternal complications of pregnancy	1,404
5	Newborn affected by maternal complications of pregnancy	1,572	Newborn affected by complications of placenta, cord and membranes	1,062
6	Intrauterine hypoxia and birth asphyxia	1,497	Respiratory distress of newborn	999
7	Unintentional injuries	1,166	Unintentional injuries	881
8	Birth trauma	1,058	Bacterial sepsis of newborn	768
9	Pneumonia and influenza	1,012	Diseases of circulatory system	663
10	Newborn affected by complications of placenta, cord, and membranes	985	Intrauterine hypoxia and birth asphyxia	630
1–4 years				
. . .	All causes	8,187	All causes	4,979
1	Unintentional injuries	3,313	Unintentional injuries	1,826
2	Congenital anomalies	1,026	Congenital malformations, deformations and chromosomal abnormalities	495
3	Malignant neoplasms	573	Malignant neoplasms	420
4	Diseases of heart	338	Homicide	356
5	Homicide	319	Diseases of heart	181
6	Pneumonia and influenza	267	Influenza and pneumonia	103
7	Meningitis	223	Septicemia	99
8	Meningococcal infection	110	Certain conditions originating in the perinatal period	79
9	Certain conditions originating in the perinatal period	84	In situ neoplasms, benign neoplasms and neoplasms of uncertain or unknown behavior	53
10	Septicemia	71	Chronic lower respiratory diseases	51
5–14 years				
. . .	All causes	10,689	All causes	7,413
1	Unintentional injuries	5,224	Unintentional injuries	2,979
2	Malignant neoplasms	1,497	Malignant neoplasms	1,014
3	Congenital anomalies	561	Congenital malformations, deformations and chromosomal abnormalities	399
4	Homicide	415	Homicide	371
5	Diseases of heart	330	Suicide	307
6	Pneumonia and influenza	194	Diseases of heart	271
7	Suicide	142	Chronic lower respiratory diseases	139
8	Benign neoplasms	104	In situ neoplasms, benign neoplasms and neoplasms of uncertain or unknown behavior	99
9	Cerebrovascular diseases	95	Influenza and pneumonia	87
10	Chronic obstructive pulmonary diseases	85	Cerebrovascular diseases	76
15–24 years				
. . .	All causes	49,027	All causes	31,307
1	Unintentional injuries	26,206	Unintentional injuries	14,113
2	Homicide	6,537	Homicide	4,939
3	Suicide	5,239	Suicide	3,994
4	Malignant neoplasms	2,683	Malignant neoplasms	1,713
5	Diseases of heart	1,223	Diseases of heart	1,031
6	Congenital anomalies	600	Congenital malformations, deformations and chromosomal abnormalities	441
7	Cerebrovascular diseases	418	Cerebrovascular diseases	199
8	Pneumonia and influenza	348	Chronic lower respiratory diseases	190
9	Chronic obstructive pulmonary diseases	141	Influenza and pneumonia	189
10	Anemias	133	Human immunodeficiency virus (HIV) disease	179
25–44 years				
. . .	All causes	108,658	All causes	130,249
1	Unintentional injuries	26,722	Unintentional injuries	27,182
2	Malignant neoplasms	17,551	Malignant neoplasms	20,436
3	Diseases of heart	14,513	Diseases of heart	16,139
4	Homicide	10,983	Suicide	11,354
5	Suicide	9,855	Human immunodeficiency virus (HIV) disease	8,356
6	Chronic liver disease and cirrhosis	4,782	Homicide	7,383
7	Cerebrovascular diseases	3,154	Chronic liver disease and cirrhosis	3,786
8	Diabetes mellitus	1,472	Cerebrovascular diseases	3,201
9	Pneumonia and influenza	1,467	Diabetes mellitus	2,549
10	Congenital anomalies	817	Influenza and pneumonia	1,432

TABLE 5.9

Leading causes of death and numbers of deaths, according to age, 1980 and 2000 [CONTINUED]

Age and rank order	1980		2000	
	Cause of death	Deaths	Cause of death	Deaths
45–64 years				
...	All causes	425,338	All causes	401,187
1	Diseases of heart	148,322	Malignant neoplasms	137,039
2	Malignant neoplasms	135,675	Diseases of heart	98,879
3	Cerebrovascular diseases	19,909	Unintentional injuries	19,783
4	Unintentional injuries	18,140	Cerebrovascular diseases	15,967
5	Chronic liver disease and cirrhosis	16,089	Diabetes mellitus	14,140
6	Chronic obstructive pulmonary diseases	11,514	Chronic lower respiratory diseases	13,990
7	Diabetes mellitus	7,977	Chronic liver disease and cirrhosis	12,428
8	Suicide	7,079	Suicide	8,382
9	Pneumonia and influenza	5,804	Human immunodeficiency virus (HIV) disease	5,381
10	Homicide	4,019	Nephritis, nephrotic syndrome and nephrosis	4,751
65 years and over				
...	All causes	1,341,848	All causes	1,799,825
1	Diseases of heart	595,406	Diseases of heart	593,707
2	Malignant neoplasms	258,389	Malignant neoplasms	392,366
3	Cerebrovascular diseases	146,417	Cerebrovascular diseases	148,045
4	Pneumonia and influenza	45,512	Chronic lower respiratory diseases	106,375
5	Chronic obstructive pulmonary diseases	43,587	Influenza and pneumonia	58,557
6	Atherosclerosis	28,081	Diabetes mellitus	52,414
7	Diabetes mellitus	25,216	Alzheimer's disease	48,993
8	Unintentional injuries	24,844	Nephritis, nephrotic syndrome and nephrosis	31,225
9	Nephritis, nephrotic syndrome, and nephrosis	12,968	Unintentional injuries	31,051
10	Chronic liver disease and cirrhosis	9,519	Septicemia	24,786

Note: . . . Category not applicable.

SOURCE: V.M. Freid, K. Prager, A.P. MacKay, H. Xia, "Table 32. Leading causes of death and numbers of deaths, according to age: United States, 1980 and 2000," in *Health, United States, 2003, with Chartbook on Trends in the Health of Americans,* Centers for Disease Control and Prevention, National Center for Health Statistics, Hyattsville, MD, September 2003

rate of infection was present among those who had used intravenous drugs (41.5 percent).

In 2000, 5.2 percent of deaths in the United States were the result of human immunodeficiency virus (HIV) infection. The highest death rate for HIV in 2000 among males and females between the ages of 25 and 44 years occurred in black men (55.4 percent), followed by black females (26.7 percent). The rate of death due to HIV infection among Hispanic males and females in the same age group was 14.3 percent and 4.6 percent, respectively. For white males and females, the death rate was 8.8 percent and 2.1 percent, respectively.

OTHER CAUSES OF DEATH

In 2000 heart disease was the leading cause of death among people 65 years of age and older, followed by cancer (malignant neoplasms) and strokes (cerebrovascular diseases). Among those 45 to 64 years of age, cancer was the leading cause of death, followed by heart disease and unintentional injuries. Heart disease was the third leading cause of death for those 25 to 44 years of age, behind unintentional injuries (first), and cancer (second). (See Table 5.9.)

For all other age groups, except those under one year of age, unintentional injuries caused the most deaths in 2000. The leading cause of death for those under one year of age was congenital abnormalities, followed by disorders caused by short gestation (premature birth) and low birth weight, sudden infant death syndrome, and maternal complications of pregnancy. (See Table 5.9.)

CHAPTER 6
EDUCATION

Despite the continuing debate over the quality and direction of U.S. education, the United States is one of the most highly educated nations in the world. In the fall of 2002 approximately 78.3 million Americans were involved, directly or indirectly, in providing or receiving formal education. About 60.3 million children were enrolled in elementary and secondary schools. Eighteen million people were enrolled in U.S. public and private universities and colleges, and 4.3 million instructors were teaching at elementary, secondary, and degree-granting institutions. Other professional, administrative, and support staff at educational institutions numbered 4.8 million.

AN INCREASINGLY EDUCATED POPULATION

Over the past three generations, the median number of school years completed has risen from 8.4 years in 1930 to 13.0 years in 2000. As late as 1940 almost 80 percent of those 25 and older had not finished high school. (See Figure 6.1.) Since that time, the proportion has steadily increased. In 2001 four out of five (84.3 percent) of those 25 and older had completed high school. (See Figure 6.2.) Among people between the ages of 25 and 29 years, 87.7 percent had completed at least four years of high school.

In 1930 only about 4 percent of the population 25 years of age and older had completed four or more years of college. By 2001 a quarter of the U.S. population (26.1 percent) 25 years of age and over had done so. Among those 25 to 29 years old, 28.6 percent had completed four or more years of college. Whites were more likely to have completed high school and college than were blacks and other minorities, but over the decades the percentages for both whites and minorities have risen steadily. In 1940 only 1.6 percent of blacks aged 25 to 29 had completed four or more years of college, compared to 6.4 percent of whites. By 2001, 17.8 percent of blacks and 11.1 percent of Hispanics in that age range had completed college, compared to 33.0 percent of whites.

In 2001, of the more than 177 million people 25 years of age and older, only 15.7 percent had not graduated high school. About one-third had completed high school but had not gone to college. Of those who had gone to college, about 17.5 percent had not completed degrees, about 8.2 percent received associate degrees, and 17.4 percent received bachelor's degrees. Master's degrees were attained by 6.0 percent of those 25 years of age and older, and 2.7 percent received doctoral or professional degrees. (See Figure 6.2.)

MOST CHILDREN STAY IN SCHOOL

According to the U.S. Census Bureau and the Department of Commerce, in October 2001 more than half (56.3 percent) of all Americans between the ages of 3 and 34 years were enrolled in school. The proportion of children at ages three and four enrolled in schools rose from 10.6 percent in 1965 to 52.4 percent in 2001. Because of compulsory attendance requirements, 97.8 percent of all young people aged 5 to 15 years were enrolled in school. This proportion dropped slightly to 93.4 percent for 16 and 17 year olds and then fell sharply to 61.0 percent among 18 and 19 year olds, as some graduated and others left high school and did not go on to college.

About 4.8 percent of all students in the 10th, 11th, and 12th grades dropped out of high school during the 2000 school year. Students of Hispanic origin had the highest dropout rate (7.4 percent), followed by blacks (6.1 percent) and whites (4.1 percent). (See Table 6.1.) Students from lower-income families (10.0 percent) were more likely to drop out of high school than those from middle- and high-income families (5.2 percent and 1.6 percent, respectively). (See Table 6.2.)

SCHOOL ENROLLMENT

Elementary and secondary school enrollment grew rapidly during the 1950s and 1960s. This jump in

FIGURE 6.1

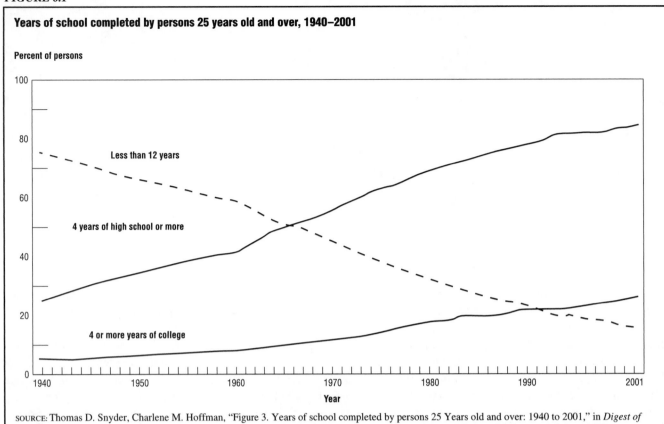

Years of school completed by persons 25 years old and over, 1940–2001

Percent of persons

SOURCE: Thomas D. Snyder, Charlene M. Hoffman, "Figure 3. Years of school completed by persons 25 Years old and over: 1940 to 2001," in *Digest of Education Statistics 2002*, vol. 2003-060, U.S. Department of Education, National Center for Education Statistics, Washington, DC, June 2003

enrollment was caused by the baby boom, the dramatic increase in births following World War II. From 1971 to 1984 total elementary and secondary school enrollment decreased steadily, reflecting the drop in the school-age population over that period. In the fall of 1985 enrollment in elementary and secondary schools began to increase once again as the children of the baby boomers became school age. (See Figure 6.3.) Public school enrollment in prekindergarten through grade eight rose from 29.8 million in the fall of 1990 and began setting new record enrollment levels in the mid-1990s. Enrollment is projected to continue climbing to 33.7 million in 2002. Enrollment is expected to decline to 33.6 million by the fall of 2012. (See Table 6.3.)

The increase in enrollment from 1985 to 2002 was concentrated in the elementary grades, but this pattern is expected to change. The growing numbers of young students that have been filling the elementary schools will mean significant increases at the secondary school level during the first decade of the 21st century. While public elementary school enrollment is expected to stay fairly stable, public secondary school enrollment is expected to rise by 2 percent between 2002 and 2012. (See Table 6.3.)

Growth in Preprimary Enrollment

Over the past 30 years, preprimary enrollment of children aged 3 to 5 years old grew substantially from 4.1

FIGURE 6.2

Highest level of education attained by persons 25 years and older, March 2001

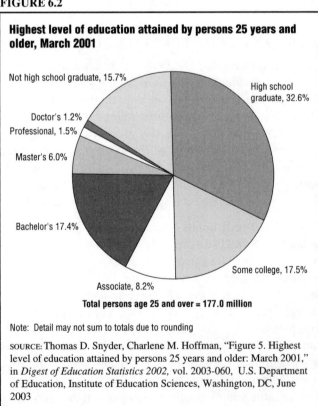

Total persons age 25 and over = 177.0 million

Note: Detail may not sum to totals due to rounding

SOURCE: Thomas D. Snyder, Charlene M. Hoffman, "Figure 5. Highest level of education attained by persons 25 years and older: March 2001," in *Digest of Education Statistics 2002*, vol. 2003-060, U.S. Department of Education, Institute of Education Sciences, Washington, DC, June 2003

TABLE 6.1

Event dropout rates of 15- through 24-year-olds who dropped out of grades 10–12, by sex and race/ethnicity, October 1972–October 2000

Year	Total (percent)	Sex (percent)		Race/ethnicity (percent)*		
		Male	Female	White non-Hispanic	Black non-Hispanic	Hispanic
1972	6.1	5.9	6.3	5.3	9.5	11.2
1973	6.3	6.8	5.7	5.5	9.9	10.0
1974	6.7	7.4	6.0	5.8	11.6	9.9
1975	5.8	5.4	6.1	5.0	8.7	10.9
1976	5.9	6.6	5.2	5.6	7.4	7.3
1977	6.5	6.9	6.1	6.1	8.6	7.8
1978	6.7	7.5	5.9	5.8	10.2	12.3
1979	6.7	6.8	6.7	6.0	9.9	9.8
1980	6.1	6.7	5.5	5.2	8.2	11.7
1981	5.9	6.0	5.8	4.8	9.7	10.7
1982	5.5	5.8	5.1	4.7	7.8	9.2
1983	5.2	5.8	4.7	4.4	7.0	10.1
1984	5.1	5.4	4.8	4.4	5.7	11.1
1985	5.2	5.4	5.0	4.3	7.8	9.8
1986	4.7	4.7	4.7	3.7	5.4	11.9
1987	4.1	4.3	3.8	3.5	6.4	5.4
1988	4.8	5.1	4.4	4.2	5.9	10.4
1989	4.5	4.5	4.5	3.5	7.8	7.8
1990	4.0	4.0	3.9	3.3	5.0	7.9
1991	4.1	3.8	4.2	3.2	6.0	7.3
1992	4.4	3.9	4.9	3.7	5.0	8.2
1993	4.5	4.6	4.3	3.9	5.8	6.7
1994	5.3	5.2	5.4	4.2	6.6	10.0
1995	5.7	6.2	5.3	4.5	6.4	12.4
1996	5.0	5.0	5.1	4.1	6.7	9.0
1997	4.6	5.0	4.1	3.6	5.0	9.5
1998	4.8	4.6	4.9	3.9	5.2	9.4
1999	5.0	4.6	5.4	4.0	6.5	7.8
2000	4.8	5.5	4.1	4.1	6.1	7.4

*Due to small sample sizes, American Indians/Alaska Natives and Asians/Pacific Islanders are included in the total but are not shown separately.

SOURCE: Phillip Kaufman, Martha Naomi Alt, and Christopher D. Chapman, "Table 3C. Event dropout rates of 15- through 24-year-olds who dropped out of grades 10–12, by sex and race/ethnicity: October 1972 through October 2000," in "Dropout Rates in the United States: 2000," *Statistical Analysis Report,* vol. 2002-114, November 2001

million in 1970, to 6.3 million in 1991, and to 7.6 million in 2001. From 1991 to 2001 preprimary enrollment rose 20 percent. This increase reflects not only the numerical growth in younger children attending preschool, but also the widespread availability and acceptance of preschool education and full-day educational programs. (See Table 6.4.)

By the mid-1980s, 55 percent of the nearly 11 million 3 to 5 year olds were enrolled in preprimary school programs. In 1990 the percentage rose to 59.4 percent before dropping to 55.1 percent in 1993. This slight decrease may be attributed to the economic recession, causing some cash-strapped parents not to send their children to preschool and some recently unemployed mothers opting to stay home with their children. When the economy began to boom in 1994, enrollment in preprimary programs again increased, reaching 65.8 percent in 1999. Due to the sluggish economy at the turn of the 21st century, enrollment decreased to 63.9 percent in 2001. (See Figure 6.4.)

Just as significant as the increase in participation rates in preschool over the past decades is the rising number of full-day programs. In 1970 only 17 percent of

young children in preprimary programs attended all-day programs. By 1990, 38.7 percent were enrolled, and by 2001 over half (51.8 percent) were in full-day programs. This growth reflects greater parental interest in the importance of early schooling, as well as more mothers of preschool-age children returning to the workforce. (See Figure 6.4.)

PUBLIC ELEMENTARY AND SECONDARY SCHOOLS

Generally, over the past decades the number of schools has decreased, usually as a result of school consolidation. In the 1930s there were more than 247,000 schools, compared to around 86,000 in 1954. The total number of schools remained relatively stable through the 1980s but slowly rose during the 1990s as consolidation generally came to an end and the growing population required more schools.

For the 2000–01 school year 47 million public school students attended the nation's 93,273 public elementary and secondary schools. An estimated 30.6 million elementary students went to the 64,601 public

TABLE 6.2

Event dropout rates of 15- through 24-year-olds who dropped out of grades 10–12, by family income, October 1972–October 2000

Year	Event dropout rate (percent)	Family income (percent)*		
		Low income	Middle income	High income
1972	6.1	14.1	6.7	2.5
1973	6.3	17.3	7.0	1.8
1974	6.7	—	—	—
1975	5.8	15.7	6.0	2.6
1976	5.9	15.4	6.8	2.1
1977	6.5	15.5	7.6	2.2
1978	6.7	17.4	7.3	3.0
1979	6.7	17.1	6.9	3.6
1980	6.1	15.8	6.4	2.5
1981	5.9	14.4	6.2	2.8
1982	5.5	15.2	5.6	1.8
1983	5.2	10.4	6.0	2.2
1984	5.1	13.9	5.1	1.8
1985	5.2	14.2	5.2	2.1
1986	4.7	10.9	5.1	1.6
1987	4.1	10.3	4.7	1.0
1988	4.8	13.7	4.7	1.3
1989	4.5	10.0	5.0	1.1
1990	4.0	9.5	4.3	1.1
1991	4.1	10.6	4.0	1.0
1992	4.4	10.9	4.4	1.3
1993	4.5	12.3	4.3	1.3
1994	5.3	13.0	5.2	2.1
1995	5.7	13.3	5.7	2.0
1996	5.0	11.1	5.1	2.1
1997	4.6	12.3	4.1	1.8
1998	4.8	12.7	3.8	2.7
1999	5.0	11.0	5.0	2.1
2000	4.8	10.0	5.2	1.6

Note: — Data not available for this year.
*Low income is defined as the bottom 20 percent of all family incomes for the year; middle income is between 20 and 80 percent of all family incomes; and high income is the top 20 percent of all family incomes.

SOURCE: "Table B3. Supporting data for figure 1: Event dropout rates of 15- through 24-year-olds who dropped out of grades 10–12, by family income: October 1972 through October 2000," in *Dropout Rates in the United States: 2000,* vol. 2002-114, November 2001

elementary schools, while approximately 15 million secondary students attended the 21,994 public secondary schools. About 1.3 million students attended the 5,096 combined elementary-secondary schools, while 82,312 students attended the 1,582 "other" schools. Typically, these schools offer special or alternative education. (See Table 6.5.)

Middle schools (sixth through eighth grades), virtually unknown a generation ago, now play a major role in the nation's education system. The number of elementary schools rose from 57,231 schools in the 1984–85 school year to 64,601 in the 2000–01 academic year. However, middle schools accounted for a disproportionate share of this increase, rising by almost 50 percent, from 6,893 schools in 1984–85 to 11,696 schools in 2000–01. On the other hand, a significant decrease has occurred in the number of one-teacher schools. In 1967–68 there were 4,146 one-teacher schools; by 2000–01 there were only 411 such schools. (See Table 6.6.)

PRIVATE SCHOOLS

A private school is defined by the U.S. Department of Education as a school not supported by public funds that teaches one or more of the grades from kindergarten to 12th grade. During the 1999–2000 school year 5.1 million children attended private schools, with 2.5 million children enrolled in Catholic schools, 1.8 million children enrolled in other religious schools, and 808,063 children enrolled in nonsectarian schools. (See Table 6.7.)

The percentage of private school enrollment in grades 9 to 12 grew more slowly than enrollment in their public school counterparts from 1991 to 2001. (See Table 6.8.) In the 2001–02 school year there were 1.3 million private school students grades 9 to 12, up from 1.2 million, an increase of 8.9 percent (114,000 students) from the 1991–92 school year. In comparison, public school enrollment in grades 9 to 12 increased from 11.5 million in the fall of 1991 to 13.7 million in the fall of 2001, an increase of 15.8 percent. Much of the growth in private school secondary education enrollment is the result of increasing enrollment in Catholic schools. From the fall of 1991 to the fall of 2001, enrollment in Catholic elementary and secondary schools increased by 173,406 students (6.6 percent).

COLLEGE AND UNIVERSITY EDUCATION

If some parents and educators consider the quality of U.S. elementary and secondary education mediocre, the nation's institutions of higher education are the envy of the world. Moreover, access to U.S. colleges and universities is almost universal for those who want to enroll. College enrollment increased more than 40 percent between 1970 and 1980. After 1980 enrollments rose more slowly, increasing about 20 percent, from almost 12.1 million to a record 15.3 million in 2000. (See Table 6.9.) College enrollment is projected to rise an additional 13 percent from 2002 to 2012.

Total enrollment increases from 1970 to the present were largely due to the increasing number of women entering college. From 1970 to 1980 the number of females entering college almost doubled, from 3.5 million to 6.2 million. From 1990 to 2000 the number of women entering college increased by 12.3 percent, from 7.5 million to 8.6 million. Over the same period, the number of men entering college increased at a slower rate (8.0 percent), from 6.3 million to 6.7 million. According to the Census Bureau, between 1990 and 2000 the number of full-time students increased from 7.8 million to 9 million (15 percent). Over the same period, the number of part-time students increased by 5 percent. (See Table 6.9.)

In 2000, 13.2 million students were attending undergraduate school, 306,625 students were going to a first-professional degree program (medical, dental, law, or theological school), and 1.9 million students were in

FIGURE 6.3

Enrollment and total expenditures in current and constant dollars, by level of education, 1960–61 to 2001–02

Enrollment, in millions

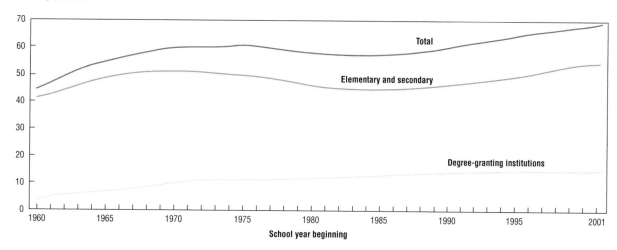

Expenditures, in billions of current dollars

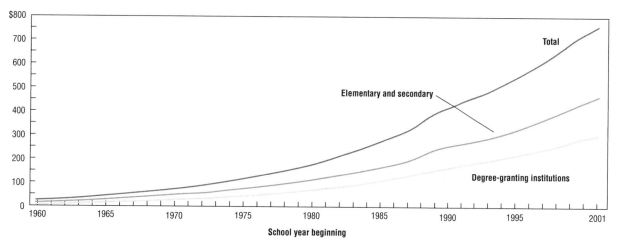

Expenditures, in billions of constant 2001-02 dollars

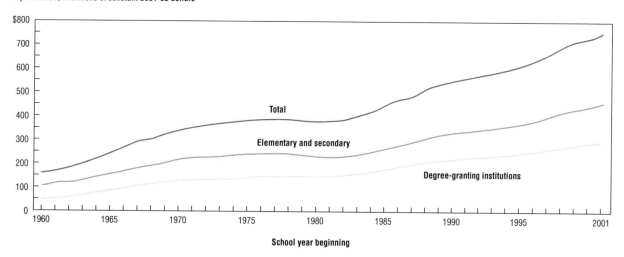

Note: Data for 2000-01 are preliminary and data for 2001-02 are estimates.

SOURCE: Thomas D. Snyder, Charlene M. Hoffman, "Figure 2. Enrollment and total expenditures in current and constant dollars, by level of education: 1960–61 to 2001–02," in *Digest of Education Statistics 2002*, vol. 2003-060, U.S. Department of Education, Institute of Education Sciences, Washington, DC, June 2003

TABLE 6.3

Enrollment in educational institutions, by level and control of institution, 1869–70 to fall 2012

[In thousands]

Year	Total enrollment, all levels	Elementary and secondary, total	Public elementary and secondary schools			Private elementary and secondary schools			Degree-granting institutions[1]		
			Total	Pre-kindergarten through grade 8	Grades 9 through 12	Total	Kindergarten through grade 8	Grades 9 through 12	Total	Public	Private
1	2	3	4	5	6	7	8	9	10	11	12
1869–70	—	—	6,872	6,792	80	—	—	—	52	—	—
1879–80	—	—	9,868	9,757	110	—	—	—	116	—	—
1889–90	14,491	14,334	12,723	12,520	203	1,611	1,516	95	157	—	—
1899–1900	17,092	16,855	15,503	14,984	519	1,352	1,241	111	238	—	—
1909–10	19,728	19,372	17,814	16,899	915	1,558	1,441	117	355	—	—
1919–20	23,876	23,278	21,578	19,378	2,200	1,699	1,486	214	598	—	—
1929–30	29,430	28,329	25,678	21,279	4,399	2,651	2,310	341	1,101	—	—
1939–40	29,539	28,045	25,434	18,832	6,601	2,611	2,153	458	1,494	797	698
1949–50	31,151	28,492	25,111	19,387	5,725	3,380	2,708	672	2,659	1,355	1,304
Fall 1959	44,497	40,857	35,182	26,911	8,271	5,675	4,640	1,035	3,640	2,181	1,459
Fall 1969	59,055	51,050	45,550	32,513	13,037	[2] 5,500	[2] 4,200	[2] 1,300	8,005	5,897	2,108
Fall 1970	59,838	51,257	45,894	32,558	13,336	5,363	4,052	1,311	8,581	6,428	2,153
Fall 1971	60,220	51,271	46,071	32,318	13,753	[2] 5,200	[2] 3,900	[2] 1,300	8,949	6,804	2,144
Fall 1972	59,941	50,726	45,726	31,879	13,848	[2] 5,000	[2] 3,700	[2] 1,300	9,215	7,071	2,144
Fall 1973	60,047	50,445	45,445	31,401	14,044	[2] 5,000	[2] 3,700	[2] 1,300	9,602	7,420	2,183
Fall 1974	60,297	50,073	45,073	30,971	14,103	[2] 5,000	[2] 3,700	[2] 1,300	10,224	7,989	2,235
Fall 1975	61,004	49,819	44,819	30,515	14,304	[2] 5,000	[2] 3,700	[2] 1,300	11,185	8,835	2,350
Fall 1976	60,490	49,478	44,311	29,997	14,314	5,167	3,825	1,342	11,012	8,653	2,359
Fall 1977	60,003	48,717	43,577	29,375	14,203	5,140	3,797	1,343	11,286	8,847	2,439
Fall 1978	58,897	47,637	42,551	28,463	14,088	5,086	3,732	1,353	11,260	8,786	2,474
Fall 1979	58,221	46,651	41,651	28,034	13,616	[2] 5,000	[2] 3,700	[2] 1,300	11,570	9,037	2,533
Fall 1980	58,305	46,208	40,877	27,647	13,231	5,331	3,992	1,339	12,097	9,457	2,640
Fall 1981	57,916	45,544	40,044	27,280	12,764	[2] 5,500	[2] 4,100	[2] 1,400	12,372	9,647	2,725
Fall 1982	57,591	45,166	39,566	27,161	12,405	[2] 5,600	[2] 4,200	[2] 1,400	12,426	9,696	2,730
Fall 1983	57,432	44,967	39,252	26,981	12,271	5,715	4,315	1,400	12,465	9,683	2,782
Fall 1984	57,150	44,908	39,208	26,905	12,304	[2] 5,700	[2] 4,300	[2] 1,400	12,242	9,477	2,765
Fall 1985	57,226	44,979	39,422	27,034	12,388	5,557	4,195	1,362	12,247	9,479	2,768
Fall 1986	57,709	45,205	39,753	27,420	12,333	[2] 5,452	[2] 4,116	[2] 1,336	12,504	9,714	2,790
Fall 1987	58,253	45,487	40,008	27,933	12,076	5,479	4,232	1,247	12,767	9,973	2,793
Fall 1988	58,485	45,430	40,189	28,501	11,687	[2] 5,242	[2] 4,036	[2] 1,206	13,055	10,161	2,894
Fall 1989	59,279	45,741	40,543	29,152	11,390	[2] 5,198	[2] 4,035	[2] 1,163	13,539	10,578	2,961
Fall 1990	60,269	46,451	41,217	29,878	11,338	5,234	4,084	1,150	13,819	10,845	2,974
Fall 1991	61,681	47,322	42,047	30,506	11,541	[2] 5,275	[2] 4,113	[2] 1,162	14,359	11,310	3,049
Fall 1992	62,633	48,145	42,823	31,088	11,735	[2] 5,322	[2] 4,175	[2] 1,147	14,487	11,385	3,103
Fall 1993	63,118	48,813	43,465	31,504	11,961	[2] 5,348	[2] 4,215	[2] 1,132	14,305	11,189	3,116

graduate school. A significant number of students also attended two-year community colleges. In 1963 barely one in six students attended public two-year schools. By the 1970s two-year schools were playing a major role in U.S. higher education, with almost two out of five students attending during the 1980s. By 2000, out of a total of 15.3 million students attending degree-granting institutions, about one out of three students (5.9 million) were attending two-year schools. (See Table 6.10.)

DEGREES CONFERRED

As attendance in U.S. colleges and universities increased, so, too, did the number of degrees granted. (See Figure 6.5.) In 1960, 365,174 bachelor's degrees, 84,609 master's degrees, and 10,575 doctoral degrees were conferred. At the end of the 2000–01 school year 578,865 associate degrees, 1.2 million bachelor's degrees,

468,476 master's degrees, 79,707 first-professional degrees, and 44,904 doctoral degrees were awarded. While more women than men earned associate, bachelor's, and master's degrees, more men than women earned first-professional and doctoral degrees.

From the founding of the U.S. colonies in the 17th century, Americans have been renown for their entrepreneurial and capitalistic endeavors. This risk-taking spirit continues today and is reflected in the types of educational degrees being earned. Of the 1.2 million bachelor's degrees conferred from public and private educational institutions in 2000–01, about 22 percent were in business. Business is the most popular major, though this percentage dropped during the 1990s from about 25 percent. Education and social sciences were also popular, and the fields of parks, recreation, leisure, and fitness; agriculture and natural resources; biological sciences; and

TABLE 6.3

Enrollment in educational institutions, by level and control of institution, 1869–70 to fall 2012 [CONTINUED]

[In thousands]

Year	Total enrollment, all levels	Elementary and secondary, total	Public elementary and secondary schools			Private elementary and secondary schools			Degree-granting institutions[1]		
			Total	Pre-kindergarten through grade 8	Grades 9 through 12	Total	Kindergarten through grade 8	Grades 9 through 12	Total	Public	Private
1	2	3	4	5	6	7	8	9	10	11	12
Fall 1994	63,888	49,609	44,111	31,898	12,213	[2]5,498	[2]4,335	[2]1,163	14,279	11,134	3,145
Fall 1995	64,764	50,502	44,840	32,341	12,500	5,662	4,465	1,197	14,262	11,092	3,169
Fall 1996	65,743	51,375	45,611	32,764	12,847	[2]5,764	[2]4,551	[2]1,213	14,368	11,120	3,247
Fall 1997	66,470	51,968	46,127	33,073	13,054	5,841	4,623	1,218	14,502	11,196	3,306
Fall 1998	66,983	52,476	46,539	33,346	13,193	[2]5,937	[2]4,702	[2]1,235	14,507	11,138	3,369
Fall 1999	67,666	52,875	46,857	33,488	13,369	6,018	4,765	1,254	14,791	11,309	3,482
Fall 2000	68,479	53,167	47,223	33,709	13,514	[2]5,944	[2]4,678	[2]1,266	15,312	11,753	3,560
Fall 2001 [3]	68,962	53,520	47,576	33,854	13,722	5,944	4,668	1,276	15,442	11,864	3,578
Fall 2002 [3]	69,174	53,566	47,613	33,756	13,857	5,953	4,660	1,292	15,608	11,986	3,622
Fall 2003 [3]	69,456	53,700	47,746	33,677	14,069	5,954	4,644	1,310	15,756	12,101	3,655
Fall 2004 [3]	69,747	53,800	47,846	33,500	14,346	5,954	4,620	1,334	15,947	12,247	3,699
Fall 2005 [3]	70,001	53,866	47,912	33,315	14,597	5,954	4,603	1,351	16,135	12,388	3,746
Fall 2006 [3]	70,183	53,862	47,912	33,174	14,739	5,950	4,592	1,358	16,321	12,528	3,793
Fall 2007 [3]	70,292	53,789	47,847	33,078	14,768	5,942	4,588	1,355	16,503	12,665	3,839
Fall 2008 [3]	70,390	53,652	47,719	33,069	14,649	5,933	4,592	1,341	16,738	12,842	3,896
Fall 2009 [3]	70,516	53,538	47,607	33,122	14,485	5,931	4,604	1,327	16,978	13,023	3,955
Fall 2010 [3]	70,683	53,498	47,561	33,244	14,317	5,937	4,625	1,313	17,185	13,179	4,007
Fall 2011 [3]	70,956	53,538	47,586	33,389	14,197	5,952	4,649	1,303	17,418	13,351	4,068
Fall 2012 [3]	71,365	53,692	47,715	33,578	14,137	5,977	4,680	1,297	17,673	13,537	4,136

—Not available.

[1] Data for 1869–70 through 1949–50 include resident degree-credit students enrolled at any time during the academic year. Beginning in 1959, data include all resident and extension students enrolled at the beginning of the fall term.

[2] Estimated.

[3] Projected.

Note: Elementary and secondary enrollment includes pupils in local public school systems and in most private schools (religiously affiliated and nonsectarian), but generally excludes pupils in subcollegiate departments of colleges, federal schools, and home-schooled children. Public elementary enrollment includes most preprimary school pupils. Private elementary enrollment includes some preprimary students. Public elementary and secondary enrollment for 2001 are state estimates. Higher education enrollment includes students in colleges, universities, professional schools, and 2-year colleges. Degree-granting institutions are 2-year and 4-year institutions that were eligible to participate in Title IV federal financial aid programs. Detail may not sum to totals due to rounding.

SOURCE: Thomas D. Snyder, Charlene M. Hoffman, "Table 3. Enrollment in educational institutions, by level and control of institution: 1869–70 to fall 2012," in *Digest of Education Statistics 2002,* vol. 2003-060, June 2003

multidisciplinary studies have been growing in recent years. Computer and information sciences, virtually unknown a generation ago, now account for nearly 3 percent of all bachelor's degrees. (See Table 6.11.)

THE INFLUENCE OF EDUCATION ON EARNINGS

Higher levels of education generally lead to higher incomes. In fact, the wage gap between more- and less-educated workers has widened over the past two decades. In 1977 the average male college graduate earned about 50 percent more than the average male high school graduate; in 2000 the male college graduate earned 80 percent more than his high school counterpart. In 1977 the average female college graduate earned 41 percent more than the average female high school graduate. By 2000 a female college graduate earned 71 percent more than a female high school graduate.

Similarly, workers without a high school degree, or its equivalent, earn less than those with high school degrees,

although the gap is not as wide as that between high school and college graduates. In 2000 the median income for men 25 years old and over who had gone beyond the ninth grade but had not completed high school was $25,095. This income was 27 percent less than males who completed high school, with a median annual income of $34,303. Women high school graduates 25 years of age and older earned a median income of $24,970 in 2000, and those who completed ninth grade but had not completed high school earned $17,919, 28 percent less. (See Table 6.12.)

HOW MUCH DO WE SPEND ON EDUCATION?

Expenditures for public and private education from preprimary through graduate school rose to an estimated record high of $745.2 billion in current dollars for the 2001–02 school year. Elementary and secondary schools were expected to expend 61 percent of this total ($454.1 billion), while institutions of higher learning would account for the remaining 39 percent ($291.1 billion). (See Table

TABLE 6.4

Enrollment of 3-, 4-, and 5-year-old children in preprimary programs by level and control of program and by attendance status, October 1965 to October 2001

[In thousands]

Year and age	Total population, 3 to 5 years old	Enrollment by level and control						Enrollment by attendance		
		Total	Percent enrolled	Nursery school		Kindergarten		Full-day	Part-day	Percent full-day
				Public	Private	Public	Private			
1	2	3	4	5	6	7	8	9	10	11

Total, 3 to 5 years old

Year and age	Total population, 3 to 5 years old	Total	Percent enrolled	Public	Private	Public	Private	Full-day	Part-day	Percent full-day
1965	12,549	3,407 (87)	27.1 (0.7)	127	393	2,291	596	—(—)	—	—(—)
1970	10,949	4,104 (71)	37.5 (0.7)	332	762	2,498	511	698 (36)	3,405	17.0 (0.8)
1975	10,185	4,955 (71)	48.7 (0.7)	570	1,174	2,682	528	1,295 (47)	3,659	26.1 (0.9)
1980	9,284	4,878 (69)	52.5 (0.7)	628	1,353	2,438	459	1,551 (51)	3,327	31.8 (1.0)
1985	10,733	5,865 (78)	54.6 (0.7)	846	1,631	2,847	541	2,144 (62)	3,722	36.6 (0.9)
1986	10,866	5,971 (78)	55.0 (0.7)	829	1,715	2,859	567	2,241 (63)	3,730	37.5 (0.9)
1987	10,872	5,931 (78)	54.6 (0.7)	819	1,736	2,842	534	2,090 (62)	3,841	35.2 (0.9)
1988	10,993	5,978 (87)	54.4 (0.8)	851	1,770	2,875	481	2,044 (68)	3,935	34.2 (1.0)
1989	11,039	6,026 (87)	54.6 (0.8)	930	1,894	2,704	497	2,238 (70)	3,789	37.1 (1.0)
1990	11,207	6,659 (82)	59.4 (0.7)	1,199	2,180	2,772	509	2,577 (71)	4,082	38.7 (0.9)
1991	11,370	6,334 (84)	55.7 (0.7)	996	1,828	2,967	543	2,408 (69)	3,926	38.0 (1.0)
1992	11,545	6,402 (85)	55.5 (0.7)	1,073	1,783	2,995	550	2,410 (69)	3,992	37.6 (1.0)
1993	11,954	6,581 (86)	55.1 (0.7)	1,205	1,779	3,020	577	2,642 (72)	3,939	40.1 (1.0)
1994	12,328	7,514 (86)	61.0 (0.7)	1,848	2,314	2,819	534	3,468 (80)	4,046	46.2 (0.9)
1995	12,518	7,739 (87)	61.8 (0.7)	1,950	2,381	2,800	608	3,689 (81)	4,051	47.7 (0.9)
1996	12,378	7,580 (90)	61.2 (0.7)	1,830	2,317	2,853	580	3,562 (83)	4,019	47.0 (0.9)
1997	12,121	7,860 (85)	64.9 (0.7)	2,207	2,231	2,847	575	3,922 (85)	3,939	49.9 (0.9)
1998	12,078	7,788 (87)	64.5 (0.7)	2,213	2,299	2,674	602	3,959 (85)	3,829	50.8 (0.9)
1999	11,920	7,844 (86)	65.8 (0.7)	2,209	2,298	2,777	560	4,154 (86)	3,690	53.0 (0.9)
2000	11,858	7,592 (86)	64.0 (0.7)	2,146	2,180	2,701	565	4,008 (85)	3,584	52.8 (0.9)
2001	11,899	7,602 (87)	63.9 (0.7)	2,164	2,201	2,724	512	3,940 (85)	3,662	51.8 (0.9)

3 years old

Year and age	Total population, 3 to 5 years old	Total	Percent enrolled	Public	Private	Public	Private	Full-day	Part-day	Percent full-day
1965	4,149	203 (24)	4.9 (0.6)	41	153	5	4	—(—)	—	—(—)
1970	3,516	454 (28)	12.9 (0.8)	110	322	12	10	142 (16)	312	31.3 (3.1)
1975	3,177	683 (33)	21.5 (1.0)	179	474	11	18	259 (22)	423	37.9 (2.6)
1980	3,143	857 (36)	27.3 (1.1)	221	604	16	17	321 (24)	536	37.5 (2.4)
1985	3,594	1,035 (41)	28.8 (1.1)	278	679	52	26	350 (27)	685	33.8 (2.2)
1986	3,607	1,041 (41)	28.9 (1.1)	257	737	26	21	399 (28)	642	38.3 (2.3)
1987	3,569	1,022 (41)	28.6 (1.1)	264	703	24	31	378 (28)	644	37.0 (2.3)
1988	3,719	1,027 (45)	27.6 (1.2)	298	678	24	26	369 (30)	658	35.9 (2.5)
1989	3,713	1,005 (45)	27.1 (1.2)	277	707	3	18	390 (31)	615	38.8 (2.6)
1990	3,692	1,205 (45)	32.6 (1.2)	347	840	11	7	447 (31)	758	37.1 (2.2)
1991	3,811	1,074 (44)	28.2 (1.2)	313	702	38	22	388 (30)	687	36.1 (2.3)
1992	3,905	1,081 (44)	27.7 (1.1)	336	685	26	34	371 (29)	711	34.3 (2.3)
1993	4,053	1,097 (45)	27.1 (1.1)	369	687	20	20	426 (31)	670	38.9 (2.3)
1994	4,081	1,385 (48)	33.9 (1.2)	469	887	19	9	670 (38)	715	48.4 (2.1)
1995	4,148	1,489 (49)	35.9 (1.2)	511	947	15	17	754 (40)	736	50.6 (2.1)
1996	4,045	1,506 (51)	37.2 (1.3)	511	947	22	26	657 (39)	848	43.7 (2.1)
1997	3,947	1,528 (51)	38.7 (1.3)	643	843	25	18	754 (41)	774	49.4 (2.1)
1998	3,989	1,498 (51)	37.6 (1.3)	587	869	27	14	735 (40)	763	49.1 (2.1)
1999	3,862	1,505 (50)	39.0 (1.3)	621	859	13	12	773 (41)	732	51.3 (2.1)
2000	3,929	1,541 (51)	39.2 (1.3)	644	854	27	16	761 (41)	779	49.4 (2.1)
2001	3,985	1,538 (51)	38.6 (1.3)	599	901	14	23	715 (40)	823	46.5 (2.1)

4 years old

Year and age	Total population, 3 to 5 years old	Total	Percent enrolled	Public	Private	Public	Private	Full-day	Part-day	Percent full-day
1965	4,238	683 (42)	16.1 (1.0)	68	213	284	118	—(—)	—	—(—)
1970	3,620	1,007 (38)	27.8 (1.1)	176	395	318	117	230 (21)	776	22.8 (1.9)
1975	3,499	1,418 (41)	40.5 (1.2)	332	644	313	129	411 (27)	1,008	29.0 (1.7)
1980	3,072	1,423 (40)	46.3 (1.3)	363	701	239	120	467 (28)	956	32.8 (1.8)
1985	3,598	1,766 (45)	49.1 (1.3)	496	859	276	135	643 (35)	1,123	36.4 (1.7)
1986	3,616	1,772 (45)	49.0 (1.3)	498	903	257	115	622 (34)	1,150	35.1 (1.7)
1987	3,597	1,717 (45)	47.7 (1.3)	431	881	280	125	548 (32)	1,169	31.9 (1.7)
1988	3,598	1,768 (50)	49.1 (1.4)	481	922	261	104	519 (35)	1,249	29.4 (1.8)
1989	3,692	1,882 (51)	51.0 (1.4)	524	1,055	202	100	592 (37)	1,290	31.4 (1.8)
1990	3,723	2,087 (48)	56.1 (1.3)	695	1,144	157	91	716 (38)	1,371	34.3 (1.6)
1991	3,763	1,994 (48)	53.0 (1.3)	584	982	287	140	667 (37)	1,326	33.5 (1.7)
1992	3,807	1,982 (49)	52.1 (1.3)	602	971	282	126	632 (36)	1,350	31.9 (1.7)
1993	4,044	2,178 (50)	53.9 (1.2)	719	957	349	154	765 (39)	1,413	35.1 (1.6)
1994	4,202	2,532 (51)	60.3 (1.2)	1,020	1,232	198	82	1,095 (45)	1,438	43.2 (1.6)
1995	4,145	2,553 (50)	61.6 (1.2)	1,054	1,208	207	84	1,104 (45)	1,449	43.3 (1.6)

TABLE 6.4

Enrollment of 3-, 4-, and 5-year-old children in preprimary programs by level and control of program and by attendance status, October 1965 to October 2001 [CONTINUED]

[In thousands]

Year and age	Total population, 3 to 5 years old	Enrollment by level and control						Enrollment by attendance		
		Total	Percent enrolled	Nursery school		Kindergarten		Full-day	Part-day	Percent full-day
				Public	Private	Public	Private			
1	2	3	4	5	6	7	8	9	10	11
4 years old										
1996	4,148	2,454 (52)	59.2 (1.3)	1,029	1,168	180	77	1,034 (46)	1,420	42.1 (1.6)
1997	4,033	2,665 (50)	66.1 (1.2)	1,197	1,169	207	92	1,161 (47)	1,505	43.5 (1.6)
1998	4,002	2,666 (49)	66.6 (1.2)	1,183	1,219	210	53	1,179 (48)	1,487	44.2 (1.6)
1999	4,021	2,769 (48)	68.9 (1.2)	1,212	1,227	207	122	1,355 (49)	1,414	48.9 (1.6)
2000	3,940	2,556 (49)	64.9 (1.3)	1,144	1,121	227	65	1,182 (48)	1,374	46.2 (1.6)
2001	3,927	2,608 (49)	66.4 (1.2)	1,202	1,121	236	49	1,255 (48)	1,354	48.1 (1.6)
5 years old										
1965	4,162	2,521 (55)	60.6 (1.3)	18	27	2,002	474	—(—)	—	—(—)
1970	3,814	2,643 (40)	69.3 (1.1)	45	45	2,168	384	326 (24)	2,317	12.3 (0.9)
1975	3,509	2,854 (33)	81.3 (0.9)	59	57	2,358	381	625 (32)	2,228	21.9 (1.1)
1980	3,069	2,598 (29)	84.7 (0.9)	44	48	2,183	322	763 (34)	1,835	29.4 (1.3)
1985	3,542	3,065 (31)	86.5 (0.9)	73	94	2,519	379	1,151 (42)	1,914	37.6 (1.3)
1986	3,643	3,157 (31)	86.7 (0.8)	75	75	2,576	432	1,220 (43)	1,937	38.6 (1.3)
1987	3,706	3,192 (32)	86.1 (0.9)	124	152	2,538	378	1,163 (43)	2,028	36.4 (1.3)
1988	3,676	3,184 (34)	86.6 (0.9)	72	170	2,590	351	1,155 (47)	2,028	36.3 (1.4)
1989	3,633	3,139 (34)	86.4 (0.9)	129	132	2,499	378	1,255 (47)	1,883	40.0 (1.5)
1990	3,792	3,367 (31)	88.8 (0.8)	157	196	2,604	411	1,414 (47)	1,953	42.0 (1.3)
1991	3,796	3,267 (34)	86.0 (0.9)	100	143	2,642	382	1,354 (47)	1,913	41.4 (1.4)
1992	3,832	3,339 (33)	87.1 (0.9)	135	127	2,688	390	1,408 (47)	1,931	42.2 (1.4)
1993	3,857	3,306 (34)	85.7 (0.9)	116	136	2,651	403	1,451 (48)	1,856	43.9 (1.4)
1994	4,044	3,597 (32)	88.9 (0.8)	359	194	2,601	442	1,704 (50)	1,893	47.4 (1.3)
1995	4,224	3,697 (34)	87.5 (0.8)	385	226	2,578	507	1,830 (51)	1,867	49.5 (1.3)
1996	4,185	3,621 (36)	86.5 (0.9)	290	202	2,652	477	1,870 (53)	1,750	51.7 (1.4)
1997	4,141	3,667 (34)	88.5 (0.8)	368	219	2,616	465	2,007 (53)	1,660	54.7 (1.4)
1998	4,087	3,624 (33)	88.7 (0.8)	442	211	2,437	535	2,044 (53)	1,579	56.4 (1.4)
1999	4,037	3,571 (34)	88.4 (0.8)	376	212	2,557	426	2,027 (52)	1,544	56.8 (1.4)
2000	3,989	3,495 (34)	87.6 (0.9)	359	206	2,447	484	2,065 (52)	1,431	59.1 (1.4)
2001	3,987	3,456 (35)	86.7 (0.9)	363	179	2,474	440	1,970 (52)	1,485	57.0 (1.4)

Note: —Not available.
*Enrollment data include only those students in preprimary programs.
Note: Detail may not sum to totals due to rounding. Standard errors appear in parentheses.

SOURCE: Thomas D. Snyder, Charlene M. Hoffman, "Table 43. Enrollment of 3-, 4-, and 5-year old children in preprimary programs, by level and control of program and by attendance status: October 1965 to October 2001," in *Digest of Education Statistics 2002,* vol. 2003-060, U.S. Department of Education, National Center for Education Statistics, Washington, DC, June 2003

6.13.) The United States is expected to spend 7.4 percent of its gross domestic product on education in 2001–02.

For the 1999–2000 school year the nation's public elementary and secondary schools received 49.5 percent of their funding from state sources, 43.2 percent from local sources, and 7.3 percent from the federal government. The percentage of federal funding for public elementary and secondary schools has remained fairly constant (between 6 and 10 percent) since 1965. (See Table 6.14.) For the 1995–96 school year, which are the most up-to-date figures available, institutions of higher education received $197.4 billion in revenue, of which 23.9 billion came from the federal government, 45.6 billion from state governments, and 5.6 billion from local governments. Federal funding for these institutions has more than doubled since the 1984–85 school year. (See Table 6.15.)

In the 1999–2000 school year private institutions received $121.5 billion from various sources. Student tuition and fees accounted for $29.6 billion, private gifts $16.5 billion, and investment returns $37.8 billion. The federal government appropriated $12.2 billion to private colleges and universities. In the same school year, revenues measured by a full-time equivalent student in a private college or university received $47,861 per year, from which $14,874 (31 percent) came from investment returns, $11,679 (24 percent) came from student tuition and fees, $6,495 (14 percent) from private gifts, $4,802 (10 percent) from the federal government, and $440 (0.9 percent) from state appropriations. (See Table 6.16.)

Expenditures Per Student

Per pupil expenditures in average daily attendance in 2001–02 for public elementary and secondary schools in the United States was $8,048. Huge differences exist in per-pupil spending by state, with New Jersey, Connecticut, New York, Rhode Island, and Alaska spending the most—

FIGURE 6.4

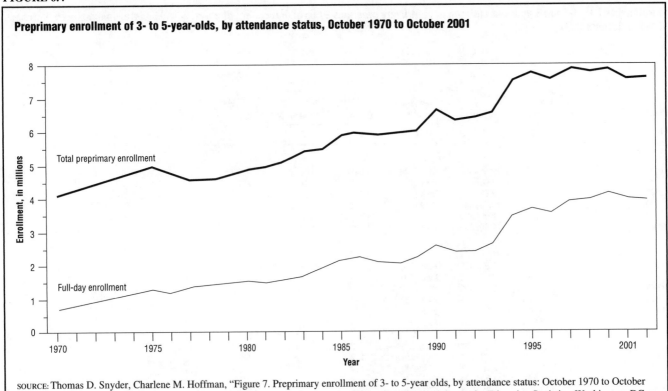

Preprimary enrollment of 3- to 5-year-olds, by attendance status, October 1970 to October 2001

SOURCE: Thomas D. Snyder, Charlene M. Hoffman, "Figure 7. Preprimary enrollment of 3- to 5-year olds, by attendance status: October 1970 to October 2001," in *Digest of Education Statistics 2002*, vol. 2003–060, U.S. Department of Education, National Center for Education Statistics, Washington, DC, June 2003

between $10,337 and $8,806 per student—and Utah, Arizona, Mississippi, Arkansas, Idaho, and Tennessee spending the least—between $5,383 and $4,378 per student—in 1999–2000. While money spent is not the only indicator of a state's commitment to education or financial ability to offer an education (it is often a reflection of the cost of living), it is one indicator of the quality of education students are receiving in that state. (See Table 6.17 and Table 6.18.)

TABLE 6.5

Public elementary and secondary schools, by type and size of school, 2000–01

	Number of schools, by type						Enrollment, by type of school[1]					
			Secondary[4]		Combined elementary/secondary[5]				Secondary[4]		Combined elementary/secondary[5]	
Enrollment size of school	Total[2]	Elementary[3]	All schools	Regular schools[6]		Other[2]	Total[2]	Elementary[3]	All schools	Regular schools[6]		Other[2]
1	2	3	4	5	6	7	8	9	10	11	12	13
Total	93,273	64,601	21,994	18,456	5,096	1,582	47,060,714	30,673,453	15,038,171	14,567,969	1,266,778	82,312
Percent[7]	100.00	100.00	100.00	100.00	100.00	100.00	100.00	100.00	100.00	100.00	100.00	100.00
Under 100	10.69	6.24	15.40	8.54	44.81	58.61	0.93	0.64	1.00	0.62	6.20	18.20
100 to 199	9.68	8.74	10.81	9.98	15.90	22.68	2.78	2.77	2.22	1.85	8.46	23.64
200 to 299	11.42	12.64	8.37	8.59	8.69	7.95	5.55	6.72	2.92	2.70	7.78	14.05
300 to 399	13.22	15.51	7.83	8.36	6.85	5.79	8.90	11.38	3.83	3.67	8.70	14.57
400 to 499	13.26	16.07	6.69	7.32	5.42	2.65	11.46	15.14	4.20	4.13	8.84	8.66
500 to 599	11.03	13.13	6.35	6.99	4.56	0.50	11.63	15.07	4.89	4.83	9.11	1.97
600 to 699	8.21	9.49	5.49	6.11	3.87	0.33	10.23	12.87	4.98	4.98	9.09	1.57
700 to 799	6.00	6.66	4.93	5.51	2.38	0.17	8.62	10.43	5.15	5.18	6.46	0.97
800 to 999	6.90	6.79	8.26	9.28	3.07	0.33	11.79	12.59	10.35	10.44	10.01	2.04
1,000 to 1,499	6.02	4.09	12.72	14.32	2.98	0.50	13.85	9.99	21.85	22.07	12.92	4.51
1,500 to 1,999	2.11	0.53	7.27	8.28	0.86	0.00	6.96	1.85	17.55	17.94	5.38	0.00
2,000 to 2,999	1.24	0.11	4.91	5.61	0.43	0.33	5.63	0.51	16.21	16.63	3.87	5.06
3,000 or more	0.24	0.01	0.96	1.10	0.17	0.17	1.68	0.06	4.85	4.95	3.18	4.76
Average enrollment[7]	519	477	714	795	274	136	519	477	714	795	274	136

[1]These enrollment data should be regarded as approximations only. This table represents data reported by schools rather than by states or school districts. Percent distribution and average enrollment calculations exclude data for schools not reporting enrollment.
[2]Includes special education, alternative, and other schools not classified by grade span.
[3]Includes schools beginning with grade 6 or below and with no grade higher than 8.
[4]Includes schools with no grade lower than 7.
[5]Includes schools beginning with grade 6 or below and ending with grade 9 or above.
[6]Excludes special education schools, vocational schools, and alternative schools.
[7]Data are for schools reporting their enrollment size.
Note: Detail may not sum to totals due to rounding.

SOURCE: Thomas D. Snyder, Charlene M. Hoffman, "Table 94. Public elementary and secondary schools, by type and size of school: 2000–01," in *Digest of Education Statistics 2002,* vol. 2003-060, U.S. Department of Education, National Center for Education Statistics, Washington, DC, June 2003

TABLE 6.6

Public elementary and secondary schools, by type of school, 1967– to 2000–01

		Schools with reported grade spans											
			Elementary schools				Secondary schools						
Year	Total, all public schools	Total	Total[1]	Middle schools[2]	One-teacher schools	Other elementary schools	Total[3]	Junior high[4]	3-year or 4-year high schools	5-year or 6-year high schools	Other secondary schools	Combined elementary/ secondary schools[5]	Other schools[6]
1	2	3	4	5	6	7	8	9	10	11	12	13	14
1967–68	—	94,197	67,186	—	4,146	63,040	23,318	7,437	10,751	4,650	480	3,693	—
1970–71	—	89,372	64,020	2,080	1,815	60,125	23,572	7,750	11,265	3,887	670	1,780	—
1972–73	—	88,864	62,942	2,308	1,475	59,159	23,919	7,878	11,550	3,962	529	2,003	—
1974–75	—	87,456	61,759	3,224	1,247	57,288	23,837	7,690	11,480	4,122	545	1,860	—
1975–76	88,597	87,034	61,704	3,916	1,166	56,622	23,792	7,521	11,572	4,113	586	1,538	1,563
1976–77	—	86,501	61,123	4,180	1,111	55,832	23,857	7,434	11,658	4,130	635	1,521	—
1978–79	—	84,816	60,312	5,879	1,056	53,377	22,834	6,282	11,410	4,429	713	1,670	—
1980–81	85,982	83,688	59,326	6,003	921	52,402	22,619	5,890	10,758	4,193	1,778	1,743	2,294
1982–83	84,740	82,039	58,051	6,875	798	50,378	22,383	5,948	11,678	4,067	690	1,605	2,701
1983–84	84,178	81,418	57,471	6,885	838	49,748	22,336	5,936	11,670	4,046	684	1,611	2,760
1984–85	84,007	81,147	57,231	6,893	825	49,513	22,320	5,916	11,671	4,021	712	1,596	2,860
1986–87	83,455	82,190	58,801	7,452	763	50,586	21,406	5,142	11,453	4,197	614	1,983	1,265
1987–88	83,248	81,416	57,575	7,641	729	49,205	21,662	4,900	11,279	4,048	1,435	2,179	1,832
1988–89	83,165	81,579	57,941	7,957	583	49,401	21,403	4,687	11,350	3,994	1,372	2,235	1,586
1989–90	83,425	81,880	58,419	8,272	630	49,517	21,181	4,512	11,492	3,812	1,365	2,280	1,545
1990–91	84,538	82,475	59,015	8,545	617	49,853	21,135	4,561	11,537	3,723	1,314	2,325	2,063
1991–92	84,578	82,506	59,258	8,829	569	49,860	20,767	4,298	11,528	3,699	1,242	2,481	2,072
1992–93	84,497	82,896	59,676	9,152	430	50,094	20,671	4,115	11,651	3,613	1,292	2,549	1,601
1993–94	85,393	83,431	60,052	9,573	442	50,037	20,705	3,970	11,858	3,595	1,282	2,674	1,962
1994–95	86,221	84,476	60,808	9,954	458	50,396	20,904	3,859	12,058	3,628	1,359	2,764	1,745
1995–96	87,125	84,958	61,165	10,205	474	50,486	20,997	3,743	12,168	3,621	1,465	2,796	2,167
1996–97	88,223	86,092	61,805	10,499	487	50,819	21,307	3,707	12,424	3,614	1,562	2,980	2,131
1997–98	89,508	87,541	62,739	10,944	476	51,319	21,682	3,599	12,734	3,611	1,738	3,120	1,967
1998–99	90,874	89,259	63,462	11,202	463	51,797	22,076	3,607	13,457	3,707	1,305	3,721	1,615
1999–2000	92,012	90,538	64,131	11,521	423	52,187	22,365	3,566	13,914	3,686	1,199	4,042	1,474
2000–01	93,273	91,691	64,601	11,696	411	52,494	21,994	3,318	13,793	3,974	909	5,096	1,582

Note: —Not available.
[1]Includes schools beginning with grade 6 or below and with no grade higher than 8.
[2]Includes schools with grade spans beginning with 4, 5, or 6 and ending with grade 6, 7, or 8.
[3]Includes schools with no grade lower than 7.
[4]Includes schools with grades 7 and 8 or grades 7 through 9.
[5]Includes schools beginning with grade 6 or lower and ending with grade 9 or above.
[6]Includes special education, alternative, and other schools not classified by grade span.

SOURCE: Thomas D. Snyder, Charlene M. Hoffman, "Table 93. Public elementary and secondary schools, by type of school: 1967–68 to 2000–01," in *Digest of Education Statistics 2002*, vol. 2003-060, U.S. Department of Education, Institute of Education Sciences, Washington, DC, June 2003

TABLE 6.7

Private elementary and secondary enrollment, teachers, and schools, by selected characteristics, fall 1999

Selected school characteristics	Kindergarten to 12th-grade enrollment				Teachers				Schools			
	Total	Catholic	Other religious	Non-sectarian	Total	Catholic	Other religious	Non-sectarian	Total	Catholic	Other religious	Non-sectarian
1	2	3	4	5	6	7	8	9	10	11	12	13
Total	5,162,684	2,511,040	1,843,580	808,063	395,317	149,600	152,915	92,801	27,223	8,102	13,232	5,889
Standard error	25,410	4,787	24,799	5,428	2,881	210	2,759	722	239	24	228	68
Level of school												
Elementary	2,831,372	1,814,676	750,026	266,669	187,833	100,565	58,386	28,882	16,530	6,707	6,843	2,981
Secondary	806,639	607,682	112,132	86,825	62,737	41,301	10,586	10,849	2,538	1,114	718	707
Combined	1,524,673	88,682	981,422	454,569	144,746	7,734	83,943	53,070	8,155	282	5,672	2,201
School enrollment												
Less than 50	196,309	5,497	128,007	62,806	26,329	769	15,898	9,662	7,565	172	5,031	2,362
50 to 149	716,129	149,542	385,184	181,403	71,676	12,543	36,431	22,702	7,738	1,408	4,280	2,050
150 to 299	1,424,018	767,888	496,825	159,306	102,457	45,928	38,371	18,157	6,571	3,450	2,364	757
300 to 499	1,228,631	720,044	357,479	151,109	84,086	41,439	26,627	16,020	3,219	1,876	946	397
500 to 749	805,490	477,806	215,910	111,774	54,078	26,057	15,964	12,057	1,352	805	360	187
750 or more	792,106	390,264	260,177	141,666	56,691	22,864	19,624	14,203	778	391	250	136
Percent minority students												
None	291,838	61,442	212,771	17,624	25,578	4,053	19,613	1,912	4,012	415	3,228	368
1 to 9 percent	2,282,659	1,216,054	806,530	260,075	164,869	72,015	64,951	27,903	9,219	3,737	4,149	1,332
10 to 29 percent	1,360,769	589,224	433,044	338,502	115,605	37,070	37,304	41,231	6,435	1,733	2,702	1,999
30 to 49 percent	414,323	190,783	139,742	83,798	32,424	11,471	10,994	9,959	2,455	604	1,007	844
50 percent or more	813,095	453,537	251,494	108,064	56,841	24,991	20,053	11,797	5,103	1,613	2,145	1,345
Community type												
Central city	2,540,516	1,293,629	870,219	376,668	189,984	76,118	71,244	42,622	10,825	3,737	4,550	2,538
Urban fringe/large town	2,051,094	1,022,949	714,090	314,056	155,436	59,815	58,053	37,568	10,359	3,142	4,725	2,492
Rural/small town	571,074	194,463	259,272	117,340	49,897	13,667	23,619	12,611	6,040	1,223	3,958	859

Note: Includes only schools that offer the first grade or a higher grade. Excludes prekindergarten students. Detail may not sum to totals due to rounding.

SOURCE: Thomas D. Snyder, Charlene M. Hoffman, "Table 59. Private elementary and secondary enrollment, teachers, and schools, by selected characteristics: Fall 1999," in *Digest of Education Statistics 2002,* U.S. Department of Education, National Center for Education Statistics, Washington, DC, vol. 2003-060, June 2003

TABLE 6.8

Enrollment in grades 9 to 12 in public and private schools compared with population 14 to 17 years of age, 1889–90 to fall 2001

[Numbers in thousands]

Year	Enrollment, grades 9 to 12 [1]			Population 14 to 17 years of age	Enrollment as a percent of population 14 to 17 years of age [3]
	All schools	Public schools	Private schools[2]		
1	2	3	4	5	6
1889–90	298	203	95	5,355	5.6
1899–1900	630	519	111	6,152	10.2
1909–10	1,032	915	117	7,220	14.3
1919–20	2,414	2,200	214	7,736	31.2
1929–30	4,741	4,399	[4] 341	9,341	50.7
1939–40	7,059	6,601	[5] 458	9,720	72.6
1949–50	6,397	5,725	672	8,405	76.1
1951–52	6,538	5,882	656	8,516	76.8
1953–54	7,038	6,290	747	8,861	79.4
1955–56	7,696	6,873	823	9,207	83.6
1957–58	8,790	7,860	931	10,139	86.7
Fall 1959	9,306	8,271	1,035	11,155	83.4
Fall 1961	10,489	9,369	1,120	12,046	87.1
Fall 1963	12,170	10,883	1,287	13,492	90.2
Fall 1965	13,010	11,610	1,400	14,146	92.0
Fall 1966	13,294	11,894	1,400	14,398	92.3
Fall 1967	13,650	12,250	1,400	14,727	92.7
Fall 1968	14,118	12,718	1,400	15,170	93.1
Fall 1969	14,337	13,037	[6] 1,300	15,549	92.2
Fall 1970	14,647	13,336	1,311	15,921	92.0
Fall 1971	15,053	13,753	[6] 1,300	16,326	92.2
Fall 1972	15,148	13,848	[6] 1,300	16,637	91.0
Fall 1973	15,344	14,044	[6] 1,300	16,864	91.0
Fall 1974	15,403	14,103	[6] 1,300	17,033	90.4
Fall 1975	15,604	14,304	[6] 1,300	17,125	91.1
Fall 1976	15,656	14,314	1,342	17,117	91.5
Fall 1977	15,546	14,203	1,343	17,042	91.2
Fall 1978	15,441	14,088	1,353	16,944	91.1
Fall 1979	14,916	13,616	[6] 1,300	16,610	89.8
Fall 1980	14,570	13,231	1,339	16,143	90.3
Fall 1981	14,164	12,764	[6] 1,400	15,609	90.7
Fall 1982	13,805	12,405	[6] 1,400	15,057	91.7
Fall 1983	13,671	12,271	1,400	14,740	92.7
Fall 1984	13,704	12,304	[6] 1,400	14,725	93.1
Fall 1985	13,750	12,388	1,362	14,888	92.4
Fall 1986	13,669	12,333	[6] 1,336	14,824	92.2
Fall 1987	13,323	12,076	1,247	14,502	91.9
Fall 1988	12,893	11,687	[6] 1,206	14,023	91.9
Fall 1989	12,553	11,390	[6] 1,163	13,536	92.7
Fall 1990	12,488	11,338	1,150	13,322	93.7
Fall 1991	12,703	11,541	[6] 1,162	13,452	94.4
Fall 1992	12,882	11,735	[6] 1,147	13,703	94.0
Fall 1993	13,093	11,961	[6] 1,132	13,953	93.8
Fall 1994	13,376	12,213	[6] 1,163	14,492	92.3
Fall 1995	13,697	12,500	1,197	14,828	92.4
Fall 1996	14,060	12,847	[6] 1,213	15,213	92.4
Fall 1997	14,272	13,054	1,218	15,499	92.1
Fall 1998	14,428	13,193	[6] 1,235	15,518	93.0
Fall 1999	14,623	13,369	1,254	15,654	93.4
Fall 2000	14,780	13,514	[6] 1,266	15,725	94.0
Fall 2001 [7]	14,998	13,722	1,276	15,821	94.8

[1] Includes a relatively small number of secondary ungraded and postgraduate students.
[2] Data for most years are partly estimated.
[3] Gross enrollment ratio based on school enrollment of all ages in grades 9 to 12 divided by the 14- to 17-year-old population. Differs from enrollment rates in other tables which are based on the enrollment of persons in the given age group only.
[4] Data are for 1927–28.
[5] Data are for 1940–41.
[6] Estimated.
[7] Projected.

Note: Allocation of ungraded students to secondary levels based on proportions derived from prior years. Includes enrollment in public schools that are a part of state and local school systems and also in most private schools, both religiously affiliated and non-sectarian. Detail may not sum to totals due to rounding.

SOURCE: Thomas D. Snyder, Charlene M. Hoffman, "Table 56. Enrollment in grades 9 to 12 in public and private schools compared with population 14 to 17 years of age: 1889–90 to fall 2001," in *Digest of Education Statistics 2002,* U.S. Department of Education, National Center for Education Statistics, Washington, DC, vol. 2003-060, June 2003

TABLE 6.9

Total fall enrollment in degree-granting institutions, by attendance status, sex of student, and control of institution, 1947–2000

Year	Total enrollment	Attendance status		Sex of student		Control of institution			
		Full-time	Part-time	Men	Women	Public	Private		
							Total	Not-for-profit	For-profit
1	2	3	4	5	6	7	8	9	10
Institutions of higher education [1]									
1947 [2]	2,338,226	—	—	1,659,249	678,977	1,152,377	1,185,849	—	—
1948 [2]	2,403,396	—	—	1,709,367	694,029	1,185,588	1,217,808	—	—
1949 [2]	2,444,900	—	—	1,721,572	723,328	1,207,151	1,237,749	—	—
1950 [2]	2,281,298	—	—	1,560,392	720,906	1,139,699	1,141,599	—	—
1951 [2]	2,101,962	—	—	1,390,740	711,222	1,037,938	1,064,024	—	—
1952 [2]	2,134,242	—	—	1,380,357	753,885	1,101,240	1,033,002	—	—
1953 [2]	2,231,054	—	—	1,422,598	808,456	1,185,876	1,045,178	—	—
1954 [2]	2,446,693	—	—	1,563,382	883,311	1,353,531	1,093,162	—	—
1955 [2]	2,653,034	—	—	1,733,184	919,850	1,476,282	1,176,752	—	—
1956 [2]	2,918,212	—	—	1,911,458	1,006,754	1,656,402	1,261,810	—	—
1957	3,323,783	—	—	2,170,765	1,153,018	1,972,673	1,351,110	—	—
1959	3,639,847	2,421,016	[3] 1,218,831	2,332,617	1,307,230	2,180,982	1,458,865	—	—
1961	4,145,065	2,785,133	[3] 1,359,932	2,585,821	1,559,244	2,561,447	1,583,618	—	—
1963	4,779,609	3,183,833	[3] 1,595,776	2,961,540	1,818,069	3,081,279	1,698,330	—	—
1964	5,280,020	3,573,238	[3] 1,706,782	3,248,713	2,031,307	3,467,708	1,812,312	—	—
1965	5,920,864	4,095,728	[3] 1,825,136	3,630,020	2,290,844	3,969,596	1,951,268	—	—
1966	6,389,872	4,438,606	[3] 1,951,266	3,856,216	2,533,656	4,348,917	2,040,955	—	—
1967	6,911,748	4,793,128	[3] 2,118,620	4,132,800	2,778,948	4,816,028	2,095,720	—	—
1968	7,513,091	5,210,155	2,302,936	4,477,649	3,035,442	5,430,652	2,082,439	—	—
1969	8,004,660	5,498,883	2,505,777	4,746,201	3,258,459	5,896,868	2,107,792	—	—
1970	8,580,887	5,816,290	2,764,597	5,043,642	3,537,245	6,428,134	2,152,753	—	—
1971	8,948,644	6,077,232	2,871,412	5,207,004	3,741,640	6,804,309	2,144,335	—	—
1972	9,214,820	6,072,350	3,142,470	5,238,718	3,976,102	7,070,635	2,144,185	—	—
1973	9,602,123	6,189,493	3,412,630	5,371,052	4,231,071	7,419,516	2,182,607	—	—
1974	10,223,729	6,370,273	3,853,456	5,622,429	4,601,300	7,988,500	2,235,229	—	—
1975	11,184,859	6,841,334	4,343,525	6,148,997	5,035,862	8,834,508	2,350,351	—	—
1976	11,012,137	6,717,058	4,295,079	5,810,828	5,201,309	8,653,477	2,358,660	2,314,298	44,362
1977	11,285,787	6,792,925	4,492,862	5,789,016	5,496,771	8,846,993	2,438,794	2,386,652	52,142
1978	11,260,092	6,667,657	4,592,435	5,640,998	5,619,094	8,785,893	2,474,199	2,408,331	65,868
1979	11,569,899	6,794,039	4,775,860	5,682,877	5,887,022	9,036,822	2,533,077	2,461,773	71,304
1980	12,096,895	7,097,958	4,998,937	5,874,374	6,222,521	9,457,394	2,639,501	2,527,787	[4] 111,714
1981	12,371,672	7,181,250	5,190,422	5,975,056	6,396,616	9,647,032	2,724,640	2,572,405	[4] 152,235
1982	12,425,780	7,220,618	5,205,162	6,031,384	6,394,396	9,696,087	2,729,693	2,552,739	[4] 176,954
1983	12,464,661	7,261,050	5,203,611	6,023,725	6,440,936	9,682,734	2,781,927	2,589,187	192,740
1984	12,241,940	7,098,388	5,143,552	5,863,574	6,378,366	9,477,370	2,764,570	2,574,419	190,151
1985	12,247,055	7,075,221	5,171,834	5,818,450	6,428,605	9,479,273	2,767,782	2,571,791	195,991
1986	12,503,511	7,119,550	5,383,961	5,884,515	6,618,996	9,713,893	2,789,618	2,572,479	217,139
1987	12,766,642	7,231,085	5,535,557	5,932,056	6,834,586	9,973,254	2,793,388	2,602,350	191,038
1988	13,055,337	7,436,768	5,618,569	6,001,896	7,053,441	10,161,388	2,893,949	2,673,567	220,382
1989	13,538,560	7,660,950	5,877,610	6,190,015	7,348,545	10,577,963	2,960,597	2,731,174	229,423
1990	13,818,637	7,820,985	5,997,652	6,283,909	7,534,728	10,844,717	2,973,920	2,760,227	213,693
1991	14,358,953	8,115,329	6,243,624	6,501,844	7,857,109	11,309,563	3,049,390	2,819,041	230,349
1992	14,487,359	8,162,118	6,325,241	6,523,989	7,963,370	11,384,567	3,102,792	2,872,523	230,269
1993	14,304,803	8,127,618	6,177,185	6,427,450	7,877,353	11,189,088	3,115,715	2,888,897	226,818
1994	14,278,790	8,137,776	6,141,014	6,371,898	7,906,892	11,133,680	3,145,110	2,910,107	235,003
1995	14,261,781	8,128,802	6,132,979	6,342,539	7,919,242	11,092,374	3,169,407	2,929,044	240,363
1996	14,300,255	8,213,490	6,086,765	6,343,992	7,956,263	11,090,171	3,210,084	2,940,557	269,527

TABLE 6.9

Total fall enrollment in degree-granting institutions, by attendance status, sex of student, and control of institution, 1947–2000 [CONTINUED]

		Attendance status		Sex of student		Control of institution			
							Private		
Year	Total enrollment	Full-time	Part-time	Men	Women	Public	Total	Not-for-profit	For-profit
1	2	3	4	5	6	7	8	9	10
				Degree-granting institutions[5]					
1996	14,367,520	8,302,953	6,064,567	6,352,825	8,014,695	11,120,499	3,247,021	2,942,556	304,465
1997	14,502,334	8,438,062	6,064,272	6,396,028	8,106,306	11,196,119	3,306,215	2,977,614	328,601
1998	14,506,967	8,563,338	5,943,629	6,369,265	8,137,702	11,137,769	3,369,198	3,004,925	364,273
1999	14,791,224	8,786,494	6,004,730	6,490,646	8,300,578	11,309,399	3,481,825	3,051,626	430,199
2000	15,312,289	9,009,600	6,302,689	6,721,769	8,590,520	11,752,786	3,559,503	3,109,419	450,084

[1] Institutions that were accredited by an agency or association that was recognized by the U.S. Department of Education, or recognized directly by the Secretary of Education.
[2] Degree-credit enrollment only.
[3] Includes part-time resident students and all extension students.
[4] Large increases are due to the addition of schools accredited by the Accrediting Commission of Career Schools and Colleges of Technology.
[5] Data are for 4-year and 2-year degree-granting institutions that were participating in Title IV federal financial aid programs.
Note: —Not available.
Trend tabulations of institutions of higher education data are based on institutions that were accredited by an agency or association that was recognized by the U.S. Department of Education, or recognized directly by the Secretary of Education.

SOURCE: Thomas D. Snyder, Charlene M. Hoffman, "Table 172. Total fall enrollment in degree-granting institutions, by attendance status, sex of student, and control of institution: 1947 to 2000," in *Digest of Education Statistics 2002,* vol. 2003-060, U.S. Department of Education, National Center for Education Statistics, Washington, DC, June 2003

TABLE 6.10

Total fall enrollment in degree granting institutions, by level of enrollment, sex, attendance status, and type and control of institution, 2000

Attendance status, and type and control of institution	Total			Undergraduate			First-professional			Graduate		
	Total	Men	Women	Total	Men	Women	Total	Men	Women	Total	Men	Women
1	2	3	4	5	6	7	8	9	10	11	12	13
Total	15,312,289	6,721,769	8,590,520	13,155,393	5,778,268	7,377,125	306,625	163,885	142,740	1,850,271	779,616	1,070,655
Full-time	9,009,600	4,111,093	4,898,507	7,922,926	3,588,246	4,334,680	273,571	145,397	128,174	813,103	377,450	435,653
Part-time	6,302,689	2,610,676	3,692,013	5,232,467	2,190,022	3,042,445	33,054	18,488	14,566	1,037,168	402,166	635,002
Total 4-year	9,363,858	4,163,169	5,200,689	7,207,289	3,219,748	3,987,541	306,625	163,885	142,740	1,849,944	779,536	1,070,408
Full-time	6,792,551	3,115,252	3,677,299	5,705,882	2,592,407	3,113,475	273,571	145,397	128,174	813,098	377,448	435,650
Part-time	2,571,307	1,047,917	1,523,390	1,501,407	627,341	874,066	33,054	18,488	14,566	1,036,846	402,088	634,758
Total 2-year	5,948,431	2,558,600	3,389,831	5,948,104	2,558,520	3,389,584	†	†	†	327	80	247
Full-time	2,217,049	995,841	1,221,208	2,217,044	995,839	1,221,205	†	†	†	5	2	3
Part-time	3,731,382	1,562,759	2,168,623	3,731,060	1,562,681	2,168,379	†	†	†	322	78	244
Public, total	11,752,786	5,132,407	6,620,379	10,539,322	4,622,098	5,917,224	124,114	63,137	60,977	1,089,350	447,172	642,178
Full-time	6,371,226	2,899,900	3,471,326	5,796,867	2,627,210	3,169,657	118,006	60,098	57,908	456,353	212,592	243,761
Part-time	5,381,560	2,232,507	3,149,053	4,742,455	1,994,888	2,747,567	6,108	3,039	3,069	632,997	234,580	398,417
Public 4-year	6,055,398	2,691,718	3,363,680	4,842,261	2,181,489	2,660,772	124,114	63,137	60,977	1,089,023	447,092	641,931
Full-time	4,371,218	2,008,618	2,362,600	3,796,864	1,735,930	2,060,934	118,006	60,098	57,908	456,348	212,590	243,758
Part-time	1,684,180	683,100	1,001,080	1,045,397	445,559	599,838	6,108	3,039	3,069	632,675	234,502	398,173
Public 2-year	5,697,388	2,440,689	3,256,699	5,697,061	2,440,609	3,256,452	†	†	†	327	80	247
Full-time	2,000,008	891,282	1,108,726	2,000,003	891,280	1,108,723	†	†	†	5	2	3
Part-time	3,697,380	1,549,407	2,147,973	3,697,058	1,549,329	2,147,729	†	†	†	322	78	244
Private, total	3,559,503	1,589,362	1,970,141	2,616,071	1,156,170	1,459,901	182,511	100,748	81,763	760,921	332,444	428,477
Full-time	2,638,374	1,211,193	1,427,181	2,126,059	961,036	1,165,023	155,565	85,299	70,266	356,750	164,858	191,892
Part-time	921,129	378,169	542,960	490,012	195,134	294,878	26,946	15,449	11,497	404,171	167,586	236,585
Private 4-year	3,308,460	1,471,451	1,837,009	2,365,028	1,038,259	1,326,769	182,511	100,748	81,763	760,921	332,444	428,477
Full-time	2,421,333	1,106,634	1,314,699	1,909,018	856,477	1,052,541	155,565	85,299	70,266	356,750	164,858	191,892
Part-time	887,127	364,817	522,310	456,010	181,782	274,228	26,946	15,449	11,497	404,171	167,586	236,585
Private 2-year	251,043	117,911	133,132	251,043	117,911	133,132	†	†	†	†	†	†
Full-time	217,041	104,559	112,482	217,041	104,559	112,482	†	†	†	†	†	†
Part-time	34,002	13,352	20,650	34,002	13,352	20,650	†	†	†	†	†	†
Not-for-profit, total	3,109,419	1,355,376	1,754,043	2,213,180	945,483	1,267,697	180,868	99,843	81,025	715,371	310,050	405,321
Full-time	2,272,698	1,018,063	1,254,635	1,794,516	785,043	1,009,473	154,680	84,815	69,865	323,502	148,205	175,297
Part-time	836,721	337,313	499,408	418,664	160,440	258,224	26,188	15,028	11,160	391,869	161,845	230,024
Not-for-profit 4-year	3,050,575	1,328,927	1,721,648	2,154,336	919,034	1,235,302	180,868	99,843	81,025	715,371	310,050	405,321
Full-time	2,226,028	996,113	1,229,915	1,747,846	763,093	984,753	154,680	84,815	69,865	323,502	148,205	175,297
Part-time	824,547	332,814	491,733	406,490	155,941	250,549	26,188	15,028	11,160	391,869	161,845	230,024
Not-for-profit 2-year	58,844	26,449	32,395	58,844	26,449	32,395	†	†	†	†	†	†
Full-time	46,670	21,950	24,720	46,670	21,950	24,720	†	†	†	†	†	†
Part-time	12,174	4,499	7,675	12,174	4,499	7,675	†	†	†	†	†	†
For-profit, total	450,084	233,986	216,098	402,891	210,687	192,204	1,643	905	738	45,550	22,394	23,156
Full-time	365,676	193,130	172,546	331,543	175,993	155,550	885	484	401	33,248	16,653	16,595
Part-time	84,408	40,856	43,552	71,348	34,694	36,654	758	421	337	12,302	5,741	6,561
For-profit 4-year	257,885	142,524	115,361	210,692	119,225	91,467	1,643	905	738	45,550	22,394	23,156
Full-time	195,305	110,521	84,784	161,172	93,384	67,788	885	484	401	33,248	16,653	16,595
Part-time	62,580	32,003	30,577	49,520	25,841	23,679	758	421	337	12,302	5,741	6,561
For-profit 2-year	192,199	91,462	100,737	192,199	91,462	100,737	†	†	†	†	†	†
Full-time	170,371	82,609	87,762	170,371	82,609	87,762	†	†	†	†	†	†
Part-time	21,828	8,853	12,975	21,828	8,853	12,975	†	†	†	†	†	†

Note: † Not applicable.
Data are for 4-year and 2-year degree-granting institutions that were participating in Title IV federal financial aid programs.

SOURCE: Thomas D. Snyder, Charlene M. Hoffman, "Table 177. Total fall enrollment in degree-granting institutions, by level of enrollment, sex, attendance status, and type and control of institution: 2000," in *Digest of Education Statistics 2002*, vol. 2003-060, U.S. Department of Education, Institute of Education Sciences, Washington, DC, June 2003

FIGURE 6.5

Enrollment, degrees conferred, and expenditures in degree-granting institutions, 1960–61 to 2001–02

Fall enrollment, in millions

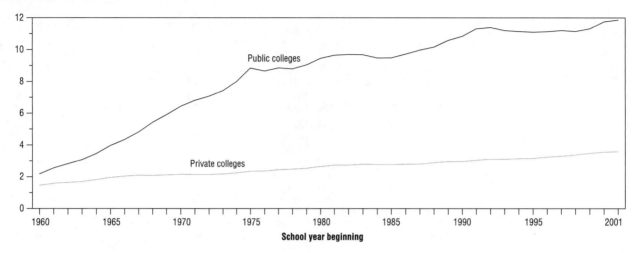

Degrees, in millions

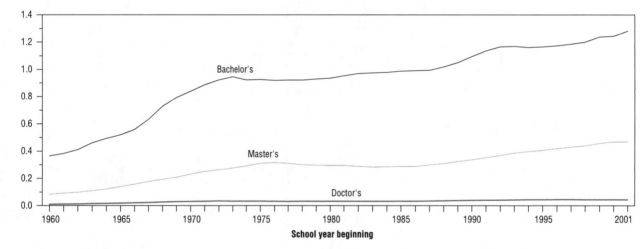

Total expenditures in billions of constant 2001–02 dollars

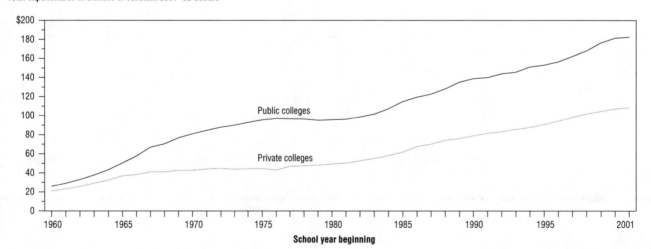

Note: Degree data for 2001–02, public finance data for 2000–01 through 2001–02, private finance data for 1996–97 through 2001–02, and enrollment data for fall 2001 are estimated.

SOURCE: Thomas D. Snyder, Charlene M. Hoffman, "Figure13. Enrollment, degrees conferred, and expenditures in degree-granting institutions, 1960–61 to 2001–02," in *Digest of Education Statistics 2002*, vol. 2003-060, U.S. Department of Education, Institute of Education Sciences, Washington, DC, June 2003

TABLE 6.11

Degrees conferred by degree-granting institutions, by control of institution, level of degree, and discipline division, 2000–01

Discipline division	Public institutions				Private institutions			
	Associate degrees	Bachelor's degrees	Master's degrees	Doctor's degrees [1]	Associate degrees	Bachelor's degrees	Master's degrees	Doctor's degrees[1]
1	2	3	4	5	6	7	8	9
Total	**456,487**	**812,438**	**246,054**	**28,187**	**122,378**	**431,733**	**222,422**	**16,717**
Agriculture and natural resources [2]	6,232	21,087	3,726	1,116	417	2,295	555	23
Architecture and related programs	361	6,517	2,804	92	56	1,963	1,498	61
Area, ethnic, and cultural studies	63	3,655	794	128	244	2,662	807	92
Biological sciences/life sciences	1,369	39,732	4,283	3,014	75	20,821	2,061	1,586
Business [3]	72,319	155,500	45,295	666	36,499	110,246	71,180	514
Communications	1,584	40,090	2,684	298	1,365	17,923	2,534	70
Communications technologies	1,493	463	92	0	490	587	441	2
Computer and information sciences	13,332	23,978	8,411	499	13,007	17,976	7,627	269
Construction trades	2,096	50	0	0	586	124	7	0
Education	7,853	75,786	72,719	4,785	1,366	29,780	56,347	1,931
Engineering	1,463	44,087	18,025	3,956	362	14,011	8,225	1,602
Engineering-related technologies	17,921	10,117	720	18	16,546	3,805	131	1
English language and literature/letters	809	34,865	5,007	1,137	68	16,554	1,934	369
Foreign languages and literatures	424	10,224	2,069	561	105	4,922	732	333
Health professions and related sciences	66,727	47,930	23,598	1,889	15,457	25,560	20,019	966
Home economics and vocational home economics	8,096	15,067	1,684	262	534	2,710	1,117	126
Law and legal studies	3,954	1,095	750	13	2,900	863	3,079	273
Liberal arts and sciences, general studies, and humanities	188,252	26,100	1,474	49	8,591	11,862	1,719	53
Library science	103	49	3,821	56	0	3	906	2
Mathematics	664	7,553	2,565	749	31	4,121	808	275
Mechanics and repairers	8,212	74	0	0	4,438	19	0	0
Multi/interdisciplinary studies	10,285	19,074	1,783	225	153	6,925	1,177	188
Parks, recreation, leisure, and fitness studies	676	14,369	2,008	166	165	5,196	479	11
Philosophy and religion	34	3,411	428	253	31	5,149	912	343
Physical sciences and science technologies	2,213	11,627	3,712	2,812	124	6,352	1,370	1,164
Precision production trades	7,193	302	0	0	4,300	45	2	0
Protective services	15,094	18,859	1,344	38	1,331	6,352	1,170	6
Psychology	1,338	48,986	6,016	1,882	216	24,548	9,180	2,777
Public administration and services	2,977	13,494	15,712	290	356	5,953	9,556	284
R.O.T.C. and military technologies	120	21	0	0	0	0	0	0
Social sciences and history	4,835	82,655	8,720	2,474	297	45,381	5,071	1,456
Theological studies/religious vocations	2	0	0	0	574	6,967	4,900	1,469
Transportation and material moving workers	689	1,472	87	0	379	2,276	669	0
Visual and performing arts	7,550	34,149	5,723	759	10,885	26,999	5,681	408
Not classified by field of study	154	0	0	0	430	783	528	63

[1] Includes Ph.D., Ed.D., and comparable degrees at the doctoral level. Excludes first-professional degrees such as M.D., D.D.S., and law degrees.
[2] Includes "Agricultural business and production," "Agricultural sciences," and "Conservation and renewable natural resources."
[3] Includes "Business management and administrative services," "Marketing operations/marketing and distribution," and "Consumer and personal services."

SOURCE: Thomas D. Snyder, Charlene M. Hoffman, "Table 257. Degrees conferred by degree-granting institutions, by control of institution, level of degree, and discipline division: 2000–01," in *Digest of Education Statistics 2002*, U.S. Department of Education, National Center for Education Statistics, Washington, DC, vol. 2003-060, June 2003

TABLE 6.12

Median annual income of year-round, full-time workers 25 years old and over, by level of education completed and sex, 1989–2000

Sex and year	Elementary/secondary						College — Bachelor's or higher degree [5]				
	Total	Less than 9th grade	9th to 12th grade, no completion [1]	High school completion (includes equivalency) [2]	Some college, no degree [3]	Associate degree [4]	Total [5]	Bachelor's [6]	Master's [4]	Professional [4]	Doctorate [4]
1	2	3	4	5	6	7	8	9	10	11	12
Men — *Current dollars*											
1990	$30,733 —	$17,394	$20,902	$26,653 —	$31,734	—	$42,671	$39,238 —	—	—	—
1991	31,613 —	17,623	21,402	26,779 —	31,663	$33,817	45,138	40,906 —	$49,734	$73,996	$57,187
1992	32,057 (120)	17,294	21,274	27,280 (175)	32,103	33,433	45,802	41,355 (304)	49,973	76,220	57,418
1993	32,359 (124)	16,863	21,752	27,370 (204)	32,077	33,690	47,740	42,757 (536)	51,867	80,549	63,149
1994	33,440 (246)	17,532	22,048	28,037 (322)	32,279	35,794	49,228	43,663 (633)	53,500	75,009	61,921
1995	34,551 (274)	18,354	22,185	29,510 (357)	33,883	35,201	50,481	45,266 (510)	55,216	79,667	65,336
1996	35,622 (150)	17,962	22,717	30,709 (183)	34,845	37,131	51,436	45,846 (458)	60,508	85,963	71,227
1997	36,678 (148)	19,291	24,726	31,215 (171)	35,945	38,022	53,450	48,616 (850)	61,690	85,011	76,234
1998	37,906 (291)	19,380	23,958	31,477 (169)	36,934	40,274	56,524	51,405 (349)	62,244	94,737	75,078
1999	40,333 (144)	20,429	25,035	33,184 (388)	39,221	41,638	60,201	52,985 (722)	66,243	100,000	81,687
2000	41,059 (156)	20,789	25,095	34,303 (457)	40,337	41,952	61,868	56,334 (573)	68,322	99,411	80,250
Women — *Current dollars*											
1990	21,372 —	12,251	14,429	18,319 —	22,227	—	30,377	28,017 —	—	—	—
1991	22,043 —	12,066	14,455	18,836 —	22,143	25,000	31,310	29,079 —	34,949	46,742	43,303
1992	23,139 (159)	12,958	14,559	19,427 (176)	23,157	25,624	32,304	30,326 (294)	36,037	46,257	45,790
1993	23,629 (166)	12,415	15,386	19,963 (158)	23,056	25,883	34,307	31,197 (310)	38,612	50,211	47,248
1994	24,399 (165)	12,430	15,133	20,373 (158)	23,514	25,940	35,378	31,741 (314)	39,457	50,615	51,119
1995	24,875 (160)	13,577	15,825	20,463 (162)	23,997	27,311	35,259	32,051 (273)	40,263	50,000	48,141
1996	25,808 (131)	14,414	16,953	21,175 (143)	25,167	28,083	36,461	33,525 (437)	41,901	57,624	56,267
1997	26,974 (134)	14,161	16,697	22,067 (148)	26,335	28,812	38,038	35,379 (295)	44,949	61,051	53,037
1998	27,956 (199)	14,467	16,482	22,780 (254)	27,420	29,924	39,786	36,559 (305)	45,283	57,565	57,796
1999	28,844 (216)	15,098	17,015	23,061 (279)	27,757	30,919	41,747	37,993 (614)	48,097	59,904	60,079
2000	30,327 (138)	15,978	17,919	24,970 (236)	28,697	31,071	42,706	40,415 (284)	50,139	58,957	57,081
Men — *Constant 2000 dollars*											
1990	40,491 —	22,917	27,539	35,116 —	41,810	—	56,220	51,697 —	—	—	—
1991	39,969 —	22,281	27,059	33,857 —	40,032	$42,755	57,069	51,718 —	$62,880	$93,554	$72,303
1992	39,346 (147)	21,226	26,111	33,483 (215)	39,402	41,035	56,216	50,758 (373)	61,335	93,550	70,473
1993	38,562 (148)	20,096	25,922	32,617 (243)	38,226	40,148	56,892	50,953 (639)	61,810	95,990	75,254
1994	38,855 (286)	20,371	25,619	32,577 (374)	37,506	41,591	57,200	50,734 (736)	62,164	87,156	71,949
1995	39,040 (310)	20,739	25,067	33,344 (403)	38,285	39,774	57,040	51,147 (576)	62,390	90,017	73,825
1996	39,096 (165)	19,714	24,932	33,704 (201)	38,243	40,752	56,452	50,317 (503)	66,408	94,346	78,173
1997	39,352 (159)	20,697	26,528	33,490 (183)	38,565	40,794	57,346	52,160 (912)	66,187	91,208	81,791
1998	40,045 (307)	20,474	25,310	33,254 (179)	39,019	42,547	59,714	54,306 (369)	65,757	100,084	79,316
1999	41,689 (149)	21,116	25,877	34,299 (401)	40,539	43,038	62,225	54,766 (746)	68,470	103,361	84,433
2000	41,059 (156)	20,789	25,095	34,303 (457)	40,337	41,952	61,868	56,334 (573)	68,322	99,411	80,250
Women — *Constant 2000 dollars*											
1990	28,158 —	16,141	19,011	24,136 —	29,285	—	40,022	36,913 —	—	—	—
1991	27,869 —	15,255	18,276	23,815 —	27,996	31,608	39,586	36,765 —	44,187	59,097	54,749
1992	28,400 (195)	15,904	17,869	23,844 (216)	28,422	31,450	39,649	37,221 (361)	44,231	56,774	56,201
1993	28,159 (198)	14,795	18,335	23,790 (206)	27,476	30,845	40,883	37,177 (369)	46,014	59,836	56,305
1994	28,350 (192)	14,443	17,584	23,672 (184)	27,322	30,141	41,107	36,881 (365)	45,847	58,812	59,397

TABLE 6.12

Median annual income of year-round, full-time workers 25 years old and over, by level of education completed and sex, 1989–2000 [CONTINUED]

		Elementary/secondary				College					
							Bachelor's or higher degree[5]				
Sex and year	Total	Less than 9th grade	9th to 12th grade, no completion[1]	High school completion (includes equivalency)[2]	Some college, no degree[3]	Associate degree[4]	Total[5]	Bachelor's[6]	Master's[4]	Professional[4]	Doctorate[4]
1	2	3	4	5	6	7	8	9	10	11	12
					Constant 2000 dollars						
Women											
1995	28,107 (181)	15,341	17,881	23,122 (183)	27,115	30,859	39,840	36,215 (308)	45,494	56,496	54,396
1996	28,325 (144)	15,820	18,606	23,240 (157)	27,621	30,821	40,016	36,794 (480)	45,987	63,243	61,754
1997	28,940 (144)	15,193	17,914	23,676 (159)	28,255	30,912	40,811	37,958 (317)	48,226	65,501	56,903
1998	29,534 (210)	15,284	17,412	24,066 (268)	28,968	31,613	42,032	38,622 (322)	47,839	60,814	61,058
1999	29,814 (223)	15,605	17,587	23,836 (288)	28,690	31,958	43,150	39,270 (635)	49,714	61,918	62,098
2000	30,327 (138)	15,978	17,919	24,970 (236)	28,697	31,071	42,706	40,415 (284)	50,139	58,957	57,081
					Number of persons with income (in thousands)						
Men											
1990	44,406 (269)	2,250	3,315	16,394 (188)	9,113	—	13,334	7,569 (133)	—	—	—
1991	44,199 (268)	1,807	3,083	15,025 (181)	8,034	2,899	13,350	8,456 (140)	3,073	1,147	674
1992	44,752 (269)	1,815	3,009	14,722 (179)	8,067	3,203	13,937	8,719 (142)	3,178	1,295	745
1993	45,873 (271)	1,790	3,083	14,604 (179)	8,493	3,557	14,346	9,178 (145)	3,131	1,231	808
1994	47,566 (273)	1,895	3,335	15,109 (182)	8,783	3,735	14,987	9,636 (148)	3,225	1,258	868
1995	48,500 (324)	1,946	3,441	15,331 (196)	8,908	3,926	15,054	9,597 (157)	3,395	1,208	853
1996	49,764 (340)	2,041	3,548	15,840 (207)	9,173	3,931	15,339	9,898 (165)	3,272	1,277	893
1997	50,807 (343)	1,914	3,613	16,225 (209)	9,170	4,086	15,864	10,349 (169)	3,228	1,321	966
1998	52,381 (347)	1,870	3,295	16,442 (210)	9,375	4,347	16,733	11,058 (174)	3,414	1,264	998
1999	53,062 (348)	1,993	3,354	16,589 (211)	9,684	4,359	17,142	11,142 (175)	3,725	1,267	1,008
2000	54,065 (351)	1,968		16,834 (213)	9,792	4,729	17,387	11,395 (177)	3,680	1,274	1,038
Women											
1990	28,636 (235)	847	1,861	11,810 (163)	6,462	—	7,655	4,704 (106)	—	—	—
1991	29,474 (237)	733	1,819	10,959 (157)	5,633	2,523	7,807	5,263 (112)	2,025	312	206
1992	30,346 (240)	734	1,659	11,039 (158)	5,904	2,655	8,355	5,604 (115)	2,192	334	225
1993	30,683 (240)	765	1,576	10,513 (154)	6,279	3,067	8,483	5,735 (116)	2,166	323	260
1994	31,379 (242)	696	1,675	10,785 (156)	6,256	3,210	8,756	5,901 (118)	2,174	398	283
1995	32,673 (276)	774	1,763	11,064 (168)	6,329	3,336	9,406	6,434 (129)	2,268	421	283
1996	33,549 (290)	750	1,751	11,363 (177)	6,582	3,468	9,636	6,689 (137)	2,213	413	322
1997	34,624 (294)	791	1,765	11,475 (177)	6,628	3,538	10,427	7,173 (141)	2,448	488	318
1998	35,628 (297)	814	1,878	11,613 (178)	7,070	3,527	10,725	7,288 (143)	2,639	468	329
1999	37,091 (302)	886	1,883	11,824 (180)	7,453	3,804	11,242	7,607 (146)	2,818	470	346
2000	37,614 (304)	930	1,950	11,789 (180)	7,391	4,118	11,436	7,899 (148)	2,823	509	353

[1] Includes 1 to 3 of years high school for 1990.
[2] Includes 4 years of high school for 1990, and equivalency certificates for the other years.
[3] Includes 1 to 3 years of college and associate degrees for 1990.
[4] Not reported separately for 1990.
[5] Includes 4 or more years of college for 1990.
[6] Includes 4 years of college for 1990.
Note: —Not available. Data for 1992 and later years are based on 1990 Census counts; prior years are based on 1980 counts. Detail may not sum to totals due to rounding. Standard errors appear in parentheses.

SOURCE: Thomas D. Snyder, Charlene M. Hoffman, "Table 381. Median annual income of year-round, full-time workers 25 years old and over, by level of education completed and sex: 1989 to 2000," in *Digest of Education Statistics 2002*, U.S. Department of Education, National Center for Education Statistics, Washington, DC, vol. 2003-060, June 2003

TABLE 6.13

Total expenditures of educational institutions related to the gross domestic product, by level of institution, 1929–30 to 2001–02

| | | | Total expenditures for education (amounts in millions of current dollars) | | | | | |
| | | | All educational institutions | | All elementary and secondary schools | | All colleges and universities | |
Year	Gross domestic product (in billions)	School year	Amount	As a percent of gross domestic product	Amount	As a percent of of gross domestic product	Amount	As a percent gross domestic product
1	2	3	4	5	6	7	8	9
1929	$103.7	1929–30	—	—	—	—	$632	0.6
1939	92.0	1939–40	—	—	—	—	758	0.8
1949	267.7	1949–50	$8,911	3.3	$6,249	2.3	2,662	1.0
1959	507.4	1959–60	23,860	4.7	16,713	3.3	7,147	1.4
1961	545.7	1961–62	28,503	5.2	19,673	3.6	8,830	1.6
1963	618.7	1963–64	34,440	5.6	22,825	3.7	11,615	1.9
1965	720.1	1965–66	43,682	6.1	28,048	3.9	15,634	2.2
1967	834.1	1967–68	55,652	6.7	35,077	4.2	20,575	2.5
1969	985.3	1969–70	68,459	6.9	43,183	4.4	25,276	2.6
1970	1,039.7	1970–71	75,741	7.3	48,200	4.6	27,541	2.6
1971	1,128.6	1971–72	80,672	7.1	50,950	4.5	29,722	2.6
1972	1,240.4	1972–73	86,875	7.0	54,952	4.4	31,923	2.6
1973	1,385.5	1973–74	95,396	6.9	60,370	4.4	35,026	2.5
1974	1,501.0	1974–75	108,664	7.2	68,846	4.6	39,818	2.7
1975	1,635.2	1975–76	118,706	7.3	75,101	4.6	43,605	2.7
1976	1,823.9	1976–77	126,417	6.9	79,194	4.3	47,223	2.6
1977	2,031.4	1977–78	137,042	6.7	86,544	4.3	50,498	2.5
1978	2,295.9	1978–79	148,308	6.5	93,012	4.1	55,296	2.4
1979	2,566.4	1979–80	165,627	6.5	103,162	4.0	62,465	2.4
1980	2,795.6	1980–81	182,849	6.5	112,325	4.0	70,524	2.5
1981	3,131.3	1981–82	197,801	6.3	120,486	3.8	77,315	2.5
1982	3,259.2	1982–83	212,081	6.5	128,725	3.9	83,356	2.6
1983	3,534.9	1983–84	228,597	6.5	139,000	3.9	89,597	2.5
1984	3,932.7	1984–85	247,657	6.3	149,400	3.8	98,257	2.5
1985	4,213.0	1985–86	269,485	6.4	161,800	3.8	107,685	2.6
1986	4,452.9	1986–87	291,974	6.6	175,200	3.9	116,774	2.6
1987	4,742.5	1987–88	313,375	6.6	187,999	4.0	125,376	2.6
1988	5,108.3	1988–89	346,883	6.8	209,377	4.1	137,506	2.7
1989	5,489.1	1989–90	381,525	7.0	230,970	4.2	150,555	2.7
1990	5,803.2	1990–91	412,652	7.1	248,930	4.3	163,722	2.8
1991	5,986.2	1991–92	432,987	7.2	261,255	4.4	171,732	2.9
1992	6,318.9	1992–93	456,070	7.2	274,335	4.3	181,735	2.9
1993	6,642.3	1993–94	477,237	7.2	287,507	4.3	189,730	2.9
1994	7,054.3	1994–95	503,925	7.1	302,400	4.3	201,525	2.9
1995	7,400.5	1995–96	529,596	7.2	318,246	4.3	211,350	2.9
1996	7,813.2	1996–97	562,871	7.2	339,151	4.3	223,720	2.9
1997	8,318.4	1997–98	597,549	7.2	361,415	4.3	236,134	2.8
1998	8,781.5	1998–99	633,532	7.2	384,038	4.4	249,494	2.8
1999	9,274.3	1999–2000	678,399	7.3	411,429	4.4	266,970	2.9
2000	9,824.6	[1] 2000–01	712,800	7.3	429,000	4.4	283,800	2.9
2001	10,082.2	[2] 2001–02	745,200	7.4	454,100	4.5	291,100	2.9

—Not available.

[1] Preliminary data for elementary and secondary schools and estimates for colleges and universities.

[2] Estimated.

Note: Total expenditures for public elementary and secondary schools include 2002 expenditures, interest on school debt, and capital outlay. Data for private elementary and secondary schools are estimated. Total expenditures for colleges and universities include current-fund expenditures and additions to plant value. Excludes expenditures of post-secondary institutions that do not confer associate or higher degrees. Data for 1995–96 and later years are for 4-year and 2-year degree-granting institutions that were eligible to participate in Title IV federal financial aid programs. Detail may not sum to totals due to rounding.

SOURCE: Thomas D. Snyder, Charlene M. Hoffman, "Table 29. Total expenditures of educational institutions related to the gross domestic product, by level of institution: 1929–30 to 2001–02," in *Digest of Education Statistics 2002,* vol. 2003-060, U.S. Department of Education, National Center for Education Statistics, Washington, DC, June 2003

TABLE 6.14

Revenues for public elementary and secondary schools, by source of funds, 1919–20 to 1999–2000

School year	In thousands				Percentage distribution			
	Total	Federal	State	Local (including intermediate)*	Total	Federal	State	Local (including intermediate)*
1	2	3	4	5	6	7	8	9
1919–20	$970,121	$2,475	$160,085	$807,561	100.0	0.3	16.5	83.2
1929–30	2,088,557	7,334	353,670	1,727,553	100.0	0.4	16.9	82.7
1939–40	2,260,527	39,810	684,354	1,536,363	100.0	1.8	30.3	68.0
1941–42	2,416,580	34,305	759,993	1,622,281	100.0	1.4	31.4	67.1
1943–44	2,604,322	35,886	859,183	1,709,253	100.0	1.4	33.0	65.6
1945–46	3,059,845	41,378	1,062,057	1,956,409	100.0	1.4	34.7	63.9
1947–48	4,311,534	120,270	1,676,362	2,514,902	100.0	2.8	38.9	58.3
1949–50	5,437,044	155,848	2,165,689	3,115,507	100.0	2.9	39.8	57.3
1951–52	6,423,816	227,711	2,478,596	3,717,507	100.0	3.5	38.6	57.9
1953–54	7,866,852	355,237	2,944,103	4,567,512	100.0	4.5	37.4	58.1
1955–56	9,686,677	441,442	3,828,886	5,416,350	100.0	4.6	39.5	55.9
1957–58	12,181,513	486,484	4,800,368	6,894,661	100.0	4.0	39.4	56.6
1959–60	14,746,618	651,639	5,768,047	8,326,932	100.0	4.4	39.1	56.5
1961–62	17,527,707	760,975	6,789,190	9,977,542	100.0	4.3	38.7	56.9
1963–64	20,544,182	896,956	8,078,014	11,569,213	100.0	4.4	39.3	56.3
1965–66	25,356,858	1,996,954	9,920,219	13,439,686	100.0	7.9	39.1	53.0
1967–68	31,903,064	2,806,469	12,275,536	16,821,063	100.0	8.8	38.5	52.7
1969–70	40,266,923	3,219,557	16,062,776	20,984,589	100.0	8.0	39.9	52.1
1970–71	44,511,292	3,753,461	17,409,086	23,348,745	100.0	8.4	39.1	52.5
1971–72	50,003,645	4,467,969	19,133,256	26,402,420	100.0	8.9	38.3	52.8
1972–73	52,117,930	4,525,000	20,699,752	26,893,180	100.0	8.7	39.7	51.6
1973–74	58,230,892	4,930,351	24,113,409	29,187,132	100.0	8.5	41.4	50.1
1974–75	64,445,239	5,811,595	27,060,563	31,573,079	100.0	9.0	42.0	49.0
1975–76	71,206,073	6,318,345	31,602,885	33,284,840	100.0	8.9	44.4	46.7
1976–77	75,322,532	6,629,498	32,526,018	36,177,019	100.0	8.8	43.2	48.0
1977–78	81,443,160	7,694,194	35,013,266	38,735,700	100.0	9.4	43.0	47.6
1978–79	87,994,143	8,600,116	40,132,136	39,261,891	100.0	9.8	45.6	44.6
1979–80	96,881,165	9,503,537	45,348,814	42,028,813	100.0	9.8	46.8	43.4
1980–81	105,949,087	9,768,262	50,182,659	45,998,166	100.0	9.2	47.4	43.4
1981–82	110,191,257	8,186,466	52,436,435	49,568,356	100.0	7.4	47.6	45.0
1982–83	117,497,502	8,339,990	56,282,157	52,875,354	100.0	7.1	47.9	45.0
1983–84	126,055,419	8,576,547	60,232,981	57,245,892	100.0	6.8	47.8	45.4
1984–85	137,294,678	9,105,569	67,168,684	61,020,425	100.0	6.6	48.9	44.4
1985–86	149,127,779	9,975,622	73,619,575	65,532,582	100.0	6.7	49.4	43.9
1986–87	158,523,693	10,146,013	78,830,437	69,547,243	100.0	6.4	49.7	43.9
1987–88	169,561,974	10,716,687	84,004,415	74,840,873	100.0	6.3	49.5	44.1
1988–89	192,016,374	11,902,001	91,768,911	88,345,462	100.0	6.2	47.8	46.0
1989–90	208,547,573	12,700,784	98,238,633	97,608,157	100.0	6.1	47.1	46.8
1990–91	223,340,537	13,776,066	105,324,533	104,239,939	100.0	6.2	47.2	46.7
1991–92	234,581,384	15,493,330	108,783,449	110,304,605	100.0	6.6	46.4	47.0
1992–93	247,626,168	17,261,252	113,403,436	116,961,481	100.0	7.0	45.8	47.2
1993–94	260,159,468	18,341,483	117,474,209	124,343,776	100.0	7.1	45.2	47.8
1994–95	273,149,449	18,582,157	127,729,576	126,837,717	100.0	6.8	46.8	46.4
1995–96	287,702,844	19,104,019	136,670,754	131,928,071	100.0	6.6	47.5	45.9
1996–97	305,065,192	20,081,287	146,435,584	138,548,321	100.0	6.6	48.0	45.4
1997–98	325,925,708	22,201,965	157,645,372	146,078,370	100.0	6.8	48.4	44.8
1998–99	347,377,993	24,521,817	169,298,232	153,557,944	100.0	7.1	48.7	44.2
1999–2000	372,864,603	27,097,866	184,613,352	161,153,385	100.0	7.3	49.5	43.2

*Includes a relatively small amount from nongovernmental private sources (gifts and tuition and transportation fees from patrons). These sources accounted for 2.4 percent of total revenues in 1999–2000.

Note: Beginning in 1980–81, revenues for state education agencies are excluded. Detail may not sum to totals due to rounding.

SOURCE: Thomas D. Snyder, Charlene M. Hoffman, "Table 156. Revenues for public elementary and secondary schools, by source of funds: 1919–20 to 1999–2000," in *Digest of Education Statistics 2002,* U.S. Department of Education, National Center for Education Statistics, Washington, DC, vol. 2003-060, June 2003

TABLE 6.15

Current-fund revenue of degree-granting institutions, by source of funds, 1919–20 to 1995–96

[In thousands]

Year	Current-fund revenue	Student tuition and fees[1]	Federal government[2]	State governments[3]	Local governments	Endowment earnings	Private gifts and grants[4]	Sales and services of educational activities	Auxiliary enterprises	Hospitals[5]	Other current income
1	2	3	4	5	6	7	8	9	10	11	12
					Higher education institutions[6]						
1919–20	$199,922	$42,255	$12,783	$61,690	(7)	$26,482	$7,584	—	$26,993	—	$22,135
1929–30	554,511	144,126	20,658	150,847	(7)	68,605	26,172	—	60,419	—	83,684
1939–40	715,211	200,897	38,860	151,222	$24,392	71,304	40,453	$32,777	43,923	—	11,383
1949–50	2,374,645	394,610	524,319	491,636	61,700	96,341	118,627	111,987	511,265	—	64,160
1959–60	5,785,537	1,157,482	1,036,990	1,374,476	151,715	206,619	382,569	102,525	1,004,283	$187,769	181,110
1969–70	21,515,242	4,419,845	4,130,066	5,873,626	778,162	516,038	1,129,438	612,777	2,900,390	619,578	535,323
1975–76	39,703,166	8,171,942	6,477,178	12,260,885	1,616,975	687,470	1,917,036	645,420	4,547,622	2,494,340	884,298
1976–77	43,436,827	9,024,932	7,169,031	13,285,684	1,626,908	764,788	2,105,070	779,058	4,919,602	2,859,376	902,377
1977–78	47,034,032	9,855,270	6,968,501	14,746,166	1,744,230	832,286	2,320,368	882,715	5,327,821	3,268,956	1,087,719
1978–79	51,837,789	10,704,171	7,851,326	16,363,784	1,573,018	985,242	2,489,366	1,037,130	5,741,309	3,763,453	1,328,991
1979–80	58,519,982	11,930,340	8,902,844	18,378,299	1,587,552	1,176,627	2,808,075	1,239,439	6,481,458	4,373,384	1,641,965
1980–81	65,584,789	13,773,259	9,747,586	20,106,222	1,790,740	1,364,443	3,176,670	1,409,730	7,287,290	4,980,346	1,948,503
1981–82	72,190,856	15,774,038	9,591,805	21,848,791	1,937,669	1,596,813	3,563,558	1,582,922	8,121,611	5,838,565	2,335,084
1982–83	77,595,726	17,776,041	9,631,097	23,065,636	2,031,353	1,720,677	4,052,649	1,723,484	8,769,521	6,531,562	2,293,706
1983–84	84,417,287	19,714,884	10,406,166	24,706,990	2,192,275	1,873,945	4,415,275	1,970,747	9,456,369	7,040,662	2,639,973
1984–85	92,472,694	21,283,329	11,509,125	27,583,011	2,387,212	2,096,298	4,896,325	2,126,927	10,100,410	7,474,575	3,015,483
1985–86	100,437,616	23,116,605	12,704,750	29,911,500	2,544,506	2,275,898	5,410,905	2,373,494	10,674,136	8,226,635	3,199,186
1986–87	108,809,827	25,705,827	13,904,049	31,309,303	2,799,321	2,377,958	5,952,682	2,641,906	11,364,188	9,277,834	3,476,760
1987–88	117,340,109	27,836,781	14,771,954	33,517,166	3,006,263	2,586,441	6,359,282	2,918,090	11,947,778	10,626,566	3,769,787
1988–89	128,501,638	30,806,566	15,893,978	36,031,208	3,363,676	2,914,396	7,060,730	3,315,620	12,855,580	11,991,265	4,268,618
1989–90	139,635,477	33,926,060	17,254,874	38,349,239	3,639,902	3,143,696	7,781,422	3,632,100	13,938,469	13,216,664	4,753,051
1990–91	149,766,051	37,434,462	18,236,082	39,480,874	3,931,239	3,268,629	8,361,265	4,054,703	14,903,127	15,149,672	4,945,998
1991–92	161,395,896	41,559,037	19,833,317	40,586,907	4,159,876	3,442,009	8,977,271	4,520,890	15,758,599	17,240,338	5,317,651
1992–93	170,880,503	45,346,071	21,014,564	41,247,955	4,444,875	3,627,773	9,659,977	5,037,901	16,662,850	18,124,015	5,714,523
1993–94	179,226,601	48,646,538	22,076,385	41,910,288	4,998,306	3,669,536	10,203,062	5,294,030	17,537,514	18,959,776	5,931,167
1994–95	189,120,570	51,506,876	23,243,172	44,343,012	5,165,961	3,988,217	10,866,749	5,603,251	18,336,094	19,100,217	6,967,023
1995–96	197,414,848	54,725,982	23,879,098	45,621,627	5,589,988	4,570,933	11,942,987	5,552,907	18,861,585	18,672,680	7,997,061
					Degree-granting institutions[8]						
1995–96	197,973,236	55,260,293	23,939,075	45,692,673	5,607,909	4,562,171	11,903,126	5,530,763	18,867,540	18,611,570	7,998,116

—Not available.

[1] Tuition and fees received from veterans under Public Law 550 are reported under student fees and are not under income from the federal government.

[2] Federally supported student aid that is received through students is included under tuition and auxiliary enterprises.

[3] Includes federal aid received through state channels and regional compacts, through 1959–60.

[4] Beginning in 1969–70, the private grants represent nongovernmental revenue for sponsored research, student aid, and other sponsored programs.

[5] Prior to 1959–60, data for hospitals are included under sales and services of educational activities.

[6] Institutions that were accredited by an agency or association that was recognized by the U.S. Department of Education, or recognized directly by the Secretary of Education.

[7] Income from state and local governments tabulated under "State governments."

[8] Data are for 4-year and 2-year degree-granting institutions that were participating in Title IV federal financial aid programs.

Note: Data for years prior to 1969–70 are not entirely comparable with data from later years. Also, some details for 1969–70 are not directly comparable with data for later years. Detail may not sum to totals due to rounding.

SOURCE: Thomas D. Snyder and Charlene M. Hoffman, "Table 333. Current-fund revenue of degree-granting institutions, by source of funds: 1919–20 to 1995–96," in *Digest of Education Statistics 2002*, U.S. Department of Education, National Center for Education Statistics, Washington, DC, June 2003

TABLE 6.16

Total revenue of private not-for-profit degree-granting institutions, by source of funds and by type of institution, 1999–2000

Type of institution	Total revenue and investment return	Student tuition and fees	Federal appropriations, grants, and contracts[1]	State appropriations, grants, and contracts	Local appropriations, grants, and contracts	Private gifts and grants[2]	Investment return	Educational activities	Auxiliary enterprises	Hospitals	Other
	2	3	4	5	6	7	8	9	10	11	12
					In thousands						
Total	**$121,509,804**	**$29,651,812**	**$12,191,827**	**$1,117,742**	**$580,237**	**$16,488,984**	**$37,763,518**	**$2,865,606**	**$8,317,607**	**$8,092,598**	**$4,439,874**
4-year	119,477,590	29,131,477	12,125,177	1,093,028	574,665	16,310,021	37,687,185	2,831,901	8,231,901	7,208,600	4,284,209
Doctoral, extensive[3]	67,148,460	8,686,143	9,445,630	380,708	278,873	8,154,228	27,113,860	2,198,726	2,923,483	6,203,323	1,763,487
Doctoral, intensive[4]	7,609,439	3,201,785	460,332	119,558	30,619	855,005	1,729,081	315,154	632,374	8,453	257,077
Master's[5]	15,464,153	8,206,000	571,622	234,646	8,856	1,921,686	1,843,632	96,141	1,847,993	80,375	653,202
Baccalaureate[6]	18,509,570	6,023,745	492,263	173,460	4,269	3,454,274	5,568,334	89,619	2,290,411	0	413,194
Specialized institutions[7]	10,745,967	3,013,803	1,155,330	184,656	252,047	1,924,828	1,432,278	131,687	537,640	916,449	1,197,249
Art, music, or design	1,183,589	567,764	24,316	9,387	956	169,867	180,017	15,946	67,906	0	147,431
Business and management	841,713	519,353	10,759	11,912	576	83,659	101,653	8,897	88,674	0	16,230
Engineering or technology	517,204	143,834	36,603	8,229	80	197,071	98,449	1,160	25,237	0	6,540
Medical or other health	5,787,285	911,498	1,026,056	144,530	247,739	740,996	643,426	77,546	138,297	916,074	941,122
Theological[8]	1,748,382	399,979	32,456	4,774	354	674,802	362,147	12,844	192,608	0	68,420
Tribal[8]	16,881	2,317	8,911	787	0	3,074	156	70	639	0	927
Other specialized	650,912	469,059	16,230	5,036	2,342	55,359	46,429	15,225	24,279	375	16,580
2-year	2,032,214	520,335	66,650	24,714	5,572	178,963	76,333	34,279	85,706	883,998	155,664
Associate of arts	1,996,171	517,343	44,894	24,613	3,914	176,319	76,190	34,247	84,915	883,998	149,739
Tribal[8]	36,043	2,992	21,756	101	1,658	2,644	143	33	791	0	5,925
					Percentage distribution						
Total	**100.0**	**24.4**	**10.0**	**0.9**	**0.5**	**13.6**	**31.1**	**2.4**	**6.8**	**6.7**	**3.7**
4-year	100.0	24.4	10.1	0.9	0.5	13.7	31.5	2.4	6.9	6.0	3.6
Doctoral, extensive[3]	100.0	12.9	14.1	0.6	0.4	12.1	40.4	3.3	4.4	9.2	2.6
Doctoral, intensive[4]	100.0	42.1	6.0	1.6	0.4	11.2	22.7	4.1	8.3	0.1	3.4
Master's[5]	100.0	53.1	3.7	1.5	0.1	12.4	11.9	0.6	12.0	0.5	4.2
Baccalaureate[6]	100.0	32.5	2.7	0.9	0.0	18.7	30.1	0.5	12.4	0.0	2.2
Specialized institutions[7]	100.0	28.0	10.8	1.7	2.3	17.9	13.3	1.2	5.0	8.5	11.1
Art, music, or design	100.0	48.0	2.1	0.8	0.1	14.4	15.2	1.3	5.7	0.0	12.5
Business and management	100.0	61.7	1.3	1.4	0.1	9.9	12.1	1.1	10.5	0.0	1.9
Engineering or technology	100.0	27.8	7.1	1.6	0.0	38.1	19.0	0.2	4.9	0.0	1.3
Medical or other health	100.0	15.8	17.7	2.5	4.3	12.8	11.1	1.3	2.4	15.8	16.3
Theological[8]	100.0	22.9	1.9	0.3	0.0	38.6	20.7	0.7	11.0	0.0	3.9
Tribal[8]	100.0	13.7	52.8	4.7	0.0	18.2	0.9	0.4	3.8	0.0	5.5
Other specialized	100.0	72.1	2.5	0.8	0.4	8.5	7.1	2.3	3.7	0.1	2.5
2-year	100.0	25.6	3.3	1.2	0.3	8.8	3.8	1.7	4.2	43.5	7.7
Associate of arts	100.0	25.9	2.2	1.2	0.2	8.8	3.8	1.7	4.3	44.3	7.5
Tribal[8]	100.0	8.3	60.4	0.3	4.6	7.3	0.4	0.1	2.2	0.0	16.4

TABLE 6.16

Total revenue of private not-for-profit degree-granting institutions, by source of funds and by type of institution, 1999–2000 [CONTINUED]

Type of institution	Total revenue and investment return	Student tuition and fees	Federal appropriations, grants, and contracts[1]	State appropriations, grants, and contracts	Local appropriations, grants, and contracts	Private gifts and grants[2]	Investment return	Educational activities	Auxiliary enterprises	Hospitals	Other
1	2	3	4	5	6	7	8	9	10	11	12
	Revenue per full-time-equivalent student										
Total	$47,861	$11,679	$4,802	$440	$229	$6,495	$14,874	$1,129	$3,276	$3,188	$1,749
4-year	48,304	11,778	4,902	442	232	6,594	15,237	1,145	3,328	2,914	1,732
Doctoral, extensive[3]	119,754	15,491	16,846	679	497	14,542	48,355	3,921	5,214	11,063	3,145
Doctoral, intensive[4]	32,489	13,670	1,965	510	131	3,650	7,382	1,346	2,700	36	1,098
Master's[5]	18,898	10,028	699	287	11	2,348	2,253	117	2,258	98	798
Baccalaureate[6]	30,804	10,025	819	289	7	5,749	9,267	149	3,812	0	688
Specialized institutions[7]	41,430	11,619	4,454	712	972	7,421	5,522	508	2,073	3,533	4,616
Art, music, or design	32,250	15,470	663	256	26	4,628	4,905	434	1,850	0	4,017
Business and management	19,802	12,218	253	280	14	1,968	2,391	209	2,086	0	382
Engineering or technology	39,484	10,981	2,794	628	6	15,045	7,516	89	1,927	0	499
Medical or other health	100,169	15,777	17,760	2,502	4,288	12,826	11,137	1,342	2,394	15,856	16,289
Theological	23,496	5,375	436	64	5	9,068	4,867	173	2,588	0	919
Other specialized	20,001	2,746	10,558	933	0	3,642	185	83	757	0	1,098
Tribal[8]	19,121	13,779	477	148	69	1,626	1,364	447	713	11	487
2-year	31,103	7,964	1,020	378	85	2,739	1,168	525	1,312	13,529	2,382
Associate of arts	31,184	8,082	701	384	61	2,754	1,190	535	1,327	13,810	2,339
Tribal[8]	27,182	2,256	16,407	76	1,251	1,994	108	25	596	0	4,469

[1] Includes independent operations.

[2] Includes contributions from affiliated entities.

[3] Doctoral, extensive institutions are committed to graduate education through the doctorate, and award 50 or more doctor's degrees per year across at least 15 disciplines.

[4] Doctoral, intensive institutions are committed to education through the doctorate and award at least 10 doctor's degrees per year across 3 or more disciplines or at least 20 doctor's degrees overall.

[5] Master's institutions offer a full range of baccalaureate programs and are committed to education through the master's degree. They award at least 40 master's degrees per year, across 3 or more disciplines.

[6] Baccalaureate institutions primarily emphasize undergraduate education.

[7] Specialized 4-year institutions award degrees primarily in single fields of study, such as medicine, business, fine arts, theology and engineering. Also, includes some institutions which have 4-year programs, but have not reported sufficient data to identify program category.

[8] Tribally controlled colleges are located on reservations and are members of the American Indian Higher Education Consortium.

Note: Detail may not sum to totals due to rounding.

source: Thomas D. Snyder, Charlene M. Hoffman, "Table 335. Total revenue of private not-for-profit degree-granting institutions, by source of funds and by type of institution: 1999–2000," in *Digest of Education Statistics 2002*, U.S. Department of Education, National Center for Education Statistics, Washington, DC, vol. 2003-060, June 2003

TABLE 6.17

Total and current expenditures per pupil in public elementary and secondary schools, 1919–20 to 2001–02

| | Expenditure per pupil in average daily attendance | | | | Expenditure per pupil in fall enrollment[1] | | | | |
| | Unadjusted dollars | | Constant 2001–02 dollars | | Unadjusted dollars | | Constant 2001–02 dollars | | |
School year	Total expenditure	Current expenditure	Total expenditure	Current expenditure	Total expenditure	Current expenditure	Total expenditure	Current expenditure	Annual percent change in current expenditure
1	2	3	4	5	6	7	8	9	10
1919–20	$64	$53	$598	$499	$48	$40	$448	$373	—
1929–30	108	87	1,129	903	90	72	935	747	—
1931–32	97	81	1,197	1,002	82	69	1,014	848	—
1933–34	76	67	1,026	908	65	57	871	771	—
1935–36	88	74	1,140	963	74	63	964	815	—
1937–38	100	84	1,240	1,043	86	72	1,065	896	—
1939–40	106	88	1,348	1,123	92	76	1,168	973	—
1941–42	110	98	1,257	1,124	94	84	1,077	962	—
1943–44	125	117	1,275	1,196	105	99	1,074	1,008	—
1945–46	146	136	1,425	1,332	124	116	1,214	1,135	—
1947–48	205	181	1,567	1,388	179	158	1,368	1,212	—
1949–50	260	210	1,959	1,583	231	187	1,738	1,404	—
1951–52	314	246	2,132	1,668	275	215	1,867	1,461	—
1953–54	351	265	2,326	1,755	312	236	2,068	1,560	—
1955–56	387	294	2,565	1,950	354	269	2,345	1,783	—
1957–58	447	341	2,792	2,129	408	311	2,546	1,941	—
1959–60	471	375	2,856	2,275	440	350	2,668	2,125	—
1961–62	517	419	3,066	2,484	485	393	2,877	2,331	—
1963–64	559	460	3,228	2,660	520	428	3,004	2,475	—
1965–66	654	538	3,651	3,003	607	499	3,390	2,788	—
1967–68	786	658	4,121	3,449	732	612	3,833	3,209	—
1969–70	955	816	4,505	3,849	879	751	4,147	3,544	—
1970–71	1,049	911	4,707	4,087	970	842	4,352	3,778	6.6
1971–72	1,128	990	4,884	4,286	1,034	908	4,479	3,931	4.0
1972–73	1,211	1,077	5,039	4,483	1,117	993	4,648	4,135	5.2
1973–74	1,364	1,207	5,213	4,614	1,244	1,101	4,753	4,207	1.7
1974–75	1,545	1,365	5,315	4,695	1,423	1,257	4,896	4,325	2.8
1975–76	1,697	1,504	5,454	4,831	1,563	1,385	5,022	4,449	2.9
1976–77	1,816	1,638	5,514	4,972	1,674	1,509	5,081	4,581	3.0
1977–78	2,002	1,823	5,697	5,186	1,842	1,677	5,240	4,770	4.1

TABLE 6.17

Total and current expenditures per pupil in public elementary and secondary schools, 1919–20 to 2001–02 [CONTINUED]

	Expenditure per pupil in average daily attendance				Expenditure per pupil in fall enrollment[1]				
	Unadjusted dollars		Constant 2001–02 dollars		Unadjusted dollars		Constant 2001–02 dollars		
School year	Total expenditure	Current expenditure	Total expenditure	Current expenditure	Total expenditure	Current expenditure	Total expenditure	Current expenditure	Annual percent change in current expenditure
1	2	3	4	5	6	7	8	9	10
1978–79	2,210	2,020	5,749	5,256	2,029	1,855	5,279	4,827	1.2
1979–80	2,491	2,272	5,717	5,214	2,290	2,088	5,255	4,794	0.7
1980–81	[2]2,742	2,502	[2]5,641	5,146	[2]2,529	2,307	[2]5,203	4,746	1.0
1981–82	[2]2,973	2,726	[2]5,630	5,161	[2]2,754	2,525	[2]5,215	4,781	0.7
1982–83	[2]3,203	2,955	[2]5,816	5,365	[2]2,966	2,736	[2]5,385	4,968	3.9
1983–84	[2]3,471	3,173	[2]6,077	5,556	[2]3,216	2,940	[2]5,630	5,147	3.6
1984–85	[2]3,722	3,470	[2]6,271	5,847	[2]3,456	3,222	[2]5,822	5,429	5.5
1985–86	[2]4,020	3,756	[2]6,583	6,150	[2]3,724	3,479	[2]6,099	5,698	5.0
1986–87	[2]4,308	3,970	[2]6,901	6,360	[2]3,995	3,682	[2]6,400	5,898	3.5
1987–88	[2]4,654	4,240	[2]7,159	6,522	[2]4,310	3,927	[2]6,630	6,040	2.4
1988–89	5,109	4,645	7,512	6,829	4,738	4,307	6,966	6,333	4.8
1989–90	5,550	4,980	7,789	6,988	5,174	4,643	7,262	6,515	2.9
1990–91	5,885	5,258	7,830	6,996	5,486	4,902	7,300	6,522	0.1
1991–92	6,074	5,421	7,832	6,989	5,629	5,023	7,257	6,476	0.7
1992–93	6,281	5,584	7,853	6,981	5,804	5,160	7,257	6,451	0.4
1993–94	6,492	5,767	7,912	7,029	5,996	5,327	7,307	6,492	0.6
1994–95	6,725	5,989	7,967	7,095	6,208	5,529	7,355	6,550	0.9
1995–96	6,962	6,147	8,029	7,090	6,443	5,689	7,431	6,562	0.2
1996–97	7,300	6,393	8,186	7,169	6,764	5,923	7,585	6,642	1.2
1997–98	7,703	6,676	8,487	7,354	7,142	6,189	7,868	6,819	2.7
1998–99	8,118	7,013	8,792	7,595	7,533	6,508	8,158	7,048	3.4
1999–2000	8,591	7,392	9,043	7,780	8,032	6,911	8,454	7,274	3.2
2000–01[2]	8,896	7,654	9,053	7,789	8,317	7,156	8,464	7,282	0.1
2001–02[2]	9,354	8,048	9,354	8,048	8,745	7,524	8,745	7,524	3.3

[1] Data for 1919–20 to 1953–54 are based on school-year enrollment.
[2] Estimated.
Note: —Not available. Beginning in 1980–81, state administration expenditures are excluded from both "total" and "current" expenditures.

SOURCE: Thomas D. Snyder, Charlene M. Hoffman, "Table 166. Total and current expenditures per pupil in public elementary and secondary schools: 1919-20 to 2001-02," in *Digest of Education Statistics 2002,* U.S. Department of Education, National Center for Education Statistics, Washington, DC, vol. 2003-060, June 2003

TABLE 6.18

Total and current expenditures per pupil in fall enrollment in public elementary and secondary education, by function and state, 1999–2000

		Current expenditures, capital expenditures, and interest on school debt													
		Current expenditures													
				Student services											
State or other area	Total	Total	Instruction	Total	Students[3]	Instruc-tional[4]	General admin-istration	School admin-istration	Operation and mainte-nance	Studen trans-portation	Other support services	Food services	Enterprise operations[2]	Capital outlay[1]	Interest on school debt
1	2	3	4	5	6	7	8	9	10	11	12	13	14	15	16
United States	**$8,032**	**$6,911**	**$4,267**	**$2,350**	**$342**	**$312**	**$143**	**$392**	**$665**	**$278**	**$217**	**$276**	**$17**	**$926**	**$195**
Alabama	6,639	5,638	3,480	1,781	247	216	155	346	477	237	103	377	0	900	101
Alaska	10,344	8,806	4,933	3,579	467	653	434	492	1,181	332	20	249	46	1,374	164
Arizona	6,878	4,999	3,056	1,702	335	134	89	256	573	180	136	242	0	1,520	360
Arkansas	5,922	5,277	3,210	1,770	236	214	182	313	481	193	151	297	0	530	114
California	7,284	6,314	3,947	2,122	248	341	46	443	607	158	280	241	4	920	50
Colorado	7,657	6,215	3,601	2,389	243	268	93	405	577	186	616	205	20	1,111	331
Connecticut	11,196	9,753	6,185	3,103	522	325	197	532	879	437	211	272	192	1,222	222
Delaware	9,157	8,310	5,113	2,809	378	119	93	459	867	456	436	389	0	726	121
District of Columbia	11,510	10,107	4,201	5,627	807	1,991	274	456	1,283	540	276	279	0	1,136	267
Florida	7,166	5,831	3,391	2,151	294	360	62	358	633	249	193	289	0	1,178	157
Georgia	7,627	6,437	4,016	2,072	311	370	84	397	501	240	170	344	5	1,069	120
Hawaii	7,388	6,530	4,117	2,007	483	251	48	395	529	118	183	406	0	640	218
Idaho	6,076	5,315	3,280	1,803	295	212	136	316	495	248	102	231	0	635	127
Illinois	8,513	7,133	4,284	2,605	425	288	243	379	740	310	221	244	0	1,215	165
Indiana	8,655	7,192	4,484	2,416	316	225	131	405	774	396	168	293	0	862	601
Iowa	7,378	6,564	3,864	2,208	425	324	196	351	548	203	162	295	198	711	103
Kansas	6,950	6,294	3,608	2,378	356	274	245	408	658	261	176	308	0	447	209
Kentucky	6,322	5,921	3,616	1,975	225	296	178	339	516	293	127	330	0	272	129
Louisiana	6,487	5,804	3,497	1,862	234	259	131	316	491	302	129	382	63	549	134
Maine	8,515	7,667	5,127	2,243	236	225	154	428	724	344	132	298	0	678	170
Maryland	8,660	7,731	4,758	2,587	320	400	64	514	710	373	207	232	153	838	90
Massachusetts	9,171	8,761	5,851	2,625	416	293	187	378	802	363	186	285	0	206	203
Michigan	9,564	8,110	4,716	3,161	534	385	191	515	852	315	369	233	0	1,157	297
Minnesota	8,588	7,190	4,521	2,369	242	389	222	297	602	393	224	299	0	1,071	327
Mississippi	5,818	5,014	3,061	1,628	208	208	155	281	483	204	87	324	1	691	114
Missouri	7,222	6,187	3,811	2,114	286	270	188	370	596	292	112	261	0	831	204
Montana	6,766	6,314	3,939	2,121	299	233	189	336	653	273	138	249	5	384	68
Nebraska	7,605	6,683	4,198	1,977	283	236	239	335	584	184	116	275	234	792	129
Nevada	7,471	5,760	3,437	2,145	214	228	93	416	559	235	400	178	0	1,317	393
New Hampshire	7,625	6,860	4,493	2,143	437	189	231	379	578	292	37	224	0	629	136
New Jersey	11,471	10,337	6,088	3,930	889	319	308	559	1,064	573	218	262	58	956	178
New Mexico	6,786	5,825	3,287	2,254	569	247	162	334	566	285	91	281	4	862	99
New York	10,819	9,846	6,707	2,874	333	274	201	419	886	482	279	265	0	675	297
North Carolina	7,303	6,045	3,835	1,872	317	214	126	407	458	218	132	339	0	1,088	170
North Dakota	6,455	5,667	3,391	1,805	206	170	280	277	496	257	119	280	192	715	73

TABLE 6.18

Total and current expenditures per pupil in fall enrollment in public elementary and secondary education, by function and state, 1999–2000 [CONTINUED]

Current expenditures, capital expenditures, and interest on school debt

State or other area	Current expenditures													Capital outlay[1]	Interest on school debt
	Total	Total	Instruction	Student services											
				Total	Students[3]	Instruc- tional[4]	General admin- istration	School admin- istration	Operation and mainte- nance	Studen trans- portation	Other support services	Food services	Enterprise operations[2]		
1	2	3	4	5	6	7	8	9	10	11	12	13	14	15	16
Ohio	7,962	7,065	4,156	2,653	375	411	183	415	654	312	302	254	1	758	140
Oklahoma	5,837	5,395	3,120	1,918	325	174	173	315	594	180	158	295	61	378	65
Oregon	8,084	7,149	4,244	2,653	429	327	120	454	615	297	411	230	21	725	210
Pennsylvania	9,160	7,772	4,876	2,605	364	291	238	344	785	361	222	276	15	1,032	356
Rhode Island	9,254	8,904	5,859	2,796	600	382	186	435	708	365	120	250	0	196	154
South Carolina	7,376	6,130	3,674	2,107	400	363	79	373	549	195	149	322	26	1,083	163
South Dakota	6,870	5,632	3,393	1,938	301	224	196	296	534	201	186	287	14	1,102	136
Tennessee	6,321	5,383	3,510	1,603	182	296	104	279	482	183	77	270	0	812	127
Texas	7,743	6,288	3,828	2,143	303	334	108	354	676	169	199	317	0	1,182	273
Utah	5,278	4,378	2,858	1,256	156	183	46	260	397	130	84	240	24	764	136
Vermont	8,837	8,323	5,379	2,714	541	289	222	555	660	279	167	224	6	375	140
Virginia	7,896	6,841	4,255	2,327	324	402	67	407	670	306	152	257	1	887	169
Washington	7,701	6,376	3,803	2,261	442	293	142	309	627	251	196	210	103	1,040	285
West Virginia	7,705	7,152	4,414	2,315	235	197	184	392	744	467	96	422	0	506	47
Wisconsin	9,164	7,806	4,860	2,701	368	399	205	406	688	320	315	246	0	1,108	250
Wyoming	8,281	7,425	4,537	2,636	437	294	162	445	773	306	220	247	5	753	102
Outlying areas															
American Samoa	3,121	2,739	1,044	1,123	444	193	32	124	194	39	97	572	0	382	0
Guam	—	—	—	—	—	—	—	—	—	—	—	—	—	—	—
Northern Marianas	5,891	5,120	4,133	667	59	0	586	0	6	8	7	320	0	771	0
Puerto Rico	3,509	3,404	2,372	648	88	30	64	0	306	59	101	384	0	74	32
Virgin Islands	6,967	6,478	4,031	2,141	398	269	366	302	448	227	131	269	36	489	0

[1]Includes expenditures for property and for building and alterations completed by school district staff or contractors.
[2]Includes expenditures for operations funded by sales of products or services (e.g., school bookstore or computer time).
[3]Includes expenditures for health, attendance, and speech pathology services.
[4]Includes expenditures for curriculum development, staff training, libraries, and media and computer centers.
Note: Excludes expenditures for state education agencies. "0" indicates none or less than $0.50. Because of rounding, details may not add to totals.
—Not available.

SOURCE: Thomas D. Snyder, Charlene M. Hoffman, "Table 167. Total and current expenditures per pupil in fall enrollment in public elementary and secondary education, by function and state: 1999–2000," in Digest of Education Statistics 2002, U.S. Department of Education, National Center for Education Statistics, Washington, DC, vol. 2003-060, June 2003

CHAPTER 7
VOTER PARTICIPATION

VOTER TURNOUT BEFORE 1920

In the early years of the American Republic, the meaning of political democracy was far different than it is today. Although the Founding Fathers were brilliant political theorists, they nevertheless believed that the "common man" should play a subservient role in the nation's political life. As illustrated in the U.S. Constitution, the Founding Fathers believed that ordinary men were endowed with certain God-given liberties to protect themselves from the intrigues of the propertied classes. However, they also assumed that the common man's social betters would always be in positions of political leadership.

For example, prior to 1824 property and tax qualifications on suffrage allowed only 1 in 30 people to vote. Furthermore, most states in the early years of the Republic prohibited voters from participating directly in presidential elections. Instead, the choice of presidential electors was determined by the state legislatures. The political landscape changed in 1828 with the rise of "Jacksonian Democracy." Between 1824 and the election of President Andrew Jackson four years later, the definition of republican citizenship was broadened to include a greater number of individuals. For example, by 1828 every state except Delaware and South Carolina adopted the system of direct election of presidential electors, thereby making the presidency a truly popular office. In addition, almost every state had eliminated property and tax qualifications to vote, which quadrupled the size of the eligible electorate. From 1824 to 1828 the popular vote increased from 365,000 (26.9 percent voter participation) to over 1 million (57.6 percent voter participation) as 1 in 11 people voted.

Mass democracy resulted in extraordinarily high voter turnout among eligible voters throughout the 19th century. In the presidential elections of 1840, 1860, and 1876, voter participation exceeded 80 percent. In fact, the lowest voter turnout in any presidential election between 1840 and 1900 was 69.6 percent in 1852. Despite tremendous voter participation among eligible white males, it is important to realize that women, slaves (and later black Americans), Native Americans, illiterates, convicted felons, and poor whites, who could not afford a poll tax, were denied the right to vote at one time or another.

Perhaps a better standard to assess the level of voter participation is the population of voting-age Americans. Using this standard, the percentage of those living in the United States who were of voting age and actually voted has been historically very low. Just one in five Americans of voting age cast a ballot in 1828 and only 37 percent voted in the 1876 presidential election between Rutherford B. Hayes (Republican) and Samuel J. Tilden (Democrat). In fact, it was not until the 1928 presidential election between Herbert Hoover (Republican) and Alfred Smith (Democrat) that over one-half of the electorate turned out to vote. Voter participation in presidential elections has remained over 50 percent ever since, with a high of 69 percent in Lyndon B. Johnson's (Democrat) landslide victory over his Republican rival Barry Goldwater in 1964. The 54.2 percent vote turnout for the 1996 contest between Bill Clinton and Bob Dole was the lowest since Harry Truman's upset victory in 1948 (51 percent) until the 2000 presidential election. According to the Center for Voting and Democracy, in 2000 the 1948 low was matched when only 51 percent of eligible voters cast their ballots.

BLACK AND WOMEN'S SUFFRAGE

The U.S. Constitution allows the states to set qualifications for conducting elections, as long as they do not violate the Constitution, particularly the 14th and 15th Amendments. In 1868 Congress ratified the 14th Amendment, granting citizenship to black Americans. Never before had newly freed slaves been granted such civil rights. Two years later the adoption of the 15th Amendment gave all citizens the right to vote, regardless of race, color, or previous condition of servitude. However, in the

TABLE 7.1

Categories of felons disenfranchised under state law, 2003

State	Prison	Probation	Parole	Ex-felons All	Ex-felons Partial
Alabama	X	X	X	X	
Alaska	X	X	X		
Arizona	X	X	X		X (2nd felony)
Arkansas	X	X	X		
California	X		X		
Colorado	X		X		
Connecticut	X		X		
Delaware	X	X	X		X (5 years)
District of Columbia	X				
Florida	X	X	X	X	
Georgia	X	X	X		
Hawaii	X				
Idaho	X				
Illinois	X				
Indiana	X				
Iowa	X	X	X	X	
Kansas	X	X	X		
Kentucky	X	X	X	X	
Louisiana	X				
Maine					
Maryland	X	X	X		X (2nd felony, 3 years)
Massachusetts	X				
Michigan	X				
Minnesota	X	X	X		
Mississippi	X	X	X	X	
Missouri	X	X	X		
Montana	X				
Nebraska	X	X	X		
Nevada	X	X	X		X (except first-time nonviolent)
New Hampshire	X				
New Jersey	X	X	X		
New Mexico	X	X	X		
New York	X		X		
North Carolina	X	X	X		
North Dakota	X				
Ohio	X				
Oklahoma	X	X	X		
Oregon	X				
Pennsylvania	X				
Rhode Island	X	X	X		
South Carolina	X	X	X		
South Dakota	X				
Tennessee	X	X	X		X (pre-1986)
Texas	X	X	X		
Utah	X				
Vermont					
Virginia	X	X	X	X	
Washington	X	X	X		X (pre-1984)
West Virginia	X	X	X		
Wisconsin	X	X	X		
Wyoming	X	X	X		X (5 years)
U.S. Total	**49**	**29**	**33**	**6**	**7**

SOURCE: "Categories of Felons Disenfranchised Under State Law," in *Felony Disenfranchisement Laws in the United States,* The Sentencing Project, Washington, DC, July 2003. Reproduced with permission.

FIGURE 7.1

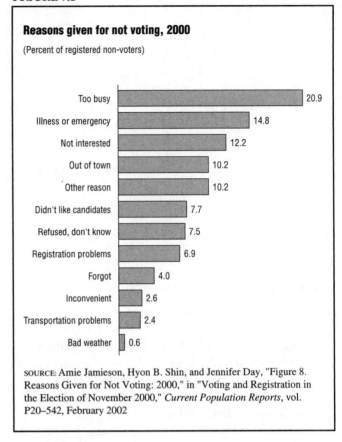

Reasons given for not voting, 2000

(Percent of registered non-voters)

Too busy	20.9
Illness or emergency	14.8
Not interested	12.2
Out of town	10.2
Other reason	10.2
Didn't like candidates	7.7
Refused, don't know	7.5
Registration problems	6.9
Forgot	4.0
Inconvenient	2.6
Transportation problems	2.4
Bad weather	0.6

SOURCE: Amie Jamieson, Hyon B. Shin, and Jennifer Day, "Figure 8. Reasons Given for Not Voting: 2000," in "Voting and Registration in the Election of November 2000," *Current Population Reports*, vol. P20–542, February 2002

1890s southern states brazenly flouted the Constitution, depriving blacks of their right to vote through the imposition of poll taxes, literacy tests, and grandfather clauses. In Louisiana, for example, 130,000 blacks voted in the presidential election of 1896. Four years later, with the enactment of these discriminatory laws, only 5,000 blacks cast a ballot. Black voter participation was violently suppressed until the 1960s.

The 15th Amendment did not grant voting rights to women. Instead of agitating for a constitutional amendment, suffragists decided to gain the right to vote by concentrating on a state-by-state approach. By 1896 Wyoming, Utah, Colorado, and Idaho recognized women's suffrage. Twenty-one years later, however, only 13 more states guaranteed full women's suffrage, 12 states allowed them to vote only in presidential elections, 2 states permitted them to vote in primary elections, and 19 states did not grant any voting rights to women. Frustrated with the pace of the suffrage movement, Progressives began campaigning for a constitutional amendment. On August 26, 1920, the 19th Amendment, granting all women the right to vote, was ratified by two-thirds of the states.

FELONY DISENFRANCHISEMENT LAWS

Under current law, all mentally competent adults have the right to vote, with one exception: felony offenders. In 2003, 48 states and the District of Columbia have laws denying the right to vote to convicted criminal offenders in prison. Only Maine and Vermont permit felons to vote. Thirty-three states prohibit felons on parole from voting, and 29 states also deny the vote to those on probation. In six states (mainly in the South), laws prohibit former offenders, those who have fully served their sentences, from ever voting. Seven additional states ban some former offenders and/or permit application for voting rights restoration for certain offenses after a waiting period.

Delaware and Wyoming ban some former felons from voting for five years and Maryland three years after the completion of their sentences. (See Table 7.1.)

According to the Sentencing Project and Human Rights Watch, two liberal nonprofit research and advocacy groups, in *Losing the Vote: The Impact of Felony Disenfranchisement Laws in the United States* (1998, updated 2003), developments in 2003 included:

• The Alabama legislature passed into law a measure allowing most felons to apply for a restoration of voting rights after completing their sentence

• The Nevada legislature passed into law a bill repealing the state's lifetime ban on former felon voting

• The Wyoming legislature passed into law a bill allowing individuals convicted of a nonviolent first-time felony to apply for voting rights restoration five years after their sentence is completed

The report also states that about 3.9 million Americans, or 1 in 50 adults, have temporarily or permanently lost their right to vote because of a felony conviction. Over one-third are former offenders who have completed their sentences, one-third are on probation or parole, and the rest are currently in prison.

Thirteen percent of black men (1.4 million) have lost their voting rights as a result of a felony conviction, a rate seven times the national average. In Alabama, Florida, Iowa, Mississippi, New Mexico, Virginia, and Wyoming, one in four black men are permanently disenfranchised. Another 2 million whites of Hispanic and non-Hispanic origin are disenfranchised, and some 500,000 women have lost their right to vote due to felony convictions. Florida reported about 600,000 former felons who were not permitted to vote in the 2000 presidential election.

LOW VOTER TURNOUT

Since 1900, when 73.2 percent of eligible voters cast a presidential ballot, voter turnout has spiraled downward. In the 1920 presidential election, Republican Warren Harding defeated James Cox the Democratic candidate in the first U.S. election where voter turnout dropped under 50 percent. It was not until the 1952 election when the Republican candidate Dwight Eisenhower defeated Adlai Stevenson that voter turnout again exceeded 60 percent. Since 1972 eligible voter turnout has not risen above this mark. In the 1996 presidential election between Bill Clinton and Bob Dole, voter turnout reached 54.2 percent. In the 2000 presidential election, eligible turnout increased to about 54.7 percent. This meager increase was primarily the result of repeated polls that predicted an extremely close race, which in turn generated extraordinary grass-roots get-out-the-vote campaigns by both political parties. (See Table 7.2.)

Various theories exist about why voter turnout is so low in the United States. Some observers believe low voter turnout indicates tacit approval of the way things are going (the people are generally happy and, therefore, see no reason to go out and vote). Others claim that low voter turnout reflects a general dissatisfaction with the system: The people are unhappy but do not think it will change anything if they go out and vote. Some say the cause is uninformed and apathetic people.

Other observers believe that if state legislatures made it easier for its citizens to register to vote and elections were not held on Tuesdays, workdays for most people, more people would go to the polls. European elections, where voter turnout often exceeds 80 percent, are generally held on Sundays. Another possible option is voting by mail. In January 1996 Oregon held its first special election in which voters could mail in their ballots. Other jurisdictions, such as Texas, allow voters to cast ballots in some elections two weeks prior to the election. However, overall, these efforts appear to have had little significant effect in increasing voter participation.

In a November 2000 survey by the U.S. Census Bureau (issued in 2002), about 21 percent of people who had registered to vote but did not vote in that year's presidential election stated that they were too busy. Other reasons given included: illness or emergency (14.8 percent), disinterest (12.2 percent), out of town (10.2 percent), didn't like the candidates (7.7 percent), and forgetting (4.0 percent). Over 5 percent of registered voters who failed to exercise their constitutional right cited inconvenience, the lack of transportation, and weather conditions. (See Figure 7.1.)

Registration

Over the past decade, many states have tried to make registration easier. Some states have mailed out registration forms, while others have permitted registration in public buildings and at public agencies. Furthermore, in 1971 the U.S. Supreme Court declared unconstitutional a Tennessee law requiring a one-year residence in the state and a three-month residence in the county as a precondition for voting (*Dunn v. Blumstein*, 405 U.S. 330, 1971).

In 1993 Congress tried to increase voter registration by enacting the National Voter Registration Act ("Motor Voter Law"—PL 103-30). This legislation permits people to register while obtaining a driving permit or visiting a public assistance office, a school, or a hospital. It also allows them to register at polls on election day and mail in their registration forms. About half of those registered since the act went into effect on January 1, 1995, have used one of these methods. Still, the downward trend in voter registration has continued. In 2000, 69.5 percent of the voting-age population reported that they had registered, a shade lower than the 71 percent of citizens registered in 1996.

TABLE 7.2

Reported voting in presidential election years by region, race, Hispanic origin, sex, and age, November 1964–2000

(Numbers in thousands)

Characteristic	Presidential elections of —									
	1964	1968	1972	1976	1980	1984	1988	1992	1996	2000
United States										
Total, voting age	110,604	116,535	136,203	146,548	157,085	169,963	178,098	185,684	193,651	202,609
Total voted	76,671	78,964	85,766	86,698	93,066	101,878	102,224	113,866	105,017	110,826
Percent voted	69.3	67.8	63.0	59.2	59.2	59.9	57.4	61.3	54.2	54.7
Race and Hispanic Origin										
White	70.7	69.1	64.5	60.9	60.9	61.4	59.1	63.6	56.0	56.4
White non-Hispanic	(NA)	(NA)	(NA)	(NA)	62.8	63.3	61.8	66.9	59.6	60.4
Black	¹58.5	57.6	52.1	48.7	50.5	55.8	51.5	54.0	50.6	53.5
Asian and Pacific Islander	(NA)	(NA)	(NA)	(NA)	(NA)	(NA)	(NA)	27.3	25.7	25.4
Hispanic (of any race)	(NA)	(NA)	37.5	31.8	29.9	32.6	28.8	28.9	26.7	27.5
Sex										
Men	71.9	69.8	64.1	59.6	59.1	59.0	56.4	60.2	52.8	53.1
Women	67.0	66.0	62.0	58.8	59.4	60.8	58.3	62.3	55.5	56.2
Age										
18 to 24 years	²50.9	²50.4	49.6	42.2	39.9	40.8	36.2	42.8	32.4	32.3
25 to 44 years	69.0	66.6	62.7	58.7	58.7	58.4	54.0	58.3	49.2	49.8
45 to 64 years	75.9	74.9	70.8	68.7	69.3	69.8	67.9	70.0	64.4	64.1
65 years and over	66.3	65.8	63.5	62.2	65.1	67.7	68.8	70.1	67.0	67.6
Northeast, Midwest, and West										
Total, voting age	78,174	81,594	93,653	99,403	106,524	112,376	117,373	122,025	125,571	130,774
Total voted	58,282	57,970	62,193	60,829	64,963	69,183	69,130	76,276	69,467	72,385
Percent voted	74.6	71.0	66.4	61.2	61.0	61.6	58.9	62.5	55.3	55.4
Race and Hispanic Origin										
White	74.7	71.8	67.5	62.6	62.4	63.0	60.4	64.9	57.4	57.5
White non-Hispanic	(NA)	(NA)	(NA)	(NA)	64.3	65.0	63.3	68.5	61.0	61.6
Black	¹72.0	64.8	56.7	52.2	52.8	58.9	55.6	53.8	51.4	53.1
Asian and Pacific Islander	(NA)	(NA)	(NA)	(NA)	(NA)	(NA)	(NA)	27.9	26.3	26.1
Hispanic (of any race)	(NA)	(NA)	(NA)	(NA)	29.8	32.8	26.8	27.4	26.3	26.8
South										
Total, voting age	32,429	34,941	42,550	47,145	50,561	57,587	60,725	63,659	68,080	71,835
Total voted	18,389	20,994	23,573	25,869	28,103	32,695	33,094	37,590	35,550	38,441
Percent voted	56.7	60.1	55.4	54.9	55.6	56.8	54.5	59.0	52.2	53.5
Race and Hispanic Origin										
White	59.5	61.9	57.0	57.1	57.4	58.1	56.4	60.8	53.4	54.2
White non-Hispanic	(NA)	(NA)	(NA)	(NA)	59.2	59.8	58.5	63.6	56.7	58.2
Black	¹44.0	51.6	47.8	45.7	48.2	53.2	48.0	54.3	50.0	53.9
Asian and Pacific Islander	(NA)	(NA)	(NA)	(NA)	(NA)	(NA)	(NA)	24.5	22.6	22.2
Hispanic (of any race)	(NA)	(NA)	(NA)	(NA)	30.1	32.4	32.9	32.0	27.6	28.7

Note: NA Not available

¹ Black category includes other races in 1964.

² Prior to 1972, data are for people 21 to 24 years of age with the exception of those aged 18 to 24 in Georgia and Kentucky, 19 to 24 in Alaska, and 20 to 24 in Hawaii.

SOURCE: Amie Jamieson, Hyon B. Shin, and Jennifer Day, "Table C. Reported Voting in Presidential Election Years, by Region, Race, Hispanic Origin, Sex, and Age: November 1964 to 2000," in "Voting and Registration in the Election of November 2000," *Current Population Reports,* vol. P20-542, February 2002

Registered Voters

Despite low voter turnout and the difficulty in getting people to register to vote, according to the Census Bureau, the vast majority of people who are registered to vote actually do so. In the 2000 presidential election, 86 percent of registered voters cast a ballot, up from 82 percent in the 1996 election. The all-time record high occurred in the 1968 presidential election when 91 percent of registered voters went to the polls.

Age

The Census Bureau attributes much of the decline in voter turnout since 1964 to the baby boom population reaching voting age and to the passage of the 26th Amendment (1971), lowering the voting age to 18 years. The earliest of the baby boomers reached the age of 18 around 1964. This amendment substantially raised the number of eligible younger voters, an age group known for being apathetic voters. Many of these baby boomers are now entering middle age and the overall voting rate does not seem to be increasing substantially.

The 1972 presidential election was the first opportunity for 18 year olds to vote, and half (49.6 percent) of the population aged 18 to 24 voted. From 1976 to 2000, however, the percentage of the youngest group voting in presidential elections declined to under 35 percent.

TABLE 7.3

Reported voting and registration by selected characteristics, November 2000

(Numbers in thousands)

Characteristic	Total population	Total citizen	Total citizen — Reported registered			Total citizen — Reported voted		
			Number	Percent	90 percent C.I. (±)[1]	Number	Percent	90 percent C.I. (±)[1]
Total, 18 years and over	202,609	186,366	129,549	69.5	0.3	110,826	59.5	0.3
Sex								
Men	97,087	88,758	60,356	68.0	0.5	51,542	58.1	0.5
Women	105,523	97,609	69,193	70.9	0.4	59,284	60.7	0.5
Race, Hispanic Origin, and Sex								
White	168,733	157,291	110,773	70.4	0.3	95,098	60.5	0.4
Men	81,720	75,728	52,299	69.1	0.5	44,879	59.3	0.5
Women	87,014	81,564	58,473	71.7	0.5	50,219	61.6	0.5
White non-Hispanic	148,035	144,732	103,588	71.6	0.4	89,469	61.8	0.4
Men	71,531	69,930	49,103	70.2	0.5	42,359	60.6	0.6
Women	76,503	74,801	54,485	72.8	0.5	47,110	63.0	0.5
Black	24,132	22,753	15,348	67.5	1.1	12,917	56.8	1.2
Men	10,771	10,048	6,416	63.9	1.7	5,327	53.0	1.8
Women	13,361	12,705	8,932	70.3	1.4	7,590	59.7	1.6
Asian and Pacific Islander	8,041	4,718	2,470	52.4	2.7	2,045	43.3	2.7
Men	3,767	2,213	1,199	54.2	4.0	980	44.3	4.0
Women	4,274	2,505	1,272	50.8	3.8	1,065	42.5	3.7
Hispanic (of any race)	21,598	13,158	7,546	57.3	2.0	5,934	45.1	2.0
Men	10,653	6,085	3,375	55.5	3.0	2,671	43.9	3.0
Women	10,945	7,073	4,171	59.0	2.7	3,263	46.1	2.8
Age								
18 to 24 years	26,712	23,915	12,122	50.7	1.0	8,635	36.1	0.9
25 to 34 years	37,304	32,233	20,403	63.3	0.8	16,286	50.5	0.8
35 to 44 years	44,476	40,434	28,366	70.2	0.7	24,452	60.5	0.7
45 to 54 years	37,504	35,230	26,158	74.2	0.7	23,362	66.3	0.7
55 to 64 years	23,848	22,737	17,551	77.2	0.8	15,939	70.1	0.9
65 to 74 years	17,819	17,233	13,573	78.8	0.9	12,450	72.2	1.0
75 years and over	14,945	14,582	11,375	78.0	1.0	9,702	66.5	1.2
Marital Status								
Married-spouse present	113,723	104,744	79,824	76.2	0.4	70,885	67.7	0.4
Married-spouse absent	2,710	1,899	1,168	61.5	3.3	982	51.7	3.4
Widowed	13,736	13,124	9,258	70.5	1.2	7,756	59.1	1.3
Divorced	19,809	19,055	12,403	65.1	1.0	10,199	53.5	1.1
Separated	4,427	3,960	2,316	58.5	2.3	1,815	45.8	2.4
Never married	48,204	43,584	24,581	56.4	0.7	19,189	44.0	0.7
Educational Attainment								
Less than 9th grade	12,894	8,784	4,655	53.0	1.6	3,454	39.3	1.6
9th to 12th grade, no diploma	20,108	17,801	9,235	51.9	1.1	6,758	38.0	1.1
High school graduate or GED	66,339	62,426	39,869	63.9	0.6	32,749	52.5	0.6
Some college or Associate degree	55,308	52,800	38,700	73.3	0.6	33,339	63.1	0.6
Bachelor's degree	32,254	30,063	24,619	81.9	0.7	22,661	75.4	0.7
Advanced degree	15,706	14,492	12,472	86.1	0.9	11,865	81.9	1.0
Annual Family Income								
Total family members	152,294	140,079	99,950	71.4	0.4	86,443	61.7	0.4
Less than $5,000	2,230	1,834	981	53.5	3.5	628	34.2	3.3
$5,000 to $9,999	4,242	3,623	2,068	57.1	2.4	1,470	40.6	2.4
$10,000 to $14,999	7,286	6,197	3,631	58.6	1.9	2,745	44.3	1.9
$15,000 to $24,999	14,600	12,337	8,013	65.0	1.3	6,330	51.3	1.3
$25,000 to $34,999	17,692	15,629	10,788	69.0	1.1	9,026	57.8	1.2
$35,000 to $49,999	22,349	20,759	15,007	72.3	0.9	12,853	61.9	1.0
$50,000 to $74,999	28,144	26,683	20,775	77.9	0.8	18,341	68.7	0.8
$75,000 and over	35,030	33,442	27,450	82.1	0.6	25,060	74.9	0.7
Income not reported	20,721	19,574	11,237	57.4	1.1	9,990	51.0	1.1
Employment Status								
In the civilian labor force	138,378	126,863	88,575	69.8	0.4	75,802	59.8	0.4
Employed	133,434	122,508	86,297	70.4	0.4	74,068	60.5	0.4
Unemployed	4,944	4,355	2,278	52.3	2.3	1,734	39.8	2.2
Not in the labor force	64,231	59,503	40,974	68.9	0.6	35,023	58.9	0.6

Over the same period, the percentage of those 65 years of age and over who voted increased from 63.5 percent in 1972 to a high of 70.1 percent in 1992, dropping somewhat to 67 percent in the 1996 presidential election.

In 2000, 72.2 percent of voters 65 to 74 years of age voted. In the 20 years from 1972 to 1992, voting rates of those aged 45 to 64 years remained close to 70 percent, dropping to 64.4 percent in the 1996 election. In 2000,

TABLE 7.3

Reported voting and registration by selected characteristics, November 2000 [CONTINUED]

(Numbers in thousands)

Characteristic	Total population	Total citizen	Total citizen Reported registered			Total citizen Reported voted		
			Number	Percent	90 percent C.I. (±)[1]	Number	Percent	90 percent C.I. (±)[1]
Tenure								
Owner-occupied units	145,362	138,929	102,442	73.7	0.4	89,886	64.7	0.4
Renter-occupied units	54,475	44,877	25,454	56.7	0.7	19,637	43.8	0.7
No cash rent units	2,773	2,561	1,653	64.5	2.8	1,302	50.8	0.3
Duration of Residence[2]								
Less than 1 month	3,009	2,520	1,363	54.1	3.0	915	36.3	2.9
1 to 6 months	17,389	14,797	8,929	60.3	1.2	6,682	45.2	1.2
7 to 11 months	8,435	7,180	4,426	61.6	1.7	3,405	47.4	1.7
1 to 2 years	28,856	24,948	17,475	70.0	0.9	14,482	58.0	0.9
3 to 4 years	26,003	23,327	17,508	75.1	0.8	14,806	63.5	0.9
5 years or longer	99,886	96,192	78,767	81.9	0.4	69,638	72.4	0.4
Not reported	19,031	17,401	1,081	6.2	0.5	898	5.2	0.5
Region and Race and Hispanic Origin								
Northeast	38,881	35,472	24,759	69.8	0.7	21,447	60.5	0.7
White	32,810	30,883	21,895	70.9	0.7	18,955	61.4	0.8
White non-Hispanic	30,194	29,175	20,916	71.7	0.7	18,179	62.3	0.8
Black	4,418	3,788	2,440	64.4	2.6	2,141	56.5	2.7
Asian and Pacific Islander	1,533	682	382	56.0	6.6	313	45.9	6.6
Hispanic (of any race)	2,978	1,930	1,094	56.7	4.9	873	45.2	4.9
Midwest	46,430	44,692	32,615	73.0	0.6	28,262	63.2	0.7
White	40,912	39,714	29,165	73.4	0.7	25,272	63.6	0.7
White non-Hispanic	39,426	38,903	28,698	73.8	0.7	24,885	64.0	0.7
Black	4,380	4,275	3,034	71.0	2.5	2,639	61.7	2.7
Asian and Pacific Islander	881	456	255	55.9	8.9	224	49.1	8.9
Hispanic (of any race)	1,561	870	500	57.5	8.0	418	48.0	8.0
South	71,835	67,153	46,321	69.0	0.6	38,441	57.2	0.6
White	56,912	53,420	37,109	69.5	0.6	30,859	57.8	0.7
White non-Hispanic	49,316	48,532	34,173	70.4	0.6	28,693	59.1	0.7
Black	13,080	12,542	8,534	68.0	1.6	7,049	56.2	1.7
Asian and Pacific Islander	1,322	698	365	52.3	7.4	293	42.0	7.3
Hispanic (of any race)	7,859	5,045	3,048	60.4	3.3	2,257	44.7	3.4
West	45,463	39,050	25,854	66.2	0.7	22,676	58.1	0.8
White	38,098	33,274	22,604	67.9	0.8	20,012	60.1	0.8
White non-Hispanic	29,099	28,121	19,801	70.4	0.8	17,711	63.0	0.9
Black	2,254	2,147	1,340	62.4	3.9	1,087	50.6	4.1
Asian and Pacific Islander	4,305	2,852	1,469	51.5	3.7	1,214	42.6	3.6
Hispanic (of any race)	9,201	5,314	2,904	54.6	3.3	2,386	44.9	3.3

[1] This figure added to or subtracted from the estimate provides the 90-percent confidence interval.
[2] Data on duration of residence were obtained from responses to the following question: "How long has (this person) lived at this address?"

SOURCE: Amie Jamieson, Hyon B. Shin, and Jennifer Day, "Table B. Reported Voting and Registration by Selected Characteristics: November 2000," in "Voting and Registration in the Election of November 2000," *Current Population Reports,* vol. P20-542, February 2002

66.3 percent of those 45 to 54 and 70.1 percent of those 55 to 64 voted. (See Table 7.3.)

Gender

For about 60 years after the ratification of the 19th Amendment, voter turnout rates for women were considerably lower than that of men. However, in every presidential election since 1984 women's rates surpassed those of men in the entire 18 years of age and older population. In the 2000 election nearly 71 percent of women were registered to vote and 60.7 percent of them voted, compared to 68.0 percent and 58.1 percent of men, respectively. (See Table 7.3.) The significant political involvement of women is correlated with other examples of female empowerment (i.e., greater educational attainment and labor force participation) since the 1960s. Because they make up an increasing share of voters, women have the potential to determine the results of elections at all levels.

Race and Ethnicity

In 1976 the voting gap between whites and blacks was 12 percentage points (60.9 percent versus 48.7 percent). By 1992 the gap had tightened to 10 points (63.6 percent and 54.0 percent, respectively). In the 2000 presidential election 60.5 percent of white and 56.8 percent of black voting-age populations turned out to vote, a difference of less than 4 percent. (See Table 7.3.)

The voting rate for persons of Hispanic origin has traditionally been recorded at about half the rate for whites. However, in the 1996 and 2000 elections Hispanic voting rates increased to 44.0 and 45.1 percent, respectively. These

TABLE 7.4

Voter registration and turnout, 2000

State	2000 VAP	2000 REG	%REG of VAP	Turnout	%TO of REG	%TO of VAP
Alabama	3,333,000	2,528,963	75.9	1,666,272	65.9	50
Alaska	430,000	473,648	110	285,560	60.3	66.4
Arizona	3,625,000	2,173,122	59.9	1,532,016	70.5	42.3
Arkansas	1,929,000	1,555,809	80.7	921,781	59.2	47.8
California	24,873,000	15,707,307	63.2	10,965,822	69.8	44.1
Colorado	3,067,000	2,274,152	74.1	1,741,368	76.6	56.8
Connecticut	2,499,000	1,874,245	75	1,459,526	77.9	58.4
Delaware	582,000	505,360	86.8	327,529	64.8	56.3
Dist. of Columbia	411,000	354,410	86.2	201,894	57	49.1
Florida	11,774,000	8,752,717	74.3	5,963,110	68.1	50.6
Georgia	5,893,000	3,859,960	65.5	2,583,208	66.9	43.8
Hawaii	909,000	637,349	70.1	367,951	57.7	40.5
Idaho	921,000	728,085	79.1	501,615	68.9	54.5
Illinois	8,983,000	7,129,026	79.4	4,742,115	66.5	52.8
Indiana	4,448,000	4,000,809	89.9	2,180,305	54.5	49
Iowa	2,165,000	1,841,346	85.1	1,314,395	71.4	60.7
Kansas	1,983,000	1,623,623	81.9	1,072,216	66	54.1
Kentucky	2,993,000	2,556,815	85.4	1,544,026	60.4	51.6
Louisiana	3,255,000	2,730,380	83.9	1,765,656	64.7	54.2
Maine	968,000	882,337	91.2	651,817	73.9	67.3
Maryland	3,925,000	2,715,366	69.2	2,023,735	74.5	51.6
Massachusetts	4,749,000	4,008,796	84.4	2,734,006	68.2	57.6
Michigan	7,358,000	6,861,342	93.3	4,232,501	61.7	57.5
Minnesota	3,547,000	3,265,324	92.1	2,438,685	74.7	68.8
Mississippi	2,047,000	1,739,858	84.9	994,184	57.1	48.6
Missouri	4,105,000	3,860,672	94	2,359,892	61.1	57.5
Montana	668,000	698,260	104.5	410,986	58.9	61.5
Nebraska	1,234,000	1,085,217	87.9	697,019	64.2	56.5
Nevada	1,390,000	898,347	64.6	608,970	67.8	43.8
New Hampshire	911,000	856,519	94	569,081	66.4	62.5
New Jersey	6,245,000	4,710,768	75.4	3,187,226	67.7	51
New Mexico	1,263,000	972,895	77	598,605	61.5	47.4
New York	13,805,000	11,262,816	81.6	6,960,215	61.8	50.4
North Carolina	5,797,000	5,122,123	88.4	2,914,990	56.9	50.3
North Dakota	477,000			288,256		60.4
Ohio	8,433,000	7,537,822	89.4	4,701,998	62.4	55.8
Oklahoma	2,531,000	2,233,602	88.2	1,234,229	55.3	48.8
Oregon	2,530,000	1,943,699	76.8	1,533,968	78.9	60.6
Pennsylvania	9,155,000	7,781,997	85	4,912,185	63.1	53.7
Rhode Island	753,000	655,107	87	408,783	62.4	54.3
South Carolina	2,977,000	2,157,006	72.5	1,386,331	64.3	46.6
South Dakota	543,000	471,152	86.8	316,269	67.1	58.2
Tennessee	4,221,000	3,181,108	75.4	2,076,181	65.3	49.2
Texas	14,850,000	10,267,639	69.1	6,407,037	62.4	43.1
Utah	1,465,000	1,123,238	76.7	770,754	68.6	52.6
Vermont	460,000	427,354	92.9	294,308	68.9	64
Virginia	5,263,000	3,770,273	71.6	2,789,808	74	53
Washington	4,368,000	3,335,714	76.4	2,487,433	74.6	56.9
West Virginia	1,416,000	1,067,822	75.4	648,124	60.7	45.8
Wisconsin	3,930,000			2,598,607		66.1
Wyoming	358,000	220,012	61.5	213,726	97.1	59.7
United States	**205,815,000**	**156,421,311**	**76**	**105,586,274**	**67.5**	**51.3**

Note: 2000 VAP refers to the total voting age population of the state. Please note that the VAP includes all persons over the age of 18—including a significant number of people not eligible to vote in U.S. elections.
2000 REG refers to the total number of registered voters as reported by the states.
Turnout in this instance refers to the total vote cast for the highest office on the ballot in 2000 (President). These figures may be inconsistent with other reported figures shown on this site and elsewhere since research suggests that approximately 2% of voters fail to vote for the highest office on a fairly consistent basis.
North Dakota has no voter registration.
Wisconsin has election day registration at the polls.
Registration and turnout statistics courtesy of state election offices.

SOURCE: "Voter Registration and Turnout 2000," Federal Election Commission, Washington, DC, 2000 [Online] http://www.fec.gov/pages/2000turnout/reg&to00.htm [accessed November 30, 2003]

higher participatory rates reflect the increase in the voting-age citizen population. Yet the overall low turnout rate among Hispanics also reflects, in part, the large proportion of noncitizens among the Hispanic population. The Current Population Survey, conducted by the Census Bureau, counts persons; it only recently included some questions on citizenship. Computing voter turnout rates for the citizen population 18 years and over, instead of for all residents (some of whom

FIGURE 7.2

Party gains in the House of Representatives, 2002

(Based on the number of seats per party)

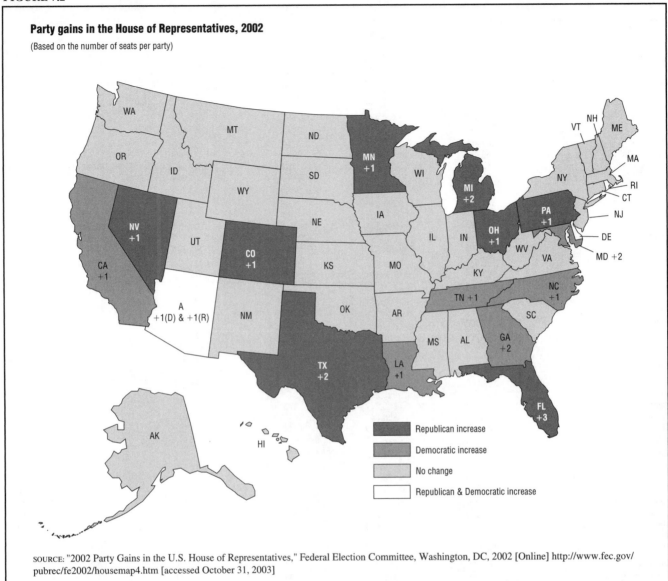

SOURCE: "2002 Party Gains in the U.S. House of Representatives," Federal Election Committee, Washington, DC, 2002 [Online] http://www.fec.gov/pubrec/fe2002/housemap4.htm [accessed October 31, 2003]

may not have the right to vote), significantly increased voter turnout rates for Hispanics in 1996 and 2000.

PRESIDENTIAL AND CONGRESSIONAL ELECTIONS

Congressional elections are held every two years. All the seats in the House of Representatives and one-third of Senate seats are contested. Every other congressional election coincides with a presidential election. Presidential elections tend to receive more interest than congressional elections, and more people vote during presidential election years than during congressional-only election years. In fact, the congressional election that occurs during the year that a presidential election does not take place is often called an "off-year" election, implying that this election is less important than the presidential election.

Since the voting and registration rates are different during these two election periods, this chapter includes studies

of both the 2000 presidential election and a preliminary assessment of the 2002 congressional elections. Every other year, the U.S. Census Bureau surveys American voting behavior as part of its Current Population Survey. Although the Census Bureau has published its analysis of the 2000 presidential election in 2002, similar voting and registration data for the 2002 congressional elections will not be released until 2004. The most reliable 2002 election analysis has been provided by the Committee for the Study of the American Electorate (CSAE), a Washington-based nonpartisan, nonprofit research institution.

THE 2000 ELECTION—A PRESIDENTIAL ELECTION YEAR

More so than in any other region, midwesterners are more apt to register and vote. In 2000, 73.0 percent of midwesterners were registered to vote and 63.2 percent cast ballots. The Midwest was followed by the Northeast

FIGURE 7.3

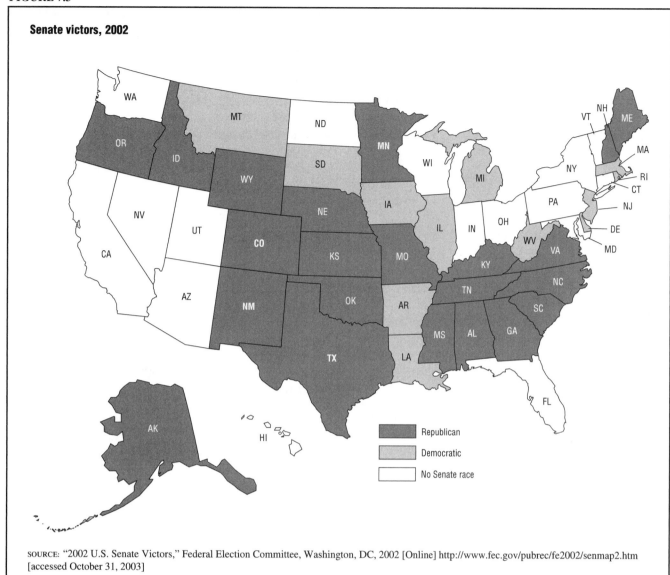

Senate victors, 2002

Republican
Democratic
No Senate race

SOURCE: "2002 U.S. Senate Victors," Federal Election Committee, Washington, DC, 2002 [Online] http://www.fec.gov/pubrec/fe2002/senmap2.htm [accessed October 31, 2003]

with 69.8 percent registered and a voting rate of 60.5 percent, the West with 66.2 percent registered and 58.1 percent voting, and the South with 69.0 percent registered and 57.2 percent voting. (See Table 7.3.)

Among the 50 states, according to the Federal Election Commission, Minnesota had the highest voter turnout, at 68.8 percent, followed by Maine (67.3 percent), Alaska (66.4 percent), Wisconsin (66.1 percent), New Hampshire (62.5 percent), and Montana (61.5 percent). The lowest voter turnouts in 2000 were seen in Hawaii (40.5 percent), Arizona (42.3 percent), Texas (43.1 percent), and Nevada and Georgia (both at 43.8 percent). (See Table 7.4.)

The election of November 7, 2000, was the closest presidential election in U.S. history. About 9.5 million more votes were cast than in the 1996 presidential election. Democratic candidate Al Gore garnered 50,996,582 votes, about 500,000 more than George W. Bush's

50,456,062 votes. Liberal Green Party candidate Ralph Nader ran a distant third, taking about 2,882,728 votes. For the Democrats, it has been 27 years since they have captured the White House with more than 50 percent of the vote. The last time that a majority of Americans voted Democratic in a presidential election occurred in 1976 when Jimmy Carter defeated President Gerald Ford in the wake of the Watergate scandal.

Because U.S. presidential elections are decided not by popular vote but by the electoral college, by the end of polling on election day November 7, 2000, neither of the two main candidates had a clear victory. The tally in electoral votes at that time was Gore, 266, and Bush, 246, with one state too close to call: Florida. With 25 electoral votes, Florida had enough to put either candidate above the 270 electoral votes needed to win. Weeks of recounts and court challenges eventually went all the way to the U.S. Supreme Court. The Court issued a bitterly divided decision (5 to 4) stating that the recounts ordered by the Florida Supreme Court were unconstitutional and that there was not enough time to conduct them prior to a December 12 deadline for states to select presidential electors. The decision stopped the recounts, giving Bush a slim majority of less than 1,000 votes. On December 13, 2001, Gore conceded the victory to his Republican rival. On January 20, 2001, Bush was inaugurated as the 43rd president of the United States.

THE 2002 ELECTIONS—A CONGRESSIONAL ELECTION YEAR

How Many Voted?

In November 2002 the CSAE released its initial post-election analysis of the 2002 midterm elections. An estimated 78.7 million citizens cast their ballots and 39.3 percent of U.S. residents reported that they had voted in the election, up 1.7 percent from 1998. Registration was down slightly from 64.6 percent in 1998 to 64.1 percent. Thirty-one states experienced increased turnout, 19 states saw declines, and 7 states set record turnout lows. Minnesota had the highest voter turnout (61.4 percent) followed by South Dakota (61.3 percent), Maine (50.6 percent), and Vermont (50.0). Ten-nessee (15.0 percent) had the highest turnout increase, followed by New Hampshire (12.1 percent), South Dakota (12.0 percent), and Louisiana (8.0 percent). California experienced the largest decrease in voter turnout (8.0 percent), followed by Alaska (6.5 percent), Colorado (5.6 percent), Hawaii (4.5 percent), and Arizona (3.0 percent).

Election Results

The 2002 congressional elections were seen by many observers as a referendum on President Bush and the "war on terrorism." To the surprise of many, Republicans not only retained political power in the House but gained six seats, increasing their majority to 24 (229 seats) over the Democrats (205 seats). Typically, the party in control of the White House loses seats in the midterm election. This was only the third time since the Civil War (1861–1865) that the president's party gained seats in the off-year elections of his first term. The 2002 congressional elections were also significant because House Republicans held their majority for the fifth straight election, a feat they have not accomplished since the 1920s. Just as important, the Republicans gained two seats in the Senate, giving them a slim 51-to-48 (1 Independent) seat advantage over the Democrats. (See Figure 7.2 and Figure 7.3.)

CHAPTER 8

CRIME

Virtually every U.S. president since John F. Kennedy has committed his administration to a "war on crime," often without much success. However, in 1994 Congress passed the Violent Crime Control and Law Enforcement Act (PL 103-322), which, in conjunction with stricter criminal justice laws passed by many state legislatures, has played a significant role in better protecting the U.S. people. Specifically, the act provided funds for thousands of new police officers and required mandatory life sentences for violent, three-time federal offenders. In addition, it expanded the federal death penalty to cover more than 60 offenses and permitted the prosecution as adults of juvenile offenders, ages 13 or older, who commit federal crimes of violence or federal crimes involving a firearm. The law increased the penalties for repeat federal sex offenders and created a program for the registration of sexual predators.

The annual *Crime in the United States,* prepared by the Federal Bureau of Investigation (FBI), is used as an indicator of the level of crime in the United States. The index is based on offenses reported by citizens to city, county, and state police agencies. The Crime Index records reports of selected offenses, including the violent crimes of murder and nonnegligent manslaughter, forcible rape, robbery, and aggravated assault and the property crimes of burglary, larceny-theft, motor vehicle theft, and arson. All offenses are reported whether anyone is arrested or not, but if any reported offense is found to be false, it is removed from the records. Updates are made each year to the previous year's information; thus, occasionally the recorded numbers of crimes change by the following year's annual report.

According to the FBI, a Crime Index offense occurred every 2.7 seconds in 2002, a violent crime occurred every 22.1 seconds, and a property crime every 3.0 seconds. (See Table 8.1.)

NUMBER AND RATE OF CRIMES

Since 1967 the number of reported crimes has almost doubled, though the figures have risen and fallen over the

TABLE 8.1

Crime Clock, 2002

Every 2.7 seconds	One crime index offense
Every 22.1 seconds	One violent crime
Every 35.3 seconds	One aggravated assault
Every 1.2 minutes	One robbery
Every 5.5 minutes	One forcible rape
Every 32.4 minutes	One murder
Every 3.0 seconds	One property crime
Every 4.5 seconds	One larceny-theft
Every 14.7 seconds	One burglary
Every 25.3 seconds	One motor vehicle theft

SOURCE: "Crime Clock," in *Crime in the United States, 2002,* Federal Bureau of Investigation, Clarksburg, WV, 2002

decades and steadily declined from 1991 to 2000. However, the number of reported crimes increased by 2.1 percent in 2001 and by another one-tenth of a percent in 2002. The volume of Crime Index offenses reported in 1967 (5.9 million reported crimes) was less than half of the total number in 1980 (13.4 million reported crimes). After several years of declines, the number of reported crimes jumped 25 percent from 1985 to 1991. Following the passage of the Violent Crime Control and Law Enforcement Act (1994) to 2000, the number of reported offenses fell from 13.9 million to 11.6 million. The biggest decline occurred from 1998 to 1999, when crime fell 6.8 percent. In 2002 the estimated number of Crime Index offenses was 11.877 million, an increase from 11.876 million the year before. (See Table 8.2.) Although the number of offenses increased slightly from 2001 to 2002, the latter figure represents a 4.9 percent decrease from 1998 and 16.0 percent decline from 1993.

The FBI report presents figures for both the total number and estimated rates of crimes. The data collected on total offenses committed is converted into a rate that estimates the incidents per 100,000 people. From 1980 through 1984, the Crime Rate index rate began to drop, reaching a low of 5,038 per 100,000 people in 1984. (See Table 8.2.) After that, the rate increased, reaching 5,898

TABLE 8.2

Index of crime, 1983–2002

Population[1]	Crime Index	Modified Crime Index[2]	Violent crime[3]	Property crime[3]	Murder and non-negligent manslaughter	Forcible rape	Robbery	Aggravated assault	Burglary	Larceny-theft	Motor vehicle theft	Arson[2]
						Number of offenses						
Population by year:												
1983– 233,791,994	12,108,630		1,258,087	10,850,543	19,308	78,918	506,567	653,294	3,129,851	6,712,759	1,007,933	
1984– 235,824,902	11,881,755		1,273,282	10,608,473	18,692	84,233	485,008	685,349	2,984,434	6,591,874	1,032,165	
1985– 237,923,795	12,430,357		1,327,767	11,102,590	18,976	87,671	497,874	723,246	3,073,348	6,926,380	1,102,862	
1986– 240,132,887	13,211,869		1,489,169	11,722,700	20,613	91,459	542,775	834,322	3,241,410	7,257,153	1,224,137	
1987– 242,288,918	13,508,708		1,483,999	12,024,709	20,096	91,111	517,704	855,088	3,236,184	7,499,851	1,288,674	
1988– 244,498,982	13,923,086		1,566,221	12,356,865	20,675	92,486	542,968	910,092	3,218,077	7,705,872	1,432,916	
1989– 246,819,230	14,251,449		1,646,037	12,605,412	21,500	94,504	578,326	951,707	3,168,170	7,872,442	1,564,800	
1990– 249,464,396	14,475,613		1,820,127	12,655,486	23,438	102,555	639,271	1,054,863	3,073,909	7,945,670	1,635,907	
1991– 252,153,092	14,872,883		1,911,767	12,961,116	24,703	106,593	687,732	1,092,739	3,157,150	8,142,228	1,661,738	
1992– 255,029,699	14,438,191		1,932,274	12,505,917	23,760	109,062	672,478	1,126,974	2,979,884	7,915,199	1,610,834	
1993– 257,782,608	14,144,794		1,926,017	12,218,777	24,526	106,014	659,870	1,135,607	2,834,808	7,820,909	1,563,060	
1994– 260,327,021	13,989,543		1,857,670	12,131,873	23,326	102,216	618,949	1,113,179	2,712,774	7,879,812	1,539,287	
1995– 262,803,276	13,862,727		1,798,792	12,063,935	21,606	97,470	580,509	1,099,207	2,593,784	7,997,710	1,472,441	
1996– 265,228,572	13,493,863		1,688,540	11,805,323	19,645	96,252	535,594	1,037,049	2,506,400	7,904,685	1,394,238	
1997– 267,783,607	13,194,571		1,636,096	11,558,475	18,208	96,153	498,534	1,023,201	2,460,526	7,743,760	1,354,189	
1998– 270,248,003	12,485,714		1,533,887	10,951,827	16,974	93,144	447,186	976,583	2,332,735	7,376,311	1,242,781	
1999– 272,690,813	11,634,378		1,426,044	10,208,334	15,522	89,411	409,371	911,740	2,100,739	6,955,520	1,152,075	
2000– 281,421,906	11,608,070		1,425,486	10,182,584	15,586	90,178	408,016	911,706	2,050,992	6,971,590	1,160,002	
2001– 285,317,559[4]	11,876,669		1,439,480	10,437,189	16,037	90,863	423,557	909,023	2,116,531	7,092,267	1,228,391	
2002– 288,368,698	11,877,218		1,426,325	10,450,893	16,204	95,136	420,637	894,348	2,151,875	7,052,922	1,246,096	
Percent change, number of offenses:												
2002/2001	*		-0.9	+0.1	+1.0	+4.7	-0.7	-1.6	+1.7	-0.6	+1.4	
2002/1998	-4.9		-7.0	-4.6	-4.5	+2.1	-5.9	-8.4	-7.8	-4.4	+0.3	
2002/1993	-16.0		-25.9	-14.5	-33.9	-10.3	-36.3	-21.2	-24.1	-9.8	-20.3	

TABLE 8.2
Index of crime, 1983–2002 [CONTINUED]

Population[1]	Crime Index	Modified Crime Index[2]	Violent crime[3]	Property crime[3]	Murder and non-negligent manslaughter	Forcible rape	Robbery	Aggravated assault	Burglary	Larceny-theft	Motor vehicle theft	Arson[2]
					Rate per 100,000 inhabitants							
Year:												
1983	5,179.2		538.1	4,641.1	8.3	33.8	216.7	279.4	1,338.7	2,871.3	431.1	
1984	5,038.4		539.9	4,498.5	7.9	35.7	205.7	290.6	1,265.5	2,795.2	437.7	
1985	5,224.5		558.1	4,666.4	8.0	36.8	209.3	304.0	1,291.7	2,911.2	463.5	
1986	5,501.9		620.1	4,881.8	8.6	38.1	226.0	347.4	1,349.8	3,022.1	509.8	
1987	5,575.5		612.5	4,963.0	8.3	37.6	213.7	352.9	1,335.7	3,095.4	531.9	
1988	5,694.5		640.6	5,054.0	8.5	37.8	222.1	372.2	1,316.2	3,151.7	586.1	
1989	5,774.0		666.9	5,107.1	8.7	38.3	234.3	385.6	1,283.6	3,189.6	634.0	
1990	5,802.7		729.6	5,073.1	9.4	41.1	256.3	422.9	1,232.2	3,185.1	655.8	
1991	5,898.4		758.2	5,140.2	9.8	42.3	272.7	433.4	1,252.1	3,229.1	659.0	
1992	5,661.4		757.7	4,903.7	9.3	42.8	263.7	441.9	1,168.4	3,103.6	631.6	
1993	5,487.1		747.1	4,740.0	9.5	41.1	256.0	440.5	1,099.7	3,033.9	606.3	
1994	5,373.8		713.6	4,660.2	9.0	39.3	237.8	427.6	1,042.1	3,026.9	591.3	
1995	5,274.9		684.5	4,590.5	8.2	37.1	220.9	418.3	987.0	3,043.2	560.3	
1996	5,087.6		636.6	4,451.0	7.4	36.3	201.9	391.0	945.0	2,980.3	525.7	
1997	4,927.3		611.0	4,316.3	6.8	35.9	186.2	382.1	918.8	2,891.8	505.7	
1998	4,620.1		567.6	4,052.5	6.3	34.5	165.5	361.4	863.2	2,729.5	459.9	
1999	4,266.5		523.0	3,743.6	5.7	32.8	150.1	334.3	770.4	2,550.7	422.5	
2000	4,124.8		506.5	3,618.3	5.5	32.0	145.0	324.0	728.8	2,477.3	412.2	
2001[4]	4,162.6		504.5	3,658.1	5.6	31.8	148.5	318.6	741.8	2,485.7	430.5	
2002	4,118.8		494.6	3,624.1	5.6	33.0	145.9	310.1	746.2	2,445.8	432.1	
Percent change, rate per 100,000 inhabitants:												
2002/2001	-1.1		-2.0	-0.9	*	+3.6	-1.7	-2.7	+0.6	-1.6	+0.4	
2002/1998	-10.9		-12.9	-10.6	-10.5	-4.3	-11.8	-14.2	-13.5	-10.4	-6.0	
2002/1993	-24.9		-33.8	-23.5	-40.9	-19.8	-43.0	-29.6	-32.1	-19.4	-28.7	

Note: * Less than one-tenth of 1 percent.
The murder and nonnegligent homicides that occurred as a result of the events of September 11, 2001, were not included in this table.
[1] Populations are estimates as of July 1 for each year except 1990 and 2000 which are decennial census counts.
[2] Although arson data are included in the trend and clearance tables, sufficient data are not available to estimate totals for this offense.
[3] Violent crimes are offenses of murder, forcible rape, robbery, and aggravated assault. Property crimes are offenses of burglary, larceny-theft, and motor vehicle theft.
[4] The 2001 crime figures have been adjusted.

SOURCE: "Table 1. Index of Crime," United States, 1983–2002," in *Crime in the United States, 2002*, Federal Bureau of Investigation, Clarksburg, WV, 2002

TABLE 8.3

Index of crime, by region, geographic division, and state, 2001–02

Area	Year	Population[1]	Crime Index		Modified Crime Index[2]		Violent crime[3]		Property crime[3]		Murder and nonnegligent manslaughter	
			Number	Rate per 100,000	Number	Rate per 100,000	Number	Rate per 100,000	Number	Rate per 100,000	Number	Rate per 100,000
United States total[4,5,6]	2001	285,317,559	11,876,669	4,162.6			1,439,480	504.5	10,437,189	3,658.1	16,037	5.6
	2002	288,368,698	11,877,218	4,118.8			1,426,325	494.6	10,450,893	3,624.1	16,204	5.6
Percent change			*	-1.1			-0.9	-2.0	+0.1	-0.9	+1.0	*
Northeast[4]	2001	53,950,802	1,617,785	2,998.6			231,126	428.4	1,386,659	2,570.2	2,277	4.2
	2002	54,227,064	1,566,645	2,889.0			225,841	416.5	1,340,804	2,472.6	2,203	4.1
Percent change			-3.2	-3.7			-2.3	-2.8	-3.3	-3.8	-3.2	-3.7
New England[4]	2001	14,052,232	424,275	3,019.3			49,578	352.8	374,697	2,666.5	330	2.3
	2002	14,144,141	419,289	2,964.4			49,065	346.9	370,224	2,617.5	333	2.4
Percent change			-1.2	-1.8			-1.0	-1.7	-1.2	-1.8	+0.9	+0.3
Connecticut	2001	3,434,602	106,791	3,109.3			11,492	334.6	95,299	2,774.7	105	3.1
	2002	3,460,503	103,719	2,997.2			10,767	311.1	92,952	2,686.1	80	2.3
Percent change			-2.9	-3.6			-6.3	-7.0	-2.5	-3.2	-23.8	-24.4
Maine[4]	2001	1,284,470	34,589	2,692.9			1,435	111.7	33,154	2,581.1	19	1.5
	2002	1,294,464	34,381	2,656.0			1,396	107.8	32,985	2,548.2	14	1.1
Percent change			-0.6	-1.4			-2.7	-3.5	-0.5	-1.3	-26.3	-26.9
Massachusetts[4]	2001	6,401,164	197,664	3,087.9			30,585	477.8	167,079	2,610.1	143	2.2
	2002	6,427,801	198,890	3,094.2			31,137	484.4	167,753	2,609.8	173	2.7
Percent change			+0.6	+0.2			+1.8	+1.4	+0.4	*	+21.0	+20.5
New Hampshire	2001	1,259,359	29,233	2,321.3			2,144	170.2	27,089	2,151.0	17	1.3
	2002	1,275,056	28,306	2,220.0			2,056	161.2	26,250	2,058.7	12	0.9
Percent change			-3.2	-4.4			-4.1	-5.3	-3.1	-4.3	-29.4	-30.3
Rhode Island	2001	1,059,659	39,020	3,682.3			3,278	309.3	35,742	3,373.0	39	3.7
	2002	1,069,725	38,393	3,589.1			3,051	285.2	35,342	3,303.8	41	3.8
Percent change			-1.6	-2.5			-6.9	-7.8	-1.1	-2.0	+5.1	+4.1
Vermont	2001	612,978	16,978	2,769.8			644	105.1	16,334	2,664.7	7	1.1
	2002	616,592	15,600	2,530.0			658	106.7	14,942	2,423.3	13	2.1
Percent change			-8.1	-8.7			+2.2	+1.6	-8.5	-9.1	+85.7	+84.6
Middle Atlantic[4]	2001	39,898,570	1,193,510	2,991.4			181,548	455.0	1,011,962	2,536.3	1,947	4.9
	2002	40,082,923	1,147,356	2,862.5			176,776	441.0	970,580	2,421.4	1,870	4.7
Percent change			-3.9	-4.3			-2.6	-3.1	-4.1	-4.5	-4.0	-4.4
New Jersey	2001	8,511,116	273,645	3,215.1			33,094	388.8	240,551	2,826.3	336	3.9
	2002	8,590,300	259,789	3,024.2			32,168	374.5	227,621	2,649.7	337	3.9
Percent change			-5.1	-5.9			-2.8	-3.7	-5.4	-6.2	+0.3	-0.6
New York[4]	2001	19,084,350	556,025	2,913.5			98,022	513.6	458,003	2,399.9	960	5.0
	2002	19,157,532	537,121	2,803.7			95,030	496.0	442,091	2,307.7	909	4.7
Percent change			-3.4	-3.8			-3.1	-3.4	-3.5	-3.8	-5.3	-5.7
Pennsylvania	2001	12,303,104	363,840	2,957.3			50,432	409.9	313,408	2,547.4	651	5.3
	2002	12,335,091	350,446	2,841.0			49,578	401.9	300,868	2,439.1	624	5.1
Percent change			-3.7	-3.9			-1.7	-1.9	-4.0	-4.3	-4.1	-4.4
Midwest[4,5]	2001	64,819,817	2,577,704	3,976.7			279,218	430.8	2,298,486	3,546.0	3,401	5.2
	2002	65,141,893	2,529,508	3,883.1			276,763	424.9	2,252,745	3,458.2	3,298	5.1
Percent change			-1.9	-2.4			-0.9	-1.4	-2.0	-2.5	-3.0	-3.5
East North Central[4,5]	2001	45,448,968	1,810,525	3,983.6			209,937	461.9	1,600,588	3,521.7	2,711	6.0
	2002	45,672,597	1,772,509	3,880.9			206,887	453.0	1,565,622	3,427.9	2,669	5.8
Percent change			-2.1	-2.6			-1.5	-1.9	-2.2	-2.7	-1.5	-2.0
Illinois[4,5]	2001	12,520,227	513,918	4,104.7			79,270	633.1	434,648	3,471.6	982	7.8
	2002	12,600,620	506,086	4,016.4			78,214	620.7	427,872	3,395.6	949	7.5
Percent change			-1.5	-2.2			-1.3	-2.0	-1.6	-2.2	-3.4	-4.0
Indiana	2001	6,126,743	234,282	3,823.9			22,734	371.1	211,548	3,452.9	413	6.7
	2002	6,159,068	230,966	3,750.0			22,001	357.2	208,965	3,392.8	362	5.9
Percent change			-1.4	-1.9			-3.2	-3.7	-1.2	-1.7	-12.3	-12.8
Michigan	2001	10,006,266	407,777	4,075.2			55,424	553.9	352,353	3,521.3	672	6.7
	2002	10,050,446	389,366	3,874.1			54,306	540.3	335,060	3,333.8	678	6.7
Percent change			-4.5	-4.9			-2.0	-2.4	-4.9	-5.3	+0.9	+0.4
Ohio	2001	11,389,785	475,138	4,171.6			40,023	351.4	435,115	3,820.2	452	4.0
	2002	11,421,267	469,104	4,107.3			40,128	351.3	428,976	3,755.9	526	4.6
Percent change			-1.3	-1.5			+0.3	*	-1.4	-1.7	+16.4	+16.1
Wisconsin	2001	5,405,947	179,410	3,318.8			12,486	231.0	166,924	3,087.8	192	3.6
	2002	5,441,196	176,987	3,252.7			12,238	224.9	164,749	3,027.8	154	2.8
Percent change			-1.4	-2.0			-2.0	-2.6	-1.3	-1.9	-19.8	-20.3

TABLE 8.3

Index of crime, by region, geographic division, and state, 2001–02 [CONTINUED]

Area	Forcible rape Number	Rate per 100,000	Robbery Number	Rate per 100,000	Aggravated assault Number	Rate per 100,000	Burglary Number	Rate per 100,000	Larceny-theft Number	Rate per 100,000	Motor vehicle theft Number	Rate per 100,000	Arson[2] Number	Rate per 100,000
United States total[4,5,6]	90,863	31.8	423,557	148.5	909,023	318.6	2,116,531	741.8	7,092,267	2,485.7	1,228,391	430.5		
	95,136	33.0	420,637	145.9	894,348	310.1	2,151,875	746.2	7,052,922	2,445.8	1,246,096	432.1		
Percent change	+4.7	+3.6	-0.7	-1.7	-1.6	-2.7	+1.7	+0.6	-0.6	-1.6	+1.4	+0.4		
Northeast[4]	12,093	22.4	80,626	149.4	136,130	252.3	252,907	468.8	962,226	1,783.5	171,526	317.9		
	12,814	23.6	80,626	148.7	130,198	240.1	248,246	457.8	929,458	1,714.0	163,100	300.8		
Percent change	+6.0	+5.4	0.0	-0.5	-4.4	-4.8	-1.8	-2.3	-3.4	-3.9	-4.9	-5.4		
New England[4]	3,802	27.1	12,461	88.7	32,985	234.7	71,350	507.7	253,529	1,804.2	49,818	354.5		
	3,851	27.2	12,905	91.2	31,976	226.1	72,038	509.3	251,008	1,774.6	47,178	333.6		
Percent change	+1.3	+0.6	+3.6	+2.9	-3.1	-3.7	+1.0	+0.3	-1.0	-1.6	-5.3	-5.9		
Connecticut	639	18.6	4,183	121.8	6,565	191.1	17,159	499.6	65,762	1,914.7	12,378	360.4		
	730	21.1	4,060	117.3	5,897	170.4	17,088	493.8	64,292	1,857.9	11,572	334.4		
Percent change	+14.2	+13.4	-2.9	-3.7	-10.2	-10.8	-0.4	-1.2	-2.2	-3.0	-6.5	-7.2		
Maine[4]	326	25.4	264	20.6	826	64.3	6,898	537.0	24,585	1,914.0	1,671	130.1		
	377	29.1	270	20.9	735	56.8	6,965	538.1	24,591	1,899.7	1,429	110.4		
Percent change	+15.6	+14.8	+2.3	+1.5	-11.0	-11.7	+1.0	+0.2	*	-0.7	-14.5	-15.1		
Massachusetts[4]	1,856	29.0	6,476	101.2	22,110	345.4	32,430	506.6	106,821	1,668.8	27,828	434.7		
	1,777	27.6	7,169	111.5	22,018	342.5	33,243	517.2	107,922	1,679.0	26,588	413.6		
Percent change	-4.3	-4.7	+10.7	+10.2	-0.4	-0.8	+2.5	+2.1	+1.0	+0.6	-4.5	-4.9		
New Hampshire	458	36.4	445	35.3	1,224	97.2	4,889	388.2	20,060	1,592.9	2,140	169.9		
	446	35.0	413	32.4	1,185	92.9	4,838	379.4	19,468	1,526.8	1,944	152.5		
Percent change	-2.6	-3.8	-7.2	-8.3	-3.2	-4.4	-1.0	-2.3	-3.0	-4.1	-9.2	-10.3		
Rhode Island	416	39.3	986	93.0	1,837	173.4	6,824	644.0	23,875	2,253.1	5,043	475.9		
	395	36.9	916	85.6	1,699	158.8	6,415	599.7	24,051	2,248.3	4,876	455.8		
Percent change	-5.0	-5.9	-7.1	-8.0	-7.5	-8.4	-6.0	-6.9	+0.7	-0.2	-3.3	-4.2		
Vermont	107	17.5	107	17.5	423	69.0	3,150	513.9	12,426	2,027.2	758	123.7		
	126	20.4	77	12.5	442	71.7	3,489	565.9	10,684	1,732.8	769	124.7		
Percent change	+17.8	+17.1	-28.0	-28.5	+4.5	+3.9	+10.8	+10.1	-14.0	-14.5	+1.5	+0.9		
Middle Atlantic[4]	8,291	20.8	68,165	170.8	103,145	258.5	181,557	455.0	708,697	1,776.2	121,708	305.0		
	8,963	22.4	67,721	169.0	98,222	245.0	176,208	439.6	678,450	1,692.6	115,922	289.2		
Percent change	+8.1	+7.6	-0.7	-1.1	-4.8	-5.2	-2.9	-3.4	-4.3	-4.7	-4.8	-5.2		
New Jersey	1,278	15.0	14,110	165.8	17,370	204.1	46,812	550.0	156,031	1,833.3	37,708	443.0		
	1,347	15.7	13,905	161.9	16,579	193.0	43,898	511.0	147,984	1,722.7	35,739	416.0		
Percent change	+5.4	+4.4	-1.5	-2.4	-4.6	-5.4	-6.2	-7.1	-5.2	-6.0	-5.2	-6.1		
New York[4]	3,546	18.6	36,555	191.5	56,961	298.5	80,400	421.3	329,316	1,725.6	48,287	253.0		
	3,885	20.3	36,653	191.3	53,583	279.7	76,700	400.4	318,025	1,660.1	47,366	247.2		
Percent change	+9.6	+9.1	+0.3	-0.1	-5.9	-6.3	-4.6	-5.0	-3.4	-3.8	-1.9	-2.3		
Pennsylvania	3,467	28.2	17,500	142.2	28,814	234.2	54,345	441.7	223,350	1,815.4	35,713	290.3		
	3,731	30.2	17,163	139.1	28,060	227.5	55,610	450.8	212,441	1,722.2	32,817	266.0		
Percent change	+7.6	+7.3	-1.9	-2.2	-2.6	-2.9	+2.3	+2.1	-4.9	-5.1	-8.1	-8.3		
Midwest[4,5]	22,757	35.1	83,079	128.2	169,981	262.2	438,675	676.8	1,614,095	2,490.1	245,716	379.1		
	24,109	37.0	82,144	126.1	167,212	256.7	446,471	685.4	1,572,181	2,413.5	234,093	359.4		
Percent change	+5.9	+5.4	-1.1	-1.6	-1.6	-2.1	+1.8	+1.3	-2.6	-3.1	-4.7	-5.2		
East North Central[4,5]	16,598	36.5	66,682	146.7	123,946	272.7	317,791	699.2	1,102,007	2,424.7	180,790	397.8		
	17,551	38.4	66,315	145.2	120,352	263.5	321,788	704.6	1,072,742	2,348.8	171,092	374.6		
Percent change	+5.7	+5.2	-0.6	-1.0	-2.9	-3.4	+1.3	+0.8	-2.7	-3.1	-5.4	-5.8		
Illinois[4,5]	4,010	32.0	24,931	199.1	49,347	394.1	79,158	632.2	306,757	2,450.1	48,733	389.2		
	4,298	34.1	25,272	200.6	47,695	378.5	81,123	643.8	301,892	2,395.9	44,857	356.0		
Percent change	+7.2	+6.5	+1.4	+0.7	-3.3	-4.0	+2.5	+1.8	-1.6	-2.2	-8.0	-8.5		
Indiana	1,716	28.0	7,171	117.0	13,434	219.3	42,758	697.9	147,291	2,404.1	21,499	350.9		
	1,843	29.9	6,612	107.4	13,184	214.1	42,605	691.7	146,073	2,371.7	20,287	329.4		
Percent change	+7.4	+6.8	-7.8	-8.3	-1.9	-2.4	-0.4	-0.9	-0.8	-1.3	-5.6	-6.1		
Michigan	5,264	52.6	12,937	129.3	36,551	365.3	72,038	719.9	226,708	2,265.7	53,607	535.7		
	5,364	53.4	11,847	117.9	36,417	362.3	70,970	706.1	214,367	2,132.9	49,723	494.7		
Percent change	+1.9	+1.5	-8.4	-8.8	-0.4	-0.8	-1.5	-1.9	-5.4	-5.9	-7.2	-7.7		
Ohio	4,466	39.2	17,199	151.0	17,906	157.2	96,910	850.9	295,976	2,598.6	42,229	370.8		
	4,809	42.1	17,871	156.5	16,922	148.2	99,164	868.2	287,045	2,513.3	42,767	374.5		
Percent change	+7.7	+7.4	+3.9	+3.6	-5.5	-5.8	+2.3	+2.0	-3.0	-3.3	+1.3	+1.0		
Wisconsin	1,142	21.1	4,444	82.2	6,708	124.1	26,927	498.1	125,275	2,317.4	14,722	272.3		
	1,237	22.7	4,713	86.6	6,134	112.7	27,926	513.2	123,365	2,267.2	13,458	247.3		
Percent change	+8.3	+7.6	+6.1	+5.4	-8.6	-9.1	+3.7	+3.0	-1.5	-2.2	-8.6	-9.2		

TABLE 8.3

Index of crime, by region, geographic division, and state, 2001–02 [CONTINUED]

Area	Year	Population[1]	Crime Index Number	Crime Index Rate per 100,000	Modified Crime Index[2] Number	Modified Crime Index[2] Rate per 100,000	Violent crime[3] Number	Violent crime[3] Rate per 100,000	Property crime[3] Number	Property crime[3] Rate per 100,000	Murder and nonnegligent manslaughter Number	Murder and nonnegligent manslaughter Rate per 100,000
West North Central	2001	19,370,849	767,179	3,960.5			69,281	357.7	697,898	3,602.8	690	3.6
	2002	19,469,296	756,999	3,888.2			69,876	358.9	687,123	3,529.3	629	3.2
Percent change			-1.3	-1.8			+0.9	+0.3	-1.5	-2.0	-8.8	-9.3
Iowa	2001	2,931,967	96,499	3,291.3			7,865	268.2	88,634	3,023.0	50	1.7
	2002	2,936,760	101,265	3,448.2			8,388	285.6	92,877	3,162.6	44	1.5
Percent change			+4.9	+4.8			+6.6	+6.5	+4.8	+4.6	-12.0	-12.1
Kansas	2001	2,702,125	116,446	4,309.4			10,909	403.7	105,537	3,905.7	92	3.4
	2002	2,715,884	110,997	4,087.0			10,229	376.6	100,768	3,710.3	78	2.9
Percent change			-4.7	-5.2			-6.2	-6.7	-4.5	-5.0	-15.2	-15.6
Minnesota	2001	4,984,535	178,191	3,574.9			13,145	263.7	165,046	3,311.2	119	2.4
	2002	5,019,720	177,454	3,535.1			13,428	267.5	164,026	3,267.6	112	2.2
Percent change			-0.4	-1.1			+2.2	+1.4	-0.6	-1.3	-5.9	-6.5
Missouri	2001	5,637,309	268,883	4,769.7			30,472	540.5	238,411	4,229.2	372	6.6
	2002	5,672,579	261,077	4,602.4			30,557	538.7	230,520	4,063.8	331	5.8
Percent change			-2.9	-3.5			+0.3	-0.3	-3.3	-3.9	-11.0	-11.6
Nebraska	2001	1,720,039	74,177	4,312.5			5,214	303.1	68,963	4,009.4	43	2.5
	2002	1,729,180	73,606	4,256.7			5,428	313.9	68,178	3,942.8	48	2.8
Percent change			-0.8	-1.3			+4.1	+3.6	-1.1	-1.7	+11.6	+11.0
North Dakota	2001	636,550	15,339	2,409.7			505	79.3	14,834	2,330.4	7	1.1
	2002	634,110	15,258	2,406.2			496	78.2	14,762	2,328.0	5	0.8
Percent change			-0.5	-0.1			-1.8	-1.4	-0.5	-0.1	-28.6	-28.3
South Dakota	2001	758,324	17,644	2,326.7			1,171	154.4	16,473	2,172.3	7	0.9
	2002	761,063	17,342	2,278.7			1,350	177.4	15,992	2,101.3	11	1.4
Percent change			-1.7	-2.1			+15.3	+14.9	-2.9	-3.3	+57.1	+56.6
South[4,5,6]	2001	101,953,947	4,873,007	4,779.6			593,711	582.3	4,279,296	4,197.3	6,842	6.7
	2002	103,347,425	4,880,003	4,721.9			590,086	571.0	4,289,917	4,151.0	6,982	6.8
Percent change			+0.1	-1.2			-0.6	-2.0	+0.2	-1.1	+2.0	+0.7
South Atlantic[4,6]	2001	52,801,462	2,539,042	4,808.7			328,088	621.4	2,210,954	4,187.3	3,411	6.5
	2002	53,632,623	2,513,263	4,686.1			322,521	601.4	2,190,742	4,084.7	3,611	6.7
Percent change			-1.0	-2.5			-1.7	-3.2	-0.9	-2.4	+5.9	+4.2
Delaware	2001	796,599	32,267	4,050.6			4,868	611.1	27,399	3,439.5	23	2.9
	2002	807,385	31,803	3,939.0			4,836	599.0	26,967	3,340.0	26	3.2
Percent change			-1.4	-2.8			-0.7	-2.0	-1.6	-2.9	+13.0	+11.5
District of Columbia[4,6]	2001	573,822	44,427	7,742.3			9,195	1,602.4	35,232	6,139.9	231	40.3
	2002	570,898	45,799	8,022.3			9,322	1,632.9	36,477	6,389.4	264	46.2
Percent change			+3.1	+3.6			+1.4	+1.9	+3.5	+4.1	+14.3	+14.9
Florida	2001	16,373,330	913,230	5,577.5			130,713	798.3	782,517	4,779.2	874	5.3
	2002	16,713,149	905,957	5,420.6			128,721	770.2	777,236	4,650.4	911	5.5
Percent change			-0.8	-2.8			-1.5	-3.5	-0.7	-2.7	+4.2	+2.1
Georgia	2001	8,405,677	389,543	4,634.3			41,671	495.7	347,872	4,138.5	598	7.1
	2002	8,560,310	385,830	4,507.2			39,271	458.8	346,559	4,048.4	606	7.1
Percent change			-1.0	-2.7			-5.8	-7.5	-0.4	-2.2	+1.3	-0.5
Maryland	2001	5,386,079	261,600	4,857.0			42,088	781.4	219,512	4,075.5	446	8.3
	2002	5,458,137	259,120	4,747.4			42,015	769.8	217,105	3,977.6	513	9.4
Percent change			-0.9	-2.3			-0.2	-1.5	-1.1	-2.4	+15.0	+13.5
North Carolina	2001	8,206,105	404,242	4,926.1			40,465	493.1	363,777	4,433.0	505	6.2
	2002	8,320,146	392,826	4,721.4			39,118	470.2	353,708	4,251.2	548	6.6
Percent change			-2.8	-4.2			-3.3	-4.7	-2.8	-4.1	+8.5	+7.0
South Carolina[4]	2001	4,062,125	219,168	5,395.4			33,114	815.2	186,054	4,580.2	330	8.1
	2002	4,107,183	217,569	5,297.3			33,761	822.0	183,808	4,475.3	298	7.3
Percent change			-0.7	-1.8			+2.0	+0.8	-1.2	-2.3	-9.7	-10.7
Virginia	2001	7,196,750	228,445	3,174.3			20,939	291.0	207,506	2,883.3	364	5.1
	2002	7,293,542	229,039	3,140.3			21,256	291.4	207,783	2,848.9	388	5.3
Percent change			+0.3	-1.1			+1.5	+0.2	+0.1	-1.2	+6.6	+5.2
West Virginia	2001	1,800,975	46,120	2,560.8			5,035	279.6	41,085	2,281.3	40	2.2
	2002	1,801,873	45,320	2,515.2			4,221	234.3	41,099	2,280.9	57	3.2
Percent change			-1.7	-1.8			-16.2	-16.2	*	*	+42.5	+42.4

crimes per 100,000 people in 1991, an increase of 16 percent. From 1996 to 1997, the rate of crime fell by 3.2 percent, then declined by 6.4 percent from 1997 to 1998 and by 6.7 percent from 1998 to 1999, respectively. In 2002 the Crime Index rate was 4,119 per 100,000, a decline of 1.1 percent from the year before, a 10.9 percent decline from the 1998 rate, and a 24.9 percent drop from the 1993 rate.

The 2002 Crime Index rate for all violent crimes, which includes murder and nonnegligent manslaughter,

TABLE 8.3

Index of crime, by region, geographic division, and state, 2001–02 [CONTINUED]

Area	Forcible rape		Robbery		Aggravated assault		Burglary		Larceny-theft		Motor vehicle theft		Arson[2]	
	Number	Rate per 100,000	Number	Rate per 100,000	Number	Rate per 100,000	Number	Rate per 100,000	Number	Rate per 100,000	Number	Rate per 100,000	Number	Rate per 100,000
West North Central	6,159	31.8	16,397	84.6	46,035	237.7	120,884	624.1	512,088	2,643.6	64,926	335.2		
	6,558	33.7	15,829	81.3	46,860	240.7	124,683	640.4	499,439	2,565.3	63,001	323.6		
Percent change	+6.5	+5.9	-3.5	-4.0	+1.8	+1.3	+3.1	+2.6	-2.5	-3.0	-3.0	-3.5		
Iowa	649	22.1	1,154	39.4	6,012	205.1	16,885	575.9	66,244	2,259.4	5,505	187.8		
	797	27.1	1,169	39.8	6,378	217.2	18,643	634.8	68,411	2,329.5	5,823	198.3		
Percent change	+22.8	+22.6	+1.3	+1.1	+6.1	+5.9	+10.4	+10.2	+3.3	+3.1	+5.8	+5.6		
Kansas	945	35.0	2,423	89.7	7,449	275.7	20,514	759.2	77,038	2,851.0	7,985	295.5		
	1,035	38.1	2,165	79.7	6,951	255.9	19,679	724.6	73,877	2,720.2	7,212	265.5		
Percent change	+9.5	+9.0	-10.6	-11.1	-6.7	-7.2	-4.1	-4.6	-4.1	-4.6	-9.7	-10.1		
Minnesota	2,236	44.9	3,758	75.4	7,032	141.1	25,496	511.5	124,519	2,498.1	15,031	301.6		
	2,273	45.3	3,937	78.4	7,106	141.6	28,034	558.5	122,150	2,433.4	13,842	275.8		
Percent change	+1.7	+0.9	+4.8	+4.0	+1.1	+0.3	+10.0	+9.2	-1.9	-2.6	-7.9	-8.6		
Missouri	1,383	24.5	7,771	137.8	20,946	371.6	42,977	762.4	167,420	2,969.9	28,014	496.9		
	1,465	25.8	7,024	123.8	21,737	383.2	42,721	753.1	159,921	2,819.2	27,878	491.5		
Percent change	+5.9	+5.3	-9.6	-10.2	+3.8	+3.1	-0.6	-1.2	-4.5	-5.1	-0.5	-1.1		
Nebraska	431	25.1	1,128	65.6	3,612	210.0	9,760	567.4	52,713	3,064.6	6,490	377.3		
	464	26.8	1,359	78.6	3,557	205.7	10,329	597.3	51,440	2,974.8	6,409	370.6		
Percent change	+7.7	+7.1	+20.5	+19.8	-1.5	-2.0	+5.8	+5.3	-2.4	-2.9	-1.2	-1.8		
North Dakota	164	25.8	60	9.4	274	43.0	2,165	340.1	11,583	1,819.7	1,086	170.6		
	163	25.7	58	9.1	270	42.6	2,243	353.7	11,501	1,813.7	1,018	160.5		
Percent change	-0.6	-0.2	-3.3	-3.0	-1.5	-1.1	+3.6	+4.0	-0.7	-0.3	-6.3	-5.9		
South Dakota	351	46.3	103	13.6	710	93.6	3,087	407.1	12,571	1,657.7	815	107.5		
	361	47.4	117	15.4	861	113.1	3,034	398.7	12,139	1,595.0	819	107.6		
Percent change	+2.8	+2.5	+13.6	+13.2	+21.3	+20.8	-1.7	-2.1	-3.4	-3.8	+0.5	+0.1		
South[4,5,6]	34,526	33.9	163,093	160.0	389,250	381.8	949,916	931.7	2,892,143	2,836.7	437,237	428.9		
	35,706	34.5	162,002	156.8	385,396	372.9	963,804	932.6	2,887,621	2,794.1	438,492	424.3		
Percent change	+3.4	+2.0	-0.7	-2.0	-1.0	-2.3	+1.5	+0.1	-0.2	-1.5	+0.3	-1.1		
South Atlantic[4,6]	16,813	31.8	92,588	175.4	215,276	407.7	485,202	918.9	1,492,066	2,825.8	233,686	442.6		
	17,173	32.0	90,015	167.8	211,722	394.8	486,178	906.5	1,467,227	2,735.7	237,337	442.5		
Percent change	+2.1	+0.6	-2.8	-4.3	-1.7	-3.2	+0.2	-1.4	-1.7	-3.2	+1.6	*		
Delaware	420	52.7	1,156	145.1	3,269	410.4	5,144	645.7	19,476	2,444.9	2,779	348.9		
	358	44.3	1,154	142.9	3,298	408.5	5,355	663.3	18,555	2,298.2	3,057	378.6		
Percent change	-14.8	-15.9	-0.2	-1.5	+0.9	-0.5	+4.1	+2.7	-4.7	-6.0	+10.0	+8.5		
District of Columbia[4,6]	181	31.5	3,780	658.7	5,003	871.9	4,949	862.5	22,313	3,888.5	7,970	1,388.9		
	262	45.9	3,834	671.6	4,962	869.2	5,170	905.6	21,708	3,802.4	9,599	1,681.4		
Percent change	+44.8	+45.5	+1.4	+1.9	-0.8	-0.3	+4.5	+5.0	-2.7	-2.2	+20.4	+21.1		
Florida	6,641	40.6	32,867	200.7	90,331	551.7	176,052	1,075.2	516,548	3,154.8	89,917	549.2		
	40.4	32,581	194.9	88,476	529.4	177,242	1,060	5	511,478	3,060.3	88,516	529.6		
Percent change	+1.7	-0.4	-0.9	-2.9	-2.1	-4.0	+0.7	-1.4	-1.0	-3.0	-1.6	-3.6		
Georgia	2,180	25.9	14,402	171.3	24,491	291.4	71,799	854.2	238,484	2,837.2	37,589	447.2		
	2,108	24.6	13,432	156.9	23,125	270.1	73,932	863.7	234,591	2,740.4	38,036	444.3		
Percent change	-3.3	-5.0	-6.7	-8.4	-5.6	-7.3	+3.0	+1.1	-1.6	-3.4	+1.2	-0.6		
Maryland	1,449	26.9	13,525	251.1	26,668	495.1	41,553	771.5	145,934	2,709.5	32,025	594.6		
	1,370	25.1	13,417	245.8	26,715	489.5	39,765	728.5	143,320	2,625.8	34,020	623.3		
Percent change	-5.5	-6.7	-0.8	-2.1	+0.2	-1.1	-4.3	-5.6	-1.8	-3.1	+6.2	+4.8		
North Carolina	2,083	25.4	13,304	162.1	24,573	299.4	101,889	1,241.6	237,241	2,891.0	24,647	300.3		
	2,196	26.4	12,205	146.7	24,169	290.5	99,535	1,196.3	229,307	2,756.0	24,866	298.9		
Percent change	+5.4	+4.0	-8.3	-9.5	-1.6	-3.0	-2.3	-3.6	-3.3	-4.7	+0.9	-0.5		
South Carolina[4]	1,769	43.5	5,987	147.4	25,028	616.1	42,611	1,049.0	126,742	3,120.1	16,701	411.1		
	1,959	47.7	5,774	140.6	25,730	626.5	43,745	1,065.1	123,196	2,999.5	16,867	410.7		
Percent change	+10.7	+9.5	-3.6	-4.6	+2.8	+1.7	+2.7	+1.5	-2.8	-3.9	+1.0	-0.1		
Virginia	1,770	24.6	6,860	95.3	11,945	166.0	31,604	439.1	157,060	2,182.4	18,842	261.8		
	1,839	25.2	6,961	95.4	12,068	165.5	31,757	435.4	157,548	2,160.1	18,478	253.3		
Percent change	+3.9	+2.5	+1.5	+0.1	+1.0	-0.3	+0.5	-0.8	+0.3	-1.0	-1.9	-3.2		
West Virginia	320	17.8	707	39.3	3,968	220.3	9,601	533.1	28,268	1,569.6	3,216	178.6		
	328	18.2	657	36.5	3,179	176.4	9,677	537.1	27,524	1,527.5	3,898	216.3		
Percent change	+2.5	+2.4	-7.1	-7.1	-19.9	-19.9	+0.8	+0.7	-2.6	-2.7	+21.2	+21.1		

forcible rape, robbery, and aggravated assaults, was at its lowest level since 1978 at 494.6 incidents per 100,000 people, a decrease of 2.0 percent from 2001. The 2002 figure reflects a 12.9 percent decrease from the 1998 rate and a 33.8 percent decrease from the 1993 rate. (See Table 8.2.)

In 2002 the number of violent crimes, which made up 12.0 percent of all reported crimes, fell by 0.9 percent from the previous year. An estimated 1.4 million violent crimes were reported in 2002, 7.0 percent lower than in 1998 and 25.9 percent lower than in 1993. An estimated 894,348

TABLE 8.3

Index of crime, by region, geographic division, and state, 2001–02 [CONTINUED]

Area	Year	Population[1]	Crime Index		Crime Index[2]		Modified Violent crime[3]		Property crime[3]		Murder and nonnegligent manslaughter	
			Number	Rate per 100,000	Number	Rate per 100,000	Number	Rate per 100,000	Number	Rate per 100,000	Number	Rate per 100,000
East South Central[4,5]	2001	17,146,859	726,084	4,234.5			82,874	483.3	643,210	3,751.2	1,265	7.4
	2002	17,248,470	729,533	4,229.6			82,769	479.9	646,764	3,749.7	1,171	6.8
Percent change			+0.5	-0.1			-0.1	-0.7	+0.6	*	-7.4	-8.0
Alabama	2001	4,468,912	192,835	4,315.0			19,582	438.2	173,253	3,876.8	379	8.5
	2002	4,486,508	200,331	4,465.2			19,931	444.2	180,400	4,020.9	303	6.8
Percent change			+3.9	+3.5			+1.8	+1.4	+4.1	+3.7	-20.1	-20.4
Kentucky[4,5]	2001	4,068,816	117,866	2,896.8			10,510	258.3	107,356	2,638.5	181	4.4
	2002	4,092,891	118,799	2,902.6			11,418	279.0	107,381	2,623.6	184	4.5
Percent change			+0.8	+0.2			+8.6	+8.0	*	-0.6	+1.7	+1.1
Mississippi	2001	2,859,733	119,615	4,182.7			10,006	349.9	109,609	3,832.8	282	9.9
	2002	2,871,782	119,442	4,159.2			9,858	343.3	109,584	3,815.9	264	9.2
Percent change			-0.1	-0.6			-1.5	-1.9	*	-0.4	-6.4	-6.8
Tennessee[4]	2001	5,749,398	295,768	5,144.3			42,776	744.0	252,992	4,400.3	423	7.4
	2002	5,797,289	290,961	5,018.9			41,562	716.9	249,399	4,302.0	420	7.2
Percent change			-1.6	-2.4			-2.8	-3.6	-1.4	-2.2	-0.7	-1.5
West South Central	2001	32,005,626	1,607,881	5,023.7			182,749	571.0	1,425,132	4,452.8	2,166	6.8
	2002	32,466,332	1,637,207	5,042.8			184,796	569.2	1,452,411	4,473.6	2,200	6.8
Percent change			+1.8	+0.4			+1.1	-0.3	+1.9	+0.5	+1.6	+0.1
Arkansas	2001	2,694,698	111,296	4,130.2			12,190	452.4	99,106	3,677.8	148	5.5
	2002	2,710,079	112,672	4,157.5			11,501	424.4	101,171	3,733.1	142	5.2
Percent change			+1.2	+0.7			-5.7	-6.2	+2.1	+1.5	-4.1	-4.6
Louisiana	2001	4,470,368	238,371	5,332.2			30,678	686.3	207,693	4,646.0	501	11.2
	2002	4,482,646	228,528	5,098.1			29,690	662.3	198,838	4,435.7	593	13.2
Percent change			-4.1	-4.4			-3.2	-3.5	-4.3	-4.5	+18.4	+18.0
Oklahoma	2001	3,469,577	159,405	4,594.4			17,726	510.9	141,679	4,083.5	185	5.3
	2002	3,493,714	165,715	4,743.2			17,587	503.4	148,128	4,239.8	163	4.7
Percent change			+4.0	+3.2			-0.8	-1.5	+4.6	+3.8	-11.9	-12.5
Texas	2001	21,370,983	1,098,809	5,141.6			122,155	571.6	976,654	4,570.0	1,332	6.2
	2002	21,779,893	1,130,292	5,189.6			126,018	578.6	1,004,274	4,611.0	1,302	6.0
Percent change			+2.9	+0.9			+3.2	+1.2	+2.8	+0.9	-2.3	-4.1
West[4]	2001	64,592,993	2,808,173	4,347.5			335,425	519.3	2,472,748	3,828.2	3,517	5.4
	2002	65,652,316	2,901,062	4,418.8			333,635	508.2	2,567,427	3,910.6	3,721	5.7
Percent change			+3.3	+1.6			-0.5	-2.1	+3.8	+2.2	+5.8	+4.1
Mountain	2001	18,665,045	884,609	4,739.4			83,798	449.0	800,811	4,290.4	977	5.2
	2002	19,057,088	931,833	4,889.7			87,096	457.0	844,737	4,432.7	1,013	5.3
Percent change			+5.3	+3.2			+3.9	+1.8	+5.5	+3.3	+3.7	+1.6
Arizona	2001	5,306,966	322,549	6,077.8			28,675	540.3	293,874	5,537.5	400	7.5
	2002	5,456,453	348,467	6,386.3			30,171	552.9	318,296	5,833.4	387	7.1
Percent change			+8.0	+5.1			+5.2	+2.3	+8.3	+5.3	-3.3	-5.9
Colorado	2001	4,430,989	186,379	4,206.3			15,492	349.6	170,887	3,856.6	158	3.6
	2002	4,506,542	195,936	4,347.8			15,882	352.4	180,054	3,995.4	179	4.0
Percent change			+5.1	+3.4			+2.5	+0.8	+5.4	+3.6	+13.3	+11.4
Idaho	2001	1,320,585	41,392	3,134.4			3,211	243.1	38,181	2,891.2	30	2.3
	2002	1,341,131	42,547	3,172.5			3,419	254.9	39,128	2,917.5	36	2.7
Percent change			+2.8	+1.2			+6.5	+4.8	+2.5	+0.9	+20.0	+18.2
Montana	2001	905,382	33,362	3,684.9			3,187	352.0	30,175	3,332.8	34	3.8
	2002	909,453	31,948	3,512.9			3,197	351.5	28,751	3,161.4	16	1.8
Percent change			-4.2	-4.7			+0.3	-0.1	-4.7	-5.1	-52.9	-53.2
Nevada	2001	2,097,722	89,845	4,283.0			12,359	589.2	77,486	3,693.8	180	8.6
	2002	2,173,491	97,752	4,497.5			13,856	637.5	83,896	3,860.0	181	8.3
Percent change			+8.8	+5.0			+12.1	+8.2	+8.3	+4.5	+0.6	-2.9
New Mexico	2001	1,830,935	97,383	5,318.8			14,288	780.4	83,095	4,538.4	99	5.4
	2002	1,855,059	94,196	5,077.8			13,719	739.5	80,477	4,338.2	152	8.2
Percent change			-3.3	-4.5			-4.0	-5.2	-3.2	-4.4	+53.5	+51.5
Utah	2001	2,278,712	96,307	4,226.4			5,314	233.2	90,993	3,993.2	67	2.9
	2002	2,316,256	103,129	4,452.4			5,488	236.9	97,641	4,215.5	47	2.0
Percent change			+7.1	+5.3			+3.3	+1.6	+7.3	+5.6	-29.9	-31.0
Wyoming	2001	493,754	17,392	3,522.4			1,272	257.6	16,120	3,264.8	9	1.8
	2002	498,703	17,858	3,580.9			1,364	273.5	16,494	3,307.4	15	3.0
Percent change			+2.7	+1.7			+7.2	+6.2	+2.3	+1.3	+66.7	+65.0

TABLE 8.3

Index of crime, by region, geographic division, and state, 2001–02 [CONTINUED]

Area	Forcible rape		Robbery		Aggravated assault		Burglary		Larceny-theft		Motor vehicle theft		Arson[2]
	Number	Rate per 100,000	Number	Rate per 100,000	Number	Rate per 100,000	Number	Rate per 100,000	Number	Rate per 100,000	Number	Rate per 100,000	Number Rate per 100,000
East South Central[4,5]	5,763	33.6	22,366	130.4	53,480	311.9	157,132	916.4	426,770	2,488.9	59,308	345.9	
	6,169	35.8	21,794	126.4	53,635	311.0	161,274	935.0	426,786	2,474.3	58,704	340.3	
Percent change	+7.0	+6.4	-2.6	-3.1	+0.3	-0.3	+2.6	+2.0	*	-0.6	-1.0	-1.6	
Alabama	1,369	30.6	5,584	125.0	12,250	274.1	40,642	909.4	119,992	2,685.0	12,619	282.4	
	1,664	37.1	5,962	132.9	12,002	267.5	42,578	949.0	123,932	2,762.3	13,890	309.6	
Percent change	+21.5	+21.1	+6.8	+6.4	-2.0	-2.4	+4.8	+4.4	+3.3	+2.9	+10.1	+9.6	
Kentucky[4,5]	1,051	25.8	3,269	80.3	6,009	147.7	26,964	662.7	71,448	1,756.0	8,944	219.8	
	1,088	26.6	3,063	74.8	7,083	173.1	27,855	680.6	70,776	1,729.2	8,750	213.8	
Percent change	+3.5	+2.9	-6.3	-6.9	+17.9	+17.2	+3.3	+2.7	-0.9	-1.5	-2.2	-2.7	
Mississippi	1,147	40.1	3,294	115.2	5,283	184.7	29,821	1,042.8	70,315	2,458.8	9,473	331.3	
	1,127	39.2	3,356	116.9	5,111	178.0	29,593	1,030.5	70,468	2,453.8	9,523	331.6	
Percent change	-1.7	-2.2	+1.9	+1.5	-3.3	-3.7	-0.8	-1.2	+0.2	-0.2	+0.5	+0.1	
Tennessee[4]	2,196	38.2	10,219	177.7	29,938	520.7	59,705	1,038.5	165,015	2,870.1	28,272	491.7	
	2,290	39.5	9,413	162.4	29,439	507.8	61,248	1,056.5	161,610	2,787.7	26,541	457.8	
Percent change	+4.3	+3.4	-7.9	-8.6	-1.7	-2.5	+2.6	+1.7	-2.1	-2.9	-6.1	-6.9	
West South Central	11,950	37.3	48,139	150.4	120,494	376.5	307,582	961.0	973,307	3,041.0	144,243	450.7	
	12,364	38.1	50,193	154.6	120,039	369.7	316,352	974.4	993,608	3,060.4	142,451	438.8	
Percent change	+3.5	+2.0	+4.3	+2.8	-0.4	-1.8	+2.9	+1.4	+2.1	+0.6	-1.2	-2.6	
Arkansas	892	33.1	2,181	80.9	8,969	332.8	22,196	823.7	69,590	2,582.5	7,320	271.6	
	754	27.8	2,524	93.1	8,081	298.2	23,229	857.1	71,129	2,624.6	6,813	251.4	
Percent change	-15.5	-16.0	+15.7	+15.1	-9.9	-10.4	+4.7	+4.1	+2.2	+1.6	-6.9	-7.5	
Louisiana	1,403	31.4	7,864	175.9	20,910	467.7	46,451	1,039.1	139,555	3,121.8	21,687	485.1	
	1,529	34.1	7,123	158.9	20,445	456.1	45,350	1,011.7	133,302	2,973.7	20,186	450.3	
Percent change	+9.0	+8.7	-9.4	-9.7	-2.2	-2.5	-2.4	-2.6	-4.5	-4.7	-6.9	-7.2	
Oklahoma	1,486	42.8	2,746	79.1	13,309	383.6	34,573	996.5	94,537	2,724.7	12,569	362.3	
	1,573	45.0	2,966	84.9	12,885	368.8	35,171	1,006.7	100,185	2,867.6	12,772	365.6	
Percent change	+5.9	+5.1	+8.0	+7.3	-3.2	-3.9	+1.7	+1.0	+6.0	+5.2	+1.6	+0.9	
Texas	8,169	38.2	35,348	165.4	77,306	361.7	204,362	956.3	669,625	3,133.3	102,667	480.4	
	8,508	39.1	37,580	172.5	78,628	361.0	212,602	976.1	688,992	3,163.4	102,680	471.4	
Percent change	+4.1	+2.2	+6.3	+4.3	+1.7	-0.2	+4.0	+2.1	+2.9	+1.0	*	-1.9	
West[4]	21,487	33.3	96,759	149.8	213,662	330.8	475,033	735.4	1,623,803	2,513.9	373,912	578.9	
	22,507	34.3	95,865	146.0	211,542	322.2	493,354	751.5	1,663,662	2,534.0	410,411	625.1	
Percent change	+4.7	+3.1	-0.9	-2.5	-1.0	-2.6	+3.9	+2.2	+2.5	+0.8	+9.8	+8.0	
Mountain	6,843	36.7	21,806	116.8	54,172	290.2	148,079	793.3	546,277	2,926.7	106,455	570.3	
	7,454	39.1	20,659	108.4	57,970	304.2	157,652	827.3	568,436	2,982.8	118,649	622.6	
Percent change	+8.9	+6.7	-5.3	-7.2	+7.0	+4.8	+6.5	+4.3	+4.1	+1.9	+11.5	+9.2	
Arizona	1,518	28.6	8,868	167.1	17,889	337.1	54,821	1,033.0	186,850	3,520.8	52,203	983.7	
	1,608	29.5	8,000	146.6	20,176	369.8	59,087	1,082.9	201,541	3,693.6	57,668	1,056.9	
Percent change	+5.9	+3.0	-9.8	-12.3	+12.8	+9.7	+7.8	+4.8	+7.9	+4.9	+10.5	+7.4	
Colorado	1,930	43.6	3,555	80.2	9,849	222.3	28,533	643.9	121,360	2,738.9	20,994	473.8	
	2,066	45.8	3,579	79.4	10,058	223.2	31,678	702.9	125,193	2,778.0	23,183	514.4	
Percent change	+7.0	+5.3	+0.7	-1.0	+2.1	+0.4	+11.0	+9.2	+3.2	+1.4	+10.4	+8.6	
Idaho	425	32.2	245	18.6	2,511	190.1	7,507	568.5	28,285	2,141.9	2,389	180.9	
	497	37.1	240	17.9	2,646	197.3	7,441	554.8	29,060	2,166.8	2,627	195.9	
Percent change	+16.9	+15.1	-2.0	-3.5	+5.4	+3.8	-0.9	-2.4	+2.7	+1.2	+10.0	+8.3	
Montana	188	20.8	230	25.4	2,735	302.1	3,670	405.4	24,684	2,726.4	1,821	201.1	
	237	26.1	283	31.1	2,661	292.6	3,289	361.6	23,679	2,603.7	1,783	196.1	
Percent change	+26.1	+25.5	+23.0	+22.5	-2.7	-3.1	-10.4	-10.8	-4.1	-4.5	-2.1	-2.5	
Nevada	883	42.1	4,932	235.1	6,364	303.4	17,711	844.3	45,073	2,148.7	14,702	700.9	
	928	42.7	5,118	235.5	7,629	351.0	18,951	871.9	47,459	2,183.5	17,486	804.5	
Percent change	+5.1	+1.4	+3.8	+0.2	+19.9	+15.7	+7.0	+3.3	+5.3	+1.6	+18.9	+14.8	
New Mexico	50	46.4	2,695	147.2	10,644	581.3	19,552	1,067.9	56,406	3,080.7	7,137	389.8	
	1,027	55.4	2,206	118.9	10,334	557.1	19,634	1,058.4	53,406	2,878.9	7,437	400.9	
Percent change	+20.8	+19.3	-18.1	19.2	-2.9	-4.2	+0.4	-0.9	-5.3	-6.5	+4.2	+2.8	
Utah	896	39.3	1,197	52.5	3,154	138.4	13,804	605.8	70,676	3,101.6	6,513	285.8	
	943	40.7	1,140	49.2	3,358	145.0	15,124	653.0	74,795	3,229.1	7,722	333.4	
Percent change	+5.2	+3.5	-4.8	-6.3	+6.5	+4.7	+9.6	+7.8	+5.8	+4.1	+18.6	+16.6	
Wyoming	153	31.0	84	17.0	1,026	207.8	2,481	502.5	12,943	2,621.3	696	141.0	
	148	29.7	93	18.6	1,108	222.2	2,448	490.9	13,303	2,667.5	743	149.0	
Percent change	-3.3	-4.2	+10.7	+9.6	+8.0	+6.9	-1.3	-2.3	+2.8	+1.8	+6.8	+5.7	

TABLE 8.3

Index of crime, by region, geographic division, and state, 2001–02 [CONTINUED]

Area	Year	Population[1]	Crime Index		Crime Index[2]		Modified Violent crime[3]		Property crime[3]		Murder and nonnegligent manslaughter	
			Number	Rate per 100,000	Number	Rate per 100,000	Number	Rate per 100,000	Number	Rate per 100,000	Number	Rate per 100,000
Pacific[4]	2001	45,927,948	1,923,564	4,188.2			251,627	547.9	1,671,937	3,640.3	2,540	5.5
	2002	46,595,228	1,969,229	4,226.2			246,539	529.1	1,722,690	3,697.1	2,708	5.8
Percent change			+2.4	+0.9			-2.0	-3.4	+3.0	+1.6	+6.6	+5.1
Alaska	2001	633,630	26,895	4,244.6			3,735	589.5	23,160	3,655.1	39	6.2
	2002	643,786	27,745	4,309.7			3,627	563.4	24,118	3,746.3	33	5.1
Percent change			+3.2	+1.5			-2.9	-4.4	+4.1	+2.5	-15.4	-16.7
California[4]	2001	34,600,463	1,347,056	3,893.2			212,867	615.2	1,134,189	3,278.0	2,206	6.4
	2002	35,116,033	1,384,872	3,943.7			208,388	593.4	1,176,484	3,350.3	2,395	6.8
Percent change			+2.8	+1.3			-2.1	-3.5	+3.7	+2.2	+8.6	+7.0
Hawaii	2001	1,227,024	65,947	5,374.5			3,117	254.0	62,830	5,120.5	32	2.6
	2002	1,244,898	75,238	6,043.7			3,262	262.0	71,976	5,781.7	24	1.9
Percent change			+14.1	+12.5			+4.7	+3.1	+14.6	+12.9	-25.0	-26.1
Oregon	2001	3,473,441	175,174	5,043.2			10,650	306.6	164,524	4,736.6	84	2.4
	2002	3,521,515	171,443	4,868.4			10,298	292.4	161,145	4,576.0	72	2.0
Percent change			-2.1	-3.5			-3.3	-4.6	-2.1	-3.4	-14.3	-15.5
Washington	2001	5,993,390	308,492	5,147.2			21,258	354.7	287,234	4,792.5	179	3.0
	2002	6,068,996	309,931	5,106.8			20,964	345.4	288,967	4,761.4	184	3.0
Percent change			+0.5	-0.8			-1.4	-2.6	+0.6	-0.6	+2.8	+1.5
Puerto Rico	2001	3,839,810	70,117	1,826.1			11,403	297.0	58,714	1,529.1	744	19.4
	2002	3,858,806	90,783	2,352.6			13,471	349.1	77,312	2,003.5	774	20.1
Percent change			+29.5	+28.8			+18.1	+17.6	+31.7	+31.0	+4.0	+3.5

aggravated assaults were reported in 2002, the largest share of all reported violent crimes (62.7 percent). That year, robbery (420,637 offenses) made up 29.5 percent of all reported violent crime; forcible rape 6.7 percent (95,136 offenses); and murder 1.1 percent. (See Table 8.2.)

An estimated 16,204 murders were recorded in 2002, an increase of 1.0 percent from the previous year. The 2002 figure, however, reflects a 4.5 percent decrease from 1998 and a 33.9 percent decrease from 1993. The nation's murder rate—5.6 per 100,000 people—remained virtually unchanged from 1999. The 2002 murder rate was 10.5 percent lower than in 1998 and 40.9 percent lower than the 1993 murder rate. (See Table 8.2.) FBI figures show that in 2001–02 U.S. cities with more than 1 million residents and cities with populations under 50,000 experienced decreases in the murder rate. In contrast, cities with populations ranging between 50,000 and 999,999 showed increases in the murder rate.

Among the other violent crimes, only forcible rape (3.6 percent) posted an increase from the previous year. In 2002 the forcible rape rate per 100,000 people was 33.0. The robbery rate per 100,000 people in 2002 was 145.9, representing a 1.7 percent decrease from the previous year. The aggravated assault rate in 2002 was 310.1 per 100,000 inhabitants, a 2.7 percent decline from 2001. (See Table 8.2.)

Crime Rate by Region and Metropolitan Area

From 2001 to 2002 the rate of crime fell in the Northeast (3.7), the Midwest (2.4), and the South (1.2), but rose in the West (1.6). Property crimes showed a similar trend from 2001 to 2002, as the rate in the West increased (2.2), but fell in the Northeast (3.8), the Midwest (2.5), and the South (1.1). (See Table 8.3.)

Since 2001 U.S. cities experienced a 1.9 percent decline in the number of violent crimes. Cities with populations of 500,000 to 999,999 showed the largest declines, 3.9 percent. Cities with populations in the 50,000 to 99,999 range recorded the smallest decrease, 1.0 percent. Suburban areas outside metropolitan statistical areas reported a 0.5 percent decline in violent crime over the same period. The greatest increase in property crimes during this period occurred in cities with populations 100,000 to 249,000, 1.1 percent. In cities of over 1 million in population, the rate of all crimes declined, except forcible rape, which increased by 2.0 percent from 2001 to 2002. (See Table 8.4.)

VICTIMS OF CRIME

Many observers believe the National Crime Victimization Survey (NCVS), prepared annually by the Bureau of Justice Statistics (BJS) since 1972, is a more accurate indicator of crime than the FBI's *Crime in the United States*. The crime increase reported in the BJS's victimization rate between 1973 and 1979 was not nearly as dramatic as the rise reported by the FBI. While the data in *Crime in the United States* indicates an increase in crime during the last half of the 1980s, the NCVS shows a general decline over the same period. However, from 2001 to 2002 BJS statistics are in general agreement with those in *Crime in the United States* for the same period.

TABLE 8.3

Index of crime, by region, geographic division, and state, 2001–02 [CONTINUED]

Area	Forcible rape Number	Forcible rape Rate per 100,000	Robbery Number	Robbery Rate per 100,000	Aggravated assault Number	Aggravated assault Rate per 100,000	Burglary Number	Burglary Rate per 100,000	Larceny-theft Number	Larceny-theft Rate per 100,000	Motor vehicle theft Number	Motor vehicle theft Rate per 100,000	Arson[2] Number	Arson[2] Rate per 100,000
Pacific[4]	14,644	31.9	74,953	163.2	159,490	347.3	326,954	711.9	1,077,526	2,346.1	267,457	582.3		
	15,053	32.3	75,206	161.4	153,572	329.6	335,702	720.5	1,095,226	2,350.5	291,762	626.2		
Percent change	+2.8	+1.3	+0.3	-1.1	-3.7	-5.1	+2.7	+1.2	+1.6	+0.2	+9.1	+7.5		
Alaska	501	79.1	514	81.1	2,681	423.1	3,847	607.1	16,695	2,634.8	2,618	413.2		
	511	79.4	489	76.0	2,594	402.9	3,908	607.0	17,739	2,755.4	2,471	383.8		
Percent change	+2.0	+0.4	-4.9	-6.4	-3.2	-4.8	+1.6	*	+6.3	+4.6	-5.6	-7.1		
California[4]	9,960	28.8	64,614	186.7	136,087	393.3	232,273	671.3	697,739	2,016.6	204,177	590.1		
	10,198	29.0	64,968	185.0	130,827	372.6	238,428	679.0	715,692	2,038.1	222,364	633.2		
Percent change	+2.4	+0.9	+0.5	-0.9	-3.9	-5.3	+2.6	+1.1	+2.6	+1.1	+8.9	+7.3		
Hawaii	409	33.3	1,142	93.1	1,534	125.0	11,162	909.7	44,925	3,661.3	6,743	549.5		
	372	29.9	1,210	97.2	1,656	133.0	12,722	1,021.9	49,344	3,963.7	9,910	796.0		
Percent change	-9.0	-10.4	+6.0	+4.4	+8.0	+6.4	+14.0	+12.3	+9.8	+8.3	+47.0	+44.9		
Oregon	1,174	33.8	2,749	79.1	6,643	191.3	26,648	767.2	123,034	3,542.1	14,842	427.3		
	1,238	35.2	2,742	77.9	6,246	177.4	25,696	729.7	118,925	3,377.1	16,524	469.2		
Percent change	+5.5	+4.0	-0.3	-1.6	-6.0	-7.3	-3.6	-4.9	-3.3	-4.7	+11.3	+9.8		
Washington	2,600	43.4	5,934	99.0	12,545	209.3	53,024	884.7	195,133	3,255.8	39,077	652.0		
	2,734	45.0	5,797	95.5	12,249	201.8	54,948	905.4	193,526	3,188.8	40,493	667.2		
Percent change	+5.2	+3.8	-2.3	-3.5	-2.4	-3.6	+3.6	+2.3	-0.8	-2.1	+3.6	+2.3		
Puerto Rico	187	4.9	7,999	208.3	2,473	64.4	19,931	519.1	26,140	680.8	12,643	329.3		
	241	6.2	8,978	232.7	3,478	90.1	24,737	641.1	39,640	1,027.3	12,935	335.2		
Percent change	+28.9	+28.2	+12.2	+11.7	+40.6	+39.9	+24.1	+23.5	+51.6	+50.9	+2.3	+1.8		

[1]Populations are Bureau of the Census provisional estimates as of July 1, 2002, and July 1, 2001.
[2]Although arson data are included in the trend and clearance tables, sufficient data are not available to estimate totals for this offense.
[3]Violent crimes are offenses of murder, forcible rape, robbery, and aggravated assault. Property crimes are offenses of burglary, larceny-theft, and motor vehicle theft.
[4]The 2001 crime figures have been adjusted.
[5]Limited data for 2002 were available.
[6]Includes offenses reported by the Zoological Police and the Metro Transit Police.
Note: *Less than one-tenth of 1 percent. Offense totals are based on all data received from reporting agencies and estimates for unreported areas. The murder and nonnegligent homicides that occurred as a result of the events of September 11, 2001, were not included in this table.

SOURCE: "Table 4. Index of Crime, by Region, Geographic Division, and State, 2001–2002," in *Crime in the United States, 2002*, Federal Bureau of Investigation, Clarksburg, WV, 2002

The BJS victimization survey asks a representative sample of U.S. households if they have been the victims of a crime and whether they reported it. Those who believe this method to be more accurate than the reporting used by the FBI note that large numbers of crimes are unreported. Many victims believe that reporting the crime to the police will bring no results. Others are too embarrassed (as in the case of fraud), or they fear they will become subjects of an investigation (as in the case of rape). Still others believe the crime is too insignificant to report (as in the case of petty larceny).

Reported Victimizations

Based on the findings of past NCVSs, researchers estimate that almost half of all violent victimizations and about one-third of all property crimes are reported to the police. Murder, the major crime most likely to be reported to the police, is not included in the victimization studies because the survey is based on victim interviews.

In 2002 crime victims reported to police 40 percent of all property crimes. These crimes—burglary, motor vehicle theft, and theft—accounted for about 75 percent of all victimizations in 2002. In the same year, victims reported to police 49 percent of all violent crimes. Violent crimes—rape, sexual assault, robbery, and aggravated and simple assault—accounted for 25 percent of victimizations.

Numbers and Rates of Crimes

In 2001–02 U.S. residents age 12 and older experienced a total of 23.7 million crimes, the lowest since the 1973 estimate of 44 million victimizations. Between 1993 and 2002 the violent victimization rate decreased 53.7 percent from 49.9 to 23.1 victimizations per 1,000 persons and the property crime victimization rate decreased 50.1 percent from 318.9 to 159.0 crimes per 1,000 households. (See Table 8.5.) According to the NCVS, from 1999 to 2002 the violent crime rate decreased 20.6 percent. Over the same period, property crimes went down 13.4 percent.

Violent Victimizations

From 1973 to 1994 violent crime rates fluctuated, but after 1994 the rate steadily declined. The rate of violent crimes fell by 10 percent from 1994–95 to 1995–96, and by

TABLE 8.4

Crime trends, by population group, 2001–02

Population group	Crime Index	Modified Crime Index[1]	Violent crime[2]	Property crime[3]	Murder and non-negligent manslaughter	Forcible rape[4]	Robbery	Aggravated assault	Burglary	Larceny-theft	Motor vehicle theft	Arson
Total all agencies; population 255,383,586												
2001	10,781,626	10,857,692	1,327,864	9,453,762	14,888	80,223	400,324	832,429	1,915,952	6,394,800	1,143,010	76,066
2002	10,758,229	10,831,504	1,308,757	9,449,472	15,031	83,631	395,474	814,621	1,942,577	6,350,026	1,156,869	73,275
Percent change	-0.2	-0.2	-1.4	*	+1.0	+4.2	-1.2	-2.1	+1.4	-0.7	+1.2	-3.7
Total cities; 8,618 cities; population 171,734,038												
2001	8,565,743	8,622,380	1,072,524	7,493,219	11,823	59,203	356,474	645,024	1,407,365	5,138,943	946,911	56,637
2002	8,523,610	8,578,483	1,052,260	7,471,350	11,750	61,551	350,974	627,985	1,420,872	5,101,814	948,664	54,873
Percent change	-0.5	-0.5	-1.9	-0.3	-0.6	+4.0	-1.5	-2.6	+1.0	-0.7	+0.2	-3.1
Group I												
69 cities, 250,000 and over; population 51,949,588												
2001	3,255,232	3,280,207	546,105	2,709,127	6,880	21,373	209,681	308,171	517,254	1,709,386	482,487	24,975
2002	3,220,348	3,244,348	532,902	2,687,446	6,823	21,773	205,183	299,123	515,935	1,692,484	479,027	24,000
Percent change	-1.1	-1.1	-2.4	-0.8	-0.8	+1.9	-2.1	-2.9	-0.3	-1.0	-0.7	-3.9
10 cities, 1,000,000 and over; population 24,682,265												
2001	1,298,118	1,306,349	262,710	1,035,408	3,222	7,239	103,827	148,422	188,589	648,583	198,236	8,231
2002	1,288,482	1,296,368	257,755	1,030,727	3,090	7,385	102,672	144,608	188,526	645,634	196,567	7,886
Percent change	-0.7	-0.8	-1.9	-0.5	-4.1	+2.0	-1.1	-2.6	*	-0.5	-0.8	-4.2
21 cities, 500,000 to 999,999; population 13,963,253												
2001	1,014,346	1,021,919	146,304	868,042	1,911	7,038	53,223	84,132	169,262	554,602	144,178	7,573
2002	1,005,707	1,013,362	140,595	865,112	1,926	7,303	50,280	81,086	169,540	552,076	143,496	7,655
Percent change	-0.9	-0.8	-3.9	-0.3	+0.8	+3.8	-5.5	-3.6	+0.2	-0.5	-0.5	+1.1
38 cities, 250,000 to 499,999; population 13,304,070												
2001	942,768	951,939	137,091	805,677	1,747	7,096	52,631	75,617	159,403	506,201	140,073	9,171
2002	926,159	934,618	134,552	791,607	1,807	7,085	52,231	73,429	157,869	494,774	138,964	8,459
Percent change	-1.8	-1.8	-1.9	-1.7	+3.4	-0.2	-0.8	-2.9	-1.0	-2.3	-0.8	-7.8
Group II												
166 cities, 100,000 to 249,999; population 24,834,622												
2001	1,398,173	1,407,385	158,920	1,239,253	1,850	9,252	55,373	92,445	241,215	837,554	160,484	9,212
2002	1,409,516	1,418,791	156,772	1,252,744	1,906	10,066	54,243	90,557	245,410	844,408	162,926	9,275
Percent change	+0.8	+0.8	-1.4	+1.1	+3.0	+8.8	-2.0	-2.0	+1.7	+0.8	+1.5	+0.7
Group III												
387 cities, 50,000 to 99,999; population 26,758,653												
2001	1,188,578	1,196,027	129,564	1,059,014	1,118	9,190	38,967	80,289	204,585	735,536	118,893	7,449
2002	1,195,535	1,202,579	128,209	1,067,326	1,198	9,456	38,858	78,697	205,909	739,275	122,142	7,044
Percent change	+0.6	+0.5	-1.0	+0.8	+7.2	+2.9	-0.3	-2.0	+0.6	+0.5	+2.7	-5.4

TABLE 8.4

Crime trends, by population group, 2001–02 [CONTINUED]

Population group	Crime Index	Modified Crime Index[1]	Violent crime[2]	Property crime[3]	Murder and non-negligent manslaughter	Forcible rape[4]	Robbery	Aggravated assault	Burglary	Larceny-theft	Motor vehicle theft	Arson
Group IV												
701 cities, 25,000 to 49,999; population 24,448,049												
2001	1,001,664	1,007,404	92,139	909,525	766	7,435	24,776	59,162	166,915	662,089	80,521	5,740
2002	989,433	995,103	90,670	898,763	763	7,683	24,372	57,852	168,453	650,184	80,126	5,670
Percent change	-1.2	-1.2	-1.6	-1.2	-0.4	+3.3	-1.6	-2.2	+0.9	-1.8	-0.5	-1.2
Group V												
1,538 cities, 10,000 to 24,999; population 24,424,834												
2001	925,269	930,000	79,164	846,105	666	6,753	17,481	54,264	150,759	634,399	60,947	4,731
2002	919,341	923,915	78,131	841,210	600	7,019	18,050	52,462	154,921	624,962	61,327	4,574
Percent change	-0.6	-0.7	-1.3	-0.6	-9.9	+3.9	+3.3	-3.3	+2.8	-1.5	+0.6	-3.3
Group VI												
5,757 cities, under 10,000; population 19,318,292												
2001	796,827	801,357	66,632	730,195	543	5,200	10,196	50,693	126,637	559,979	43,579	4,530
2002	789,437	793,747	65,576	723,861	460	5,554	10,268	49,294	130,244	550,501	43,116	4,310
Percent change	-0.9	-0.9	-1.6	-0.9	-15.3	+6.8	+0.7	-2.8	+2.8	-1.7	-1.1	-4.9
Suburban counties												
1,259 agencies; population 55,661,496												
2001	1,672,347	1,687,324	193,253	1,479,094	2,050	14,739	39,076	137,388	354,044	965,598	159,452	14,977
2002	1,688,437	1,702,611	195,127	1,493,310	2,289	15,524	39,763	137,551	363,406	959,610	170,294	14,174
Percent change	+1.0	+0.9	+1.0	+1.0	+11.7	+5.3	+1.8	+0.1	+2.6	-0.6	+6.8	-5.4
Rural counties[5]												
2,393 agencies; population 27,988,052												
2001	543,536	547,988	62,087	481,449	1,015	6,281	4,774	50,017	154,543	290,259	36,647	4,452
2002	546,182	550,410	61,370	484,812	992	6,556	4,737	49,085	158,299	288,602	37,911	4,228
Percent change	+0.5	+0.4	-1.2	+0.7	-2.3	+4.4	-0.8	-1.9	+2.4	-0.6	+3.4	-5.0
Suburban area[6]												
5,893 agencies; population 101,022,671												
2001	3,279,354	3,303,201	325,394	2,953,960	3,082	25,157	72,353	224,802	605,950	2,060,715	287,295	23,847
2002	3,277,268	3,300,133	323,799	2,953,469	3,259	26,079	72,917	221,544	619,687	2,035,813	297,969	22,865
Percent change	-0.1	-0.1	-0.5	*	+5.7	+3.7	+0.8	-1.4	+2.3	-1.2	+3.7	-4.1

[1]The Modified Crime Index is the sum of the seven offenses making up the Crime Index, with the addition of arson.

[2]Violent crimes are offenses of murder, forcible rape, robbery, and aggravated assault.

[3]Property crimes are offenses of burglary, larceny-theft, and motor vehicle theft.

[4]Forcible rape figures furnished by the state Uniform Crime Reporting (UCR) Program administered by the Illinois State Police were not in accordance with national UCR guidelines; therefore, the figures were excluded from the forcible rape, violent crime, Crime Index, and Modified Crime Index categories.

[5]Includes state police agencies that report aggregately for the entire state.

[6]Suburban area includes law enforcement agencies in cities with less than 50,000 inhabitants and county law enforcement agencies that are within a Metropolitan Statistical Area. Suburban area excludes all metropolitan agencies associated with a central city. The agencies associated with suburban areas also appear in other groups within this table.

Note: *Less than one-tenth of 1 percent. The murder and nonnegligent homicides that occurred as a result of the events of September 11, 2001, were not included in this table.

SOURCE: "Table 12. Crime Trends, by Population Group, 2001–2002," in *Crime in the United States, 2002*, Federal Bureau of Investigation, Clarksburg, WV, 2002

TABLE 8.5

Rates of criminal victimization and percent change, 1993–2002

Type of crime	Victimization rates (per 1,000 persons age 12 or older or per 1,000 households)		
	1993	2002	Percent change[1,2] 1993-2002
Personal crimes[3]	52.2	23.7	-54.6%*
Crimes of violence	49.9	23.1	-53.7*
Completed violence	15.0	7.6	-49.3*
Attempted/threatened violence	34.9	15.5	-55.6*
Rape/sexual assault	2.5	1.1	-56.0*
Rape/attempted rape	1.6	0.7	-56.3*
Rape	1.0	0.4	-60.0*
Attempted rape	0.7	0.3	-57.1*
Sexual assault	0.8	0.3	-62.5*
Robbery	6.0	2.2	-63.3*
Completed robbery	3.8	1.7	-55.3*
With injury	1.3	0.7	-46.2*
Without injury	2.5	0.9	-64.0*
Attempted robbery	2.2	0.5	-77.3*
With injury	0.4	0.2	-50.0*
Without injury	1.8	0.4	-77.8*
Assault	41.4	19.8	-52.2*
Aggravated	12.0	4.3	-64.2*
With injury	3.4	1.4	-58.8*
Threatened with weapon	8.6	2.9	-66.3*
Simple	29.4	15.5	-47.3*
With minor injury	6.1	3.9	-36.1*
Without injury	23.3	11.6	-50.2*
Personal theft[4]	2.3	0.7	-69.6*
Property crimes	318.9	159.0	-50.1%*
Household burglary	58.2	27.7	-52.4*
Completed	47.2	23.5	-50.2*
Forcible entry	18.1	9.2	-49.2*
Unlawful entry without force	29.1	14.3	-50.9*
Attempted forcible entry	10.9	4.2	-61.5*
Motor vehicle theft	19.0	9.0	-52.6*
Completed	12.4	7.1	-42.7*
Attempted	6.6	1.9	-71.2*
Theft	241.7	122.3	-49.4*
Completed[5]	230.1	118.2	-48.6*
Less than $50	98.7	37.9	-61.6*
$50-$249	76.1	40.4	-46.9*
$250 or more	41.6	29.6	-28.8*
Attempted	11.6	4.1	-64.7*

Note: Completed violent crimes include rape, sexual assault, robbery with or without injury, aggravated assault with injury, and simple assault with minor injury.
In 1993 the total population age 12 or older was 211,524,770; and in 2002; 231,589,260. The total number of households in 1993 was 99,927,410; and in 2002; 110,323,840.
*The difference between the indicated years is significant at the 95%-confidence level.
[1]Differences between the annual rates shown do not take into account changes that may have occurred during interim years.
[2]Percent change calculated using unrounded rates.
[3]The data is based on interviews with victims and therefore cannot measure murder.
[4]Includes pocket picking, purse snatching, and attempted purse snatching.
[5]Includes thefts with unknown losses.

SOURCE: Callie Marie Rennison and Michael R. Rand, "Table 3. Rates of criminal victimization and percent change, 1993–2002," in *Criminal Victimization, 2002*, U.S. Department of Justice, Bureau of Justice Statistics, August 2003

7 percent from 1996–97 to 1997–98. The 5.5 million violent crimes that occurred in 2001–02 included 247,990 rapes and sexual assaults (down from 322,060 in 1999–2000), 571,590 robberies (down from 771,000 in 1999–2000), 1.1 million aggravated assaults (down from 1.3 million in 1999–2000), and 3.6 million simple assaults (down from 4.3 million in 1999–2000). Rates of victimization for violent crimes in 2001–02 were 0.4 for rape (down from 0.5 in 1999–2000), 1.8 completed robberies (down from 2.3 in 1999–2000), 4.8 aggravated assaults (down from 6.2 in 1999–2000), and 15.7 simple assaults per 1,000 persons age 12 and older (down from 19.3 in 1999–2000).

Property Crimes

For every 1,000 households in 2001–02 there were 28.2 burglaries, or a total of 3 million household burglaries, down from 3.5 million in 1999–2000. About 6 percent of all property crimes were forcible entries, and about 6 percent were unlawful entries without force. Some 998,740 motor vehicles were reported stolen in 2001–02 (or 9.1 motor vehicle thefts per 1,000 households), down slightly from just over 1 million in 1999–2000.

Characteristics of Victims

PERSONAL CRIMES. Males were victims of violent crimes more often than females in 2002, although females were victims of rape or sexual assaults at significantly higher rates than males. Males were more likely to experience aggravated assault. Blacks and the poor tended to have higher rates of victimization as well. According to the NCVS, those between 16 and 19 years old were most likely to be victimized (58.2 per 1,000 persons), with those 20 to 24 years of age being second most likely (47.4 per 1,000 persons). After the age of 25, the crime rate drops with age; those 65 and older experienced a rate of 3.4 per 1,000 persons. (See Table 8.6.)

In 2002 the rate of violent crime for blacks was 27.9 per 1,000 persons, compared to 23.6 for Hispanics and 22.8 for whites. Non-Hispanics had slightly lower violent victimization rates (23.0) than Hispanics (23.6), but were more likely than Hispanics to fall victim to rape and sexual assault. Blacks were victims of robbery at a rate of 4.1, significantly higher than the rate for Hispanics (3.2) or whites (1.9). In 2002 there were 6.7 aggravated assaults per 1,000 among black persons age 12 and older, compared to 6.1 for Hispanics and 4.1 for whites. (See Table 8.6.)

Victimization rates usually decrease with increases in family income. People with household incomes of less than $7,500 were the victims of violent crimes at a rate of 45.5 per 1,000, more than double the rate of 19.0 for those with household incomes of $75,000 or more in 2002. Urban residents were more often victims of violent crime than were residents of the suburbs or of rural areas. Also, residents of the West (29.4), home to 22.8 percent of the total population, were more likely to be victims of violent crime than midwesterners (25.7), who comprise 22.6 percent of the population, southerners (19.7), who account for 35.8 percent of the population, and northeasterners (18.8), who make up 18.8 percent of the population. The rates of victimization for violent crime were significantly

TABLE 8.6

Rates of violent crime and personal theft, by gender, age, race, and Hispanic origin, 2002

		Victimizations per 1,000 persons age 12 or older						
		Violent crimes						Per- sonal theft
Characteristic of victim	Population	All	Rape/ sexual assault	Robbery	Assault			
					Total	Aggra- vated	Simple	
Gender								
Male	112,241,930	25.5	0.3	2.9	22.3	5.2	17.1	0.6
Female	119,347,330	20.8	1.8	1.6	17.4	3.4	14.0	0.7
Race								
White	192,956,980	22.8	0.8	1.9	20.0	4.1	15.9	0.7
Black	28,871,440	27.9	2.5	4.1	21.3	6.7	14.6	0.7*
Other	9,760,850	14.7	1.2*	2.4*	11.0	0.9*	10.1	0.4*
Hispanic origin								
Hispanic	26,991,490	23.6	0.7*	3.2	19.7	6.1	13.7	0.4*
Non-Hispanic	203,062,880	23.0	1.1	2.1	19.8	4.1	15.8	0.7
Age								
12-15	16,676,560	44.4	2.1	3.0	39.3	5.0	34.3	0.9*
16-19	16,171,800	58.2	5.5	4.0	48.6	11.9	36.7	0.6*
20-24	19,317,740	47.4	2.9	4.7	39.8	10.1	29.7	1.6*
25-34	37,329,720	26.3	0.6*	2.8	22.8	5.2	17.6	0.5*
35-49	65,263,580	18.1	0.5*	1.5	16.1	3.5	12.7	0.7
50-64	43,746,850	10.7	0.2*	1.6	8.9	1.7	7.2	0.3*
65 or older	33,083,000	3.4	0.1*	1.0	2.2	0.7*	1.5	0.6*

Note: The data includes as violent crime: rape, sexual assault, robbery, and assault. Murder and manslaughter cannot be included.
*Based on 10 or fewer sample cases.

SOURCE: Callie Marie Rennison and Michael R. Rand, "Table 6. Rates of violent crime and personal theft, by gender, age, race, and Hispanic origin, 2002," in *Criminal Victimization, 2002,* U.S. Department of Justice, Bureau of Justice Statistics, August 2003

higher among those who never married (43.3) and those who divorced or separated (30.7) than for those who were married (10.6) or widowed (7.1) in 2002. (See Table 8.7.)

PROPERTY CRIMES. In 2002 households with an income of $7,500 or less were victimized at the highest rate, 188.9 per 1,000 households. Those with annual family incomes over $75,000 were victimized by household property crimes at 169.8 per 1,000 households, which was at a lower rate than households earning $15,000 to $24,999 a year and $35,000 to $49,999 a year. Households with annual incomes of $50,000 or more were victims of property crimes at the lowest rate of 158.3 per 1,000 households. Like violent crime victims in the West, households in this region (219.9) were more apt to be victims of property crime than households in the Northeast (117.0), the Midwest (155.8), and the South (147.8). (See Table 8.8.)

For each type of property crime in 2002, urban households had consistently higher rates than suburban or rural households. For example, urban households experienced burglaries at a rate of 40.5 per 1,000 households, compared to rural households (22.6) and suburban households (22.4). Householders who rented their domiciles had significantly higher victimization rates than householders who owned their homes. Householders who rented sustained motor vehicle thefts at rates twice that of householders who owned their residences, with 14.2

thefts per 1,000 renter householders, compared to 6.5 thefts per 1,000 owner householders. Urban households experienced motor vehicle thefts at almost eight times the rate of rural households. (See Table 8.8.)

Use of Weapons

According to the FBI, 31.2 percent of all violent crimes (murder, rape, sexual assault, robbery, and aggravated assault) in 2002 involved hands, fists, feet, and so on; firearms were involved in 26.8 percent; and knives and other cutting instruments were used in 14.9 percent. Other types of weapons were used in 27.1 percent of these violent crimes. Among aggravated assaults, 59.3 per 1,000 assaults involved firearms. Firearms were used in 60.2 per 1,000 robberies, knives and cutting instruments were used in 12.5 per 1,000 robberies, and other weapons were used in 13.4 per 1,000 robberies. Firearms were used as murder weapons in 71.1 percent of all murders, with knives and other cutting instruments accounting for 13.4 percent, and other weapons such as blunt objects and personal weapons (hands, fists, and so on) making up most of the remainder.

TERRORISM

September 11, 2001

At 8:45 A.M. eastern daylight time, American Airlines Flight 11, hijacked out of Logan Airport in Boston,

TABLE 8.7

Rates of violent crime and personal theft, by household income, marital status, region, and location of residence of victims, 2002

Characteristic of victim	Population	Victimizations per 1,000 persons age 12 or older						Per-sonal theft
		Violent crimes						
					Assault			
		All	Rape/ sexual assault	Robbery	Total	Aggra-vated	Simple	
Household income								
Less than $7,500	8,347,650	45.5	2.5*	6.3	36.7	11.2	25.5	1.7*
$7,500 - $14,999	15,608,210	31.5	3.2	4.1	24.2	5.8	18.4	0.5*
$15,000 - $24,999	23,872,200	30.0	2.1	2.9	25.0	6.1	18.9	0.8*
$25,000 - $34,999	24,104,810	27.0	1.2*	2.9	22.9	4.1	18.9	0.3*
$35,000 - $49,999	31,655,160	25.6	0.9*	2.2	22.4	5.2	17.2	0.4*
$50,000 - $74,999	33,713,640	18.7	0.2*	2.1	16.5	2.5	14.0	0.6*
$75,000 or more	43,139,380	19.0	0.4*	1.0	17.6	2.8	14.8	0.7
Marital status								
Never married	74,029,810	43.3	2.6	3.7	37.0	7.3	29.7	1.1
Married	117,296,790	10.6	0.2*	0.9	9.5	2.2	7.2	0.3
Divorced/separated	24,768,200	30.7	1.1*	4.0	25.6	5.9	19.7	1.1*
Widowed	13,699,370	7.1	0.3*	2.0*	4.8	2.2*	2.7	0.6*
Region								
Northeast	43,705,120	18.8	0.7	1.5	16.7	2.7	13.9	1.2
Midwest	54,065,070	25.7	1.0	2.2	22.6	4.3	18.3	0.5*
South	83,470,930	19.7	1.0	2.6	16.2	4.7	11.5	0.6
West	50,348,150	29.4	1.6	2.3	25.5	5.0	20.6	0.5*
Residence								
Urban	64,533,840	33.1	2.2	4.3	26.7	6.5	20.2	1.2
Suburban	111,164,070	20.0	0.7	1.8	17.6	3.5	14.1	0.6
Rural	55,891,360	17.5	0.6	0.7	16.2	3.3	12.9	0.2*

Note: Data includes as violent crime: rape, sexual assault, robbery, and assault. Murder and manslaughter cannot be included.
*Based on 10 or fewer sample cases.

SOURCE: Callie Marie Rennison and Michael R. Rand, "Table 7. Rates of violent crime and personal theft, by household income, marital status, region, and location of residence of victims, 2002," in *Criminal Victimization, 2002,* U.S. Department of Justice, Bureau of Justice Statistics, August 2003

TABLE 8.8

Property crime victimization, by household income, region, residence, and home ownership of households victimized, 2002

Characteristic of household or head of household	Number of households, 2002	Victimizations per 1,000 households			
		Total	Burglary	Motor vehicle theft	Theft
Household income					
Less than $7,500	5,157,750	188.9	51.4	3.2*	134.3
$7,500 - $14,999	9,038,620	166.7	31.8	8.1	126.8
$15,000 - $24,999	12,231,090	172.1	33.8	9.9	128.5
$25,000 - $34,999	11,586,530	161.7	27.8	12.6	121.2
$35,000 - $49,999	14,391,310	175.4	27.3	11.3	136.9
$50,000 - $74,999	14,283,610	158.3	24.6	9.2	124.5
$75,000 or more	17,532,840	169.8	21.0	5.9	142.9
Region					
Northeast	20,821,680	117.0	18.4	6.4	92.1
Midwest	26,238,340	155.8	30.7	7.9	117.2
South	40,202,070	147.8	28.2	7.9	111.8
West	23,061,760	219.9	31.9	14.3	173.8
Residence					
Urban	31,937,800	215.3	40.5	17.1	157.7
Suburban	51,446,980	145.3	22.4	7.5	115.4
Rural	26,939,060	118.3	22.6	2.2	93.5
Home ownership					
Owned	75,023,210	136.4	23.9	6.5	105.9
Rented	35,300,630	207.0	35.7	14.2	157.1

*Based on 10 or fewer sample cases.

SOURCE: Callie Marie Rennison and Michael R. Rand, "Table 8. Property crime victimization, by household income, region, residence, and home ownership of households victimized, 2002," in *Criminal Victimization, 2002,* U.S. Department of Justice, Bureau of Justice Statistics, August 2003

Massachusetts, crashed into the north tower of the World Trade Center in Manhattan, New York. Eighteen minutes later, at 9:03 A.M., the south tower was hit by United Airlines Flight 175, also hijacked from Boston.

President George W. Bush, traveling in Sarasota, Florida, announced at 9:30 A.M. that the United States had suffered an "apparent terrorist attack." Only 13 minutes later, at 9:43 A.M., a third hijacked airliner, American Airlines Flight 77, exploded into the Pentagon in Washington, D.C. At 10:10 A.M., United Airlines Flight 93, a fourth hijacked commercial jetliner, crashed in Somerset County, Pennsylvania, due to the apparent resistance of several passengers intent on preventing the hijackers from reaching their intended target, suspected to be in Washington, D.C.

More than 3,000 people from 78 countries were killed in what would be confirmed as the worst act of domestic terrorism in U.S. history. Previously, the worst act of terrorism on U.S. soil had been the bombing on April 19, 1995, of the Murrah Federal Building in Oklahoma City, Oklahoma, which killed 168 people. Timothy McVeigh and Terry Nichols were convicted of terrorism, murder, and conspiracy in connection with that bombing. Nichols was sentenced to life in prison, while McVeigh was executed on June 11, 2001.

Domestic Terrorism

In *Terrorism in the United States: 1999* (2000), the FBI defines a terrorist incident as "a violent act or an act dangerous to human life, in violation of the criminal laws of the United States, or of any state, to intimidate or coerce a government, the civilian population, or any segment thereof, in furtherance of political or social objectives."

According to the FBI, there were 272 terrorist incidents, 55 suspected incidents, and 130 prevented incidents of domestic terrorism from 1980 to 1999. Of these, 321 were bombings and 21 were assassinations, while arson and shootings each accounted for 19 such acts. The targets of these terrorist acts included 232 civilian commercial sites, 101 government facilities, 61 diplomatic foreign government targets, and 13 military targets, resulting in 205 deaths and 2,037 injuries. (See Figure 8.1.)

Of the 327 actual incidents or suspected incidents of terrorism in the United States between 1980 and 1999, domestic terrorists were responsible for 239 attacks, while 88 attacks were carried out by international terrorists or terrorist groups. As defined by the FBI, a suspected terrorist incident is "a potential act of terrorism for which responsibility cannot be attributed to a known or suspected group."

The 130 planned acts of terrorism that were prevented by U.S. law enforcement included 83 that were being planned by domestic terrorists and 47 plots linked to

international terrorists or terrorist groups. The FBI defines a terrorism prevention to be "a documented instance in which a violent act by a known or suspect terrorist group or individual with means and a proven propensity for violence is successfully interdicted."

Domestic Terrorist Groups

The FBI has identified three broad categories of domestic terrorist groups: right wing, left wing, and special interest. From 1980 to 1999, of 457 terrorist events, left-wing terrorists were linked to 130 terrorist events, right-wing terrorists to 83, and special-interest terrorists were responsible for 61 (the others were individuals, international terrorist groups, or unknown). (See Figure 8.2.)

Right-wing terrorist groups often espouse racial supremacy and antigovernment beliefs. Certain patriot and militia movements are examples of right-wing terrorist groups. Their small, tight-knit nature can make it difficult for law enforcement to infiltrate them or to anticipate their actions. According to the FBI, such groups often file bogus legal actions against law enforcement, the government, and other citizens. Known as "paper terrorism," these acts are not counted in official FBI terrorism statistics.

Left-wing terrorist groups tend to be of a socialist bent and see themselves as a force in the fight against what they view as the dehumanizing effects of globalization and U.S. imperialism. According to the FBI, such left-wing groups posed the most serious terrorist threat from the 1960s through the 1980s, but have since declined dramatically, in part due to law enforcement's success in infiltrating them. The FBI cites anarchists such as those who disrupted the 1999 World Trade Organization meeting in Seattle, Washington, as examples of left-wing terrorist groups.

Special-interest terrorism tends to focus on specific issues in society, such an animal rights or environmentalism. According to the FBI, the threat posed by such groups appears to be rising, as does their level of violent activity.

The International Terrorist Threat

According to the U.S. Department of State, which tracks international terrorism, there were 77 anti-U.S. terrorist attacks that occurred in foreign countries in 2002, down significantly from the 219 anti-U.S. attacks in 2001. Of these, the most by far (46) occurred in Latin America, followed by the Middle East (16), Asia (10), and western Europe and Africa (1 each). Bombings accounted for almost all such incidents (66), followed by armed attack (8) and kidnapping (2). Of 85 total U.S. targets attacked in 2002, 51 were business related. Only four such targets were government facilities. (See Figure 8.3.) From 1997 to 2002, 1,513 U.S. citizens were killed and 210 were wounded in international terrorist attacks. In 2002, 26

FIGURE 8.1

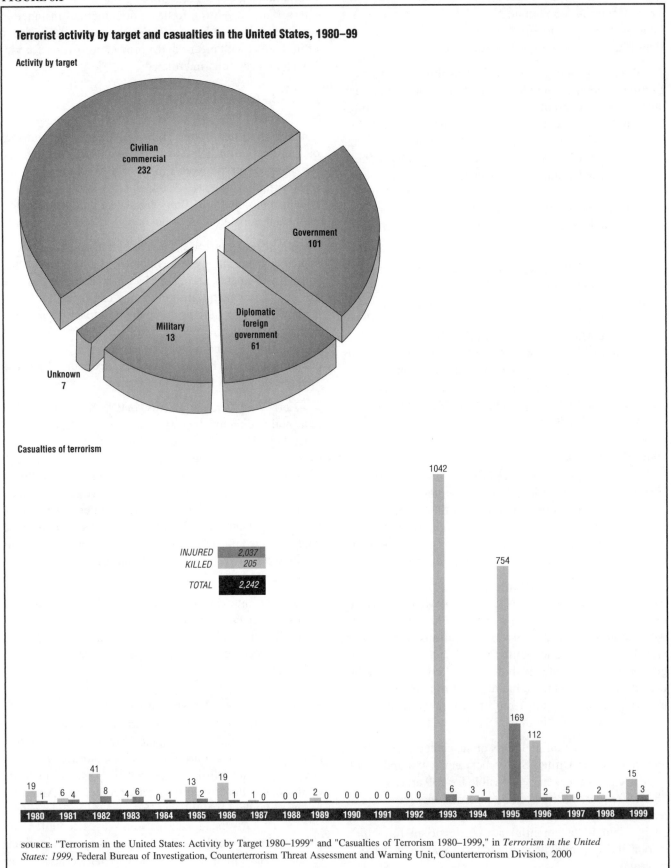

Terrorist activity by target and casualties in the United States, 1980–99

Activity by target

Civilian commercial 232

Government 101

Military 13

Diplomatic foreign government 61

Unknown 7

Casualties of terrorism

INJURED	2,037
KILLED	205
TOTAL	2,242

SOURCE: "Terrorism in the United States: Activity by Target 1980–1999" and "Casualties of Terrorism 1980–1999," in *Terrorism in the United States: 1999,* Federal Bureau of Investigation, Counterterrorism Threat Assessment and Warning Unit, Counterterrorism Division, 2000

FIGURE 8.2

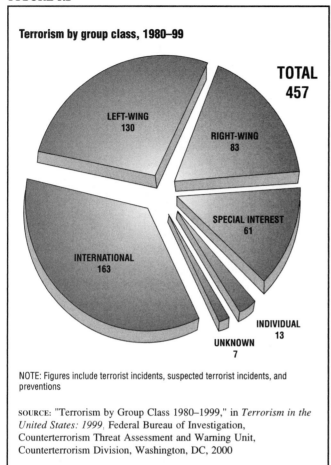

Terrorism by group class, 1980–99

TOTAL
457

LEFT-WING
130

RIGHT-WING
83

SPECIAL INTEREST
61

INTERNATIONAL
163

INDIVIDUAL
13

UNKNOWN
7

NOTE: Figures include terrorist incidents, suspected terrorist incidents, and preventions

SOURCE: "Terrorism by Group Class 1980–1999," in *Terrorism in the United States: 1999,* Federal Bureau of Investigation, Counterterrorism Threat Assessment and Warning Unit, Counterterrorism Division, Washington, DC, 2000

FIGURE 8.3

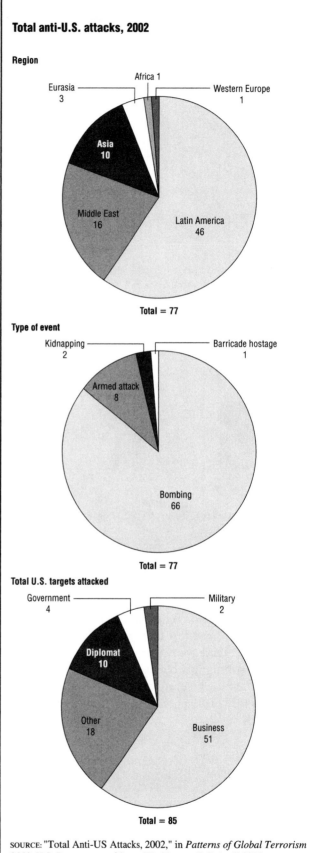

Total anti-U.S. attacks, 2002

Region

Eurasia 3

Africa 1

Western Europe 1

Asia 10

Middle East 16

Latin America 46

Total = 77

Type of event

Kidnapping 2

Barricade hostage 1

Armed attack 8

Bombing 66

Total = 77

Total U.S. targets attacked

Government 4

Military 2

Diplomat 10

Other 18

Business 51

Total = 85

SOURCE: "Total Anti-US Attacks, 2002," in *Patterns of Global Terrorism 2002*, U.S. Department of State, Washington, DC, April 2003

U.S. civilians were murdered by terrorists, compared to 2001 when 1,440 were killed. (See Figure 8.4.)

In *Patterns of Global Terrorism: 2002* (2003), the U.S. State Department's Designated Foreign Terrorist Organization List identified 38 groups that engage in worldwide acts of terrorism against various governments (not just the United States). Over the past 21 years, international terrorist attacks reached a high of 665 in 1987 and a low of 199 such acts committed in 2002.

Weapons of Mass Destruction

Between 1997 and 2000 the FBI investigated 779 reports involving the use of weapons of mass destruction (chemical and biological weapons) for possible terrorist acts, most of which proved to be false or fabricated. In 2000, 90 of the 115 threats of biological terrorism investigated by the FBI threatened the use of anthrax, a bacteria spread by spores that can cause skin lesions if touched or death if inhaled. Of those, all proved false and no anthrax was found, according to the FBI.

On October 5, 2001, Robert Stevens, a photo editor for American Media Inc. in Boca Raton, Florida, died of inhalation anthrax after being exposed to spores sent via the U.S. mail in an apparent terrorist attack against U.S.

FIGURE 8.4

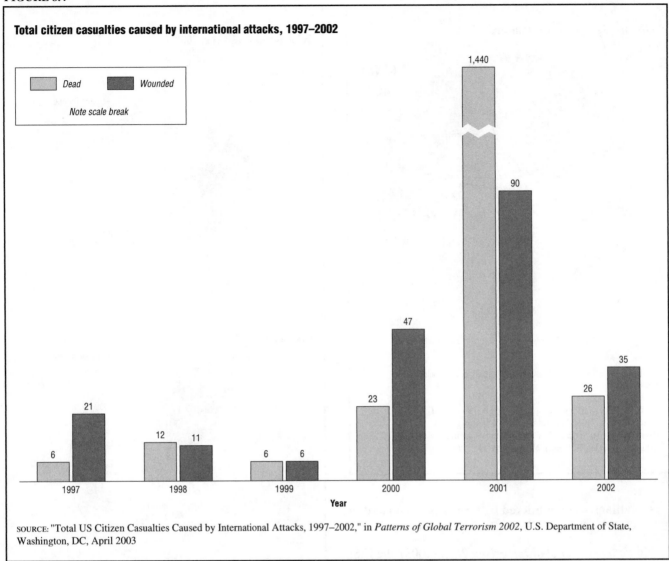

Total citizen casualties caused by international attacks, 1997–2002

SOURCE: "Total US Citizen Casualties Caused by International Attacks, 1997–2002," in *Patterns of Global Terrorism 2002*, U.S. Department of State, Washington, DC, April 2003

citizens. Subsequent letters sent to CBS and NBC News departments in New York City and to the Washington, D.C., offices of Senator Tom Daschle also tested positive for anthrax. As a result of these and other mailings, by November 2001 there were 16 confirmed cases of anthrax infections, resulting in 4 deaths from inhalation anthrax. Two of the fatalities were postal workers who came in contact with the deadly anthrax spores by handling contaminated mail.

Cyberterrorism

The FBI reports an increasing use of information technology by terrorist groups and individuals. In addition to the use of cybertools to shut down or infiltrate national infrastructures such as energy, transportation, communications, and government services, terrorist groups are also using the Internet to recruit members, raise funds, spread propaganda, and communicate between terrorist cells and their members.

CHAPTER 9
SPENDING OUR MONEY

The U.S. Census Bureau, under contract to the Bureau of Labor Statistics (BLS), conducts an ongoing two-part Consumer Expenditure Survey of the spending habits of the American people. The first part is the Interview Survey, which obtains data on the types of expenditures respondents can be expected to recall for a period of three months or longer. Respondents are interviewed every three months over a period of fifteen months. In general, these recollections include those about relatively large expenditures, such as real property, automobiles, and major appliances, or expenditures that occur on a fairly regular basis, such as rent, utilities, or insurance premiums. Overnight trips are also included in this category, but business-related expenditures are not. Approximately 95 percent of all expenditures are covered in this survey.

Part two, the Diary Survey, is designed to determine expenditures on small, frequently purchased items, which are normally difficult for people to remember. In the Diary Survey, 5,000 households are asked to keep a diary of all expenses for two one-week periods, resulting in a total of 10,000 diaries. These diaries cover spending for groceries, eating out, tobacco, housekeeping supplies, nonprescription drugs, and personal care products and services.

The Consumer Expenditure Survey is the only national survey that thoroughly examines consumer spending in all types of households. Government and private agencies and companies use the survey results to determine the spending patterns of Americans.

GENERAL SPENDING

In 2001 the average family earned about $47,507 before taxes, had 2.5 people in the household, was headed by a 48.1-year-old person, and had 1.9 vehicles. (See Table 9.1.) The typical family spent 32.9 percent of its total expenditures on housing, 19.3 percent on transporta-tion, and 13.5 percent on food. The distribution of expenditures among the major spending components changed very little from 1998 to 2001. (See Table 9.2.)

From 1999 to 2001 average annual expenditures per consumer unit rose about 3.9 percent. This increase continued the trend of modest increases over the previous several years. Spending on utilities, fuels, and public services increased 11.2 percent; personal insurance and pensions, 11.1 percent; housing and health care, 5.6 percent each; cash contributions, 5.5 percent; dining, 4.6 percent; education, 2.5 percent; and transportation, 2.9 percent. Some expenditures that showed decreases were personal care products and services (14.0 percent), public transportation (6.3 percent), alcoholic beverages (6.2 percent), house furnishings and equipment (5.9 percent), and tobacco products and supplies (3.4 percent). (See Table 9.1.)

CHARACTERISTICS OF CONSUMERS

In 2001 the greater the number of working household members, the more the family earned, with those in the highest income bracket of $70,000 and over averaging 2.1 earners per family. Not surprisingly, the more a family earned, the more vehicles it owned. Those in the highest income bracket averaged 2.9 vehicles. Families earning less than $5,000 and those earning between $5,000 and $9,999 had one vehicle per household. Furthermore, the more a family earned, the more likely it was to own a home. (See Table 9.3.)

Black families in general earned less in 2001 than white families, Hispanics less than non-Hispanics, renters less than home owners, and rural residents less than those in urban settings. Although the number of wage earners was almost the same for black families (1.3 wage earners) as for white families (1.4 wage earners), blacks earned much less ($33,739) compared with whites ($49,334). Hispanic families had 1.6 wage earners per family but

TABLE 9.1

Average annual expenditures of all consumer units and percent changes, 1999–2001

Item	1999	2000	2001	Percent change 1999–2000	Percent change 2000–2001
Number of consumer units (in thousands)	108,465	109,367	110,339		
Income before taxes*	$43,951	$44,649	$47,507		
Averages:					
Age of reference person	47.9	48.2	48.1		
Number of persons in consumer unit	2.5	2.5	2.5		
Number of earners	1.3	1.4	1.4		
Number of vehicles	1.9	1.9	1.9		
Percent homeowner	65	66	66		
Average annual expenditures	$36,995	$38,045	$39,518	2.8	3.9
Food	5,031	5,158	5,321	2.5	3.2
Food at home	2,915	3,021	3,086	3.6	2.2
Cereals and bakery products	448	453	452	1.1	-.2
Meats, poultry, fish, and eggs	749	795	828	6.1	4.2
Dairy products	322	325	332	.9	2.2
Fruits and vegetables	500	521	522	4.2	.2
Other food at home	896	927	952	3.5	2.7
Food away from home	2,116	2,137	2,235	1.0	4.6
Alcoholic beverages	318	372	349	17.0	-6.2
Housing	12,057	12,319	13,011	2.2	5.6
Shelter	7,016	7,114	7,602	1.4	6.9
Utilities, fuels, and public services	2,377	2,489	2,767	4.7	11.2
Household operations	666	684	676	2.7	-1.2
Housekeeping supplies	498	482	509	-3.2	5.6
Housefurnishings and equipment	1,499	1,549	1,458	3.3	-5.9
Apparel and services	1,743	1,856	1,743	6.5	-6.1
Transportation	7,011	7,417	7,633	5.8	2.9
Vehicle purchases (net outlay)	3,305	3,418	3,579	3.4	4.7
Gasoline and motor oil	1,055	1,291	1,279	22.4	-.9
Other vehicle expenses	2,254	2,281	2,375	1.2	4.1
Public transportation	397	427	400	7.6	-6.3
Health care	1,959	2,066	2,182	5.5	5.6
Entertainment	1,891	1,863	1,953	-1.5	4.8
Personal care products and services	408	564	485	38.2	-14.0
Reading	159	146	141	-8.2	-3.4
Education	635	632	648	-.5	2.5
Tobacco products and supplies	300	319	308	6.3	-3.4
Miscellaneous	867	776	750	-10.5	-3.4
Cash contributions	1,181	1,192	1,258	.9	5.5
Personal insurance and pensions	3,436	3,365	3,737	-2.1	11.1
Life and other personal insurance	394	399	410	1.3	2.8
Pensions and Social Security	3,042	2,966	3,326	-2.5	12.1

*Income values are derived from "complete income reporters" only.

SOURCE: "Table A. Average annual expenditures of all consumer units and percent changes, Consumer Expenditure Survey, 1999–2001," in *Consumer Expenditures in 2001,* U.S. Department of Labor, Bureau of Labor Statistics, Washington, DC, April 2003

earned significantly less income ($35,886) than non-Hispanics ($48,726). (See Table 9.4.)

Black families owned 1.3 cars, compared to 2.0 cars for white families. Ownership of vehicles differed slightly between Hispanics (1.6 per family) and non-Hispanics (2.0 per family). Black and Hispanic families were much less likely to own their homes (49 and 47 percent, respectively) than whites (69 percent) and non-Hispanic families (68 percent). (See Table 9.4.)

SPENDING PATTERNS

Just as the U.S. economy is affected by wars, economic declines, technological advances, and changes in population demographics and the labor force, spending patterns also change. In the mid-1930s the average family spent over one-third of its total expenditures on food. By 1960 to 1961 housing had replaced food as the largest portion of total spending and continues to be the largest portion on average, at about one-third of total spending from 1998 to 2001. Food expenditures during the same four years averaged about 13.5 percent of spending. (See Table 9.2.)

Not surprisingly, spending varies dramatically depending on the earnings of the household. On average, in 2001 those in the three lowest income brackets spent more than they earned, reflecting at least some dependence on government assistance, support from friends and/or family, and debt.

Generally, for virtually every income bracket, the more the family earned the more it spent on most categories. However, the proportion of the income spent varied

TABLE 9.2

Percent distribution of total annual expenditures by major category, 1998–2001

Item	1998	1999	2000	2001
Average annual expenditures	100.0	100.0	100.0	100.0
Food	13.5	13.6	13.6	13.5
Food at home	7.8	7.9	7.9	7.8
Food away from home	5.7	5.7	5.6	5.7
Housing	33.0	32.6	32.4	32.9
Apparel and services	4.7	4.7	4.9	4.4
Transportation	18.6	19.0	19.5	19.3
Vehicles	8.3	8.9	9.0	9.1
Gasoline and motor oil	2.9	2.9	3.4	3.2
Other transportation	7.4	7.2	7.1	7.0
Health care	5.4	5.3	5.4	5.5
Entertainment	4.9	5.1	4.9	4.9
Personal insurance and pensions	9.5	9.3	8.8	9.5
Life and other personal insurance	1.1	1.1	1.0	1.0
Pensions and Social Security	8.4	8.2	7.8	8.4
Other expenditures*	10.4	10.5	10.5	10.0

*Includes spending for alcoholic beverages, personal care products and services, reading, education, tobacco products and supplies, cash contributions, and miscellaneous.

SOURCE: "Table B. Percent distribution of total annual expenditures by major category, Consumer Expenditure Survey, 1998–2001," in *Consumer Expenditures in 2001*, U.S. Department of Labor, Bureau of Labor Statistics, Washington, DC, April 2003

Little Left Over

In 2001 many American households had little money left over for college education for their children, the down payment on a home, retirement (above and beyond what they contributed to a pension fund or to Social Security), or investments that might earn them money. Even those earning from $40,000 to $49,999 per year had just $3,518 left over for taxes and other payments after their other expenditures were considered. Consequently, the amount of money saved for retirement among 80 percent of the population was little more than the Social Security contributions automatically taken from their salaries.

significantly. According to the BLS, those in the top quintile (top 20 percent) spent a total of more than four times as much as those in the lowest quintile ($77,125 and $18,883, respectively). Yet, the richest spent only 21 percent ($23,953) of their pretax income on housing, while the poorest spent 86 percent ($6,834) of their income on housing. Similarly, while the richest 20 percent spent almost three times as much on food as the poorest 20 percent ($9,101 and $3,269, respectively), this amount was only 8 percent of their total pretax income, compared to the poorest quintile, at 41 percent. There were similar disparities for transportation and health care.

TABLE 9.3

Income before taxes, average annual expenditures and characteristics, 2001

	Complete reporting of income								
Item	Total complete reporting	Less than $5,000	$5,000 to $9,999	$10,000 to $14,999	$15,000 to $19,999	$20,000 to $29,999	$30,000 to $39,999	$40,000 to $49,999	$50,000 to $69,999	$70,000 and over
Number of consumer units (in thousands)	88,735	4,100	6,829	8,099	7,014	12,075	10,508	8,737	12,480	18,892
Consumer unit characteristics:										
Income before taxes*	$47,507	$1,666	$7,675	$12,380	$17,282	$24,494	$34,456	$44,418	$58,943	$113,978
Age of reference person	48.0	39.4	54.1	55.4	53.0	49.5	46.8	45.3	44.8	45.5
Average number in consumer unit:										
Persons	2.5	1.7	1.6	1.9	2.1	2.3	2.4	2.7	2.9	3.1
Children under 18	.7	.4	.3	.5	.5	.6	.6	.8	.8	.9
Persons 65 and over	.3	.2	.5	.5	.5	.4	.3	.2	.2	.1
Earners	1.4	.8	.5	.7	.8	1.1	1.4	1.6	1.8	2.1
Vehicles	2.0	1.0	.9	1.1	1.5	1.7	1.9	2.2	2.5	2.9
Percent homeowner	65	33	43	51	54	58	62	69	77	87
Average annual expenditures	$41,395	$20,517	$16,625	$20,642	$25,028	$28,623	$35,430	$40,900	$50,136	$76,124
Food	5,662	3,497	3,051	3,406	3,763	4,499	5,071	5,904	6,851	9,066
Food at home	3,253	1,974	2,101	2,210	2,524	2,904	3,136	3,488	3,742	4,565
Cereals and bakery products	481	296	313	340	376	436	450	501	543	683
Meats, poultry, fish, and eggs	869	553	594	599	729	821	883	910	974	1,145
Dairy products	352	198	211	218	274	315	334	378	410	513
Fruits and vegetables	545	332	357	395	439	501	527	572	603	754
Other food at home	1,007	596	627	658	707	831	941	1,127	1,212	1,470
Food away from home	2,409	1,523	950	1,195	1,238	1,595	1,935	2,415	3,109	4,501
Alcoholic beverages	386	385	186	223	249	227	326	412	436	695
Housing	13,120	7,307	6,021	7,472	8,305	9,525	11,006	12,248	15,356	23,622
Shelter	7,583	4,323	3,276	4,097	4,747	5,382	6,238	6,978	8,969	13,913
Owned dwellings	4,905	1,902	1,289	1,705	2,063	2,558	3,396	4,192	6,306	11,035
Rented dwellings	2,197	2,056	1,865	2,253	2,494	2,601	2,589	2,497	2,108	1,656
Other lodging	481	365	122	138	191	223	253	289	556	1,222
Utilities, fuels, and public services	2,739	1,599	1,654	2,002	2,170	2,457	2,661	2,841	3,102	3,841
Household operations	672	248	290	353	323	428	509	541	688	1,465
Housekeeping supplies	566	298	299	312	369	414	495	579	747	930
Household furnishings and equipment	1,561	839	502	709	695	844	1,103	1,309	1,850	3,473
Apparel and services	1,846	1,102	748	869	1,272	1,063	1,636	1,894	2,173	3,479
Transportation	7,919	3,417	2,727	3,539	4,624	5,644	7,549	8,672	9,888	13,892
Vehicle purchases (net outlay)	3,778	1,712	1,349	1,684	2,163	2,704	3,874	4,155	4,617	6,505
Gasoline and motor oil	1,290	646	522	645	861	1,048	1,236	1,473	1,615	2,027
Other vehicle expenses	2,447	850	723	1,021	1,362	1,669	2,148	2,788	3,197	4,447
Public transportation	405	209	132	189	237	223	292	257	459	913
Health care	2,222	1,154	1,277	1,792	2,143	2,089	2,200	2,239	2,512	2,908
Entertainment	2,028	923	630	790	1,292	1,187	1,620	1,958	2,638	3,986
Personal care products and services	514	349	262	287	346	402	543	541	600	794
Reading	148	69	54	82	93	103	121	137	180	274
Education	638	878	486	259	359	271	292	433	748	1,358
Tobacco products and smoking supplies	327	284	234	266	313	326	353	415	372	315
Miscellaneous	768	370	264	362	447	608	666	802	865	1,412
Cash contributions	1,324	433	357	591	609	901	1,053	1,181	1,616	2,743
Personal insurance and pensions	4,494	350	329	704	1,213	1,779	2,994	4,065	5,900	11,579
Life and other personal insurance	423	179	140	236	308	250	323	368	496	844
Pensions and Social Security	4,071	171	188	468	906	1,529	2,670	3,698	5,405	10,736

*Components of income and taxes are derived from "complete income reporters" only.

SOURCE: "Table 2. Income before taxes: Average annual expenditures and characteristics, Consumer Expenditure Survey, 2001," in *Consumer Expenditures in 2001,* U.S. Department of Labor, Bureau of Labor Statistics, Washington, DC, April 2003

TABLE 9.4

Housing tenure, type of area, race and Hispanic origin of reference person, average annual expenditures and characteristics, 2001

Item	All consumer units	Housing tenure		Type of area		Race of reference person		Hispanic origin of reference person	
		Homeowner	Renter	Urban	Rural	White and other	Black	Hispanic	Non-Hispanic
Number of consumer units (in thousands)	110,339	73,010	37,329	96,492	13,847	97,056	13,283	9,621	100,718
Consumer unit characteristics:									
Income before taxes*	$47,507	$56,709	$30,415	$48,856	$37,921	$49,334	$33,739	$35,886	$48,726
Age of reference person	48.1	52.1	40.3	47.6	51.7	48.5	45.1	42.4	48.7
Average number in consumer unit:									
Persons	2.5	2.6	2.2	2.5	2.5	2.5	2.7	3.4	2.4
Children under 18	.7	.7	.6	.7	.6	.6	.9	1.2	.6
Persons 65 and over	.3	.4	.2	.3	.4	.3	.2	.2	.3
Earners	1.4	1.4	1.2	1.4	1.4	1.4	1.3	1.6	1.3
Vehicles	1.9	2.3	1.2	1.9	2.5	2.0	1.3	1.6	2.0
Percent homeowner	66	100	n.a.	64	82	69	49	47	68
Average annual expenditures	$39,518	$45,399	$28,016	$40,355	$33,681	$40,968	$28,903	$34,361	$40,009
Food	5,321	5,871	4,244	5,431	4,549	5,463	4,271	5,648	5,288
Food at home	3,086	3,380	2,509	3,119	2,851	3,124	2,804	3,551	3,039
Cereals and bakery products	452	495	369	458	413	459	402	490	448
Meats, poultry, fish, and eggs	828	900	687	833	792	813	941	1,098	801
Dairy products	332	367	263	335	307	344	241	355	329
Fruits and vegetables	522	569	430	534	439	530	460	663	508
Other food at home	952	1,050	760	959	899	978	759	946	952
Food away from home	2,235	2,491	1,735	2,312	1,697	2,339	1,467	2,097	2,249
Alcoholic beverages	349	361	325	369	206	375	156	308	353
Housing	13,011	14,713	9,683	13,563	9,167	13,353	10,510	11,747	13,132
Shelter	7,602	8,197	6,437	8,043	4,524	7,831	5,925	7,018	7,657
Owned dwellings	4,979	7,490	67	5,216	3,320	5,252	2,981	3,349	5,134
Rented dwellings	2,134	73	6,166	2,318	850	2,048	2,762	3,503	2,003
Other lodging	489	634	205	508	354	531	182	167	520
Utilities, fuels, and public services	2,767	3,242	1,836	2,781	2,667	2,741	2,955	2,429	2,799
Household operations	676	852	332	723	349	711	417	430	699
Housekeeping supplies	509	609	313	518	447	532	336	432	517
Household furnishings and equipment	1,458	1,813	764	1,498	1,180	1,537	877	1,437	1,460
Apparel and services	1,743	1,930	1,377	1,814	1,243	1,745	1,729	1,857	1,732
Transportation	7,633	8,861	5,232	7,514	8,468	7,969	5,184	7,083	7,686
Vehicle purchases (net outlay)	3,579	4,174	2,414	3,426	4,644	3,769	2,193	3,360	3,600
Gasoline and motor oil	1,279	1,466	915	1,247	1,506	1,322	968	1,265	1,281
Other vehicle expenses	2,375	2,762	1,618	2,412	2,120	2,459	1,766	2,134	2,398
Public transportation	400	459	285	429	198	419	257	323	407
Health care	2,182	2,697	1,174	2,139	2,478	2,307	1,264	1,343	2,262
Entertainment	1,953	2,330	1,216	1,970	1,837	2,085	988	1,246	2,021
Personal care products and services	485	538	380	499	386	487	468	467	486
Reading	141	169	86	147	102	152	62	59	149
Education	648	665	614	700	285	688	352	428	669
Tobacco products and smoking supplies	308	298	329	299	373	323	203	177	321
Miscellaneous	750	879	498	782	527	773	585	457	778
Cash contributions	1,258	1,558	672	1,284	1,078	1,324	776	727	1,309
Personal insurance and pensions	3,737	4,530	2,186	3,845	2,983	3,926	2,356	2,814	3,825
Life and other personal insurance	410	541	156	401	473	424	310	209	430
Pensions and Social Security	3,326	3,989	2,030	3,444	2,510	3,501	2,046	2,605	3,395

*Components of income and taxes are derived from "complete income reporters" only.
Note: n.a. Not applicable.

SOURCE: "Table 7. Housing tenure, type of area, race of reference person, and Hispanic origin of reference person: Average annual expenditures and characteristics, Consumer Expenditure Survey, 2001," in *Consumer Expenditures in 2001,* U.S. Department of Labor, Bureau of Labor Statistics, Washington, DC, April 2003

IMPORTANT NAMES AND ADDRESSES

Bureau of Economic Analysis
U.S. Department of Commerce
1441 L St., NW
Washington, DC 20230
(202) 606-9900
Fax: (202) 606-5310
E-mail: customerservice@bea.gov
URL: http://www.bea.doc.gov

Bureau of Justice Statistics
U.S. Department of Justice
810 7th St., NW
Washington, DC 20531
(202) 307-0765
Fax: (202) 307-5846
E-mail: askbjs@ojp.usdoj.gov
URL: http://www.ojp.usdoj.gov/bjs

Bureau of Labor Statistics
U.S. Department of Labor
Postal Square Building
2 Massachusetts Ave., NE
Washington, DC 20212-0001
(202) 691-5200
Fax: (202) 691-6325
E-mail: blsdata_staff@bls.gov
URL: http://www.bls.gov

Center for Voting and Democracy
6930 Carroll Ave., Suite 601
Takoma Park, MD 20912
(301) 270-4616
Fax: (301) 270-4133
E-mail: cvd@fairvote.com
URL: http://www.fairvote.org

Centers for Disease Control
and Prevention
1600 Clifton Rd., NE
Atlanta, GA 30333
(404) 639-3311
(800) 311-3435
URL: http://www.cdc.gov

Centers for Medicare and Medicaid
Services (formerly Health Care
Financing Administration)
7500 Security Blvd.
Baltimore, MD 21244-1850
(410) 786-3000
(877) 267-2323
URL: http://cms.hhs.gov/

Children's Defense Fund
25 E St., NW
Washington, DC 20001
(202) 628-8787
Fax: (202) 662-3540
E-mail: cdfinfo@childrensdefense.org
URL: http://www.childrensdefense.org/

Economic Research Service
U.S. Department of Agriculture
1800 M St., NW
Washington, DC 20036-5831
(202) 694-5050
Fax: (202) 694-5757
URL: http://www.ers.usda.gov

Federal Bureau of Investigation
J. Edgar Hoover Building
935 Pennsylvania Ave., NW
Washington, DC 20535-0001
(202) 324-3000
Fax: (202) 324-4705
URL: http://www.fbi.gov

Federal Reserve Board
20th Street and Constitution Ave., NW
Washington, DC 20551
(202) 452-3000
URL: http://www.federalreserve.gov/

Human Rights Watch
1630 Connecticut Ave., NW, Suite 500
Washington, DC 20009
(202) 612-4321
Fax: (202) 612-4333
E-mail: hrwdc@hrw.org
URL: http://www.hrw.org/

International Labour Organization
1828 L St., NW, Suite 600
Washington, DC 20036
(202) 653-7652
Fax: (202) 653-7687
E-mail: washilo@ilowbo.org
URL: http://www.ilo.org/

Justice Research and
Statistics Association
777 N. Capitol St., NE, Suite 801
Washington, DC 20002
(202) 842-9330
Fax: (202) 842-9329
E-mail: cjinfo@jrsa.org
URL: http://www.jrsa.org

National Agricultural Statistics Service
U.S. Department of Agriculture
Room 5829-South
Washington, DC 20250
(202) 720-3878
(800) 727-9540
Fax: (202) 690-2090
E-mail: nass@nass.usda.gov
URL: http://www.usda.gov/nass/

National Center for Education Statistics
U.S. Department of Education
1990 K St., NW
Washington, DC 20006
(202) 502-7300
Fax: (202) 502-7466
URL: http://nces.ed.gov

National Center for Health
Statistics Centers for Disease Control
and Prevention
1600 Clifton Rd.
Atlanta, GA 30333
(404) 639-3311
(800) 311-3435
URL: http://www.cdc.gov/nchs

National Institute of Justice
U.S. Department of Justice
810 7th St., NW
Washington, DC 20531
(301) 519-5500
(800) 851-3420
Fax: (202) 307-6394
E-mail: askncjrs@ncjrs.org
URL: http://www.ojp.usdoj.gov/nij/welcome.
html

National Partnership for Women
and Families
1875 Connecticut Ave., NW, Suite 650
Washington, DC 20009
(202) 986-2600
Fax: (202) 986-2539
E-mail: info@nationalpartnership.org
URL: http://www.nationalpartnership.org

Population Reference Bureau
1875 Connecticut Ave., NW, Suite 520
Washington, DC 20009-5728
(202) 483-1100
(800) 877-9881
Fax: (202) 328-3937
E-mail: popref@prb.org
URL: http://www.prb.org

The Sentencing Project
514 10th St., NW, Suite 1000
Washington, DC 20004
(202) 628-0871
Fax: (202) 628-1091
URL: http://www.sentencingproject.org

The Urban Institute
2100 M St., NW
Washington, DC 20037
(202) 833-7200
E-mail: paffairs@ui.urban.org
URL: http://www.urban.org/

U.S. Census Bureau
Washington, DC 20233-6900
(301) 457-4608
Fax: (301) 457-3761
E-mail: comments@census.gov
URL: http://www.census.gov

U.S. Citizenship and
Immigration Services
4420 N. Fairfax Drive
Arlington, VA 22203
(800) 870-3676
URL: http://uscis.gov/graphics/index.htm

U.S. Conference of Mayors
1620 I St., NW
Washington, DC 20006
(202) 293-7330
Fax: (202) 293-2352
E-mail: info@usmayors.org
URL: http://www.usmayors.org/uscm/
home.asp

U.S. Department of Agriculture
1400 Independence Ave., SW
Washington, DC 20250
(202) 720-2791
Fax: (202) 690-0228
E-mail: barbara.robinson@usda.gov
URL: http://www.usda.gov

U.S. Department of Commerce
1401 Constitution Ave., NW
Washington, DC 20230
(202) 482-2112
Fax: (202) 482-4576
URL: http://www.commerce.gov/

U.S. Department of Education
400 Maryland Ave., SW
Washington, DC 20202
(800) 872-5327

Fax: (202) 401-0689
E-mail: customerservice@inet.ed.gov
URL: http://www.ed.gov/index.jhtml

U.S. Department of Health and
Human Services
200 Independence Ave., SW
Washington, DC 20201
(202) 619-0257
(877) 696-6775
URL: http://www.os.dhhs.gov

U.S. Department of Housing and
Urban Development
451 7th St., SW
Washington, DC 20410
(202) 708-1112
URL: http://www.hud.gov

U.S. Department of the Interior
1849 C St., NW
Washington, DC 20240
(202) 208-3100
Fax: (202) 208-5048
E-mail: webteam@ios.doi.gov
URL: http://www.doi.gov

U.S. Department of Justice
950 Pennsylvania Ave., NW
Washington, DC 20530-0001
(202) 353-1555
Fax: (202) 514-4371
E-mail: askdoj@usdoj.gov
URL: http://www.usdoj.gov

U.S. Department of Labor
200 Constitution Ave., NW
Washington, DC 20210
(202) 219-8271
(866) 487-2365
Fax: (202) 219-8822
URL: http://www.dol.gov

RESOURCES

The Census Bureau of the U.S. Department of Commerce provides the most complete statistics on the life of the American people. The most valuable information comes from the national census, taken every 10 years, most recently in 2000. In addition to the national census, the Census Bureau surveys the nation in its annual Current Population Surveys.

The dozens of valuable reports based on these statistics and surveys include the biannual *American Housing Survey for the United States: 2001* (2002); *State Population Estimates from July 1, 2000 to July 1, 2002* (2003); *The Foreign-Born Population of the United States, March 2002* (2003); *Income in the United States: 2002* (2003); *Household Net Worth and Asset Ownership: 1995* (2001); *Poverty in the United States: 2002* (2003); *Health Insurance Coverage in the United States: 2002* (2003); *Voting and Registration in the Election of November 2000* (2002); *Housing Vacancy Survey: Third Quarter 2003* (2003); *Expenditures for Residential Improvement and Repairs: 2002* (2003); and *Children's Living Arrangements and Characteristics: March 2000* (2003). Other publications by the Census Bureau include *Number, Timing, and Duration of Marriages and Divorces: 1996* (2002) and *The Big Payoff: Educational Attainment and Synthetic Estimates of Work-Life Earnings* (2002).

The National Agricultural Statistics Service of the U.S. Department of Agriculture prepared the *2002 Census of Agriculture* (2003). The Office of Immigration Statistics of the U.S. Department of Homeland Security published the annual report *2002 Yearbook of Immigration Statistics* (2003). The Bureau of Labor Statistics (BLS) of the U.S. Department of Labor maintains the nation's employment and occupation statistics. Its monthly and annual compilation *Employment and Earnings* statistically covers the subject. Its *Monthly Labor Review* magazine provides monthly statistical updates and articles on the U.S. labor force. The annual BLS study, Consumer

Expenditure Survey, based on Census Bureau surveys, traces how Americans spend their money. The Federal Reserve surveys family finances in *Recent Changes in U.S. Family Finances: Results from the 2001 and 1998 Surveys of Consumer Finances* (2003).

The National Center for Health Statistics is the primary source for statistical information on health. Its annual *Health, United States* offers a statistical overview, while its *National Vital Statistics Reports* provide the most recent health information. The Health Care Financing Administration, in its quarterly *Health Care Financing Review,* maintains statistics and prepares valuable studies on health care spending. Among its valuable publications is *National Health Care Expenditures 2001* (2002).

America's Children: Key National Indicators of Well-Being (2003) is the fifth report in an annual series prepared by the Interagency Forum on Child and Family Statistics. The annual *Digest of Education Statistics,* prepared by the National Center for Education Statistics of the U.S. Department of Education, provides a complete overview of education.

The Federal Bureau of Investigation (FBI), in the annual *Crime in the United States,* and the Bureau of Justice Statistics of the U.S. Department of Justice, in the yearly National Crime Victimization Survey, keep track of crime and justice statistics. The FBI also tracks terrorism in the United States in a series previously published annually, the latest of which (as of early 2004) is *Terrorism in the United States: 1999* (2000). The U.S. State Department tracks worldwide terrorism in *Patterns of Global Terrorism: 2002* (2003).

The Federal Reserve Board studies patterns of consumer finances and debt in its yearly Survey of Consumer Finances.

Human Rights Watch and the Sentencing Project jointly published *Losing the Vote: The Impact of Felony Disen-*

franchisement Laws in the United States (1998, updated 2003). The U.S. Conference of Mayors, in *A Status Report on Hunger and Homelessness in America's Cities 2002* (December 2002), by Eugene T. Lowe, details the status of the homeless in 25 U.S. cities.

INDEX

Page references in italics refer to photographs. References with the letter t following them indicate the presence of a table. The letter f indicates a figure. If more than one table or figure appears on a particular page, the exact item number for the table or figure being referenced is provided.

A

Acquired immunodeficiency syndrome (AIDS), 80, 82
Age/aging, 20–21
    criminal victimization and, 137t
    death/death rates, 81t–82t
    dentist visits, 76
    employment status, 38t–41t
    health insurance coverage, 72, 73t–74t, 75t–77t, 78t
    of householders, 27
    Medicaid, 71t–72t
    Medicare, 79–80
    poverty by, 61f, 64t, 65t
    presidential elections, participation in, 116t
    unemployment, 37
Agriculture industry, 41, 42
AIDS (acquired immunodeficiency syndrome), 80, 82
Alabama, 115
Alaska, 3, 35, 121, 122
American Indians/Alaska Natives, 16, 18
    dentist visits, 76
    health insurance coverage, 73t–74t, 75t–77t
    Medicaid coverage, 71t–72t
Arizona, 3, 121
Asian/Pacific Islander Americans, 16, 18
    dentist visits, 76
    health insurance coverage, 73t–74t, 75t–77t
    income, median, 54
    Medicaid coverage, 71t–72t
    in poverty, 61
    presidential elections, participation in, 116t

Assets, 59–60
Associate degrees, 83, 88
    conferred, 101t
    income of holders of, 102t–103t
Austria, 35

B

Baby boomers, 2, 21
    forming households, 27
    in labor force, 33
    school enrollment, 84
Bachelor's degrees, 83, 88
    conferred, 101t
    income of holders of, 102t–103t
Bangladesh, 1
Benefit plans, 50–51
Births/birthrates, 2–3, 21–23
BJS (Bureau of Justice Statistics), 132
Black/African Americans, 16, 18
    children's living arrangements, 30t, 31
    criminal victimization, 136, 137t
    dentist visits, 76
    disenfranchised felons, 115
    dropout rates, 83, 85t
    educational attainment, 83
    employment status, 38t–41t
    Food Stamp Program, 66
    health insurance coverage, 72, 73t–74t, 75t–77t
    hospital stays, 75
    housing tenure, 147t
    income, median, 54
    income and spending patterns, 143–144
    infant mortality, 23
    life expectancy, 24t
    mammograms, 80
    marital status of population, 28t
    married couples, same or mixed race/ethnicity, 29t
    Medicaid coverage, 71t–72t
    net worth, 59
    occupations, 35
    in poverty, 61, 62, 63–64
    presidential elections, participation in, 116t
    reemployment of displaced workers, 43

unemployment, 37
    union affiliation, 48t
    voter participation, 113–114
BLS. *See* Bureau of Labor Statistics
Blue-collar workers, 49
Bombings, 141t
Brazil, 1
Bureau of Justice Statistics (BJS), 132
Bureau of Labor Statistics (BLS), 33, 37, 47, 143, 145
Bush, George W., 121–122, 139

C

California, 3, 20, 72, 122
Canada, 67
Cars per household, 143
Carter, Jimmy, 121
Catholic schools, 95t
    See also Private elementary/secondary schools
Census Bureau
    assets, 59–60
    births/birth rates, 21–23
    categories of households, 25
    college enrollment, 86
    foreign-born population, 19
    immigrants, 20
    income inequality, 56
    marriage statistics, 27
    median age, 21
    median household net worth, 56
    median incomes, 53
    most populous counties, 3
    population of United States, 1
    poverty, 63–64
    race/ethnicity, 16
    spending money, patterns of, 143
    on voter turnout, 115
Chicago, IL, 6
Children, 18–19
    dentist and doctor visits, 76
    in household by presence of married parents, 30t
    living arrangements of, 30–32, 31t–32t
    as percentage of population, 20
    in poverty, 60–61, 62, 63–64

China, 1
Cities, 5, 6, 8*t*
   See also Metropolitan statistical areas (MSAs)
Civilian labor force, 33, 34*t*–35*t*
   See also Labor force
Clinton, Bill, 113, 115
Cohabitation of couples, 29
College and university education, 86, 88–89
   See also Postsecondary education
Colorado, 3, 122
Communication technology, 45
Congressional elections, 120, 120*f*, 121*f*, 122
Constitution of the United States, 113–114
Construction work, 33, 41
Consumer Expenditure Survey, 143
Consumer information, 143–147
   See also Spending money by consumers
Contingent workers, 46–47
Cook County, IL, 3
Corporations, agricultural, 12
Counties, 3–4, 5*t*, 6*t*
Cox, James, 115
Credit card debts, 57*t*–59*t*
Crime, 123–142
   cyberterrorism, 142
   disenfranchised felons, 114–115, 114*t*
   index of, 124*t*–125*t*, 126*t*–133*t*
   number and rate of, 123, 128–129, 132
   property crime victimization, 138*t*
   terrorism, 137, 139, 141–142
   trends by metropolitan status, 134*t*–135*t*
   victims of, 132–133, 136–137, 136*t*, 137*t*
   violent crime victimization, 138*t*
Crime in the United States, 123, 132
Cuban Americans, 16
Current-fund revenues for postsecondary education, 106*t*
Cyberterrorism, 142

D

Death/death rates, 23*t*, 81*t*–82*t*
   from murders, 124*t*–125*t*
   from occupational injuries, 47
   from terrorism, 140*f*, 142*f*
Death penalty, 123
Deaths
   murders, 123*t*
Debts, 57*t*–59*t*, 60
Degrees conferred, 101*t*
   See also Postsecondary education
Degrees earned, 83, 100*f*
   See also Postsecondary education
Delaware, 3, 115
Democratic party, 120*f*, 121*f*, 122
Dentist visits, 76
Department of Education, 86
Department of Health and Human Services, 70
Detroit, MI, 6
Displaced workers, 42–43
District of Columbia, 3, 114
Divorce, 29
Doctor visits, 75–76
Doctor's degrees, 83, 88
   conferred, 101*t*
   income of holders of, 102*t*–103*t*

Dole, Bob, 113, 115
Domestic terrorist groups, 139
Douglas County, CO, 3
Dropouts/dropout rates, 83, 85*t*, 86*t*

E

Early retirement, 33
Education, 83–112
   attainment, 84*f*
   college and university education, 86, 88–89
   enrollment in elementary/secondary schools, 83–86, 96*t*
   enrollment in school, 87*f*
   enrollment in school by level and control, 88*t*–89*t*
   expenditures on, 89, 91–92
   expenditures on compared to gross domestic product (GDP), 104*t*
   income influenced by, 55, 89
   lack of health insurance coverage, 78*t*
   poverty rate by, 65*t*
   preprimary, 84–85, 90*t*–91*t*, 92*f*
   private elementary/secondary schools, 86, 88*t*–89*t*, 95*t*, 96*t*
   public elementary/secondary schools, 85–86, 93*t*, 94*t*
Eisenhower, Dwight, 115
Elbert County, CO, 3
Elderly population, 20–21
   See also Age/aging
Elections, 113–122
   See also Voter participation
Electoral college, 121
Elementary schools, 94*t*
   See also Education
Employee benefit plans, 50–51
Employment, 34*t*–35*t*
   See also Labor force
Enrollment in elementary/secondary education, 83–84, 87*f*
   See also Education
Enrollment in postsecondary education, 87*f*, 99*t*.
See also Postsecondary education
Expenditures, 143–147
   Consumer Expenditure Survey, 143
   on education, 89, 91–92, 104*t*
   enrollment in school, 87*f*
   health care, 67
   per pupil for public elementary/secondary schools, 109*t*–110*t*, 111*t*–112*t*
   See also Spending money by consumers

F

Faculty at colleges/universities, 46
Families and households, 25–32
   age in, 27
   children's living arrangements, 30–32, 30*t*, 31*t*–32*t*
   debts for, 57*t*–59*t*
   definitions of, 53
   difficulties in meeting basic needs, 65*t*
   divorce, 29
   headed by women, 27
   income, 55

   marital status of population, 28*t*
   marriage, 27–29
   net worth, 59
   in poverty, 62–63, 63*t*, 64*t*, 65*t*
   size of household, 26–27
   solitary living arrangements, 29
   types of households, 26*t*
   unmarried couples, 29
   young adults' living arrangements, 30
Farms, 12, 18*t*, 19*t*
Fatalities, 81*t*–82*t*
   murders, 123*t*, 124*t*–125*t*
   from occupational injuries, 47
   from terrorism, 140*f*, 142*f*
Fathers, 30
FBI (Federal Bureau of Investigation), 123, 132–133, 139
Federal Bureau of Investigation (FBI), 123, 132–133, 139
Federal Employee Program, 70
Federal government, 91
   current-fund revenues for postsecondary education, 106*t*
   revenues for public elementary/secondary schools, 105*t*
Felons, disenfranchised, 114–115, 114*t*
Firearms, 137
First-professional degree programs, 86, 88
   enrollment in, 99*t*
   income of holders of, 102*t*–103*t*
Flagler County, FL, 3
Florida, 3, 121–122
Fluctuations in income, 56
Food Stamp Program, 66
Ford, Gerald, 121
Foreign-born population, 18–20
   See also Immigrants/immigration
Forsyth County, GA, 3
Four-year colleges, 99*t*, 107*t*–108*t*
France, 35, 67
Full-day attendance for preprimary education, 90*t*–91*t*, 92*f*
Full-time college attendance, 97*t*–98*t*, 99*t*
Full-time jobs, 44*t*, 48*t*

G

GDP (Gross Domestic Product), 45
Gender, 21
   acquired immunodeficiency syndrome (AIDS), 80, 82
   criminal victimization, 136, 137*t*
   death rates, 23
   dentist visits, 76
   dropout rates, 85*t*
   employment status by, 36*t*–37*t*, 37, 38*t*–41*t*, 41
   enrollment in postsecondary education, 97*t*–98*t*, 99*t*
   families and households headed by women, 27
   Food Stamp Program, 66
   health insurance coverage, 73*t*–74*t*, 78*t*
   income, median, 54–55
   influence of education on income, 89
   labor force, 33
   life expectancy, 23
   marital status of population, 28*t*

Medicaid coverage, 71*t*–72*t*
multiple jobholders, 45–46
net worth, 59
occupations, 35
poverty, 65*t*
presidential elections, participation in, 116*t*
reemployment of displaced workers, 43
union affiliation, 48*t*
See also Men; Women
Georgia, 3, 121
Germany, 35, 67
Goldwater, Barry, 113
Goods-producing industries, 56
Gore, Al, 121
Government. *See* Federal government; Local governments; States
Government assistance, 64–66, 69–70
Graduate students, 99*t*
Grandparents, 31*t*–32*t*, 32
Great Depression, 1
Green Party, 121
Gross Domestic Product (GDP), 45
    compared to expenditures on education, 104*t*
    health care expenditures, 67, 68*t*
Guam, 19
Guns, 137

H

Harding, Warren, 115
Harris County, TX, 3
Hawaii, 3, 121, 122
Hayes, Rutherford B., 113
Health, United States, 80
Health care, 67–82
    acquired immunodeficiency syndrome (AIDS), 80, 82
    death/death rates, 81*t*–82*t*
    doctor visits, 75–76
    expenditures on as part of gross domestic product, 68*t*
    expenditures on by type of, 69*t*–70*t*
    hospital care, 73–75
    insurance for, 70–73
    mammograms, 78, 80
    Medicare and Medicaid, 69–70
Health insurance, 70–73
    for the elderly, 75*t*–77*t*
    employee benefit plans, 50–51, 50*t*
    health maintenance organizations (HMOs), 72–73
    lack of coverage, 71–72, 73*t*–74*t*, 74, 78*t*, 79*t*
    Medicaid coverage, 71*t*–72*t*
    poverty, 66
    private companies for, 67, 69
Health maintenance organizations (HMOs), 72–73
Heart disease, 82
Henry County, GA, 3
High school completion, 102*t*–103*t*
High schools, 94*t*
Hispanic Americans, 16, 18
    children's living arrangements, 30*t*, 31
    criminal victimization, 136, 137*t*
    dentist visits, 76
    disenfranchised felons, 115

dropout rates, 83, 85*t*
educational attainment, 83
Food Stamp Program, 66
health insurance coverage, 72, 73*t*–74*t*, 75*t*–77*t*
hospital stays, 75
housing tenure, 147*t*
income, median, 54
income and spending patterns, 143–144
mammograms, 80
marital status of population, 28*t*
married couples, same or mixed race/ethnicity, 29*t*
Medicaid coverage, 71*t*–72*t*
net worth, 59
in poverty, 61, 62, 63–64
presidential elections, participation in, 116*t*
reemployment of displaced workers, 43
unemployment, 37
union affiliation, 48*t*
HIV (human immunodeficiency virus), 80, 82
HMOs (health maintenance oganizations), 72–73
Home ownership, 138*t*, 143, 147
Home-secured debts, 57*t*–59*t*, 60
Hoover, Herbert, 113
Hospital care, 73–75
Hostages, 141*f*
Hours per workweek, 43–45
House of Representatives, 120*f*, 122
Households, 25–32
    definition of, 53
    types of, 26*t*
    See also Families and households
Housing tenure, 147*t*
Human immunodeficiency virus (HIV), 80, 82

I

Illinois, 3
Immigrants/immigration, 3, 18–20
    admitted by state, 22*t*
    by country of birth, 21*t*
    in poverty, 61, 64*t*
    by region of birth, 18*f*
Income, 53–66, 143
    assets, 59–60
    children living with grandparents, 31*t*–32*t*
    consumption and, 143–144
    criminal victimization and, 136, 137, 138*t*
    debts, 57*t*–59*t*, 60
    distribution of, 55–56
    dropout rates by, 86*t*
    education, influence of, 89, 102*t*–103*t*
    government assistance, 64–66
    health insurance coverage, 72, 78*t*
    median, 53–55
    net worth, 56, 59–60
    poverty, 60–66, 65*t*
    spending patterns and, 144–145, 146*t*
Income in the United States: 2002, 54
Independent contractors, 46–47
Index of crime, 124*t*–125*t*, 126*t*–133*t*

India, 1
Indonesia, 1
Inequality in income, 55–56
    See also Income
Infant mortality, 23, 82
Inflation and health care costs, 67
Information technology, 45
Inpatient care at hospitals, 74
International comparisons
    health care expenditures, 67, 68*t*
    hours of working per week, 43–45
    population, 1–2
    unemployment rate, 35, 37*f*
International terrorist groups, 139, 141*f*
Interracial marriages, 29*t*
Iowa, 3, 72
Italy, 35

J

Jackson, Andrew, 113
Japan, 2
Johnson, Lyndon B., 113
Junior high schools, 94*t*

K

Kaiser Permanente, 72
Kennedy, John F., 123
Kidnapping, 141*f*
Kindergarten, 90*t*–91*t*
Korea, 45

L

Labor force, 33–51
    alternative work arrangements, 47
    contingent workers, 46–47
    displaced workers, 42–43
    employee benefit plans, 50–51
    employment status, 34*t*–35*t*, 36*t*–37*t*, 38*t*–41*t*
    hours of working per week, 43–45
    multiple jobs, 45–46, 46*t*
    occupational injuries and illnesses, 47
    occupations, 35, 43*t*, 44*t*
    service economy, 33
    unemployment, 35, 37, 41–43
    union affiliation, 47–49, 48*t*, 49*t*
    women working outside of home, 53–54
    work stoppages, 49–50
Las Vegas, NV-AZ, 6
Left-wing terrorist groups, 139, 141*f*
Legislation and international treaties
    National Voter Registration Act (1993), 115
    Tax Equity and Fiscal Responsibility Act (1982), 73
    Violent Crime Control and Law Enforcement Act (1994), 123
Life expectancy, 23, 24*t*
Local governments, 91
    current-fund revenues for postsecondary education, 106*t*
    revenues for public elementary/secondary schools, 105*t*
Los Angeles, CA, 6
Los Angeles County, CA, 3

Losing the Vote: The Impact of Felony Disenfranchisement Laws in the United States, 115
Loudon County, VA, 3
Louisiana, 3, 72, 122

M

Maine, 114, 121, 122
Mammograms, 78, 80
Marriage/marital status, 27–29
    couples by race/ethnicity, 29*t*
    crime trends by, 137
    criminal victimization and, 138*t*
    family households, 25
    multiple jobholders, 46*t*
    net worth of couples, 59
    poverty rate for couples, 62, 63*t*
    women working, 54
Maryland, 115
Massachusetts, 72
Master's degrees, 83, 88
    conferred, 101*t*
    income of holders of, 102*t*–103*t*
McVeigh, Timothy, 139
Mean population center for U. S., 1, 2*f*
Median income, 53–55
    See also Income
Medicaid, 69–70, 71*t*–72*t*
Medicare, 69–70, 73
Men
    criminal victimization, 136, 137*t*
    employment status, 36*t*–37*t*, 37, 38*t*–41*t*,
      41
    in labor force, 33
    median income, 54–55
    multiple jobholders, 45–46
    net worth, 59
    reemployment of displaced workers, 43
    See also Gender
Metropolitan statistical areas (MSAs), 4–12
    cities, 5, 6, 8*t*
    population for incorporated places over
      100,000, 9*t*–12*t*, 13*t*–16*t*, 17*t*
    ranked by population, 7*t*
Metropolitan status
    crime trends by, 132, 134*t*–135*t*, 136, 137
    criminal victimization and, 138*t*
    health insurance for the elderly, 75*t*–77*t*
    housing tenure, 147*t*
    income and, 53
    Medicaid coverage, 71*t*–72*t*
    metropolitan statistical areas (MSAs),
      4–12
    poverty, 64*t*, 65*t*
Mexican Americans, 16
Mexico, 4
Michigan, 3, 6
Middle schools, 86, 94*t*
Minnesota, 4, 72, 121, 122
Mobility of population, 20
Montana, 3, 121
Mortgages, 57*t*–59*t*, 60
Mothers, 30
"Motor Voter Law," 115
MSAs (metropolitan statistical areas), 4–12
Multiple jobholders, 45–46, 46*t*

N

Nader, Ralph, 121
National Center for Health Statistics, 27
National Crime Victimization Survey
    (NCVS), 132
National Voter Registration Act (1993), 115
NCVS (National Crime Victimization
    Survey), 132
Nebraska, 35
Net worth, 56, 59–60
*Net Worth and Asset Ownership of
    Households: 1998 and 2000,* 56
Netherlands, 35
Nevada, 3, 6, 115, 121
Never-married population, 28–29
New Hampshire, 3, 121, 122
New Jersey, 3
New Mexico, 72
New York, 3, 20
New York City, NY, 6, 53, 139
Nichols, Terry, 139
Nigeria, 2
Nonfamily households, 25–26, 27
North Dakota, 3, 35
Norway, 35
Nursery school, 90*t*–91*t*

O

Occupations, 35
    employment by, 43*t*
    by full- or part-time status, 44*t*
    hours of working per week, 43
    injuries and illnesses, 47
    unemployment in, 41
    union affiliation, 49*t*
Ohio, 3
Oklahoma City, OK, 139
Orange County, CA, 3
Oregon, 35, 115
Outpatient care at hospitals, 74

P

Pakistan, 1
Park County, CO, 3
Part-day attendance for preprimary
    education, 90*t*–91*t*
Part-time college attendance, 97*t*–98*t*, 99*t*
Part-time jobs, 44*t*, 45, 48*t*
Pennsylvania, 3, 6
Pension plans, 51
    See also Retirement
Per capita health expenditures, 68
Per capita income, 54
Per student expenditures, 91–92
Philadelphia, PA, 6
Political parties, 120*f*
Population, 1–24
    age/aging, 20–21
    cities, 8*t*
    compared to world, 1–2
    deaths, 23*t*
    farms, 12, 18*t*, 19*t*
    gender, 21
    geographic mobility, 20
    growth of, 3*f*
    immigrants, 18–20

    for incorporated places over 100,000,
      9*t*–12*t*, 13*t*–16*t*, 17*t*
    in labor force, 34*t*–35*t*
    life expectancy, 23, 24*t*
    marital status, 28*t*
    mean population center for U. S., 1, 2*f*
    metropolitan areas, 4–12
    race/ethnicity, 16–19
    rural, 12, 16
Postsecondary education, 86, 88–89
    current-fund revenues for, 106*t*
    degrees conferred, 88–89, 101*t*
    degrees earned, 83, 100*f*
    enrollment in, 88*t*–89*t*, 97*t*–98*t*, 99*t*
    expenditures and enrollment in, 100*f*
    income influenced by, 102*t*–103*t*
    private colleges and universities,
      revenues for, 107*t*–108*t*
    See also Education
Poverty, 60–66, 64*t*
    by age, 61*f*
    children living with grandparents,
      31*t*–32*t*
    health insurance for the elderly, 75*t*–77*t*
    hospital stays, 75
    mammograms, 80
    Medicaid coverage, 71*t*–72*t*
    rate of, 60*f*
    ratio of family income to, 55
    by type of household, 63*t*
Preprimary education, 84–85, 90*t*–91*t*, 92*f*
Presidential elections, 120–122
Private colleges and universities, 88*t*–89*t*,
    97*t*–98*t*
    degrees conferred, 101*t*
    enrollment in, 99*t*, 100*f*
    revenues for, 107*t*–108*t*
Private elementary/secondary schools, 86,
    88*t*–89*t*, 95*t*, 96*t*
Property crimes, 133, 136, 137*t*, 138*t*
    See also Crime
Public assistance to family, 31*t*–32*t*
Public colleges and universities, 88*t*–89*t*,
    97*t*–98*t*
    degrees conferred, 101*t*
    enrollment in, 99*t*, 100*f*
Public elementary/secondary schools, 84,
    85–86
    enrollment in, 88*t*–89*t*, 96*t*
    expenditures per pupil, 109*t*–110*t*,
      111*t*–112*t*
    organization of, 93*t*, 94*t*
    revenues for, 105*t*
Puerto Rico, 3, 16

R

Race/ethnicity, 16–19
    children's living arrangements, 30*t*, 31,
      31*t*–32*t*
    criminal victimization, 136, 137*t*
    debts, 57*t*–59*t*
    dentist visits, 76
    disenfranchised felons, 115
    dropout rates, 83, 85*t*
    educational attainment, 83
    employment status, 38*t*–41*t*
    family households, 25

Food Stamp Program, 66
　health insurance coverage, 72, 73t–74t, 75t–77t
　hospital stays, 75
　housing tenure, 147t
　income, median, 54
　income and spending patterns, 143–144
　life expectancy, 24t
　mammograms, 80
　marital status of population, 28t
　married couples by same or mixed, 29t
　Medicaid coverage, 71t–72t
　net worth, 59
　occupations, 35
　poverty, 61, 62, 63–64, 65t
　presidential elections, participation in, 116t
　reemployment of displaced workers, 43
　unemployment, 37
　union affiliation, 48t
Recession, 35, 43
Regions
　crime index for, 126t–133t
　crime rate, 132, 138t
　dentist visits, 76
　employee benefit plans for health insurance and retirement, 50t
　farms, 12
　health insurance coverage, 72, 75t–77t, 78t, 79t
　immigrants/immigration, 19
　income, median, 54
　Medicaid coverage, 71t–72t
　population, 2, 20f
　poverty, 63, 64t
　poverty rate by, 65t
　presidential elections, participation in, 116t
　voter registration, 120–121
Registering to vote, 115–116
Religious schools, 95t
Rental properties, 147t
Republican party, 120f, 121f, 122
Residence. See Metropolitan status
Retirement, 33, 50t
Rhode Island, 3, 72
Right-wing terrorist groups, 139, 141f
Rockwall County, TX, 3
Rural areas, 134t–135t
　See also Metropolitan status
Russia, 2

S

San Francisco, CA, 53
San Jose, CA, 53
Saving money, 145
Secondary education, 87f, 102t–103t
　See also Education
Senate, 121f, 122
Sentencing Project and Human Rights Watch, 115
September 11, 2001 terrorist attacks, 35, 137, 139
Service economy, 33, 35, 56
Service occupations, 35
Single-parent families, 30–32, 62–64, 63t
Smith, Alfred, 113

Solitary living arrangements, 29, 30
South Dakota, 3, 35, 122
Spain, 35
Special-interest terrorist groups, 139, 141f
Spending money by consumers, 143–147
　average annual expenditures, 144t
　average annual expenditures by major category, 145t
　housing tenure, 147t
　income and spending patterns, 146t
　See also Expenditures
States
　crime index, 126t–133t
　current-fund revenues for postsecondary education, 106t
　disenfranchised felons, 114–115, 114t
　expenditures on education, 91–92
　expenditures per pupil for public elementary/secondary schools, 111t–112t
　health insurance coverage, 72, 79t
　income, median, 54
　population, 3, 4t
　revenues for public elementary/secondary schools, 105t
　southern suppressing Black Americans right to vote, 114
　unemployment rate, 35
　voter turnout, 121, 122
Statistical Abstract of the United States, 20
Statistical information
　average annual expenditures for consumer units, 144t
　average annual expenditures of consumers by major category, 145t
　casualties from terrorism, 140f
　children's living arrangements, 30t, 31t–32t
　crime clock, 123t
　crime index, 124t–125t, 126t–133t
　crime trends by metropolitan status, 134t–135t
　criminal victimization, rate of, 136t, 137t
　current-fund revenues for postsecondary education, 106t
　death/death rates, 23t, 81t–82t
　debts for families and households, 57t–59t
　degrees conferred by control of institution, 101t
　disenfranchised felons by state, 114t
　dropout rates, 85t, 86t
　employee benefit plans for health insurance and retirement, 50t
　employment by occupation, 43t
　employment status by gender, 36t–37t
　enrollment in college and university education, 99t
　enrollment in colleges and universities, 97t–98t
　enrollment in elementary/secondary education, 96t
　enrollment in school by level and control, 88t–89t
　expenditures by type of health care, 69t–70t

　expenditures on education compared to gross domestic product, 104t
　expenditures on health care as part of gross domestic product, 68t
　expenditures per pupil for public elementary/secondary schools, 109t–110t, 111t–112t
　farms, 18t
　health insurance coverage, 73t–74t, 75t–77t, 78t, 79t
　housing tenure, 147t
　immigrants by country of birth, 21t
　immigrants by state admitted to, 22t
　income and spending patterns, 146t
　income by education, 102t–103t
　life expectancy, 24t
　marital status of population, 28t
　married couples by race/ethnicity, 29t
　Medicaid coverage, 71t–72t
　metropolitan statistical areas (MSAs) ranked by population, 7t
　multiple jobholders, 46t
　occupations by full- or part-time status, 44t
　population for incorporated places over 100,000, 9t–12t, 13t–16t, 17t
　population of counties of U. S., 5t, 6t
　population of states, 4t
　poverty, 63t, 64t, 65t
　preprimary education enrollment, 90t–91t
　presidential elections, participation in, 116t
　private elementary/secondary schools, 95t
　property crime victimization, 138t
　public elementary/secondary schools, 93t, 94t, 105t
　revenues for private colleges and universities, 107t–108t
　sales of farms, 19t
　types of households, 26t
　unemployment by gender and age, 42t
　union affiliation, 48t, 49t
　violent crime victimization, 138t
Stevenson, Adlai, 115
Strikes, 49–50
Students with jobs, 46
Suburban areas, 134t–135t
　See also Metropolitan status
Surgeries, 74
Switzerland, 67

T

Tax Equity and Fiscal Responsibility Act (1982), 73
Teachers at private schools, 95t
Technology, 74
Temporary help agency workers, 47
Terrorism, 137, 139, 141–142
　casualties from, 140f, 142f
　cyberterrorism, 142
　by group, 141f
　total attacks, 141f
Terrorism in the United States: 1999, 139
Texas, 3, 72, 115, 121
Tilden, Samuel J., 113

Truck drivers, 47
Truman, Harry, 113
Two-year colleges, 99*t*, 107*t*–108*t*

U

Undergraduates, 99*t*
Unemployment, 35, 37, 41–43
    by age, gender and race, 38*t*–41*t*
    displaced workers, 42–43
    duration of, 41–42
    by gender and age, 42*t*
    international comparisons, 37*f*
Unions, 47–50
United Nations International Labor
    Organization (ILO), 43
United Parcel Service, 48
United States Census Bureau. *See* Census
    Bureau
United States Constitution, 113–114
Unmarried couples, 29
Urban areas, 134*t*–135*t*
    See also Metropolitan status

V

Vehicles per household, 143
Vermont, 3, 114, 122
Victims of crime, 132–133, 136–137, 136*t*,
    137*t*
    See also Crime
Violent Crime Control and Law
    Enforcement Act (1994), 123
Violent crimes, 133, 136, 138*t*
    See also Crime
Virginia, 35

Voter participation, 113–122
    Black/African Americans, 113–114
    congressional elections, 120, 120*f*, 121*f*,
        122
    disenfranchised felons, 114–115
    low voter turnout, 115–120
    presidential elections, 116*t*, 120–122
    reasons given for not voting, 114*f*
    turnout before 1920, 113
    women, 114

W

Watergate scandal, 121
Wealth. *See* Net worth
Wealth gap, 145
Weapons, 137
West Virginia, 3
White Americans, 16–17
    children's living arrangements, 30*t*, 31
    criminal victimization, 136, 137*t*
    dentist visits, 76
    disenfranchised felons, 115
    dropout rates, 83, 85*t*
    educational attainment, 83
    employment status, 38*t*–41*t*
    Food Stamp Program, 66
    health insurance coverage, 72, 73*t*–74*t*,
        75*t*–77*t*
    hospital stays, 75
    housing tenure, 147*t*
    income, median, 54
    income and spending patterns, 143–144
    life expectancy, 24*t*
    mammograms, 80
    marital status of population, 28*t*

    married couples, same or mixed
        race/ethnicity, 29*t*
    Medicaid coverage, 71*t*–72*t*
    net worth, 59
    occupations, 35
    in poverty, 61, 62
    presidential elections, participation in,
        116*t*
    reemployment of displaced workers, 43
    unemployment, 37
    union affiliation, 48*t*
Wisconsin, 72, 121
Women
    criminal victimization, 136, 137*t*
    disenfranchised felons, 115
    employment status, 36*t*–37*t*, 37, 38*t*–41*t*,
        41
    families and households headed by, 27
    Food Stamp Program, 66
    income, median, 54–55
    in labor force, 33
    as multiple jobholders, 45–46
    net worth, 59
    reemployment of displaced workers, 43
    single-parent families, 62–63, 63–64
    suffrage for, 114
    working outside of home, 53–54
    See also Gender
Work stoppages, 49–50
Work week, 43–45
World Trade Center, New York City, 139
Wyoming, 3, 115

Y

Years of school completed, 84*f*
Young adults, 30